behavioral science

April 92
Read   marked c̄
pencil. i in question read
only   circled ⓞ

Psychiatry , Kaplan + Sadock.

The National Medical Series for Independent Study

behavioral science

EDITOR

Jerry M. Wiener, M.D.

*Leon Yochelson Professor
and Chairman
Department of Psychiatry and
Behavioral Sciences
George Washington University
Medical Center
Washington, D.C.*

A WILEY MEDICAL PUBLICATION
JOHN WILEY & SONS
New York • Chichester • Brisbane • Toronto • Singapore

Harwal Publishing Company, Media, Pennsylvania

Library of Congress Cataloging in Publication Data

Behavioral science.

(The National medical series for independent study)
(A Wiley medical publication)
   Includes index.
   1. Medicine and psychology—Outlines, syllabi, etc.
2. Medicine and psychology—Examinations, questions,
etc.   3. National Board of Medical Examiners—
Examinations—Study guides.   I. Wiener, Jerry M.,
1933-   . II. Series.   III. Series: A Wiley medical
publication.   [DNLM: 1. Behavior—examination questions. 2. Behavior—outlines.   3. Behavioral
Medicine—examination questions.   4. Behavioral
Medicine—outlines. WB 18 B419]
R726.5.B4267   1987   616'.001'9   86-25693

ISBN 0-471-82924-2

10 9 8 7 6 5 4 3 2

Contents

Contributors

Joan K. Barber, M.D.
Associate Professor of Psychiatry
and Behavioral Sciences
George Washington University
Medical Center
Washington, D.C.

Philip S. Birnbaum, M.S.
Professor of Health Services
Administration
George Washington University
Dean for Administrative Affairs
George Washington University
Medical Center
Washington, D.C.

James H. Egan, M.D.
Professor of Psychiatry
and Behavioral Sciences
George Washington University
Medical Center
Chairman, Department of
Child Psychiatry
Children's Hospital National
Medical Center
Washington, D.C.

Richard P. Foa, M.D.
Assistant Professor of Neurology
Georgetown University Medical Center
Washington, D.C.

Bernard L. Frankel, M.D.
Associate Professor of Psychiatry
and Behavioral Sciences
Director, Consultation-Liaison Psychiatry
George Washington University
Medical Center
Washington, D.C.

William J. Freed, Ph.D.
Chief, Preclinical Neurosciences Section
Neuropsychiatry Branch
National Institute of Mental Health
Washington, D.C.

Warren Greenberg, Ph.D.
Associate Professor of Health
Services Administration
George Washington University
Washington, D.C.

Robert L. Hendren, D.O.
Medical Director, Children's
Psychiatric Hospital
University of New Mexico
Albuquerque, New Mexico
formerly, Associate Professor of
Psychiatry and Behavioral Sciences
George Washington University
Medical Center
Washington, D.C.

Marc Hertzman, M.D.
Professor of Psychiatry and
and Behavioral Sciences
Director, Inpatient Services
Department of Psychiatry
George Washington University
Medical Center
Washington, D.C.

Robert L. Jenkins, Ph.D.
Associate Professor of Psychiatry
and Behavioral Sciences
George Washington University
Medical Center
Washington, D.C.

Dilip V. Jeste, M.D.

Professor of Psychiatry and
  Neurosciences
Director, Neuropsychiatry/Geropsychiatry
  Program and Neuropathology Research
  Laboratory
University of California, San Diego,
  School of Medicine
La Jolla, California
formerly, Associate Clinical Professor
  of Psychiatry and Behavioral Sciences
George Washington University
  Medical Center
Washington, D.C.

Charles A. Kaufmann, M.D.

Assistant Professor of Clinical
  Psychiatry
College of Physicians and Surgeons
Columbia University
New York, New York

Darrell G. Kirch, M.D.

Clinical Assistant Professor of
  Psychiatry and Behavioral Sciences
George Washington University
  Medical Center
Senior Staff Fellow
Neuropsychiatry Branch
National Institute of Mental Health
Washington, D.C.

James B. Lohr, M.D.

Director, Tardive Dyskinesia Program
Unit on Movement Disorders
  and Dementia
Neuropsychiatry Branch
National Institute of Mental Health
Washington, D.C.

John M. Morihisa, M.D.

Professor and Chairman
Department of Psychiatry
Georgetown University School of Medicine
Psychiatry Service
Veterans Administration Medical Center
Washington, D.C.

Seymour Perlin, M.D.

Professor of Psychiatry and Behavioral
  Sciences
Director, Residency Training
  in Psychiatry
George Washington University
  Medical Center
Washington, D.C.

Richard B. Rosse, M.D.

Assistant Professor of Psychiatry
Georgetown University School of Medicine
Psychiatry Service
Veterans Administration Medical Center
Washington, D.C.

Richard F. Southby, Ph.D.

Professor and Chairman
Department of Health Services
  Administration
George Washington University
Professor of Health Care Sciences
George Washington University
  Medical Center
Washington, D.C.
Adjunct Professor of Preventive
  Medicine and Biometrics
Uniformed Services University
  of the Health Sciences
Bethesda, Maryland

Frederick S. Wamboldt, M.D.

Assistant Professor of Psychiatry
  and Behavioral Sciences
Research Staff, Center for
  Family Research
George Washington University
  Medical Center
Washington, D.C.

Jerry M. Wiener, M.D.

Leon Yochelson Professor and Chairman
Department of Psychiatry and
  Behavioral Sciences
George Washington University
  Medical Center
Washington, D.C.

Preface

The term "behavioral science" has always seemed to be nebulous and so overinclusive as to defy definition. In the medical school curriculum, behavioral science is generally classified as one of the basic sciences along with standards such as physiology, biochemistry, and pharmacology. However, behavioral science differs from the others in that it is defined in a variety of ways, is taught under a variety of disciplines, and is of varying relevance to the education of the physician and to the clinical practice of medicine. Behavioral science has come to include everything that cannot be categorized in one of the traditional basic sciences; at the same time, it encompasses material that is fundamental to modern medical practice, including odd bedfellows such as brain–behavior correlations, ethical issues, and the economic forces affecting the future of medicine.

I considered the task of assembling this review of behavioral science to be challenging, if not impractical. To my advantage, however, were prior service on a National Board task force, which defined the subject matter to be included in the behavioral science category of the Part I exam, and an active role in the development of the behavioral science curriculum at the George Washington University School of Medicine. In addition, I found significant support in the superb and broadly qualified faculty of the Department of Psychiatry and Behavioral Sciences, with whom I collaborated on this book.

Although this project was first undertaken with a sense of obligation to the Department, the writing and development of this book turned into a stimulating and exciting experience. I hope that some of the excitement and reward I felt is transmitted through the book to its readers.

Jerry M. Wiener

Acknowledgments

I must give special thanks to the chapter authors for their splendid contributions, to Jane Velker at Harwal for her gifted and patient editorial work, and to Carol Lundy, my secretary, who kept everything straight.

Publisher's Note

The objective of the *National Medical Series* is to present an extraordinarily large amount of information in an easily retrievable form. The outline format was selected for this purpose of reducing to the essentials the medical information needed by today's student and practitioner.

While the concept of an outline format was well received by the authors and publisher, the difficulties inherent in working with this style were not initially apparent. That the series has been published and received enthusiastically is a tribute to the authors who worked long and diligently to produce books that are stylistically consistent and comprehensive in content.

The task of producing the *National Medical Series* required more than the efforts of the authors, however, and the missing elements have been supplied by highly competent and dedicated developmental editors and support staff. Editors, compositors, proofreaders, and layout and design staff have all polished the outline to a fine form. It is with deep appreciation that I thank all who have participated, in particular the staff at Harwal—Debra L. Dreger, Jane Edwards, Gloria Hamilton, Deborah G. Huey, Susan Kelly, Wieslawa B. Langenfeld, Keith LaSala, June Sangiorgio Mash, and Jane Velker.

The Publisher

Introduction

Behavioral Science is one of 10 basic science review books in the *National Medical Series for Independent Study*. This series has been designed to provide students and house officers, as well as physicians, with a concise but comprehensive instrument for self-evaluation and review within the basic sciences. Although *Behavioral Science* would be most useful for students preparing for the National Board of Medical Examiners examinations (Part I, FLEX, and FMGEMS), it should also be useful for students studying for course examinations. These books are not intended to replace the standard basic science texts but, rather, to complement them.

The books in this series present the core content of each basic science, using an outline format and featuring 300 study questions. The questions are distributed throughout the book, at the end of each chapter and in a pretest and post-test. In addition, each question is accompanied by the correct answer, a paragraph-length explanation of the correct answer, and specific reference to the outline points under which the information necessary to answer the question can be found.

We have chosen an outline format to allow maximal ease in retrieving information, assuming that the time available to the reader is limited. Considerable editorial time has been spent to ensure that the information required by all medical school curricula has been included and that the question format parallels that of the National Board examinations. We feel that the combination of the outline and the board-type study questions provides a unique teaching device.

We hope you will find this series interesting, relevant, and challenging. The authors, as well as the John Wiley and Harwal staffs, welcome your comments and suggestions.

Pretest

QUESTIONS

Directions: Each question below contains five suggested answers. Choose the **one best** response to each question.

1. A 21-year-old single woman is brought to the emergency room by her parents who report the patient to be intensely anxious and withdrawn. She has had deteriorating performance in college over the last year. The school psychologist administered several psychological tests to her, and his report states that on the Rorschach test she demonstrated markedly poor form quality with evidence of autistic logic and a poorly controlled strong emphasis on pure color. These findings are most consistent with which one of the following diagnostic possibilities?

(A) Cyclothymic disorder
(B) Panic disorder
(C) Schizophrenia
(D) Adjustment disorder with anxious mood
(E) Organic brain syndrome

2. All the following societal expectations of the sick role are basic EXCEPT

(A) the obligation to get well
(B) functioning as usual until symptoms become severe
(C) exemption from usual social-role responsibilities
(D) the obligation to seek technically competent help
(E) exemption from blame for the illness

3. The term bureaucracy is used by sociologists and political scientists to describe an organization that is characterized by

(A) public ownership
(B) participation in the internal decision-making process by members of all levels of the organization
(C) a hierarchy of offices designed on a rational basis in order to achieve specified goals
(D) staffing patterns that do not vary as missions and requirements are modified
(E) procedures and practices that follow the model developed in the civil service in France (from which is derived the term)

4. What percentage of female offspring would be expected to demonstrate a trait with a Y-linked pattern of inheritance?

(A) 100
(B) 50
(C) 25
(D) 5
(E) 0

5. The adrenogenital syndrome results in

(A) a genetic female born with an enlarged clitoris or a normal-appearing penis and scrotal sac
(B) a genetic male born with female genitalia
(C) a genetic male born with incompletely developed or absent male genitalia
(D) an XXY chromosomal pattern
(E) an XYY chromosomal pattern

6. The benzodiazepines show all of the following characteristics EXCEPT

(A) metabolism resulting in pharmacologically active compounds
(B) the ability to ameliorate the effects of alcohol withdrawal
(C) development of tolerance with chronic use
(D) anticonvulsant properties
(E) high lethal potential with an oral overdose

7. All of the following statements concerning the association of alcohol use and sexual functioning are true EXCEPT

(A) alcohol interferes with sexual functioning by its depressant effect on the central nervous system
(B) alcohol may enhance sexual desire by decreasing inhibitions
(C) common sexual dysfunctions in alcoholic women include inhibited desire, dyspareunia, and orgasmic dysfunction
(D) common sexual dysfunctions in alcoholic men include inhibited desire, erectile dysfunction, and ejaculatory incompetence
(E) alcohol-related sexual dysfunction is reversed with abstinence from alcohol

8. The term informal organization applies to

(A) social groups that develop outside the work environment
(B) the modifications that occur in the formal structure as a result of personal and social factors that interact with the formal organization
(C) those aspects of the organizational structure that are beyond the influence of administrators within the organization
(D) the interactions that the organization has with its clients
(E) the relationship of the governing board and the executive staff of the institution

9. Normal parent–infant behavior is best described interactionally as an example of

(A) autonomous functioning
(B) a power struggle
(C) socialization by modeling
(D) complementary, affiliative behavior
(E) ethnocentrism

10. Which type of procedure would be most likely to succeed in teaching a bird to ride a bicycle?

(A) Operant conditioning
(B) Classical conditioning
(C) Autoshaping
(D) Imprinting
(E) Self-stimulation

11. Most noradrenergic (norepinephrine-containing) neurons in the brain arise from the

(A) raphe nucleus
(B) locus ceruleus
(C) cingulate gyrus
(D) septal area
(E) stria terminalis

12. The Medicare program is best described as

(A) an entitlement health care program for the elderly poor
(B) an insurance program for catastrophic illness–related hospital bills
(C) a direct provider for specific categorized diseases (e.g., end-stage renal disease)
(D) a form of insurance under which the federal government pays certain health care costs for specific, eligible groups
(E) a national health insurance plan shared by the state and the federal governments

13. When guarded, suspicious individuals become ill, they typically manifest all of the following characteristics EXCEPT

(A) marked self-confidence and snobbishness
(B) a tendency to blame others for their illness
(C) difficulties in cooperating fully with their physicians
(D) misinterpretation of the physician's behavior
(E) hypervigilance about all aspects of their care and treatment

14. Which of the following statements concerning eating and drinking behaviors is true?

(A) Postingestional factors are more important in drinking behavior than in eating behavior
(B) Postingestional factors are more important in eating behavior than in drinking behavior
(C) Oral factors are more important in the regulation of drinking behavior than eating behavior
(D) Oral factors are more important in the regulation of eating behavior than drinking behavior
(E) Oral factors are equally important in eating and drinking behaviors

15. The clinical use of antihypertensive drugs is most likely to be associated with which of the following psychiatric symptoms?

(A) Depression
(B) Delusions
(C) Hypersexuality
(D) Tardive dyskinesia
(E) Paranoia

16. A form of learning that takes place only during a critical stage of development describes which of the following?

(A) Operant conditioning
(B) Classical conditioning
(C) Autoshaping
(D) Imprinting
(E) Habituation

17. Sex-typing the brain is the process by which the hypothalamus is influenced to determine gonadotropin release. Which of the following hormones has the greatest significance in this process for both males and females?

(A) Testosterone
(B) Estrogen
(C) Progesterone
(D) Prolactin
(E) Growth hormone

18. The primary reason for the substantial growth in health care expenditures has been the increase in

(A) the age of the population
(B) health care payments by public and private health insurers
(C) new health care technology
(D) the relative number of physicians
(E) the absolute number of physicians

19. What area of the brain when damaged is associated most with the appearance of snout and grasp reflexes?

(A) Parietal lobe
(B) Frontal lobe
(C) Occipital lobe
(D) Temporal lobe
(E) Raphe nucleus

20. Opioid withdrawal is most likely to be characterized by

(A) respiratory depression
(B) rapid alleviation of symptoms with naloxone
(C) exacerbation of symptoms by methadone
(D) piloerection, chilling, and sweating
(E) seizures

21. The type of Down syndrome that results from a translocation is characterized by all of the following conditions EXCEPT

(A) 46 chromosomes
(B) clinical differences from the mongolism due to trisomy
(C) a lower frequency than the mongolism due to nondisjunction
(D) a higher incidence in offspring of mothers over 35
(E) mental retardation

22. Masturbation and sexual play with other children in early childhood are generally regarded as

(A) developmental disturbances
(B) indications of sexual overstimulation at home
(C) normal behavior at this developmental age
(D) indications of immaturity
(E) indications of early sexual deviancy

23. Utilitarian theory is best described as

(A) the philosophy of Immanuel Kant
(B) goodness in the act itself
(C) a set of absolute standards
(D) action in terms of consequences
(E) religious justification of an act as good

Directions: Each question below contains four suggested answers of which **one or more** is correct. Choose the answer

A   if **1, 2, and 3** are correct
B   if **1 and 3** are correct
C   if **2 and 4** are correct
D   if **4** is correct
E   if **1, 2, 3, and 4** are correct

24. Characteristics that qualify a cluster of signs and symptoms as a psychiatric disease include

(1) replicability (e.g., independent examiners agree upon the same cluster)
(2) the presence of central nervous system signs and symptoms, in the absence of cranial nerve, peripheral nervous system, motor, or sensory findings
(3) response to treatment with psychotherapy with or without major tranquilizers
(4) consistent and reproducible patient histories

25. Structures of the limbic system include the

(1) hippocampus
(2) cingulate gyrus
(3) amygdaloid complex
(4) raphe nucleus

26. Principles of reward and reinforcement propose that

(1) rewarding a behavior on an intermittent, variable basis will establish the strongest and most persistent learning
(2) a continuous and predictable reward is the most satisfactory method to elicit long-term behavior change
(3) disapproval or criticism may either discourage (extinguish) or reinforce a behavior
(4) a reward is related to primary needs, and reinforcement is related to learned needs

27. When a physician asks his patient for a date, he is violating which of the societal expectations of the physician's role?

(1) Collectivity orientation
(2) Medical role universalism
(3) Specificity of competence
(4) Affective neutrality

28. What is stranger anxiety?

(1) A differentiation of self from the mother
(2) A reaction to the mother's absence
(3) A reflection of object permanence
(4) A reflection of insecure attachment

29. Animals with the Klüver-Bucy syndrome characteristically display

(1) oral exploration of objects
(2) lack of fear
(3) inappropriate sexual behavior
(4) aggressive behavior

30. Demographic trends of family life in the United States that have demonstrated no significant change in recent times include

(1) the number of children born per couple
(2) the importance of extended family members as sources of social support
(3) the number of childless married couples
(4) the percentage of the population that eventually marries

31. Maturationally based ego functions include

(1) motor activity
(2) sensory activity
(3) cognition and memory
(4) defenses

32. A patient with a fluent or mixed aphasia may be misdiagnosed as schizophrenic because of which of the following findings on mental status examination (MSE)?

(1) Delusions
(2) Neologisms
(3) Auditory hallucinations
(4) Word salad

33. True statements concerning behavior patterns include

(1) dependence on learned behavior patterns places humans at a biological disadvantage
(2) mammals do not have inherited behavior patterns
(3) humans do not have inherited behavior patterns
(4) most of the behavior patterns of invertebrates are inherited

34. True statements concerning substance abuse include

(1) elevated blood pressure is common with drug withdrawal
(2) half of the dose may be given on the second day for treatment of benzodiazepine withdrawal
(3) hallucinogen intoxication may simulate anxiety disorders
(4) there is only symptomatic treatment for hallucinogen-induced delirium

35. A child continually wets the bed while asleep. An attempt is made to change this behavior: Each time he begins to wet, a buzzer sounds and wakes him up, and soon he stops the wetting. What can be said concerning this example of behavior modification?

(1) The waking up is the desired learned response
(2) The buzzer serves as the learned stimulus
(3) Stopping the wetting is the reinforcement
(4) This is an operant conditioning paradigm

36. Currently, the typical or modal American family with school-aged children is one in which

(1) half of the members are likely to develop a definable mental illness
(2) the parents will divorce during their children's school years
(3) contacts with the extended family are maintained
(4) both the mother and father work outside the home

37. The role of hospitals has been changing in recent years. True statements concerning the current status of hospitals include

(1) hospitals have recently increased the number of outpatient services that are offered
(2) hospitals have recently developed excess capacity
(3) hospitals can be members of multi-institutional systems
(4) most hospitals operate for profit

38. A physician typically perceives a patient as "good" when the patient

(1) shows appreciation for the physician's efforts
(2) seeks help prior to the appearance of symptoms
(3) has objective signs of a treatable disease
(4) displays an emotional reaction to being sick

39. Attachment behaviors include

(1) crying
(2) visual pursuit
(3) clinging
(4) smiling

40. Tardive dyskinesia is a movement disorder characterized mainly by choreoathetoid movements of the upper extremities. It occurs after chronic use of neuroleptic medications. Anticholinergic drugs and amphetamines have been reported to exacerbate the condition. Some cases closely resemble Huntington's disease. Considering this information, which neurotransmitter systems may be involved in the pathophysiology of tardive dyskinesia?

(1) Norepinephrine
(2) Acetylcholine (ACh)
(3) Dopamine
(4) Gamma-aminobutyric acid (GABA)

41. A 65-year-old man has recently been admitted to the psychiatric ward for evaluation and treatment of depression. The psychiatrist wants to do a dexamethasone suppression test (DST). What would be important factors to consider in evaluating the results of the test?

(1) Recent heavy alcohol use
(2) A concurrent diagnosis of dementia
(3) Concurrent use of steroids
(4) Possible underlying Addison's disease

42. Examples of assimilation in cognitive theory include

(1) a child who identifies flying objects as birds identifies an airplane as a "bird"
(2) an infant sucks on each object as if it were a nipple
(3) a child identifies all four-footed animals as "horses"
(4) an infant smiles preferentially at the sound of his mother's voice

43. Margaret Mahler conceptualized a framework within which normal and deviant development could be understood. This framework includes

(1) a sequence of protest, despair, and detachment
(2) the development of the social smile
(3) a sequence of behaviors between 6 and 12 months when the infant and caretaker are separated
(4) the development of object relations within the basic structure of psychoanalytic theory

---

SUMMARY OF DIRECTIONS

A	B	C	D	E
1, 2, 3 only	1, 3 only	2, 4 only	4 only	All are correct

---

44. Changes in sleep that are usually associated with depression include

(1) decreased rapid eye movement (REM) sleep
(2) decreased REM latency
(3) increased total sleep time
(4) decreased stage 4 sleep

45. Hallucinogen intoxication may cause

(1) hypersexual behavior
(2) aggressive behavior
(3) depression and anxiety
(4) symptoms of schizophrenia

Directions: The groups of questions below consist of lettered choices followed by several numbered items. For each numbered item select the **one** lettered choice with which it is **most** closely associated. Each lettered choice may be used once, more than once, or not at all.

Questions 46–49

Specific chromosomal abnormalities have been associated with specific diseases. For each disorder listed below, select the chromosome with which it is associated.

(A) Chromosome 5
(B) X chromosome
(C) Chromosome 4
(D) Chromosome 21
(E) Chromosome 22

46. Huntington's disease
47. Down syndrome
48. Cri du chat syndrome
49. Turner syndrome

Questions 50–53

Listed below are major metabolites that are found in blood and cerebrospinal fluid. Match each with its associated neurotransmitter.

(A) Norepinephrine
(B) Serotonin
(C) Dopamine
(D) Histamine
(E) Acetylcholine (ACh)

50. 3-Methoxy-4-hydroxyphenylglycol (MHPG)
51. 5-Hydroxyindoleacetic acid (5-HIAA)
52. Homovanillic acid (HVA)
53. Vanillylmandelic acid (VMA)

Questions 54–57

For each phase of the sexual response cycle listed below, match the corresponding physiologic response.

(A) Secretion of Bartholin's glands in women and Cowper's glands in men
(B) Descent of the cervix in women and descent of the testes in men
(C) Rhythmic contractions of the pelvic floor in women and of the anal sphincter in men and women
(D) Lubrication of the vagina in women; penile tumescence in men
(E) Intense stimulation of the sympathetic nervous system

54. Excitement phase

55. Plateau phase

56. Orgasmic phase

57. Resolution phase

Questions 58–60

For each person described below, select the appropriate diagnosis.

(A) Alcohol abuse
(B) Schizotypal personality disorder
(C) Narcissistic personality disorder
(D) Dysthymic disorder
(E) Sociopathic personality disorder

58. After being fired from her management position, a 36-year-old woman drives her car into a ditch at 90 miles an hour, but she is so relaxed that she suffers only minor cuts.

59. A flashily dressed young man is brought to a psychiatrist's office by his fiancée, who thinks he needs therapy. The couple argues about petty items in the psychiatrist's presence. After the woman leaves, the young man demands to see the psychiatrist again that afternoon, even though the physician explains that the office schedule is full.

60. Mary has no friends. She lives alone, dresses oddly, and is sometimes identified as a bag lady by her neighbors. She comes to the emergency room occasionally and is so vague that no one can figure out why she is there. However, she does not have obvious delusions or hallucinations, and she always seems about the same.

ANSWERS AND EXPLANATIONS

1. The answer is C. [*Chapter 8 III F 3 b (4); Table 8-4*] Rorschach determinants of form quality and color are believed to reflect perceptual accuracy and emotional responsiveness and control. In this case, the presumption is that the young woman has poor perceptual accuracy and reality testing along with poorly controlled emotional responsiveness. Such clinical characteristics along with autistic logic are most often found in schizophrenia. They are not likely to be found in this combination in cyclothymic disorder, panic disorder, adjustment disorder with anxious mood, or organic brain syndrome.

2. The answer is B. (*Chapter 12 II A*) Sociologist Talcott Parsons has described four societal expectations that are basic to the sick role. These include the obligation to get well, the obligation to seek technically competent help, exemption from blame for the illness, and exemption from usual social-role responsibilities. The sick person is **not** expected to function as usual until his symptoms become severe.

3. The answer is C. (*Chapter 15 II C 2*) Based on Max Weber's original study of large-scale organizations, the definition of a bureaucracy is a hierarchy of offices designed on a rational basis in order to achieve specified goals in a predictable and efficient manner. A bureaucracy can be either public or private. Inefficiency, inflexibility, and overstaffing can be faults of any organizational form and are not peculiar to bureaucracies.

4. The answer is E. (*Chapter 4 II A 2*) The Y chromosome is the determinant of maleness, and no females carry it. No matter how many X chromosomes are present, the presence of a Y chromosome determines a male phenotype. The YO chromosomal constitution is not compatible with life.

5. The answer is A. (*Chapter 10 I A 3*) An elevated level of androgen in a genetic female produces an enlarged clitoris or a normal-looking penis and scrotal sac. This condition is known as the adrenogenital syndrome. The infant has a normal XX chromosomal pattern.

6. The answer is E. (*Chapter 2 V E 3*) Although other sedative–hypnotic drugs such as barbiturates and meprobamate may cause respiratory arrest in the case of an overdose, the benzodiazepines have a high therapeutic index and oral overdoses are usually uncomplicated if the stupor or coma is managed supportively. However, when given intravenously or when combined with another central nervous system depressant such as alcohol, benzodiazepine overdoses may be lethal.

7. The answer is E. (*Chapter 10 VI E 1*) Chronic abuse of alcohol can cause irreversible sexual dysfunction. Small amounts of alcohol can enhance sexual desire by decreasing inhibitions, but larger amounts depress the central nervous system and interfere with sexual excitement and performance in both men and women.

8. The answer is B. (*Chapter 15 II C 3*) A formal organization is the structure as it exists on the official organization chart. An informal organization is the structure as it actually operates. The modifications that occur in the formal structure, creating the informal structure, are the result of personal and social factors that interact with the formal organization. Many social groups operate both within and without work environments. An informal organization cannot be described as being beyond the influence of administrators within the organization because administrators can use the informal structure to help achieve the established goals of the institution. Although institution–client interactions and the relationship of the governing board and the executive staff of the institution may involve some aspects of an informal organization, they are not definitive.

9. The answer is D. (*Chapter 11 II B 3*) Normal parent–infant interaction is affiliative behavior that is mutual, interdependent, and complementary. Although socialization undoubtedly occurs (we learn to parent in large measure from how we have been parented), this is not a very specific interactional description. Ethnocentrism, the tendency to see one's own cultural values and beliefs as superior, is an unrelated concept.

10. The answer is A. (*Chapter 5 III B 2*) Inasmuch as birds do not normally ride bicycles, the individual components of bicycle riding would have to be trained one component at a time by reinforcing individual components of the ultimately desired behavior. This would be done through operant conditioning.

11. The answer is B. (*Chapter 3 II D 1*) Most noradrenergic neurons in the brain arise from the locus ceruleus. Stimulation of this nucleus can produce fearful, anxiety-like responses in animals. The locus ceruleus is thought to play a role in anxiety and panic disorders in humans.

12. The answer is D. (*Chapter 15 I B 2 a*) Medicare was designed to provide the elderly and certain other specific groups, such as patients suffering from end-stage renal disease, with basic coverage for both physician- and hospital-provided health care. It provides coverage, with the exception of a relatively modest deductible and copayments, for all services; and, at least at present, it covers all elderly individuals, regardless of income. It is not to be confused with Medicaid, which is a medical assistance program that is directed at the indigent and is shared by the federal and state governments.

13. The answer is A. [*Chapter 12 II B 4 a (5)*] The guarded, suspicious individual's difficulty in trusting others is intensified when he is ill. As a patient, he is overly concerned about being harmed, exploited, and criticized. Thus, cooperating fully with his physician is perceived as dangerous.

14. The answer is C. (*Chapter 5 II A 1 c, B 4*) Oral factors are more important in the regulation of drinking behavior than eating behavior. Postingestional consequences of both food and water ingestion are important; that is, both drinking and eating are regulated in correspondence with body needs for fluid and nutrients. Much of the immediate feedback for drinking as well as metering of amounts of fluid ingested, however, occurs through cooling of the mouth and tactile feedback from the oral cavity.

15. The answer is A. (*Chapter 2 X A 1*) Several antihypertensive drugs, especially reserpine, methyldopa, and propranolol, have been associated with depression. In most cases the side effect of depression is best treated by changing to another antihypertensive agent. The emergence of depression may relate to the ability of antihypertensive drugs to block central nervous system catecholamines. A primary theory of the neurochemistry of depression is that it is caused by low levels of amine neurotransmitters.

16. The answer is D. (*Chapter 5 III A 1*) Imprinting is a type of animal behavior in which young birds learn to follow their mothers or any other large, moving, noise-making animal or object, and it occurs only during a critical period shortly after hatching. Because of the nature of the behavior that is usually learned by imprinting (following the mother), imprinting would only be of adaptive value to a young infant. Other forms of learning, such as operant conditioning, habituation, and classical conditioning, can involve a wide variety of behaviors and stimuli and can continue to be of adaptive value through all stages of development.

17. The answer is A. (*Chapter 10 I A 2*) The presence of testosterone influences the hypothalamus to develop the male acyclic pattern of gonadotropin release. The absence of testosterone results in the cyclic pattern of gonadotropin release of the female-typed brain.

18. The answer is B. (*Chapter 15 II E 1 b*) Although increases in the age of the population and in the relative and absolute number of physicians as well as new health care technology may have contributed to increases in health care costs, most observers have suggested that increased insurance coverage has made patients insensitive to prices and services delivered by providers. It has been, therefore, by all measures, the most important reason for the rising cost of health care in the United States.

19. The answer is B. [*Chapter 3 II A 1 b (2), 2 b, 3 b, 4 b, D 2*] Damage to the frontal lobes seems to be associated most with the appearance of snout and grasp reflexes as well as sucking and palmomental reflexes. Symptoms of parietal lobe damage include problems with sensory discrimination. Symptoms of occipital lobe damage include visual illusions, visual distortion, and blindness. Temporal lobe damage is associated with a variety of findings, including Klüver-Bucy–like syndromes and partial complex (psychomotor) seizures.

20. The answer is D. (*Chapter 2 IX D*) Cross-dependence exists between opioids. Therefore, methadone alleviates symptoms of withdrawal. Narcotic antagonists such as naloxone precipitate or exaggerate withdrawal in a dependent patient and may be used to treat opioid overdoses. Seizures are not common in opioid withdrawal. Typical symptoms of withdrawal include piloerection ("gooseflesh"), chilling, and sweating. This skin appearance gave rise to the expression "cold turkey" to describe abrupt withdrawal.

21. The answer is D. [*Chapter 4 II A 3 d (1)*] Down syndrome (mongolism) is commonly associated with trisomy 21 due to nondisjunction, a condition that is seen most frequently in the offspring of older mothers. A less common form of Down syndrome results from translocation of chromosome 21, and the total number of chromosomes is 46; this form is seen in the offspring of mothers of all ages. The clinical features of the two forms of the syndrome (including moderate mental retardation) are indistinguishable.

22. The answer is C. (*Chapter 10 I C 1 b*) In early childhood, children's exploration of their own bodies and those of other children of similar age is not unusual and is not indicative of other problems. A child who has been sexually overstimulated may exhibit more intense sexual behavior in public, but sexual play alone does not suggest this overstimulation. Often the most harmful aspect of this sexual exploration is the negative reaction it may illicit from parents and other authority figures.

23. The answer is D. (*Chapter 14 V E 2 a, b*) Utilitarianism originates with the philosophies of David Hume, Jeremy Bentham, and John Stuart Mill. Utilitarian theory places ultimate value on the net benefits generated by a particular action. In contrast, in nonconsequential theories, actions themselves are believed to have inherent qualities that make them right or wrong.

24. The answer is E (all). (*Chapter 9 I*) Reliability, one definition of which is replicability, is necessary to the agreement that a disease exists, although reliability may not be sufficient unto itself. Diseases can exist in which the only presenting findings are patients' reports of their mental symptoms; examples include delirium, schizophrenia, and depression. The response to treatment is an accepted measure of whether the initial judgment of the presence of an illness was correct. In psychiatric illnesses, as well as in other medical illnesses, patient histories may be sufficient to suggest or establish correct diagnoses; examples include migraine, irritable bowel syndrome, and depression.

25. The answer is A (1, 2, 3). (*Chapter 3 II B 1*) The limbic lobe was first identified as such by Paul Broca, and this original concept later was expanded to be called the limbic system, which is a network of nuclei and tracts composed of both cortical and subcortical tissue. The limbic system is thought to be the center of emotion. The raphe nucleus, although connected to the limbic system, is not considered to be a part of it.

26. The answer is B (1, 3). (*Chapter 6 II B 5*) Empiric studies document that unpredictably intermittent rewards are the most effective reinforcement for behavior and that continuous reward is an effective short-term, not long-term, reinforcement. Disapproval or criticism may be experienced as attention and be reinforcing of behavior. A reward, as defined by the subject, is reinforcing for behavior and is related to the gratification of both primary and learned needs.

27. The answer is D (4). (*Chapter 12 III A 4*) Affective neutrality refers to the expectation of society that the physician's attitude will be one of professional concern and compassion. In his effort to achieve and maintain objectivity and empathy in his interaction with patients, he is not to become emotionally involved with them.

28. The answer is A (1, 2, 3). (*Chapter 7 II B 2*) Stranger anxiety (or eight-month anxiety), as described by Spitz, is of importance on several grounds. First, it is an indication that a significant, differentiated attachment to the caretaker has taken place, and, therefore, it is a reaction to the absence of the caretaker. Second, it reflects the development of the capacity for evocative memory and for object permanence; that is, the capacity to retain, albeit briefly, the mental representation of an object (or person) even when it is not present.

29. The answer is A (1, 2, 3). [*Chapter 5 II D 3 b (1)*] Animals with the Klüver-Bucy syndrome are generally tame rather than aggressive, although they frequently show inappropriate social interactions with members of their own species. Klüver-Bucy syndrome also includes a lack of fear of natural enemies, hyperactive and indiscriminate sexuality, and a tendency to explore objects orally and indiscriminately.

30. The answer is C (2, 4). (*Chapter 11 IV B 2, 3, 5, 8*) There has been no significant change in the percentage of the population that eventually marries. Marriage remains as popular as ever, with 95% of individuals marrying at least once during their lifetime. Although the average geographic distance between extended family members continues to grow, extended families continue to be major sources of social support.

31. The answer is A (1, 2, 3). (*Chapter 6 I B 6*) Maturationally based ego functions are those that depend on and emerge out of neurologic maturation and, as such, develop along a more or less predetermined sequential timetable. Defenses, on the other hand, are individualized and dependent on the interaction with the environment and the influence of specific experience.

32. The answer is C (2, 4). [*Chapter 8 II E 1 c (2) (c), 2 a (9), (12)*] Word salad and neologisms were assumed in the past to be important and common findings in schizophrenia. Recent studies have shown their rarity in schizophrenia and their frequent occurrence in fluent and mixed aphasias. While there may be great similarity between schizophrenia and fluent and mixed aphasias on the basis of these items, aphasic patients generally have highly reduced overall verbal output.

33. The answer is D (4). (*Chapter 5 I A, B*) Most of the behavior patterns of invertebrates are inherited. Although humans and other mammals have some inherited behavior patterns, higher animals have increasingly less dependence on inherited patterns of behavior. This is not overall a biological disadvantage, although it may be related to a lower reproductive rate because of the increased amount of time then devoted to child rearing.

34. The answer is E (all). (*Chapter 9 VII A, B 4 b, C 1 b, c*) Transient hypertension, usually with an elevated pulse rate and often with a generalized increased metabolism, is characteristic of the withdrawal states of alcohol and a number of other drugs. In treating withdrawal, a reasonable guideline is that the drug dosage can be halved on successive days until the dose is zero. (Barbiturates and alprazolam may be exceptions because more cautious schedules are required, with perhaps a 10% reduction in dosage per day.) The response to small to moderate dosages of phencyclidine (PCP) and other hallucinogens, especially on a chronic basis, may mimic many psychiatric disorders, including anxiety states. Some hallucinogens (e.g., PCP) may need to be combated by drugs such as major tranquilizers and antianxiety agents or by acidification of the urine in order to speed up renal clearance of the offending agent.

35. The answer is C (2, 4). (*Chapter 6 II C 2*) The situation discussed in this question demonstrates eliciting new behavior (i.e., the bed-wetting stops) by the introduction of an aversive consequence (i.e., the buzzer causes awakening, which extinguishes the undesirable behavior). This is a classic paradigm of operant conditioning.

36. The answer is E (all). (*Chapter 11 IV B 4, 5, 6, 8, D 2 a*) Current demographics indicate that for all children under the age of 18 years, 40% live in families in which both the mother and father work outside the home, 30% will experience the divorce of their parents, and 20% live in families in which the father is the sole wage earner. In at least 50% of families, one or more members will develop a diagnosable mental illness at one time or another. Additionally, even though the geographic distance that separates members of extended families has increased, contact among members (e.g., telephone calls and holiday visits) remains high.

37. The answer is A (1, 2, 3). (*Chapter 15 I A 1*) Although hospitals that operate for profit might be a growing and an important segment of health care delivery, they still account for no more than 20% of all hospitals. Some of the more important trends in the hospital sector involve the hospital's provision of community service; for example, hospitals have recently increased the number of outpatient services that are offered.

38. The answer is B (1, 3). (*Chapter 12 III C 1*) The "good" patient typically does not seek help prior to the appearance of symptoms lest he be perceived as a hypochondriac, and he does not display much emotion lest he be referred to a psychiatrist. The "good" patient is explicitly appreciative of the physician's efforts at treating his detectable, significant disease.

39. The answer is E (all). (*Chapter 7 II A 2 a, B 1, 2*) According to attachment theory, the human organism is preadapted for survival. These biologically based, built-in behaviors that seem to serve the process of maintaining contact with the mother are referred to as attachment behaviors. Included among them are crying, smiling, looking, following, approaching, sucking, and clinging.

40. The answer is E (all). (*Chapter 1 III A 5, B 4 c; IV E; V A 5*) It has been proposed that tardive dyskinesia may be the result of dopamine receptor supersensitivity following chronic postsynaptic dopamine receptor blockade with neuroleptics. This dopamine receptor supersensitivity is thought to upset the dopamine–acetylcholine (ACh) balance in the extrapyramidal motor system, resulting in the choreoathetoid movements. Recent evidence, including exacerbation of the condition with amphetamines and elevated norepinephrine and dopamine-β-hydroxylase concentrations in a subgroup of tardive dyskinesia patients, indicates that norepinephrine may also be important in the pathophysiology of tardive dyskinesia. Finally, the clinical resemblance of some tardive dyskinesia patients to patients with Huntington's disease, another choreoathetoid disorder, plus the efficacy of GABAergic agonists in some patients with tardive dyskinesia suggest that GABAergic mechanisms may also be involved.

41. The answer is E (all). (*Chapter 3 VII A*) False-positive results of the dexamethasone suppression test (DST) have been associated with a number of underlying medical conditions such as uncontrolled diabetes, Cushing's disease, and acute withdrawal from alcohol. False-negative results are associated with Addison's disease and steroid therapy. A significant proportion of patients with psychiatric disorders other than depression, such as dementia, have abnormal DST results. There are no clear indications at this time for routine use of the DST in the diagnosis or management of depression, although research on the DST continues. While it might have less predictive value than most diagnostic laboratory tests in medicine, it may be helpful in monitoring clinical recovery.

42. The answer is A (1, 2, 3). (*Chapter 6 III B 2 a*) Assimilation is the incorporation of a stimulus into an existing reflex pattern or preexisting comprehension without altering or modifying the pattern to fit the new stimulus. An infant who has learned to smile preferentially at the sound of his mother's voice has passed beyond assimilation, since the innate reflex pattern of smiling has been modified by experience.

43. The answer is D (4). (*Chapter 7 II B 4*) Margaret Mahler described object relations from normal autism, to the symbiotic phase, through differentiation and practicing phases, into the rapprochement crisis, when the infant's illusion of invincibility crumbles. As a consequence of individuation, object constancy is established.

44. The answer is C (2, 4). (*Chapter 3 III C 1*) Disturbances in sleep usually accompany depression. Depression has been associated with increased rapid eye movement (REM) sleep and decreased REM latency. REM latencies after the intravenous administration of acetylcholine (ACh)-like drugs are reported to be much shorter in patients with major depression than in normal controls. Decreased stage 4 sleep has been found both in depressed patients and in some patients with chronic schizophrenia. Although hypersomnia can occur in depressive illness, insomnia of some type is more common.

45. The answer is E (all). (*Chapter 9 VII B 4*) Most hallucinogen intoxication produces dilated pupils, increased heart rate and blood pressure, illusions, hallucinations (both visual and tactile), altered mood, and depressed cognition. Aggressive and hypersexual behavior also are commonly seen in hallucinogen abusers. Hallucinogen intoxication causes psychiatric symptoms, especially psychotic symptoms of schizophrenia and mania as well as depression and anxiety.

46–49. The answers are: 46-C, 47-D, 48-A, 49-B. (*Chapter 4 II A 2, 3, B 7*) Down syndrome is most often associated with three instead of the normal two chromosomes 21 (i.e., trisomy 21). Cri du chat syndrome is associated with a deletion of the short arm of chromosome 5. Turner's syndrome is associated with a single X chromosome. Recently, Huntington's disease, which is autosomal dominant with full penetrance, has been found to be associated with a gene marker located on chromosome 4.

50–53. The answers are: 50-A, 51-B, 52-C, 53-A. (*Chapter 1 III A 2 b, B 2 a, C 2 a*) 3-Methoxy-4-hydroxyphenylglycol (MHPG) is a metabolite of norepinephrine that is formed in the brain and in the periphery; it is estimated that between 30% and 50% of urinary MHPG is derived from brain norepinephrine. Decreased levels of MHPG have been observed in patients with bipolar disorder. Vanillylmandelic acid (VMA), the major metabolite of norepinephrine, has less clinical use in psychiatry, but it is routinely measured in suspected cases of pheochromocytoma, in which excess amounts of norepinephrine are produced. Very little VMA is found in the brain. Homovanillic acid (HVA) is a very useful indicator of dopaminergic function when it is measured in the cerebrospinal fluid or in the brain. Decreased amounts of HVA in the cerebrospinal fluid have been associated with Parkinson's disease. 5-Hydroxyindoleacetic acid (5-HIAA) is the major metabolite (and in the brain, possibly the only metabolite) of serotonin. Some depressed patients have been found to have altered cerebrospinal fluid levels of 5-HIAA.

54–57. The answers are: 54-D, 55-A, 56-C, 57-B. (*Chapter 10 II A*) During the excitement phase of the sexual response cycle, pelvic congestion and myotonia result in enlargement of the clitoris and ballooning and sweating (lubrication) of the vagina in women. In men, there is penile tumescence and elevation of the scrotal sac.

There is retraction of the clitoris, tenting of the vagina, and mucoid secretions from Bartholin's glands during the plateau phase in women. In men, the testes enlarge and elevate further, and there are mucoid secretions from Cowper's glands.

During the orgasmic phase, contraction of the orgasmic platform, including the pelvic floor, uterus, and anal sphincter, occurs in women. In men, there are contractions of the prostate gland, seminal vesicles, urethra, and anal sphincter.

During the resolution phase, decreased vasoconstriction of the vaginal wall and descent of the cervix into the dorsal area of the vagina occurs in women. In men, there is penile detumescence along with descent of the testes.

58–60. The answers are: 58-A, 59-C, 60-B. (*Chapter 9 II A, C; III A, E; VII A 1, B 1 a; VIII A, B 1 b, 2 c*) Difficulties with one's occupation or responsibilities, traffic accidents, and diminution of anxiety all suggest serious alcohol abuse. Approximately 50% of fatal automobile accidents in the United States are associated with alcohol.

The young man in the question is characterized by attention-seeking, demanding and shallow relationships and, apparently, little empathy. Although sociopathy is possible, there is no evidence of such in the question. The young man demonstrates narcissistic personality traits, which include an inflated sense of self-importance with little concern for the needs of other people.

An effort should be made to discern whether schizophrenia or an organic brain syndrome is present in Mary. However, the stability of the pattern argues for a personality disorder.

1

Biochemistry and Behavior

James B. Lohr
Charles A. Kaufmann
Dilip V. Jeste

I. INTRODUCTION. It is well-known that certain chemical substances may influence mood, thought, and action. With the discovery of neuroleptics, antidepressants, lithium, levodopa (L-dopa), lysergic acid diethylamide (LSD), and other drugs that have a profound effect on both normal and abnormal behavior, the field of psychopharmacology has grown enormously and, with it, interest in the basic biochemistry of behavior.

II. NEURONAL TRANSMISSION OF INFORMATION. About 75 years ago Ramon y Cajal developed the **"neuron doctrine."** According to this doctrine, the neuron is the basic unit of the nervous system. **Information basic to behavior is transferred** in the form of specific chemicals and energy, both **within neurons** (intraneuronal) **and between neurons** (interneuronal).

A. MEMBRANES. In both intraneuronal and interneuronal processes, neuronal membranes play an important role. They contain the means by which information is transferred from one neuron to the next. Information transfer across neurons occurs via electrical or chemical changes.

1. Ion channels. The **electrical** means of neuronal transfer involves the **action potential**: When a neuron is stimulated, a dramatic change in the electrical potential across the axonal membrane is propagated down the length of the axon.
   a. The action potential is dependent upon the opening and closing of membrane-associated proteins known as **ion channels**, which allow for the passage of ions such as sodium, potassium, chloride, and calcium.
   b. The passage of these ions across the neuronal membrane causes depolarization (in which the electrical potential difference across the membrane rises from approximately -70 mV to -15 mV), followed by repolarization (whereby the baseline high potential difference is restored).

2. Receptors. The **chemical means** of information transfer across neurons involves **neurochemical receptors** located in the membrane itself.
   a. Neurochemical receptors are proteins that bind to specific chemical substances. This binding results in the eventual triggering of specific processes within the neuron.
   b. These receptors are important for the action of **neurotransmitters**, **neuromodulators**, and **neurohormones** (see section II C 2).

B. INTRANEURONAL TRANSPORT. Information, in the form of specific chemical substances, can pass through the body of a neuron from one portion to another, often along axons or dendrites, and can influence some specific aspect of neuronal functioning, such as nuclear processes and energy metabolism. **Cyclic nucleotides, calcium,** and **phosphatidylinositol** are believed to be important intraneuronal "messengers."

1. Cyclic nucleotides are substances such as cyclic adenosine $3',5'$-monophosphate **(cAMP)** and cyclic guanosine $3',5'$-monophosphate **(cGMP)**. They are sometimes called **second messengers** because they help translate the information received from extracellular messengers (such as neurotransmitters and hormones) into an intracellular response.
   a. Certain neurotransmitters, by binding to receptors, **activate adenylate cyclase**, which is the enzyme that catalyzes the formation of cAMP from adenosine triphosphate (ATP). The increase in cAMP concentration may then activate cAMP-dependent protein phosphorylation, which may, in turn, cause a change in ion permeability in the neuronal membrane.
   b. Instead of activating adenylate cyclase, some receptors [possibly including α_2-adrenergic receptors, dopamine D_2 receptors, somatostatin receptors, gamma-aminobutyric acid (GABA) B receptors, and certain muscarinic and opiate receptors] are believed to inhibit it.
   c. Not all neurotransmitters exert their effects through the cyclic nucleotide system.

2. Calcium

a. Another **second messenger** system consists of calcium along with a number of associated binding proteins, most importantly a protein known as **calmodulin**.

b. Depolarization of neurons is associated with significant quantities of calcium entering the neuron, and this **calcium binds with calmodulin**, triggering it to associate with and modulate a number of calcium-dependent enzymes such as certain types of adenylate cyclase, phosphodiesterase, and adenosinetriphosphatase (ATPase).

3. Phosphatidylinositol is a membrane phospholipid that may regulate membrane permeability during synaptic transmission.

C. INTERNEURONAL TRANSPORT

1. **Synapses.** Interneuronal transfer of information takes place primarily through the synapse, which is a term derived from the Greek word for connection or conjunction. Three different types of synapses have been described: chemical, electrical, and conjoint.

   a. **Chemical synapses** are perhaps the most important type of synapses. They consist of a specific region where the membranes of two neurons are in close approximation. A chemical messenger released from the presynaptic membrane travels across the synaptic cleft and acts on a specific receptor on the postsynaptic membrane. In some cases the messenger may act on receptors on the presynaptic membrane as well.

   b. **Electrical synapses**, the function of which is poorly understood, transmit information directly through the transfer of an electrical charge and do not employ chemical messengers.

   c. **Conjoint synapses** operate through both chemical and electrical means.

2. **Neuroregulators** are chemicals that carry information between neurons. They **include neurotransmitters**, **neuromodulators**, and **neurohormones**.

   a. **Neurotransmitters** are neuroregulators that **exert their effects on specific pre- or postsynaptic receptors**. The transfer of information by neurotransmitters usually takes only 1 to 2 msec, in contrast to that by other neuroregulators, which takes much longer.

   b. **Neuromodulators**, like neurotransmitters, may be released from presynaptic membranes and exert their effects on receptors. However, neuromodulators may be released from membranes other than synaptic ones, and they may act on receptors located on large numbers of neurons. Their effects last longer than those of neurotransmitters (up to minutes). Neuromodulators may control the action of neurotransmitters on certain synapses.

   c. **Neurohormones** also act on receptors located on neurons. The main difference between neurohormones and the other neuroregulators is that neurohormones are released into the systemic circulation and thus travel throughout the body.

3. **Types of neurotransmitters**

   a. Neurotransmitters may be divided in two ways, depending on their effects on the postsynaptic neuron.

      (1) **Excitatory neurotransmitters** increase the likelihood of the firing of the postsynaptic neuron.

      (2) **Inhibitory neurotransmitters** decrease the likelihood of firing.

   b. Some neurotransmitters appear to be solely excitatory or inhibitory (such as glutamate, which appears to be solely excitatory, and GABA and glycine, which appear to be solely inhibitory). Other neurotransmitters may function either way [such as dopamine and acetylcholine (ACh)].

   c. Some transmitters function as excitatory or inhibitory at different synapses on the same neuron.

4. **Neurotransmitter criteria**

   a. In order to be considered a definite neurotransmitter, neurochemicals must meet specific criteria, as follows.

      (1) The neurotransmitter must be present in nerve terminals.

      (2) Stimulation of the nerve must cause the release of the transmitter in sufficient amounts to exert its actions on the postsynaptic neuron.

      (3) The effects of the transmitter on the postsynaptic membrane must be similar to those of transmitter stimulation of the presynaptic nerve (such as activating the same ion channels).

      (4) Pharmacologic agents should alter the dose-response curve of the applied neurotransmitter in the same magnitude and direction that they alter the naturally occurring synaptic potential.

      (5) A mechanism for inactivation or metabolism of the transmitter must exist in the vicinity of the synapse.

   b. Neurotransmitters that meet these criteria are considered **proven or definite neurotransmitters** and include ACh, dopamine, norepinephrine, epinephrine, GABA, serotonin, and glycine. Those that meet a few of the criteria are considered **putative neurotransmitters** and include glutamate, aspartate, and substance P. Those that only meet one or two criteria are considered **neurotransmitter candidates** and include adenosine, cAMP, prostaglandins, and most peptides.

5. **Steps in neurochemical transmission**
   a. **Synthesis** of a specific neurotransmitter may take place near the presynaptic membrane where it is to be released or elsewhere in the neuron.
   b. **Transport.** The neurotransmitter is moved from the site of its synthesis to that of its storage or release.
   c. **Storage** of a neurotransmitter often takes place in vesicles specific to that purpose.
   d. **Release.** The exact mechanism of release of many neuroregulators is not apparent.
      (1) Some neuroregulators appear to be released by a process in which a vesicle containing the regulator liberates its contents. It is not always clear, however, if the regulator simply diffuses out of the vesicle and the neuron or if the vesicle combines with the neuron plasma membrane, externalizing its contents through the process of **exocytosis**.
      (2) The process of release is **dependent on the influx of calcium** that occurs with depolarization of the presynaptic membrane.
      (3) In some cases, neurotransmitter receptors on the presynaptic neuron can modulate the release of that transmitter. Such receptors are called **autoreceptors**.
   e. **Termination.** The action of a particular neuroregulator may be terminated by **diffusion** of the regulator out of the receptor area, **metabolism** of the regulator, or **reuptake** of the regulator, usually into the presynaptic neuron. Reuptake is probably the most common process.

6. **Mechanisms of neuroregulator effects**
   a. **Binding** to the recognition site of specific receptors is the first step in the action of neurotransmitters.
   b. **Transduction**
      (1) This is the process by which the binding of the receptor results in a biological response of the neuron. This process takes place through so-called **effector proteins**, which are closely linked to the receptor protein. There are two basic types of effector proteins: nucleotide cyclases that catalyze the formation of cyclic nucleotides; and ion channels that control passage of certain ions through the membrane.
      (2) **Modulator proteins** may be interposed between the receptor and effector proteins and may themselves have binding sites for neuromodulators and neurohormones. Modulator proteins, such as guanine nucleotide binding protein (see section III C 3), may provide the means through which neuromodulators and neurohormones affect synaptic function.
         (a) Some neuromodulators coexist with neurotransmitters in the same neuron. These neuromodulators, which are usually peptides, may regulate the time course and the magnitude of the postsynaptic activity of the neurotransmitter.
         (b) It used to be thought that one neuron could possess only one neuroregulator and that this neuroregulator had the same function (excitation or inhibition) at every synapse of that neuron. This was referred to as **Dale's principle**, but it is now known to be incorrect.
   c. **Amplification.** Following transduction, the full response of the neuron to the neurotransmitter occurs through amplification of the initial response. This may take place through activation of enzymes, protein phosphorylation, hormone release, and a number of other mechanisms.

III. BIOGENIC AMINES

A. DOPAMINE

1. **Synthesis.** Tyrosine hydroxylation is the rate-limiting step in the synthesis of all of the major catecholamines (i.e., dopamine, norepinephrine, and epinephrine).

$$\text{Phenylalanine} \xrightarrow[\text{O}_2\text{, pteridine, NADPH}]{\text{phenylalanine hydroxylase}} \text{Tyrosine}$$

$$\text{Tyrosine} \xrightarrow[\text{O}_2\text{, pteridine, NADPH}]{\text{tyrosine hydroxylase}} \text{L-Dopa (3,4-dihydroxy-L-phenylalanine)}$$

$$\text{L-Dopa} \xrightarrow[\text{pyridoxal PO}_4]{\text{aromatic L-amino acid decarboxylase}} \text{Dopamine}$$

2. Metabolism
 a. Two enzymes are important for the inactivation of catecholamines: monoamine oxidase (MAO) and catechol-*O*-methyltransferase (COMT).
  (1) MAO is located on the outer membrane of mitochondria and is important for the oxidative deamination of intracellular, extravesicular catecholamines. Two forms of MAO have been identified. Dopamine is deaminated by both forms.
   (a) MAO-A deaminates norepinephrine and serotonin.
   (b) MAO-B deaminates β-phenylethylamine and benzylamine.
  (2) COMT is found on the outer plasma membranes of most cells and methylates most extracellular catecholamines.
 b. A major metabolite of dopamine in urine and plasma is homovanillic acid (HVA), which is formed through the action of both MAO and COMT, in either order.

3. Receptors. The action of dopamine may be either inhibitory or excitatory, but inhibition appears to be the more common effect. It is uncertain exactly how many types of dopamine receptors there are; however, there are at least two (D_1 and D_2) and perhaps four (D_3 and D_4), although D_3 and D_4 may be high-affinity forms of D_1 and D_2.
 a. D_1 receptors are postsynaptic and activate adenylate cyclase, but their exact function is uncertain.
 b. D_2 receptors are also postsynaptic and probably inhibit adenylate cyclase.
 c. D_3 receptors are presynaptic and inhibit dopamine release.

4. Important brain tracts
 a. Several important dopaminergic tracts have been identified in the brain.
  (1) Nigrostriatal tract. This pathway runs from the pars compacta of the substantia nigra to the striatum, which is comprised of the caudate nucleus and the putamen. The nigrostriatal pathway is **important in the initiation of movement** in animals and man, as its destruction causes a reduction or loss of movement.
  (2) Mesolimbic and mesocortical tracts. The dopaminergic neurons that form these tracts are found in the ventral tegmental area of Tsai, which lies superior and medial to the substantia nigra. The neurons project to the limbic system, including the amygdala, nucleus accumbens, septum, and cingulate gyrus, and to the cerebral cortex, predominately to the frontal lobes. These tracts are believed to be **important in affect, cognition**, and **motivation** in man.
  (3) Tuberoinfundibular (tuberohypophyseal) tract. The dopaminergic neurons of this tract are located in the arcuate nuclei and periventricular nuclei of the **hypothalamus** and project to the median eminence of the hypothalamus and to the intermediate lobe of the **pituitary gland**. Dopamine is thought to act as a prolactin-inhibiting factor, and the tuberoinfundibular pathway is believed to be **important in the regulation of prolactin release**.
  (4) Medullary periventricular tract. Dopaminergic cell bodies are located in the motor nucleus of the vagus nerve and in the nucleus of the solitary tract and probably project to the periventricular and periaqueductal gray areas, the reticular formation, and the spinal cord gray areas. Their exact function is unknown.
  (5) Incertohypothalamic tract. A small group of neurons in the zona incerta project from the dorsal posterior hypothalamus to the dorsal anterior hypothalamus and to the septum. Their function is unknown.
 b. In addition to the above-mentioned tracts, dopaminergic neurons are located in the interplexiform cells of the inner nuclear layer of the retina and in the periglomerular cells of the olfactory bulb. These neurons lack axons and make connections via dendrodendritic synapses.

5. Behavioral functions. From a behavioral perspective, **the three most important dopaminergic tracts are the nigrostriatal, mesolimbic, and mesocortical**.
 a. The nigrostriatal tract is the pathway that degenerates in Parkinson's disease, resulting in the clinical picture of akinesia, tremor, rigidity, and loss of postural reflexes.
  (1) Neuroleptic drugs, because they block postsynaptic dopamine receptors, and reserpine, because it depletes dopamine, also cause parkinsonism.
  (2) A relative excess of dopamine transmission is thought to be important in some **disorders of excessive movement** (hyperkinetic disorders) such as tardive dyskinesia, which occurs after long-term treatment with neuroleptic drugs and usually appears as choreoathetoid movements of the mouth and hands. One hypothesis of tardive dyskinesia is that long-term treatment with neuroleptic drugs causes supersensitivity of postsynaptic D_2 dopamine receptors.
 b. Dopamine is also important for the **organization of thought and feeling**.
  (1) Schizophrenia, a disorder marked by hallucinations, delusions, thought disorder, and inappropriate or blunted affect, has been postulated to be related to **abnormalities in**

dopamine transmission in the mesolimbic and possibly mesocortical areas of the brain. This is known as the **dopamine hypothesis of schizophrenia**. (Although dopamine probably plays a role in schizophrenia as well as in other psychotic illnesses, dopaminergic abnormalities alone do not account for the entire clinical picture.)

(2) Basically, the psychotic symptoms of schizophrenia are believed to result from a hyperdopaminergic state.

(a) The ability of neuroleptic drugs to block dopamine receptors correlates significantly with their antipsychotic potency.

(b) Dopamine agonist drugs such as amphetamine and L-dopa tend to make schizophrenic symptoms worse.

(c) There is some evidence of increased concentrations of dopamine and increased dopamine receptor activity in patients with schizophrenia (although it is not always clear if increased dopamine concentrations and receptor activity are secondary to treatment with neuroleptic drugs).

B. NOREPINEPHRINE

1. Synthesis

$$\text{Dopamine} \xrightarrow[\text{Cu}^{2+},\ O_2,\ ascorbate]{\textit{dopamine-}\beta\textit{-hydroxylase}} \text{Norepinephrine} \atop \downarrow \atop \text{Epinephrine*}$$

2. Metabolism

a. Two metabolites of norepinephrine are commonly measured in plasma or urine: 3-methoxy-4-hydroxyphenylglycol (MHPG) and 3-methoxy-4-hydroxymandelic acid (vanillylmandelic acid or VMA). Thirty to fifty percent of urinary MHPG is formed in the brain. Both MHPG and VMA are formed through the oxidative deamination of norepinephrine involving the enzyme MAO-A.

b. At least in some instances, it appears that norepinephrine is released into the synaptic cleft from vesicles in which it is stored by the process of exocytosis. After release, there is an active reuptake process that removes norepinephrine from the synaptic cleft.

3. Receptors

a. There are four types of norepinephrine (noradrenergic) receptors: α_1, α_2, β_1, and β_2.

(1) α_1-**Receptors** are postsynaptic and are not linked to adenylate cyclase. Prazosin exerts relatively selective α_1-receptor blockade.

(2) α_2-**Receptors** are mainly (although not exclusively) presynaptic, are linked to adenylate cyclase, and decrease the synthesis of norepinephrine in the presynaptic neuron when stimulated. At low doses, clonidine is an α_2-agonist and piperoxan and yohimbine are selective α_2-antagonists.

(3) β_1-**Receptors** are mainly (but not exclusively) postsynaptic and are linked to adenylate cyclase. Practolol, metoprolol, atenolol, acebutolol, and tolamolol are selective antagonists.

(4) β_2-**Receptors** are postsynaptic and also are linked to adenylate cyclase. Terbutaline and albuterol are selective agonists.

b. There is also a variety of **nonselective β-agonists** and **β-antagonists**.

(1) Nonselective β-agonists include epinephrine and norepinephrine (which are equipotent on β_1-receptors, although epinephrine is more potent than norepinephrine on β_2-receptors).

(2) Nonselective β-antagonists include propranolol, alprenolol, nadolol, and timolol.

(3) In the periphery, β_1-receptors are found predominantly in the heart, whereas β_2-receptors are found mainly in the lungs.

4. Important brain tracts

a. There are **two major groups of noradrenergic neuron tracts in the brain**.

(1) The first group arises from the **locus ceruleus**, which is a cluster of pigmented neurons located within the pontine central gray area along the lateral aspect of the fourth ventricle. This nucleus sends projections to the cerebellum and spinal cord and through the median forebrain bundle to the hippocampus, ventral striatum, and entire cerebral cortex.

(2) The second group of tracts originates in the lateral ventral tegmental areas and projects to basal forebrain areas such as the septum and amygdala.

b. There is considerable intermingling of noradrenergic neurons, making analysis of projection systems difficult.

---

*Epinephrine, which is formed from norepinephrine, is found primarily in the adrenal medulla; in the brain, it is only found in a small group of neurons in the brain stem.

5. Behavioral functions

a. Noradrenergic axons project to most areas of the brain, and it is likely that norepinephrine is an important neuromodulator in the related areas. For example, norepinephrine enhances locomotor responses to dopamine. Norepinephrine is also thought to play a role in various physiologic functions, including the sleep–wake cycle, pain, anxiety, and arousal. It has been proposed that the norepinephrine system mediates the organism's orientation to the environment: When unexpected external sensory stimuli arise, norepinephrine neuronal firing increases, whereas it decreases during tonic vegetative activities.

b. Norepinephrine is considered to be important in the genesis and maintenance of mood, and it may be related to mood and anxiety disorders.

  (1) The **catecholamine theory of mood disorders** states that reduced activity of catecholaminergic systems (usually the noradrenergic system) in certain brain areas may be associated with depression and high levels with mania. This theory is based on indirect pharmacologic evidence, such as the following.

  (a) Reserpine, which depletes norepinephrine, causes a state similar to depression.

  (b) MAO inhibitors such as iproniazid have antidepressant properties.

  (c) Amphetamines, which cause the release of norepinephrine, also cause an elevation of mood.

  (d) Tricyclic antidepressants increase the availability of norepinephrine.

  (e) Propranolol, a nonselective β-blocker, has been reported to cause symptom improvement in some patients with manic-depressive illness.

  (2) Similarly, there is some indirect pharmacologic evidence of norepinephrine hyperactivity in a subset of schizophrenic patients and in patients with anxiety disorders.

c. It has been proposed that norepinephrine is involved in a number of different movement disorders, including autosomal dominant torsion dystonia, Parkinson's disease, Tourette's syndrome (which is marked by vocal and motor tics), akathisia (a disorder of motor restlessness that may be associated with neuroleptic drugs), and tardive dyskinesia.

C. SEROTONIN [5-HYDROXYTRYPTAMINE (5-HT)]

1. Synthesis

$$\text{Tryptophan} \xrightarrow{\textit{tryptophan-5-hydroxylase}} \text{5-Hydroxytryptophan}$$

$$\text{5-Hydroxytryptophan} \xrightarrow{\textit{aromatic L-amino acid decarboxylase}} \text{Serotonin}$$

2. Metabolism

a. The catabolism of serotonin involves oxidation of the amino group, which is catalyzed by MAO (primarily MAO-A). Usually this is rapidly oxidized further to 5-hydroxyindoleacetic acid (5-HIAA).

  (1) **Melatonin** is an *N*-acetylated derivative of serotonin that is made in the pineal gland.

  (2) *N*-Methylated and *N*-formylated derivatives may also be formed in the brain. They have received attention because they may cause psychosis.

b. Apart from degradation, serotonin may be inactivated by reuptake into the presynaptic neuron, a process that is inhibited by tricyclic antidepressants. Drugs such as reserpine and tetrabenazine deplete serotonin from the granules.

3. Receptors

a. Two types of serotonergic receptors are thought to exist.

  (1) S_1 **(or 5-HT$_1$) receptors** preferentially bind serotonin, are regulated by guanine nucleotides, and possibly activate adenylate cyclase.

  (2) S_2 **(or 5-HT$_2$) receptors** preferentially bind spiperone and are less affected by guanine nucleotides than are S_1 receptors. The S_2 receptor is thought to be more important in mediating the behavioral effects of serotonin.

b. The **predominant action** of serotonin on receptors **is inhibition**, although excitation has been described in some cases.

c. Presynaptic serotonin receptors also exist, although their type is not known. LSD acts as both a receptor blocker and a partial agonist, and it exerts more potent effects on presynaptic serotonin receptors.

4. Important brain tracts.

The most important serotonergic neurons in the brain are located in clusters in or around the midline (or raphe) of the pons and mesencephalon, including the **median and dorsal raphe nuclei.**

a. The median raphe neurons innervate limbic structures including the amygdala.

b. The dorsal raphe neurons innervate the striatum, cerebral cortex, thalamus, and cerebellum.

5. **Behavioral functions**
   a. **Serotonin** is considered to be **important in many central processes**, including pain perception, aggression, memory, appetite, thermoregulation, blood pressure control, heart rate, and respiration. It is probably important in the induction of both sleep and wakefulness.
   b. **Serotonin** has also been proposed to be **involved in the pathophysiology of both affective disorders and schizophrenia.**
      (1) **Affective disorders**
         (a) One theory has held that low activity of serotonin in the brain is associated with depression and high activity is associated with mania.
         (b) Another theory, known as the **permissive serotonin hypothesis**, states that lowered serotonin activity "permits" low levels of catecholamines to cause depression and also permits high levels to cause mania.
      (2) In **schizophrenia**, it has been hypothesized that certain methylated derivatives of serotonin, formed as a result of errors in metabolism, may cause psychosis. This is known as the **transmethylation hypothesis of schizophrenia**, and it is supported by the finding that LSD and serotonin derivatives such as dimethyltryptamine, harmaline, and psilocybin cause psychosis and behavioral abnormalities. Direct proof for this hypothesis is lacking, however. Overall, the evidence for serotonin involvement in schizophrenia is much weaker than that for dopamine involvement.

D. HISTAMINE

1. **Synthesis**

$$\text{Histidine} \xrightarrow{\textit{L-histidine decarboxylase}} \text{Histamine}$$

2. **Metabolism.** Histamine is methylated to methylhistamine and subsequently is oxidized to 1,4-methylimidazoleacetic acid.

3. **Receptors.** Two types of histamine receptors have been identified, H_1 and H_2. They appear to exist in the brain as well as in the periphery. Both types of receptors probably activate adenylate cyclase, although the evidence is more conclusive for H_2 receptors. Histamine appears to be excitatory in the hypothalamus, while it is mainly inhibitory in the cerebral cortex.

4. **Important brain tracts.** Histamine has been found in high concentrations in the hypothalamus and in moderate concentrations in the mesencephalon, hippocampus, thalamus, basal ganglia, and cerebral cortex. The exact histaminergic pathways are unclear, although histaminergic axons travel through the medial forebrain bundle.

5. **Behavioral functions.** It has been proposed that histamine is important in arousal, water intake, vasopressin release, thermoregulation, and cardiovascular function. Blockade of histamine receptors leads to weight gain, sedation, and hypotension.
   a. Anorexia nervosa, an illness characterized by excessive weight loss, has been reported to be treated successfully with cyproheptadine, a drug that blocks H_2 receptors.
   b. The tricyclic antidepressant doxepin also has powerful H_1 and H_2 receptor-blocking abilities, although it is not clear how this relates to its antidepressant potential.

IV. ACETYLCHOLINE

A. SYNTHESIS

$$\text{Acetyl CoA and choline} \xrightarrow{\textit{choline acetyltransferase}} \text{ACh}$$

Choline cannot be synthesized in neurons and is, therefore, transported into the brain by high-affinity and low-affinity transport processes. The high-affinity process (which is inhibited by hemicholinium-3) appears to be the primary factor regulating the amount of ACh present in neurons.

B. METABOLISM

1. ACh is inactivated by cholinesterases, including both acetylcholinesterase and pseudo-cholinesterase. Acetylcholinesterase is reversibly inhibited by physostigmine and almost irreversibly inhibited by organophosphorus compounds such as those used in insecticides.

2. Exactly how ACh is released into the synapse is not clear, but its release is known to be controlled by an influx of calcium ions.

C. **RECEPTORS.** The two main types of **ACh receptors are nicotinic and muscarinic**. Both types occur in the brain.

1. **Nicotinic receptors**
   a. Nicotinic receptors are excitatory.
   b. In the peripheral nervous system, cholinergic neurons whose cell bodies lie in the spinal cord or brain stem (such as those that innervate skeletal muscles) are predominantly nicotinic.
   c. Nicotinic receptor agonists include nicotine, and antagonists include curare drugs, gallamine, and decamethonium.

2. **Muscarinic receptors**
   a. Muscarinic receptors may be excitatory or inhibitory.
   b. Neurons whose cell bodies lie outside of the central nervous system (such as those in sympathetic and parasympathetic ganglia that innervate smooth muscles and glands) are predominantly muscarinic.
   c. Muscarinic receptor agonists include muscarine (a mushroom alkaloid), pilocarpine, and oxotremorine. Antagonists include atropine.
   d. Presynaptic ACh receptors are mainly muscarinic.
   e. Muscarinic receptors have been divided into two types, M_1 and M_2.
      (1) **M_1 receptors**
         (a) M_1 receptors appear to be widespread throughout the neocortex.
         (b) M_1 receptors are postsynaptic and excitatory.
      (2) **M_2 receptors**
         (a) M_2 receptors are concentrated in the cortical laminae that demonstrate the greatest choline acetyltransferase activity.
         (b) M_2 receptors may be presynaptic and modulate the release of ACh, probably through inhibition of adenylate cyclase.
         (c) There is evidence of a decreased amount of M_2 (but not M_1) receptors in Alzheimer's disease.

D. **IMPORTANT BRAIN TRACTS.** There is an important cholinergic pathway from the basal forebrain to the hippocampus and also probably to the cerebral cortex. The striatum is rich in ACh, where it is found mainly in short intrastriatal neurons. There appear to be very few intracortical cholinergic neurons.

E. **BEHAVIORAL FUNCTIONS.** In animals, ACh is believed to be important in movement, sleep, aggression, exploratory behavior, sexual behavior, and memory. For humans, the most important known effects involve movement and memory.

1. **ACh is important in movement** both peripherally and centrally.
   a. **Peripherally,** ACh is the main neurotransmitter for skeletal muscles, and many powerful neurotoxins (such as curare and α-bungarotoxin) paralyze by binding to ACh receptors.
   b. **Centrally,** ACh and dopamine appear to exist in a sort of balance in the extrapyramidal motor system. A decrease in one (such as a decrease in dopamine in Parkinson's disease) can be somewhat offset by decreasing the other (e.g., by using anticholinergic drugs). A variety of synthetic antimuscarinic drugs, such as benztropine and trihexyphenidyl, that cross the blood–brain barrier are currently used in the treatment of Parkinson's disease and neuroleptic-induced parkinsonism.

2. **ACh is also important in memory and cognition.** Dementing illnesses such as Alzheimer's disease appear to be associated with a loss of cholinergic transmission in the brain, both to the hippocampus and to the cerebral cortex. A decreased number of cholinergic neurons in the nucleus basalis of Meynert (located in the basal forebrain) has been reported in patients with Alzheimer's disease and certain other dementing disorders, although it is not clear if this is the primary pathologic change.

V. AMINO ACIDS

A. **GAMMA-AMINOBUTYRIC ACID (GABA)**

1. **Synthesis**

$$\text{Glutamic acid} \xrightarrow{\text{glutamic acid decarboxylase}} \text{GABA}$$

2. **Metabolism.** GABA is catabolized via transamination (catalyzed by GABA transaminase) to succinic semialdehyde. Succinic semialdehyde is then oxidized to succinic acid, which enters the citric acid cycle.

3. Receptors
    a. GABA was the **first amino acid demonstrated to be a neurotransmitter**. Unlike most of the other neurotransmitters discussed, GABA is almost entirely limited to the central nervous system. To date, studies have proved it to be **purely inhibitory**. It is probably the most abundant neurotransmitter in the central nervous system, present in as many as 60% of synapses and two hundred to one thousand times more abundant than dopamine, ACh, norepinephrine, and other transmitters.
    b. There are probably at least **two different types of GABAergic receptors** in the central nervous system.
        (1) GABA-A receptors are the classical postsynaptic GABA receptors. Muscimol is a selective agonist, and bicuculline, a convulsant, is an antagonist.
        (2) GABA-B receptors. Baclofen, a drug used to treat spasticity, is a selective agonist. GABA-B receptors are resistant to bicuculline.
        (3) Some GABA receptors, which may comprise a third type of receptor, are coupled to a recognition site for benzodiazepines, which potentiate the inhibitory action of GABA. Benzodiazepine receptors also appear to exist in two forms, but the distinctions between the two are as yet unclear.

4. Important brain tracts. There are many different pathways in the brain that contain GABA.
    a. GABA is the neurotransmitter for Purkinje cells, which are the only efferent neurons for the entire cerebellar cortex.
    b. Inhibitory interneurons in almost all areas of the brain, including the brain stem, striatum, amygdala, and cerebral cortex, and the spinal cord, contain GABA.
    c. GABAergic pathways extend from the striatum to the substantia nigra and to the globus pallidus, which may be important in movement disorders such as Parkinson's and Huntington's diseases. This tract may be regulated by endogenous opiates, as morphine and β-endorphin cause a decrease in GABA turnover.
    d. Finally, there is recent evidence of a GABAergic pathway from the magnocellular neurons of the posterior hypothalamus to the neocortex.

B. GLYCINE, structurally the simplest amino acid, like GABA, has been proposed to be an inhibitory neurotransmitter.

1. Its action is probably much more restricted than that of GABA, however, as it is found only in the brain stem and spinal cord and possibly is present in the retina and diencephalon. Strychnine blocks its action.

2. Other possible inhibitory amino acids include alanine, cystathionine, and serine.

C. GLUTAMATE AND ASPARTATE are the only amino acids believed to serve as excitatory neurotransmitters. Both are synthesized from glucose.

1. Glutamate is thought to be present in the corticostriatal pathway and in cerebellar granule cells, and aspartate is thought to be present in the hippocampal commissural pathway, although both of these transmitters probably are present in many other pathways as well. They may, in fact, be the primary excitatory transmitters of the brain.

2. These excitatory neurotransmitters as well as some of their analogues (such as kainic acid) are **neurotoxic** under certain conditions.

VI. OTHER NONPEPTIDE NEUROTRANSMITTER CANDIDATES

A. PROSTAGLANDINS AND THROMBOXANES belong to a family of substances known as **eicosanoids,** which are derivatives of 20-carbon polyunsaturated fatty acids. Their actions are diverse and complicated and vary from species to species.

1. Prostaglandins and thromboxane are released by afferent stimulation of the cortex and also by certain pharmacologic agents, such as picrotoxin, pentylenetetrazol, and strychnine.

2. Prostaglandins do not appear to function as neurotransmitters, but they may have a neuromodulatory role. They have significant effects on cAMP (either to decrease or increase it) and have been shown to block the inhibitory action of norepinephrine (probably mediated by cAMP) on Purkinje cells in the cerebellum.

B. PURINES

1. ATP may function as a neurotransmitter in the intrinsic, nonadrenergic, noncholinergic neurons of visceral smooth muscle.

2. Adenosine may serve as an inhibitory neuromodulator of excitatory cells in the cerebellum, hippocampus, medial geniculate body, and septum.

VII. NEUROPEPTIDES

A. The previous sections of this chapter primarily considered neurotransmitters and neuromodulators. In this final section, neuropeptides, which **function principally as neurohormones** and are important in psychoneuroendocrinology, will be considered.

1. Some investigators believe that neuropeptides may also serve as neuromodulators and in some cases as neurotransmitters as well, although their course of action is much slower than that of substances such as ACh, dopamine, and norepinephrine. Although hormones may be steroids, amino acids, and peptides, most of the recent interest in neurohormones has surrounded peptide hormones.

2. An interesting finding that has emerged in recent years concerns the coexistence within a neuron of peptides and the "simpler" or "classical" transmitters, which violates Dale's principle [see section II C 6 b (2) (b)]. Definitive proof that peptides function as neurotransmitters is lacking, however. Some of the combinations currently believed to exist are listed in Table 1-1.

B. ENDOGENOUS OPIOIDS

1. General considerations
  a. Opium has been used as a pain reliever and psychotomimetic drug for millenia. In the nineteenth century, it was determined that most of this action is due to the alkaloid, morphine. In the 1970s, it was discovered that there is stereospecific binding of opiates to animal brain homogenates. A class of endogenous neuropeptides was then identified that binds to receptors that mediate response to opioids. These neuropeptides originally were called **enkephalins** (meaning "in the head"). Later, other substances were discovered that also bind to these receptors, and these were called **endorphins** (which is a contraction of "endogenous" and "morphine").
  b. The entire class of enkephalins and endorphins is usually called endogenous opioids, although sometimes the term endorphin is used in reference to the whole class of endogenous opioids. Most investigators, however, use the term endorphin to refer to endogenous opioids with a longer peptide chain than the enkephalin chain (which is only 5 amino acids in length).

2. A large number of endogenous opioids now have been identified, including **methionine enkephalin and leucine enkephalin (met- and leu-enkephalin, respectively)** and α-, β-, and γ-endorphins. All of these substances are chemically related peptides, although the relationships are complex and are defined in ways that continually change as more is discovered about them.

3. Associated disorders
  a. Many behavioral states and neuropsychiatric disorders are currently postulated to be associated with alterations in endogenous opioids, especially β-endorphin. These conditions include thermoregulation, seizure induction, alcoholism, schizophrenia, general effects on locomotion (especially hypomotility and some movement disorders), and analgesia.
  b. Except in the case of narcotic overdose, the treatment of behavioral disorders with opioid antagonists (such as naloxone and naltrexone) has so far yielded inconsistent results.

Table 1-1. Coexisting "Classical" Neurotransmitters and Neuropeptides

"Classical" Neurotransmitter	Coexisting Neuropeptides
Acetylcholine (ACh)	Vasoactive intestinal polypeptide Enkephalins
Norepinephrine	Somatostatin Neurotensin Enkephalins
Dopamine	Cholecystokinin Enkephalins
Serotonin	Substance P Thyrotropin-releasing hormone Vasoactive intestinal polypeptide

C. "GUT" PEPTIDES are found in both the brain and the digestive tract.

   1. Substance P is an 11–amino acid peptide that was first discovered in 1931 in extracts of brain and intestine. Substance P has been found in the spinal cord, substantia nigra, striatum, amygdala, hypothalamus, and cerebral cortex.
   a. It may be the principal neurotransmitter for the primary afferent sensory fibers that travel through the dorsal roots to the substantia gelatinosa of the spinal cord and carry information about pain.
   b. It may also be involved in a major excitatory outflow tract from the striatum to the substantia nigra and globus pallidus and may be important for movement. Substance P abnormalities have been implicated in the pathophysiology of Huntington's disease, in which substance P levels have been reported to be reduced.

   2. Cholecystokinin is a polypeptide that is released from the gut in response to chyme, amino acids, fats, and other substances, whereupon it stimulates gallbladder motility and secretion of pancreatic enzymes. It is found in the hippocampus and neocortex as well as in the brain stem, basal ganglia, hypothalamus, and amygdala.
   a. Behaviorally, cholecystokinin may be associated with satiety, which has led to proposals that the polypeptide may be useful in appetite reduction.
   b. Cholecystokinin has been reported to coexist with dopamine in neurons in the ventral tegmental area of the brain stem and in the nucleus accumbens, brain regions that are thought to be important in the pathophysiology of schizophrenia.

   3. Vasoactive intestinal polypeptide is a 29–amino acid peptide originally discovered in the intestine and named for its ability to alter blood flow in the gut.
   a. It is extremely common in the neocortex, where it has been found in a distribution indicating that vasoactive intestinal polypeptide neurons may be localized to single cortical columns.
   b. It appears to be excitatory in action and to be coupled to cAMP.

   4. Somatostatin is a 14–amino acid peptide that was first isolated and characterized in the early 1970s.
   a. Somatostatin is found in the gastrointestinal tract, in the islets of Langerhans, and in a number of areas in the nervous system (including dorsal root ganglia, the amygdala, and the cerebral cortex).
   b. Its hormonal actions include suppression of the release of growth hormone (GH) and thyroid-stimulating hormone (TSH) in the brain and suppression of the release of glucagon and insulin in the pancreas.
   c. It is thought to be important in the production of slow wave sleep and rapid eye movement (REM) sleep, in appetite, and in motor control.
   d. Somatostatin injection in animals is associated with decreased spontaneous motor activity.
   e. Increased somatostatin levels have been reported in the corpus striatum of patients with Huntington's disease, whereas decreased levels have been reported in the cortex of patients with Alzheimer's disease.
   f. Somatostatin may modulate the activity of the nigrostriatal dopamine tract.

   5. Neurotensin is a 13–amino acid peptide.
   a. It is found in the substantia gelatinosa of the spinal cord, the brain stem (especially in the motor nucleus of the trigeminal nerve and substantia nigra), hypothalamus, amygdala, nucleus accumbens, septum, and anterior pituitary gland.
   b. It appears to be excitatory and may play a role in arousal, thermoregulation, and pain perception.

D. HYPOTHALAMIC, PITUITARY, AND PINEAL PEPTIDES

   1. General considerations. This section considers neuroregulators of the hypothalamus, pituitary gland, and pineal gland.
   a. The **pituitary gland** consists of two parts, the anterior and posterior.
      (1) The **anterior pituitary** secretes six hormones, most of which have **trophic properties**. These hormones are:
         (a) Adrenocorticotropic hormone (ACTH)
         (b) GH (which is also called somatotropin)
         (c) TSH
         (d) Luteinizing hormone (LH)
         (e) Follicle-stimulating hormone (FSH)
         (f) Prolactin
      (2) The **posterior pituitary** secretes vasopressin and oxytocin.

     b. The hypothalamus secretes a number of factors that control the release of hormones from the anterior pituitary, which in turn control the release of hormones in the periphery.

     c. Melanocyte-stimulating hormone (MSH) is an important hypothalamic–pineal hormone, and melatonin is synthesized by the pineal gland.

  2. ACTH is found in areas of the brain in addition to the pituitary gland, such as the limbic system, brain stem, and thalamus, and it may be important in learning, memory, and attention. ACTH regulates the release of the adrenal steroid **cortisol**, and ACTH in turn is regulated by the hypothalamic **corticotropin-releasing factor**. The levels of both ACTH and cortisol exhibit a diurnal variation, and cortisol levels peak at approximately 7 A.M.

CRF

     a. Excess amounts of cortisol are seen in Cushing's syndrome, which may be associated with depression, mania, hallucinations, delusions, and delirium.

     b. A deficit of cortisol is seen in Addison's disease, which may be accompanied by depression, lethargy, and fatigue.

     c. A subset of patients with endogenous depression have high cortisol levels, loss of the normal diurnal variation in cortisol levels, and "early escape" from suppression of cortisol secretion following administration of dexamethasone in the **dexamethasone suppression test**. These findings are not unique to depressed patients, as some patients with mania, schizoaffective disorders, bulimia, and anorexia nervosa may also exhibit them. However, suppression of cortisol levels during the dexamethasone suppression test is thought to indicate the presence of treatment-responsive endogenous depressive illness.

  3. GH is a protein consisting of 190 amino acids. It increases protein synthesis and decreases the utilization of carbohydrates. It also facilitates the mobilization of fats.

     a. Its secretion and synthesis are controlled by GH-releasing factor and GH-release inhibiting factor (which is somatostatin).

     b. The somatic effects of GH appear to require the involvement of a family of polypeptides called **somatomedins**.

     c. Norepinephrine, dopamine, and serotonin alter GH concentrations, and stress causes increased release of GH.

     d. GH exhibits a diurnal pattern of release, with higher levels secreted during sleep.

  4. TSH causes the release of the thyroid hormones triiodothyronine (T_3) and thyroxine (T_4). The release of TSH is controlled by TSH-releasing factor.

     a. TSH-releasing factor is believed to be localized in the dorsomedial and periventricular nuclei of the hypothalamus, which send processes to other hypothalamic nuclei, the median eminence, medial forebrain bundle, septum, nucleus accumbens, and certain motor cranial nerve nuclei (i.e., III, V, VII, and XII), as well as to the anterior pituitary.

     b. TSH-releasing factor is largely inhibitory to postsynaptic neurons, and it is believed to be involved in mood and behavior, apart from its effects on thyroid function. Some patients with major depression show a blunted TSH response to intravenous infusion of TSH-releasing factor, which has been taken to implicate hypothalamic–pituitary dysfunction in major depression.

  5. The release of **LH** and **FSH** from the anterior pituitary is regulated by LH-releasing hormone, which is also known as gonadotropin-releasing hormone.

     a. LH and FSH regulate ovarian follicle growth and spermatogenesis and testosterone secretion.

     b. LH-releasing hormone injection in males causes an increase in sexual arousal, and injections have been used with some success in the treatment of delayed puberty.

     c. LH-releasing hormone may function as a neurotransmitter or neuromodulator as well as a hormone, and it may be excitatory or inhibitory.

  6. Prolactin is a 198–amino acid protein released from the anterior pituitary. Its release is controlled by prolactin-inhibiting factor and prolactin-releasing factor.

     a. Prolactin regulates the activity of the mammary glands during lactation. Sleep, exercise, pregnancy, and breast-feeding increase circulating levels of prolactin.

     b. Dopamine may function physiologically as prolactin-inhibiting factor. Most neuroleptic medications block dopamine receptors in the tuberoinfundibular dopamine tract, causing an increase in circulating prolactin and, therefore, inducing lactation, which is a common side effect of neuroleptics in women.

  7. Vasopressin and oxytocin are 9–amino acid peptides formed from larger precursor hormones known as neurophysins.

     a. They are synthesized in large neurons in the supraoptic and paraventricular hypothalamic nuclei as well as in the suprachiasmatic, arcuate, dorsomedial, and ventromedial nuclei of the hypothalamus.

      (1) The neurons from the supraoptic and paraventricular nuclei project to the posterior pituitary, where the hormones are released into the circulation.

      (2) Neurons containing vasopressin and oxytocin from these and other hypothalamic nuclei project to the medial amygdaloid nucleus, lateral septum, hippocampus, thalamus, nucleus of the solitary tract, ventral tegmental area, area postrema, and locus ceruleus.

    b. Vasopressin

      (1) The release of vasopressin (which is also known as antidiuretic hormone because it **facilitates water absorption in the distal tubule**) is increased by stress, pain, exercise, and a variety of drugs including morphine, nicotine, and barbiturates. Alcohol decreases its release, resulting in diuresis.

      (2) Vasopressin is believed to be mainly inhibitory, and it may be important in **learning**, **memory**, and **attention**. Vasopressin has been reported to improve memory in a few patients with dementia and brain damage, although the results are inconsistent. It may also be important in depression and psychosis.

    c. Oxytocin

      (1) The **main peripheral effects of oxytocin** include stimulation of the myoepithelial cells lining ducts of the breast, causing **expression of milk**, and inducing **contraction of uterine smooth muscles during parturition**.

      (2) Centrally, oxytocin may be an inhibitory neurotransmitter or neuromodulator. It may act in a way opposite to vasopressin in terms of its effects on memory and may actually cause amnesia.

8. MSH is structurally similar to ACTH, and it is important in the control of pigmentation. Its release is regulated by MSH-inhibiting factor and MSH-releasing factor.

    a. It is found in the pineal gland as well as in the cerebral cortex (especially in the occipital cortex), septum, cerebellum, thalamus, hypothalamus, amygdala, mammillary bodies, pons, and medulla.

    b. Its behavioral function is unclear, although it may have a role in learning and memory.

    c. MSH and MSH-inhibiting factor have been reported to have antidepressant effects. MSH-inhibiting factor may also have antiparkinsonian effects.

9. Melatonin is synthesized from serotonin in the pineal gland.

    a. Although it is not a peptide, melatonin has important neuroendocrinologic effects. It is thought to be involved in the regulation of circadian rhythms. Melatonin synthesis is regulated by the day–night or light–dark cycle, and levels are increased during darkness.

    b. Because the pineal gland can transform information contained in light into chemical information contained in melatonin, the pineal gland has been called a "neuroendocrine transducer."

VIII. COMPLEXITIES IN THE NEUROCHEMISTRY OF BEHAVIORAL DISORDERS

    A. During the course of this chapter the authors have mentioned a number of behavioral disorders, especially psychiatric and movement disorders, that have been proposed to be associated with disturbances of specific neurotransmitters. Yet, the current state of knowledge is far from being as simple as to suggest associations of one disease–one neurotransmitter. Although disorders such as schizophrenia, tardive dyskinesia, and Parkinson's disease are believed to be associated with dopaminergic abnormalities and depression is thought to be associated with dysfunction in norepinephrine pathways, myriad different neurochemical abnormalities have been proposed to be associated with each of these conditions. Response to pharmacotherapeutic agents is also a complex issue, for very few psychopharmacologic drugs affect a single transmitter system.

    B. All behavioral abnormalities not only represent the primary pathologic process but also the brain's attempt to correct it or compensate for it. Thus, even in those conditions in which a limited number of neurochemical systems may be involved in the primary disease process, changes will usually be observed in other neurochemical systems.

    C. Other factors influence the neurochemical status of an individual as well, including age, gender, diet, and pharmacotherapy, all of which have effects on behavior.

    D. Finally, we probably understand only a small fraction of the neurochemistry of the brain, as new neuroactive substances and transmitter candidates are continually being discovered. Much remains to be investigated in the field of behavioral biochemistry.

BIBLIOGRAPHY

Cooper JR, Bloom FE, Roth RH: *The Biochemical Basis of Neuropharmacology.* New York, Oxford University Press, 1982

Emson PC (ed): *Chemical Neuroanatomy.* New York, Raven Press, 1983

Jeste DV, Wyatt RJ: *Understanding and Treating Tardive Dyskinesia.* New York, Guilford Press, 1982

Krieger DT, Martin JB: Brain peptides. *New Engl J Med* 304:876–884, 944–951, 1981

McGeer PL, Eccles JC, McGeer EG: *Molecular Neurobiology of the Mammalian Brain.* New York, Plenum Press, 1978

Reinis S, Goldman JM: *The Chemistry of Behavior: A Molecular Approach to Neuronal Plasticity.* New York, Plenum Press, 1982

Siegel GJ, Albers RW, Agranoff BW, et al (eds): *Basic Neurochemistry.* Boston, Little, Brown, 1981

Snyder SH: Drug and neurotransmitter receptors in the brain. *Science* 224:22–31, 1984

STUDY QUESTIONS

Directions: Each question below contains five suggested answers. Choose the **one best** response to each question.

1. All of the following statements regarding neurotransmitter receptors are true EXCEPT

(A) muscarinic receptors are found in the central nervous system of primates
(B) presynaptic receptors (autoreceptors) usually facilitate the release of the type of neurotransmitter that binds to them
(C) although benzodiazepines increase GABAergic transmission in the brain, they do not bind directly to gamma-aminobutyric acid (GABA) receptors
(D) modulator proteins are often associated with receptors
(E) effector proteins are often associated with receptors

2. Which of the following ions is most important for the release of a transmitter?

(A) Sodium
(B) Potassium
(C) Calcium
(D) Iron
(E) Manganese

Directions: Each question below contains four suggested answers of which **one or more** is correct. Choose the answer

    A   if **1, 2, and 3** are correct
    B   if **1 and 3** are correct
    C   if **2 and 4** are correct
    D   if **4** is correct
    E   if **1, 2, 3, and 4** are correct

3. Behavioral processes proposed to be associated with serotonin transmission include

(1) REM sleep
(2) depression
(3) thermoregulation
(4) slow wave sleep

4. Substances commonly found both in the central nervous system and in the periphery include

(1) vasoactive intestinal polypeptide
(2) gamma-aminobutyric acid (GABA)
(3) serotonin
(4) epinephrine

5. Peptides that have been proposed to function as either neurotransmitters or neuroregulators include

(1) substance P
(2) somatostatin
(3) thyrotropin-releasing factor
(4) prostaglandin E

6. Dopaminergic excess in schizophrenia is evidenced by which of the following statements?

(1) Neuroleptics block dopamine receptors to a degree that correlates highly with their antipsychotic potency
(2) It takes weeks of neuroleptic administration for the antipsychotic potency of the drug to reach full effect
(3) Amphetamines can cause a psychosis very similar to schizophrenia
(4) Amphetamines may improve certain schizophrenic symptoms such as apathy and anhedonia

7. Monoamine oxidase (MAO) is an enzyme important in the metabolism of which of the following neurotransmitters?

(1) Dopamine
(2) Serotonin
(3) Norepinephrine
(4) Substance P

Directions: The group of questions below consists of lettered choices followed by several numbered items. For each numbered item select the **one** lettered choice with which it is **most** closely associated. Each lettered choice may be used once, more than once, or not at all.

Questions 8–11

Match the upper brain stem and basal forebrain nuclei listed below with the associated neurotransmitter.

(A) Norepinephrine
(B) Serotonin
(C) Dopamine
(D) Histamine
(E) Acetylcholine (ACh)

C 8. Substantia nigra

A 9. Locus ceruleus

B 10. Raphe nuclei

E 11. Nucleus basalis

ANSWERS AND EXPLANATIONS

1. The answer is B. (*IV C 2; V A 5*) Presynaptic receptors usually inhibit the release of the neurotransmitter that binds to them. Some receptor agonists, such as apomorphine, in low concentrations bind preferentially to presynaptic receptors, thus inhibiting the neurotransmitter release, whereas in higher concentrations they bind to postsynaptic receptors, and their agonist qualities become apparent. Both muscarinic and nicotinic receptors are present in the central nervous system of primates, including man. Benzodiazepines bind to separate receptors that are linked to certain gamma-aminobutyric acid (GABA) receptors. Benzodiazepine receptors may exist in two forms, I and II. It is possible, although not proven, that one of these receptors may mediate the anxiolytic effect of benzodiazepines and that the other may mediate the hypnotic effect. Benzodiazepine antagonists also exist, and these may elicit extreme anxiety in humans. Modulator proteins are frequently interposed between neurotransmitter receptors and effectors (which effect the biological response of the neuron to the neurotransmitter). Modulator proteins may be a means by which neuromodulators modify synaptic function.

2. The answer is C. (*II B*) Calcium influx has been shown to be necessary for transmitter release, whereas the other ions do not appear to be necessary. The amount of the transmitter released depends on the amount of calcium influx. Depolarization of neurons is associated with a significant amount of calcium entering the neuron.

3. The answer is E (all). (*III C 5*) Serotonin is involved in a wide variety of behavioral processes. In addition to serving a role in thermoregulation, it has been proposed to be involved in the genesis of rapid eye movement (REM) and slow wave sleep. The permissive serotonin hypothesis of depression states that low levels of serotonin allow low levels of norepinephrine to cause depression and high levels of norepinephrine to cause mania. The idea that there may be two types of depression, one more "noradrenergic" and one more "serotonergic," has now been challenged by many investigators.

4. The answer is B (1, 3). (*III C; V A; VII D 3*) Gamma-aminobutyric acid (GABA) is unusual in that it is almost entirely limited to the central nervous system, whereas epinephrine is almost entirely limited to the periphery and only occurs centrally in small areas of the brain stem. Vasoactive intestinal polypeptide and serotonin, in contrast, are more typical in that they occur both in the brain and in other parts of the body as well. The reasons for the selective localization of certain neurotransmitters in specific regions of the body are not known.

5. The answer is A (1, 2, 3). (*VI A; VII C 1, D 3–4*) Prostaglandin E belongs to a group of substances called eicosanoids, which are derivatives of fatty acids; it is not a peptide. Substance P, somatostatin, and thyrotropin-releasing factor are all short chains of amino acids called peptides.

6. The answer is B (1, 3). (*III A 5 b*) Schizophrenia is generally thought to be a hyperdopaminergic state; therefore, the fact that it takes several weeks for neuroleptics to exert their antipsychotic effects while their ability to block dopamine receptors occurs much more rapidly has been regarded as evidence against the validity of the dopamine hypothesis (i.e., that schizophrenia is associated with abnormalities of dopamine transmission in the brain). Also, the fact that amphetamines, which are dopamine agonists, improve certain schizophrenic symptoms, especially the so-called "negative" symptoms such as affective flattening and social withdrawal, indicates that more is involved in the schizophrenic process than mere dopaminergic hyperactivity. For example, it is likely that noradrenergic dysfunction or dopaminergic hypoactivity characterizes a subset of schizophrenic patients.

7. The answer is A (1, 2, 3). (*III A 2; VII A, D 1*) Substance P is a peptide, and, to date, there is no absolute proof that peptides function as neurotransmitters. Monoamine oxidase (MAO) is an important enzyme in the inactivation of biogenic amines. Norepinephrine and serotonin are deaminated preferentially by MAO-A, whereas dopamine is deaminated by both MAO-A and MAO-B.

8–11. The answers are: 8-C, 9-A, 10-B, 11-E. (*III A 4, B 3, C 3; IV D, E*) Dopamine is the major neurotransmitter in the pigmented cells of the substantia nigra, which degenerates in Parkinson's disease. The pigmented cells of the locus ceruleus contain norepinephrine and are thought to be important in the manifestation of anxiety, depression, mania, and other disorders. The midline raphe nuclei contain serotonin, which is important in sleep and other functions. Finally, the nucleus basalis contains cholinergic neurons, and its degeneration is thought to be associated with the clinical symptomatology of Alzheimer's disease. Histamine has, thus far, not been associated with specific nuclei in the brain stem or basal forebrain.

2
Pharmacology and Behavior
Darrell G. Kirch

I. INTRODUCTION. This chapter reviews the pharmacology of those classes of drugs that have a significant impact upon behavior and includes a discussion of their use in various clinical disorders.

A. DEFINITIONS

1. **Pharmacology** involves the chemistry, mechanisms of action, absorption, distribution, metabolism, excretion, and effects of drugs.

2. A **drug** is any substance, other than food, that has an effect on living processes.

3. **Behavior** includes all of the actions and activities of an individual.

B. PHARMACOKINETIC PRINCIPLES

1. **Absorption** of a drug is a function of the **dose** given and the **route of administration** (i.e., alimentary, parenteral, topical, or via inhalation).

2. **Distribution** of a drug throughout the body occurs as a result of passage across membranes via diffusion, transport (active or passive), or endocytosis. Drugs that have a wide deposition throughout body fluids and tissues have a greater **volume of distribution**.

3. **Elimination** of a drug is a function of **metabolism** within and **excretion** from the body. Metabolites of a drug may themselves have pharmacologic activity. **Half-life** is the amount of time required for the plasma concentration of a drug to fall by 50%.

4. **Therapeutic index** refers to the ratio between a lethal dose of a drug and a clinically effective dose. Thus, the higher the therapeutic index, the safer a drug is in clinical use.

C. CENTRAL NERVOUS SYSTEM NEUROTRANSMITTERS AND RECEPTORS

1. **Behavior is ultimately the result of the transmission of messages** through complex neuronal pathways in the central nervous system. The passage of an impulse across the synaptic cleft is dependent upon the release of a **neurotransmitter** from the presynaptic axonal terminal. This neurotransmitter then binds to a specific **receptor** on another neuron, causing a response in the postsynaptic cell.

2. **Primary neurotransmitters** in the central nervous system include:
   a. The catecholamines **dopamine** and **norepinephrine**
   b. **5-hydroxytryptamine [5-HT] (serotonin)**
   c. **Acetylcholine (ACh)**
   d. **Gamma-aminobutyric acid (GABA)**
   e. Various **peptides**, such as the enkephalins, somatostatin, and cholecystokinin

II. ANTIPSYCHOTIC AGENTS

A. GENERAL CONSIDERATIONS

1. **Psychosis** is a state of global cognitive impairment.
   a. It involves deficits in the ability to think, remember, communicate, respond emotionally, behave appropriately, perceive sensory stimuli correctly, and interpret reality.
   b. **Primary symptoms** of psychosis include **disordered thought processes, hallucinations**, and **delusions**.
   c. This state is **commonly seen in schizophrenic disorders**. It may also be present in **major**

affective disorders (i.e., **depression** and **bipolar disorder**) and in **organic brain syndromes**.

2. **Antipsychotic agents improve cognition, mood, and behavior** in a psychotic individual **without producing physical dependence**. This antipsychotic effect appears to be independent of any sedating effects that the drugs might have.

B. CLASSES OF DRUGS

1. Historically, the first agents used to treat psychotic states were **alkaloid derivatives of** the plant *Rauwolfia serpentina*. **Reserpine** was isolated in 1952 and, in addition to having antihypertensive properties, was found to be an effective antipsychotic.

2. **Phenothiazines** were first investigated as anthelmintic and antihistaminic agents, and then in the early 1950s, they were found to have antipsychotic properties. Three subgroups are determined by the side chain attached to the phenothiazine nucleus. This basic nucleus is a three-ring structure, with two benzene rings joined centrally by a sulfur and a nitrogen atom. These subgroups include:
   a. **Aliphatic compounds** (**chlorpromazine, triflupromazine**)
   b. **Piperidine compounds** (**thioridazine, mesoridazine, piperacetazine**)
   c. **Piperazine compounds** (**trifluoperazine, fluphenazine, perphenazine**)

3. **Butyrophenone compounds** (**haloperidol**) were developed in the late 1950s.

4. **Thioxanthene compounds** (**chlorprothixene, thiothixene**) chemically resemble the phenothiazines, with substitution of a carbon for a nitrogen atom in the central ring of the phenothiazine nucleus.

5. Other antipsychotic agents include **loxapine, molindone, clozapine**, and **diphenylbutylpiperidine** derivatives (**pimozide, penfluridol**).

C. PHARMACOLOGY AND PHARMACOKINETICS

1. **All antipsychotic agents block dopamine receptors** in the central nervous system. This has led to **the theory** (as yet not conclusively proven) **that schizophrenia is the result of a hyperdopaminergic state**. In addition to **antipsychotic effects**, these agents have multiple other pharmacologic properties, including:
   a. **Sedation**, probably via activity in the reticular activating system
   b. **Extrapyramidal side effects** resulting from the blockade of dopamine receptors in the basal ganglia
   c. An **antiemetic effect** by suppression of the chemoreceptor trigger zone
   d. **Hypothalamic effects**, including altered temperature regulation, weight gain, and increased prolactin secretion
   e. **Peripheral α-adrenergic blockade**, which may result in orthostatic hypotension
   f. Central and peripheral **anticholinergic effects**
   g. **Antihistaminic effects** (for most phenothiazines)

2. **Antipsychotic agents are generally well absorbed** after oral or parenteral administration, with rapid distribution throughout the body.

3. **Metabolism may result in multiple active and inactive metabolites**. A large number of metabolites have been postulated for chlorpromazine, perhaps the agent best studied in this regard. Hydroxylation and formation of sulfoxides are common. For some antipsychotic agents, relatively few metabolites are known.

4. **Slow excretion** occurs in urine and feces. For most compounds a relatively **long half-life** allows once-a-day dosing.

D. CLINICAL USE

1. **Indications.** Antipsychotic agents are indicated in a number of disorders.
   a. They are used for the control of psychotic symptoms in acute and chronic **schizophrenia** and **schizoaffective disorder**.
   b. They are used in the acute treatment of the **manic phase of bipolar illness**, although lithium is the preferred maintenance agent for affected patients.
   c. Psychotic manifestations of some severe major depressions, personality disorders, and chronic organic brain syndromes can be treated with antipsychotic agents.
   d. Haloperidol is the current treatment of choice for the tics and involuntary vocalizations of **Tourette's disorder**.

2. **Dosage.** The potencies of the antipsychotic drugs and, therefore, the doses vary widely.

a. In general, they have a **high therapeutic index**.

b. Assays to measure antipsychotic drug concentrations in the blood have become available. Firm therapeutic ranges have not yet been established, although blood levels may help identify patients who, for reasons of compliance or pharmacokinetics, have subtherapeutic concentrations.

c. Although divided doses may aid in minimizing sedation in early phases of treatment, a **single daily dose** at bedtime is usually adequate in the maintenance phase of treatment.

E. SIDE EFFECTS AND TOXICITY

1. **Sedation** is more common with the low-potency phenothiazines such as chlorpromazine and thioridazine.

2. **Extrapyramidal side effects**, including dystonia, akathisia, and parkinsonian tremor and rigidity, are more commonly seen with high-potency drugs such as haloperidol and fluphenazine. They **may be treated with anticholinergic agents** such as trihexyphenidyl and benztropine.

3. **Anticholinergic side effects** include dry mouth, blurred vision, constipation, urinary retention, and tachycardia.

4. **Hypotension** may occur, especially in elderly patients.

5. **Endocrine effects** include elevated levels of prolactin. Galactorrhea and amenorrhea may occur in women, and loss of libido may occur in men. Men may experience **retrograde ejaculation** with thioridazine.

6. **Allergic reactions**, including agranulocytosis and cholestatic jaundice, have been rarely noted.

7. Antipsychotic drugs may cause a **lower seizure threshold**.

8. They also may impair **hypothalamic temperature regulation**, predisposing a patient to either hypothermia or heat stroke.

9. Thioridazine has been associated with a **pigmentary retinopathy** in higher doses.

10. **Tardive dyskinesia** is a syndrome involving abnormal involuntary movements and has been associated with the chronic use of antipsychotic agents. In a significant number of cases, it appears to be irreversible. No treatment is known other than discontinuation of the drug if the clinical status of the patient allows.

11. **Neuroleptic malignant syndrome** involves fever, rigidity, and deterioration in mental status and has been increasingly recognized in association with the use of antipsychotic drugs.

12. **Overdose of antipsychotic drugs** may result in coma, hypotension, seizures, hypothermia, extrapyramidal reactions, and cardiac arrhythmias.

III. ANTIDEPRESSANT DRUGS

A. GENERAL CONSIDERATIONS

1. **Depression** varies in its clinical manifestations.
   a. It may be a **normal mood in reaction to a loss**.
   b. As a psychiatric syndrome, it involves dysphoric mood, loss of interest in usual activities, appetite and sleep disturbances, psychomotor agitation or retardation, fatigue, feelings of guilt or self-reproach, impaired concentration, and suicidal ideation.
   c. Depressive syndromes vary in severity and may include psychotic symptoms such as delusions and hallucinations.

2. Antidepressants improve mood and the other manifestations of the major depressive syndromes. They have minimal value, however, in the short-term management of acute depression (grief) as a normal emotional response to a loss.

B. CLASSES OF DRUGS

1. **Tricyclic antidepressants** are the primary drugs used to treat depression.
   a. They structurally resemble the phenothiazines.
   b. Specific drugs include **imipramine** and **amitriptyline** and their demethylated derivatives **desipramine** and **nortriptyline**, respectively. Other tricyclic antidepressants include **doxepin, clomipramine, trimipramine**, and **protriptyline**.
   c. Structurally "atypical" antidepressants include **maprotiline, nomifensine, zimelidine,**

trazodone, and the dibenzoxazepine derivative, **amoxapine** (which is structurally similar to loxapine, an antipsychotic drug).

  2. Monoamine oxidase (MAO) inhibitors are of two types.
    a. Hydrazide derivatives include **isocarboxazid** and **phenelzine**.
    b. Tranylcypromine structurally resembles dextroamphetamine.

C. PHARMACOLOGY AND PHARMACOKINETICS

  1. The mechanism of the antidepressant action of these drugs remains unclear.
    a. Tricyclic antidepressants block reuptake of amine neurotransmitters, especially norepinephrine and serotonin, at the synapse. Therefore, these drugs might reverse a deficiency in central amine neurotransmission.
      (1) Although these drugs have immediate effects on amine reuptake, **antidepressant effects usually do not emerge until after 2 to 3 weeks of treatment**.
      (2) The tricyclic antidepressants have significant central and peripheral **anticholinergic properties**.
    b. MAO inhibitors bind irreversibly with the amine degrading enzyme MAO, thereby increasing central and peripheral nervous system stores of catecholamines and serotonin.
      (1) Except for tranylcypromine, which directly increases norepinephrine release, **MAO inhibitors require 2 to 3 weeks to exert antidepressant effects**.
      (2) They **interfere with metabolism** of many drugs and may enhance effects of narcotic, sedative-hypnotic, anesthetic, and tricyclic antidepressant agents.
      (3) They may **block degradation of tyramine** from certain aged cheeses, wines, and beers, resulting in massive release of stored catecholamines and a **hypertensive crisis** after these foods are consumed.

  2. All antidepressants are **well absorbed** from the gastrointestinal tract.
    a. Tricyclic antidepressants have **long half-lives** and may be metabolized to active compounds by microsomal enzymes.
    b. MAO inhibitors are inactivated by acetylation. Even after stopping drug administration, sufficient enzyme regeneration to end the drug effect may require weeks.

D. CLINICAL USE

  1. Indications. These drugs are indicated in a number of disorders.
    a. All are effective in **major depression** and the **depressed phase of bipolar illness**.
    b. They may also be effective in some cases of **bulimia** and **phobic-anxiety disorders**.
    c. The tricyclic antidepressants, in particular **imipramine**, are used to treat **enuresis**.
    d. MAO inhibitors are effective in the treatment of narcolepsy.
    e. Clomipramine appears to be particularly effective in the treatment of **obsessive-compulsive disorder**.

  2. Dosage. The dose of an antidepressant is ultimately limited by side effects and by the clinical response of the individual patient.
    a. The average daily dose for tricyclic antidepressants is 75 mg to 150 mg (more for doxepin and clomipramine and less for protriptyline). The average MAO inhibitor dose ranges from 15 mg to 75 mg daily, depending upon the drug.
    b. Divided doses may minimize side effects early in treatment, but **once-a-day dosing** is usually feasible given the long half-life of these drugs.
    c. Therapeutic blood concentrations have been determined for the tricyclic antidepressants. This information may be useful, especially for patients treated with nortriptyline, which appears to have a well-defined "therapeutic window" (i.e., a range of blood concentrations above and below which less than maximal clinical response occurs).

  3. Psychotherapy is also effective in the treatment of depression. This is particularly true in cases in which a significant loss, real or perceived, is identified.

  4. In patients with severe depression who are unresponsive to antidepressant drugs or in whom active suicidal behavior makes it difficult to tolerate the lag time required for response to an antidepressant, **electroconvulsive therapy (ECT)** may be the most effective treatment approach.

E. SIDE EFFECTS AND TOXICITY

  1. The side effects of antidepressants include:
    a. Sedation (in the case of tricyclic antidepressants), especially in combination with sedative-hypnotic drugs

   b. Sympathomimetic effects, including tachycardia, tremor, diaphoresis, agitation, and in-somnia
   c. Anticholinergic effects, including constipation, urinary retention and hesitancy, visual blurring, worsening of glaucoma, and (in severe cases) a confusional state
   d. Cardiac complications, including **orthostatic hypotension** and (in the case of tricyclic antidepressants) **conduction delays** and **arrhythmias** (especially at higher doses)
   e. Neurologic side effects, most commonly **tremor**, but also (in some cases) **paresthesias**
   f. Less common side effects such as **cholestatic jaundice**, **agranulocytosis**, **sexual disturbances**, and **weight gain**

2. All antidepressants have a **relatively low therapeutic index** and may be very toxic, especially in cases of tricyclic overdose.
   a. Symptoms of antidepressant overdose include agitation, delirium, hyperpyrexia, seizures, and coma.
   b. Tricyclic antidepressant overdose often results in severe cardiac conduction abnormalities and arrhythmias.
   c. Given the **risk of suicide** in depressed patients, care must be exercised in prescribing antidepressants. In high-risk cases, a limited amount of medication should be prescribed at one time or a family member might be enlisted to help monitor medication.

IV. ANTIMANIC DRUGS

A. GENERAL CONSIDERATIONS

1. Manic-depressive illness, a disorder involving alternating cycles of elevated and depressed mood, is now referred to as **bipolar disorder**.

2. Characteristic **symptoms of mania** are elevated mood, hyperactivity, pressured speech, grandiosity, decreased need for sleep, distractibility, and excessive involvement in potentially self-damaging activities.

3. The full manic syndrome is characteristic of bipolar disorder, although many of these individual symptoms may be seen in other psychiatric illnesses, including schizophrenia and some organic brain syndromes.

B. CLASSES OF DRUGS

1. The **lithium ion**, administered in the form of lithium carbonate or citrate, is **effective in treating acute mania and controlling the mood swings of bipolar disorder**.

2. Antipsychotic drugs may be especially useful in treating acute mania, and antidepressant drugs are indicated in the treatment of the depressed phase (see sections II and III, respectively).

C. PHARMACOLOGY AND PHARMACOKINETICS

1. The mechanism of action by which lithium stabilizes mood is unknown, but insofar as it is an ion, it may interact functionally with the cell membrane.

2. Lithium is **rapidly absorbed** gastrointestinally and is primarily **excreted by the kidney**, where it is subject to reabsorption in the proximal tubule.

3. The half-life of lithium is 20 to 24 hours.

D. CLINICAL USE

1. **Screening** of white blood cell count, renal function, thyroid function, and cardiac conduction **is required prior to initiation of lithium therapy**.

2. **Dosage.** The average dose is usually in the range of 900 mg to 1500 mg daily, starting low and increasing gradually. **Because of a low therapeutic index, serum lithium concentrations should be monitored**. Levels of 0.9 to 1.4 mEq/L are usually required in the acute phase of bipolar disorder, although lower serum concentrations may be adequate for maintenance treatment. Models exist for predicting the dose required.

3. The long half-life allows **once-a-day dosing**, if side effects (usually gastrointestinal) from peak levels after a large oral dose are not a problem.

E. SIDE EFFECTS AND TOXICITY

1. Common **early side effects** include nausea, diarrhea, polyuria, and tremor.

2. Chronic lithium ingestion is associated with several effects.

    a. Later side effects from chronic treatment include **edema** and **weight gain**, which may occur even if the patient is maintained at a therapeutic serum concentration.

    b. **Polydipsia** and **polyuria** are common. It is possible that lithium is also associated with a nephropathy, and renal function should be monitored during chronic treatment.

    c. Lithium may interfere with thyroxine synthesis, leading to **hypothyroidism**.

3. Lithium is contraindicated in the presence of significant **cardiac conduction abnormalities**.

4. Lithium is contraindicated in pregnancy because of possible **fetal cardiac abnormalities**.

5. **Acute lithium toxicity** (which may be observed at serum concentrations near 2.0 mEq/L) may include slurred speech, drowsiness, coarse tremor, vertigo, and hyperreflexia. Severe toxicity may lead to coma and convulsions.

V. ANTIANXIETY DRUGS

A. GENERAL CONSIDERATIONS

1. **Anxiety is a ubiquitous phenomenon that may be a normal response** to a fear-inducing situation or may represent a pathologic symptom.

2. Anxiety is **emotionally characterized by apprehension** and may be somatically accompanied by **motor tension** and **autonomic responses** including tachycardia, diaphoresis, mouth dryness, urinary frequency, and diarrhea.

3. Some individuals develop a well-defined **panic disorder**, characterized by recurrent acute episodes of intense anxiety.

B. CLASSES OF DRUGS

1. In the mid-1800s, bromides were introduced to alleviate anxiety; however, their potential toxicity became clear and their use fell into disfavor.

2. **Barbiturates**, especially the longer-acting forms such as **phenobarbital**, have been used since the early 1900s to treat anxiety. Problems of tolerance, dependence, and withdrawal gradually became clear. Other barbiturates include **amobarbital**, **mephobarbital**, **pentobarbital**, and **secobarbital**.

3. **Meprobamate**, a glycerol derivative, was developed in the early 1950s. It was widely used until it was displaced by the benzodiazepines, a class of drugs that now has become the pharmacologic treatment of choice for anxiety.

4. The first **benzodiazepine** was **chlordiazepoxide**. Subsequent structural modifications have yielded others, including **alprazolam**, **clonazepam**, **chlorazepate**, **diazepam**, **flurazepam**, **lorazepam**, **oxazepam**, **prazepam**, **temazepam**, and **triazolam**.

5. **Antihistamines** such as **diphenhydramine** and **hydroxyzine** have some antianxiety properties, as do some antipsychotic drugs and tricyclic antidepressants.

C. PHARMACOLOGY AND PHARMACOKINETICS

1. The barbiturates, meprobamate, and the benzodiazepines have **common properties as antianxiety and sedative agents**.

    a. At higher doses they have the ability to act as **hypnotic** drugs (inducing sleep).

    b. After chronic administration they also have in common the **induction of metabolic enzymes**.

    c. Chronic use leads to **tolerance**, the need to use higher doses to achieve the same degree of response.

    d. At sufficiently high doses, chronic use also may lead to physical **dependence**, a state in which withdrawal of the drug is associated with a specific abstinence syndrome.

    e. They also **suppress rapid eye movement (REM) sleep**.

2. The central nervous system activity of both barbiturates and benzodiazepines appears to involve **facilitation of GABA activity as an inhibitory neurotransmitter**. The two classes of drugs differ, however, in terms of their ability to affect neuronal membrane ion channels.

3. **Barbiturates and benzodiazepines vary widely in their absorption time and half-lives**. In addition, some benzodiazepines are metabolized to a succession of active compounds. Thus, these drugs vary from short-acting (e.g., pentobarbital and triazolam) to long-acting (e.g., phenobarbital and diazepam).

D. CLINICAL USE

1. Indications
   a. Anxiety is often a normal reaction to life events, requiring no pharmacologic intervention.
   b. In the specific treatment of severe or prolonged anxiety or in cases of panic disorder, the **benzodiazepines have become overwhelmingly preferred** over barbiturates and other agents.
   c. Benzodiazepines are also effective for **muscle spasm** (especially diazepam), acute control of **seizures,** treatment of **alcohol withdrawal,** and as **preoperative medications and intravenous anesthetics.**

2. Dosage. Benzodiazepines **vary in potency and in usual therapeutic doses.**
   a. Lower doses in general have antianxiety and sedative properties, while higher doses may be hypnotic, inducing sleep.
   b. Dosing schedules depend upon the drug half-life. Short-acting compounds may require several divided doses each day to avoid the emergence of symptoms of withdrawal during chronic treatment.
   c. In general, the benzodiazepines have a **high therapeutic index.**

E. SIDE EFFECTS AND TOXICITY

1. The primary side effect of antianxiety agents is **sedation,** which may cause **impaired judgment and slow the performance of motor tasks.**

2. Tolerance, leading to the use of increasing doses, and the ultimate development of **dependence** must be monitored with the chronic use of barbiturates, meprobamate, and benzodiazepines. The time course of withdrawal symptoms after discontinuation of a drug is dependent upon the half-life.

3. Overdoses of barbiturates and meprobamate may be lethal, primarily due to respiratory arrest. Benzodiazepines alone in an oral overdose may cause stupor or coma, but ventilatory assistance is rarely needed. However, the **sedative effects of benzodiazepines in combination with other drugs, especially alcohol, may be extremely dangerous.**

VI. HYPNOTIC DRUGS

A. GENERAL CONSIDERATIONS

1. Insomnia is the inability to initiate or maintain sleep. Hypnotic drugs assist in inducing sleep.

2. In general, agents that have significant antianxiety properties may be used as hypnotics, although usually a somewhat higher dose is required than that which is effective for anxiety. Sedating drugs with **rapid absorption and relatively short half-lives** are especially effective in this regard.

B. CLASSES OF DRUGS

1. In the late 1800s, **chloral hydrate,** a halogenated hydrocarbon, was introduced as a hypnotic. Subsequently, short-acting **barbiturates** became popular. Other drugs used as hypnotics include the barbiturate-like piperidinedione compounds, **glutethimide** and **methyprylon,** and the antihistamine, **diphenhydramine.**

2. As is the case in the treatment of anxiety, the use of other agents as hypnotics has been largely replaced by the use of **benzodiazepines,** in particular **flurazepam, nitrazepam, temazepam,** and **triazolam.**

C. PHARMACOLOGY AND PHARMACOKINETICS

1. Hypnotic drugs depress the central nervous system, involving not only the reticular activating system but multiple other levels from brain stem to cortex. One possible mode of action is their ability to potentiate GABA-related inhibition.

2. In terms of sleep stages, **both barbiturates and benzodiazepines reduce REM and stage 4 (slow wave) sleep.** Moreover, their discontinuation may be marked by a "rebound" insomnia.

3. These drugs are **well absorbed gastrointestinally** and easily cross the blood-brain barrier. The benzodiazepines (especially flurazepam and nitrazepam) may be **metabolized to active com-**

pounds with relatively long half-lives, allowing **accumulation** and possibly causing chronic sedation if used nightly.

D. CLINICAL USE

1. Prior to the use of hypnotic drugs, other **disorders that may be associated with insomnia should be ruled out**, including nocturnal myoclonus, sleep apnea, chronic obstructive pulmonary disease, substance abuse, and other significant psychiatric disorders such as major depression, bipolar disorder, or schizophrenia.

2. **The benzodiazepines are now the hypnotic drugs of choice**. The barbiturates and other hypnotics have significant toxicity, overdose lethality, and abuse potential.

3. **Basic principles** in the clinical use of hynoptic drugs are:
   a. Use of the **lowest effective dose**
   b. **Avoidance of chronic administration**, relying as much as possible on nonpharmacologic approaches such as establishing regular sleep patterns, avoiding caffeine and other stimulants, and using relaxation techniques

E. SIDE EFFECTS AND TOXICITY

1. Hypnotic drugs in excessive doses may cause **oversedation**. **Residual daytime sedation** may occur after nighttime use, resulting in impaired cognitive and motor performance.

2. Habitual use may result in **dependence**, and subsequent discontinuation may be accompanied by a **withdrawal syndrome**. **Rebound insomnia** may also occur after chronic use.

VII. PSYCHOPHARMACOLOGY OF DISORDERS IN CHILDREN AND ADOLESCENTS

A. GENERAL CONSIDERATIONS

1. The specific diagnoses of depression, anxiety, psychosis, and other general psychiatric problems in children may be obscured, and **symptoms may appear indirectly in behavioral manifestations such as poor school performance or impaired social interactions**.

2. Special considerations in the psychopharmacology of children and adolescents include the following.
   a. Rates of **absorption, metabolism, and excretion may be markedly different in children** when compared with adults, and adult doses may not simply be converted by weight to determine appropriate doses for children.
   b. The ability of a child to accept and respond to a drug is closely related to the specific level of psychosocial development of that child and to the context of the family of which the child is a part.

B. DEPRESSION

1. **Tricyclic antidepressants**, in particular imipramine, have been used with success in treating childhood depression.

2. Low starting doses are indicated, and plasma concentrations are monitored in unresponsive cases.

3. For side effects, see section VII E 2 c.

C. PSYCHOSIS

1. Antipsychotic drugs may be indicated in the treatment of **schizophrenia, autism, pervasive developmental disorder**, some cases of **aggressive conduct disorders**, and **Tourette's disorder**.

2. The full range of antipsychotic drug side effects may be observed in children. In particular, **sedation** and **weight gain** may be bothersome. Children are also at risk for **tardive dyskinesia**.

D. ATTENTION DEFICIT DISORDER

1. This disorder has, in the past, been referred to as "hyperkinetic syndrome," "hyperactivity," and "minimal brain dysfunction."
   a. Attention deficit disorder (ADD) is characterized by inappropriate **inattention**, including distractibility and poor concentration, and **impulsiveness**.

b. The disorder may or may not be accompanied by **motor hyperactivity**.

2. The drugs of choice are stimulants, such as **methylphenidate**, **dextroamphetamine**, and **pemoline**. In most cases, these drugs decrease motor activity and increase attention span. In cases that are unresponsive to stimulants, tricyclic antidepressants may be effective.
   a. Side effects of stimulants include headache, nausea, anorexia, insomnia, and a decrease in the rate of growth.
   b. Barbiturates and other sedatives may cause **paradoxical excitement** in cases of ADD.

3. There is a lack of firm evidence that dietary manipulations are effective in the control of ADD.

4. Additional nonpharmacologic treatment measures that may be effective in ADD include psychotherapy, family therapy, behavior modification, and special educational approaches.

E. ENURESIS

1. Enuresis is **repeated involuntary urination**, not due to a physical disorder, after the age of 5 years.

2. **Treatment**
   a. Prior to drug therapy, physical disorders such as infection, urinary tract structural abnormalities, and diabetes mellitus must be ruled out.
   b. In most cases, behavioral therapy should be tried before drug treatment.
   c. The drug of choice is **imipramine**, although other tricyclic antidepressants also are effective in decreasing the frequency of enuresis. The most common **side effects** of imipramine in children are irritability, insomnia, and nightmares.

F. EATING DISORDERS

1. Eating disorders involve gross **disturbances in eating behavior**.
   a. Anorexia nervosa is characterized by an intense fear of being overweight and a refusal to eat, even with a body weight below the normal minimum.
   b. Bulimia involves repeated eating binges, often accompanied by restrictive diets, self-induced vomiting, or the use of laxatives, emetics, and diuretics to maintain or lose weight.
   c. Both disorders are much more common in females than in males.

2. **Treatment**
   a. The primary immediate **treatment of anorexia nervosa** involves **medical management** of fluids and electrolytes and nutritional status combined with structured **behavior modification** programs (often requiring inpatient treatment). Many advocate longer-term individual or group psychotherapy.
   b. Bulimia treatment also involves **medical management**, **cognitive therapy**, and **behavior modification**. **Drug therapy** with tricyclic antidepressants or MAO inhibitors has proven effective in some patients, especially as these patients often have a significant coexisting depression.

VIII. PSYCHOPHARMACOLOGY OF DISORDERS IN THE ELDERLY

A. GENERAL CONSIDERATIONS

1. Drug absorption, metabolism, and excretion may be altered in the elderly, often leading to **increased blood and tissue concentrations** after a given drug dose, in comparison with younger patients.

2. The elderly may also be more **vulnerable to side effects** of psychopharmacologic agents, including **sedation** and **cardiac effects**.

B. DEMENTIA

1. The cognitive impairments seen in a degenerative dementia such as Alzheimer's disease have not been shown conclusively to be responsive to drug therapy.

2. **Psychotic symptoms and behavioral agitation** in a patient with dementia may respond favorably to a high-potency, less sedating antipsychotic drug such as **haloperidol**.

C. OTHER DISORDERS

1. **Depression is relatively common in the elderly** and may be accompanied by cognitive impairments referred to as "pseudodementia." Treatment with **tricyclic antidepressants** may be indicated, although close monitoring for excessive sedation, hypotension, and anticholinergic side effects is necessary.

2. Benzodiazepines, especially those with long half-lives, should be used with caution in the elderly because of their ability to impair cognitive and motor performance, in some cases resulting in a toxic confusional state.

IX. DRUGS OF ABUSE

A. GENERAL CONSIDERATIONS

1. Drug abuse involves a pattern of pathologic use of a substance, either prescription or nonprescription, which results in **social or occupational impairment**. Drug abuse may cause or exacerbate other medical disorders.

2. Drug dependence physiologically involves the development of **tolerance**, the requirement for increasing amounts of a substance to achieve a given effect, and **withdrawal**, the presence of a specific syndrome following drug cessation. This may be accompanied by the psychological factor of an ongoing subjective desire for the drug. Furthermore, animal models have shown that, even in the absence of physical dependence, drugs of abuse are themselves **strong reinforcers for ongoing self-administration**.

B. ALCOHOL

1. Alcohol is used by approximately two-thirds of the adult population in the United States. Effects sought by users of alcohol include **the relief of anxiety or depression or the disinhibition of emotions**.

2. Chronic alcohol abuse may lead to complications including hepatic dysfunction, myopathy, peripheral neuropathy, and encephalopathic syndromes due to direct toxic effects.

3. In individuals dependent upon alcohol, **withdrawal** may result in a tremulous syndrome, seizures, hallucinosis, or delirium tremens.

4. Disulfiram is a drug that is given to patients with a history of alcohol abuse in order to help them maintain sobriety. It alters the metabolism of alcohol, leading to high concentrations of acetaldehyde. If an individual taking disulfiram ingests alcohol, **a reaction occurs that is characterized by flushing, headache, nausea, and hypotension**.

C. SEDATIVE-HYPNOTIC DRUGS

1. Abuse of **barbiturates**, **benzodiazepines**, and related drugs may vary from episodic intoxication to chronic use accompanied by dependence. The abuse may have begun when the drug was prescribed for anxiety or insomnia.

2. Cross-dependence occurs between these drugs and alcohol; therefore, one drug may be substituted for another to ameliorate the effects of withdrawal. It is for this reason that the alcohol or sedative-hypnotic abuser may misuse several different drugs from this class.

3. The **withdrawal syndrome** from sedative-hypnotic drugs may range from tremor, weakness, anxiety, and insomnia to delirium and seizures. In a drug with a long half-life such as diazepam, withdrawal symptoms (including seizures) may not emerge until several days after the drug is discontinued. Because of cross-dependence, **withdrawal symptoms** for any sedative-hypnotic drug (including alcohol) **may be alleviated by a gradually tapering dose of another** long-acting **sedative-hypnotic** agent such as chlordiazepoxide.

D. OPIOID DRUGS

1. Opioid abuse (via either oral ingestion or intravenous injection) involves naturally occurring compounds and synthetic drugs. Opioid drugs include **heroin, morphine, methadone, codeine**, and related compounds.

2. These substances are **analgesics**, and they **blunt sensory awareness**. They also cause **euphoria, sedation**, and (in higher doses) **decreased respiratory drive**.

3. Patterns of use, the degree of social and occupational impairment, and the accompanying medical complications vary greatly among opioid abusers.

4. Withdrawal
   a. Cross-dependence exists among opioids. For example, a patient who is dependent upon heroin may be switched to maintenance on oral methadone or may be slowly withdrawn from heroin by a gradually tapering dose of methadone.
   b. The untreated **withdrawal syndrome** is marked by yawning, piloerection, lacrimation, rhinorrhea, sweating, nausea, vomiting, diarrhea, abdominal cramps, and hypertension.

    c. An immediate and short-lived (lasting approximately 2 hours) withdrawal syndrome may be precipitated in a dependent patient by the administration of an **opioid antagonist** such as **naloxone** or **naltrexone**. Likewise, maintenance on oral naltrexone may help an opioid abuser maintain abstinence insofar as it will block the effects of a narcotic injection.

    5. The **characteristic symptoms of an opioid overdose** are pinpoint pupils, coma, and depressed respiration.

E. STIMULANT DRUGS

    1. The most commonly abused stimulants are sympathomimetic drugs such as **cocaine**, **amphetamine**, and related compounds.

    2. Although in the past these drugs were used medically to decrease appetite or to combat drowsiness and fatigue, constraints have been placed on prescribing them. Abuse now tends to occur in individuals seeking **elevation of mood**.

    3. The central nervous system activity of sympathomimetic drugs relates to **actions on central nervous system amines**, especially dopamine. For example, amphetamine appears to stimulate release of catecholamines from presynaptic terminals.

    4. Tolerance to some effects of these drugs occurs. **Withdrawal** from stimulants may lead to depression, fatigue, and sleep disturbance.

F. HALLUCINOGENIC DRUGS

    1. These drugs have the ability to **alter perceptions, thought processes, and emotional states** in a dramatic fashion. In some cases this may include the production of illusions (distortions of real stimuli) or hallucinations.

    2. Several groups of drugs have prominent hallucinogenic properties:
        a. Indolealkylamines, including **lysergic acid diethylamide (LSD)**, **dimethyltryptamine (DMT)**, and **psilocybin**
        b. Phenylethylamines, including **mescaline** and **2,5-dimethoxy-4-methylamphetamine (DOM or "STP")**
        c. Arylcyclohexylamines, primarily **phencyclidine (PCP)**

    3. The **mode of action** of LSD-like compounds appears to involve agonist actions at presynaptic serotonin receptors. PCP was initially developed as an anesthetic, but it has mixed analgesic, stimulant, depressant, and hallucinogenic properties.

    4. These drugs typically are used episodically. Therefore, although tolerance to their effects may develop, physical dependence and withdrawal syndromes are not commonly observed. They clearly do present **psychological hazards**, however, in terms of both producing severe psychotic symptoms during intoxication and possibly also inducing long-term cognitive impairment and psychiatric syndromes.

G. CANNABIS

    1. Cannabis (marijuana), a drug derived from the hemp plant, contains a large number of cannabinoid compounds. **Tetrahydrocannabinol (THC)** is thought to be the primary active compound. The drug is usually self-administered by smoking.

    2. The **pharmacologic effects** of THC are as follows.
        a. Low doses induce a feeling of well-being, drowsiness, altered sensory and time perception, and impairment of short-term memory and complex motor function (such as that required for driving).
        b. Higher doses may cause anxiety, hallucinations, delusions, paranoia, confusion, and depersonalization.
        c. Cardiovascular effects include tachycardia, increased supine blood pressure, and decreased standing blood pressure.

    3. Tolerance develops with chronic cannabis use, and abstinence may result in withdrawal symptoms including irritability, insomnia, anxiety, and anorexia.

    4. Apparent **adverse effects** of chronic cannabis use may include an **"amotivational syndrome,"** characterized by apathy and cognitive impairment. Smoking may produce bronchitis and bronchospasm.

H. TOBACCO

    1. Approximately one-third of the adults in the United States regularly smoke tobacco.

2. Although a large number of gases and particles are contained in cigarette smoke, **nicotine appears to be primarily responsible for the reinforcement of tobacco smoking**.

3. The **pharmacologic effects** of nicotine are paradoxical insofar as they include an alerting response, with increased attention and memory, combined with skeletal muscle relaxation and decreased irritability.

4. Chronic tobacco use has been decisively linked to a number of diseases, including **cardiac and peripheral vascular disease**, and **cancer** of the lung, oropharynx, and bladder.

5. Tolerance develops to nicotine, and tobacco **withdrawal** is associated with anxiety, irritability, impaired concentration, headache, and drowsiness.

I. CAFFEINE

1. Caffeine is a **methylxanthine** compound that is found in a number of beverages including coffee, tea, cocoa, and cola drinks. It also is often included in nonprescription drugs sold as stimulants.

2. The **pharmacologic effects** of caffeine include central nervous system stimulation, diuresis, cardiac stimulation, and smooth muscle relaxation.

3. **Caffeine intoxication** may be marked by restlessness, agitation, insomnia, flushing, gastrointestinal disturbances, diuresis, muscle twitching, cardiac arrhythmias, and rambling speech.

4. Although physical dependence is not well documented, some tolerance and psychological dependence are observed with chronic use of caffeine-containing beverages.

X. BEHAVIORAL EFFECTS OF NONPSYCHIATRIC DRUGS

A. CARDIOVASCULAR DRUGS

1. Antihypertensive drugs, in particular **reserpine**, **methyldopa**, and **propranolol**, may cause depression.

2. **Digitalis** in low doses may cause weakness, apathy, and anorexia. Toxicity may be manifested by delirium with hallucinations.

3. The antiarrhythmic agents **quinidine**, **lidocaine**, and **procainamide** may cause confusion and delirium.

B. ANTICHOLINERGIC DRUGS

1. Many **nonprescription drugs for colds**, **motion sickness**, and **insomnia** include anticholinergic agents that may cause drowsiness, impaired concentration, blurred vision, and dry mouth.

2. In higher doses, anticholinergic agents such as **atropine** and **scopolamine** may cause a toxic delirium accompanied by fever and decreased sweating.

C. ANTIMICROBIAL DRUGS

1. The antibacterial agents **nalidixic acid** and **nitrofurantoin** may cause headache, drowsiness, or even confusional states.

2. The antitubercular drugs **isoniazid**, **iproniazid**, and **cycloserine** may cause confusion and delirium, including delusions and hallucinations.

D. ANALGESIC AND ANTI-INFLAMMATORY DRUGS

1. In high doses, the analgesic agents **propoxyphene** and **pentazocine** may cause acute psychotic states. They also are associated with the development of physical dependence.

2. The anti inflammatory drug **indomethacin** may cause depression or, in rare cases, an acute psychosis.

E. HORMONES

1. Chronic treatment with **corticosteroids** is commonly associated with depression. Less commonly, confusion, delusions, and hallucinations may occur.

2. **Oral contraceptives** are frequently associated with depression. In rare cases, treatment with or withdrawal from oral contraceptives may be associated with psychosis, especially in individuals with a past history of a psychotic disorder.

F. LEVODOPA

1. As a **precursor of dopamine**, levodopa (L-dopa) is frequently used to treat Parkinson's disease. Behavioral side effects are relatively common with prolonged therapy.

2. Reported **side effects** include depression, restlessness, hyperactivity, confusion, delirium, and dyskinesia.

XI. PRINCIPLES OF PRESCRIBING

A. INFORMING THE PATIENT

1. As with any medical procedure, when a drug is prescribed for a patient an explanation must be made of both the expected benefits from the drug and the risks of potential side effects and toxicity.

2. **Patient compliance.** An extremely common cause of failure to respond to a prescribed drug regimen is patient **noncompliance**, which may involve failure to take a drug or overuse of the drug. Several factors contribute to noncompliance.
   a. The physician is responsible for explaining both **the nature of the patient's disorder and the rationale for prescribing** a specific drug.
   b. **Outpatients**, especially if they are elderly or live alone, **are much less likely to comply** with a prescription than patients in a hospital or day-care situation.
   c. The emergence of **side effects**, especially in a patient not forewarned, often leads to noncompliance.
   d. **Simple drug-treatment regimens**, especially once-a-day dosing when pharmacokinetic factors allow it, contribute to greater compliance.

B. PLACEBO EFFECTS

1. Nonspecific placebo effects, responses other than those due to the pharmacologic properties of the drug, may be observed even when a patient is taking an active medication.

2. These nonspecific effects, whether positive or negative, may be in large part **the result of the quality of the physician–patient relationship** and the set of expectations for a drug on the part of the physician and the patient.

C. DRUG INTERACTIONS

1. **Drugs have the potential for interacting with one another in beneficial or adverse ways**. All drugs (including nonprescription agents) that the patient is taking must be considered before a new drug is prescribed.

2. An example of a beneficial interaction is the reduction in tremor and rigidity (common side effects in a patient taking an antipsychotic drug) that may result from the addition of an anticholinergic drug such as benztropine.

3. An extremely common adverse interaction between psychopharmacologic agents is excess drowsiness and impaired motor performance caused by their **cumulative sedative effects**.

D. INDIVIDUALIZATION OF TREATMENT

1. The decision to prescribe a given drug in a given dose is dependent upon the **physiology and psychology** of the individual patient.
   a. An **accurate diagnosis** is crucial. In psychiatry, this is often dependent upon a longitudinal, rather than a cross-sectional, view of the patient. Moreover, **other medical disorders presenting with psychiatric symptoms must be ruled out**.
   b. Common physiologic parameters involve the age, weight, cardiovascular status, and the hepatic and renal functioning of the patient as well as drugs that the patient is currently taking.
   c. The **attitude of patients** regarding a drug may be strongly influenced by past experiences of their own or others close to them and by their understanding of and reactions to their illness.

2. **Frequent reevaluation** of a prescribed regimen in terms of both therapeutic response and adverse reactions is crucial. Large prescriptions and frequent renewals without close monitoring are to be avoided.

STUDY QUESTIONS

Directions: Each question below contains five suggested answers. Choose the **one best** response to each question.

1. The anticholinergic side effects of drugs may include all of the following EXCEPT

(A) mouth dryness
(B) constipation
(C) bradycardia
(D) blurred vision
(E) urinary hesitancy

2. Tardive dyskinesia is a potentially irreversible movement disorder that is associated with the long-term use of

(A) barbiturates
(B) phenothiazines
(C) alcohol
(D) tricyclic antidepressants
(E) lithium

3. Cross-dependence is most likely to exist between

(A) imipramine and phenelzine
(B) secobarbital and diazepam
(C) haloperidol and chlorpromazine
(D) amitriptyline and lithium
(E) alcohol and phencyclidine (PCP)

4. A 40-year-old man presents to the emergency room with rapid speech, grandiose delusions, insomnia, and hypersexual behavior of several weeks duration. The history reveals similar past episodes, interspersed with periods of psychomotor retardation, hypersomnia, weight gain, and poor job performance. The drug most likely to be of long-term benefit for this patient is

(A) thioridazine
(B) desipramine
(C) carbamazepine
(D) lithium
(E) chlordiazepoxide

5. Tricyclic antidepressants are often effective in the treatment of all of the following disorders EXCEPT

(A) agoraphobia
(B) bulimia
(C) schizophrenia
(D) bipolar disorder
(E) enuresis

6. A withdrawal syndrome is likely to occur after discontinuation of chronic high doses of all of the following drugs EXCEPT

(A) alprazolam
(B) amphetamine
(C) chlorpromazine
(D) diazepam
(E) nicotine

Directions: Each question below contains four suggested answers of which **one or more** is correct. Choose the answer

A   if **1, 2, and 3** are correct
B   if **1 and 3** are correct
C   if **2 and 4** are correct
D   if **4** is correct
E   if **1, 2, 3, and 4** are correct

7. Side effects associated with a serum lithium concentration of 1.0 mEq/L include

(1) constipation
(2) tremor
(3) hyperthyroidism
(4) polyuria

8. The pharmacologic properties of the benzodiazepines and barbiturates include

(1) sedative effects
(2) induction of metabolic enzymes
(3) development of tolerance
(4) increases in rapid eye movement (REM) sleep

9. Effective drugs in the treatment of attention deficit disorder (ADD) in children include

(1) dextroamphetamine
(2) pemoline
(3) methylphenidate
(4) barbiturates

10. A 55-year-old woman is admitted to the hospital with severe depression, weight loss, early morning awakening, and poor concentration. She has unremitting suicidal ideas and, even after hospitalization, makes a serious attempt to commit suicide. Immediate treatment options for this patient should include

(1) lithium
(2) electroconvulsive therapy (ECT)
(3) phenobarbital
(4) doxepin

11. A 28-year-old man with a 10-year history of chronic schizophrenia has been started on fluphenazine because of a recurrence of his delusional thoughts and auditory hallucinations. He returns to the outpatient clinic for his next appointment and is noted to have cogwheel rigidity of his extremities, a mask-like facial expression, hand tremor, and a shuffling gait. The treatment approach to these symptoms includes

(1) the addition of lithium carbonate
(2) immediate discontinuation of fluphenazine
(3) addition of a bedtime dose of flurazepam
(4) addition of benztropine

ANSWERS AND EXPLANATIONS

1. The answer is C. (*II E 3; III E 1 c*) The anticholinergic side effects of drugs may include tachycardia, possibly due to decreased vagal tone. Cholinergic antagonism would also decrease salivation and sweating, lessen gastrointestinal motility, cause urinary hesitancy and retention, and impair visual accommodation. In particular, the phenothiazines and the tricyclic antidepressants are associated with anticholinergic side effects.

2. The answer is B. (*II E 10*) Tardive dyskinesia is characterized by involuntary choreoathetoid movements, which may involve the face, mouth, tongue, trunk, and extremities. It is seen in as many as 20% of patients who are chronically treated with phenothiazines and other antipsychotic agents. Other neuromuscular side effects associated with antipsychotic drugs include acute dystonia, akathisia (motor restlessness), and parkinsonian symptoms such as tremor and rigidity. Tremor is the most common neuromuscular side effect seen with the use of tricyclic antidepressants and lithium, and it is also common in withdrawal from barbiturates and alcohol.

3. The answer is B. (*IX C 2*) Physical dependence refers to a state in which a drug has been chronically administered and discontinuation of the drug results in a specific abstinence syndrome. Many psychopharmacologic agents cause dependence with chronic use; in particular, this is true of sedative–hypnotic and opioid drugs. Cross-dependence refers to the ability of one substance to ameliorate the withdrawal symptoms of another. The benzodiazepines, barbiturates, and alcohol exhibit cross-dependence with one another.

4. The answer is D. (*IV B*) The alternating manic and depressed episodes exhibited by this patient make the diagnosis of bipolar disorder likely. Treatment of the acute manic phase may be facilitated by use of an antipsychotic drug such as thioridazine, and the depression may be treated with an antidepressant such as desipramine. Chronic treatment with lithium, however, has proven to be the most effective means of decreasing the frequency and severity of mood swings and in some cases eliminating them altogether. Certain treatment-resistant or rapidly cycling cases of bipolar disorder have been successfully treated with carbamazepine, an anticonvulsant, but lithium remains the drug of choice.

5. The answer is C. (*III D 1*) Treatment with tricyclic antidepressants has been fairly successful in a variety of disorders in which depression may not be prominent, including agoraphobia, bulimia, and enuresis. Tricyclic antidepressants also may be used to treat the depressed phase of bipolar disorder, but caution is required to avoid precipitation of a manic phase. The primary symptoms of schizophrenia, however, are typically unresponsive to antidepressant therapy. Schizophrenic patients usually do not benefit from antidepressants except in cases in which there is a significant coexisting depression.

6. The answer is C. (*II A 2; V C 1 d; IX C, E, H*) Although some tolerance may develop to their sedating effects, the antipsychotic drugs such as chlorpromazine are not associated with prominent physical dependence or a well-defined withdrawal syndrome. The withdrawal syndrome in a patient dependent on a benzodiazepine is a function of the half-life of the specific drug. A drug with a long half-life like diazepam is much more likely to produce a delayed withdrawal syndrome in comparison with a short-acting agent like alprazolam.

7. The answer is C (2, 4). (*IV E*) Lithium is a drug with a relatively narrow therapeutic range. Serum concentrations between 0.6 and 1.4 mEq/L are generally therapeutic, whereas levels above 2.0 mEq/L are toxic. Side effects that may be common even at therapeutic blood levels include gastrointestinal irritation manifested by nausea and diarrhea, fine tremor, polydipsia, polyuria, weight gain, and edema. Chronic use may also be associated with hypothyroidism, which is thought to be related to impaired thyroxine synthesis. Toxic blood levels may lead to confusion and seizures.

8. The answer is A (1, 2, 3). (*V C 1; VI E 2*) The benzodiazepines and barbiturates have many properties in common, including antianxiety and hypnotic effects. They induce enzymes involved in their own metabolism, and tolerance to their effects and physical dependence may develop with chronic administration. They consistently reduce rapid eye movement (REM) and stage 4 sleep. Although they may have sleep-inducing properties, when chronic use of these drugs is discontinued, rebound insomnia often occurs.

9. The answer is A (1, 2, 3). (*VII D 2*) A number of agents are effective in the treatment of attention deficit disorder (ADD), in particular, stimulants such as dextroamphetamine, methylphenidate, and pemoline. In patients who do not respond to stimulants, the tricyclic antidepressant, imipramine, should be tried. In spite of the frequent appearance of motor hyperactivity in ADD, sedatives are ineffective and may actually result in a paradoxical exacerbation of hyperactivity.

10. The answer is C (2, 4). (*III D 4*) The diagnosis in this case is that of a severe major depression. If the patient also has a history of past manic episodes, indicating a possible bipolar disorder, lithium might be considered for long-term maintenance. It would not be an effective treatment, however, for the acute depression. Sedative–hypnotic drugs such as the barbiturates are in general not effective as antidepressants. An antidepressant such as doxepin may be effective. In this case, however, the suicide risk may make it difficult to wait the 2 to 3 weeks often necessary for a response to tricyclic antidepressants. In such situations, treatment with electroconvulsive therapy (ECT) may be more rapidly effective. There is no evidence that ECT combined with an antidepressant is more effective in the acute treatment of depression than ECT alone. However, placing a patient on a maintenance dose of an antidepressant after ECT treatment may aid in preventing relapse.

11. The answer is D (4). (*II E 2*) Rigidity, mask-like facies, shuffling gait, and "pill-rolling" tremor are characteristic extrapyramidal side effects of the antipsychotic drugs. They are thought to result from the blockade of dopamine receptors in the basal ganglia, and they resemble the clinical features of Parkinson's disease (a disorder caused by degeneration of nigrostriatal dopaminergic pathways). The side effects usually respond to the addition of an anticholinergic drug such as benztropine or trihexyphenidyl while treatment with the antipsychotic drug is continued.

3
Psychophysiology

John M. Morihisa
Richard B. Rosse

I. INTRODUCTION. Many of the concepts presented in this chapter are derived from pioneering research in the neurosciences and are in large part hypothetical. Ideas founded on the frontiers of knowledge are subject to change as new data are reported. Thus, the reader should use these concepts as learning tools in a dynamic process rather than as items of knowledge to be committed to memory.

II. NEUROANATOMICAL CORRELATES OF PSYCHOPHYSIOLOGY. Functional neuroanatomy and psychophysiology are evolving fields, and some of the concepts discussed in this chapter no doubt will be modified. The functions performed by different areas of the brain cannot always be confined neatly to certain neuroanatomical areas, and the fact that some areas of the brain are not discussed here does not mean that they are not associated with behavior, but that their role is unclear. The categories and systems described here may overlap and at times even contradict descriptions found elsewhere, due to differing conventions and interpretations of research findings.

A. CEREBRAL CORTEX

1. **Frontal lobe**
   a. **Function.** The frontal lobes are responsible for the **initiation and organization of voluntary movement**, including conjugate eye movement. Motor control of speech is a function of the dominant frontal lobe. The frontal lobes integrate sensory information and help direct motor movements. **Intellectual processes** such as problem solving, judgment, planning, and goal direction as well as understanding socially acceptable behavior are functions associated with the frontal lobe.
   b. **Dysfunction.** Symptoms of frontal lobe dysfunction can include contralateral hemiplegia, impairment in problem solving, and expressive aphasia. Psychological symptoms involve personality changes such as poor judgment; inappropriate, silly, or childlike behavior; apathy; impulsiveness; and irritability. Frontal lobe dysfunction might also play a role in schizophrenia and depression.
      (1) Some clinicians differentiate between the **"pseudodepressed"** and the **"pseudopsychopathic"** types of **frontal lobe syndromes**, which are usually due to some type of frontal lobe damage such as a stroke. The pseudodepressed type is characterized by apathy and slowed mentation. The pseudopsychopathic type is characterized by silliness, lack of social tact, hyperactivity, impulsiveness, crudity, and antisocial behavior.
      (2) Damage to the frontal lobes is believed to be associated with the appearance of certain reflexes (i.e., snout, sucking, palmomental, and grasp reflexes).

2. **Temporal lobe**
   a. **Function.** The temporal lobe receives auditory input and is involved in the **comprehension of spoken language** as well as with particular memory processes. **Emotions and sexual activity** are also associated with the temporal lobe, which is intimately related to the limbic system (see section II B).
   b. **Dysfunction**
      (1) Bilateral **destructive lesions** cause symptoms of the **Klüver-Bucy syndrome** (first demonstrated as an experiment in rhesus monkeys in which the temporal limbic system was removed, resulting in visual agnosia, a tendency toward the oral exploration of objects, altered sexual behavior, loss of fear and anger, and placidity).
      (2) **Partial complex (psychomotor) seizures** are associated with irritative lesions of the temporal lobe. These seizures are believed to be able to mimic many different psychiatric disorders.

The authors would like to thank Deborah L. Warden, M.D., for her valuable comments and review of the manuscript.

(a) Psychomotor seizures can involve sensory, psychic, or autonomic symptoms as well as somatomotor automatisms. These seizures can be divided into three components, which can be recalled by using the mnemonic **three ''A's,''** for **aura**, **alterations in consciousness**, and **automatisms**.

    (i) **Aura** is generally the first sign of a seizure. It can involve a wide range of sensations, including autonomic symptoms such as the feeling of epigastric fullness, butterflies in the stomach, cardiac arrhythmia, sweating, blushing, and urinary incontinence or mental symptoms such as déjà vu, jamais vu, hallucinations, fear, dysphoria, euphoria, derealization, and depersonalization.

    (ii) **Alterations in consciousness.** A brief lapse in consciousness can be the only symptom of a complex partial seizure.

    (iii) **Automatisms** can involve simple motor acts such as grimacing, chewing, and blinking or complex motor behaviors.

(b) The particular symptom picture depends on the site of seizure focus and the locations to which the seizure activity might spread. For instance, the presence of autonomic symptoms probably represents seizure activity spread to the hypothalamus, an area of the brain intimately involved in controlling autonomic functioning. The electrical activity can also spread throughout the brain to the point that the patient experiences a generalized seizure.

3. Parietal lobe

  a. Function. The parietal lobe includes the primary somatosensory area of the brain. The reception, interpretation, and **integration of multimodal sensory stimuli** are controlled by the parietal lobe. It is responsible for complex sensory discrimination, including a sense of body position and body image; the size, shape, texture, and weight of objects; pain; touch; pressure; and temperature. *loss of sensa(tion) / inability to make proper use*

  b. Dysfunction. Parietal lobe dysfunction is associated with **impairment in sensory discrimination**, including distortion of body image, agnosia, and apraxia. Parietal lobe lesions in the nondominant (generally right) hemisphere may be associated with anosognosia (an inability to recognize one's own bodily defects) and constructional apraxia (characterized by inability to copy drawings or replicate patterns via construction). *of an object*

4. Occipital lobe

  a. Function. The occipital lobe receives and interprets visual stimuli (i.e., it processes visual information concerning objects and patterns).

  b. Dysfunction. Pathology of the occipital lobe can result in visual illusions and hallucinations (both formed and unformed), distortion of images, cortical blindness, and visual agnosia.

B. LIMBIC SYSTEM. The limbic system is composed of both cortical and subcortical tissue.

1. Structures. Major limbic system structures include the hippocampus, parahippocampal area, cingulate gyrus, subcallosum, amygdala, septum, anterior thalamic nuclei, hypothalamus, and major tracts connecting the system.

2. Function. The limbic system is closely associated with the temporal lobe, frontal lobe, and autonomic nervous system. The **hypothalamus is** often considered to be **a central element of the limbic system**, and it seems to be involved in the control of many vegetative functions of the body (e.g., regulation of body temperature, hunger, and thirst). Limbic system functions involve the elaboration of impulses to and from higher cortical centers, and the limbic system has been hypothesized to play an important role in mediating emotions (e.g., fear, pleasure, sexual response).

3. Dysfunction

  a. Irritative lesions of the limbic system may be associated with psychomotor seizures, which can include many psychiatric symptoms such as hallucinations, alterations in sex drive, anxiety and fear, rage, and aggression.

  b. Hippocampal lesions can result in memory deficits.

  c. A few investigators believe that some episodic psychoses may be associated with dysrhythmias (seizure-like activity) in certain areas of the brain such as the limbic system.

C. DIENCEPHALON

1. Structures. The major elements of the diencephalon consist of the thalamus, hypothalamus, epithalamus, and subthalamus.

2. Function. The diencephalon seems to function as an integrating system for multiple brain structures. It perhaps is involved in processing sensory stimuli and the body's reaction to them as well as helping facilitate mechanisms associated with memory. For instance, there have been patients with thalamic lesions who have had resultant memory problems.

3. **Dysfunction.** Pathologic lesions in the diencephalon are thought possibly to be associated with a variety of disorders and behaviors [e.g., Kleine-Levin syndrome (hyperphagia, hypersomnia, hypersexuality, and hyperirritability), eating disorders, and certain pain syndromes].

D. MIDBRAIN AND BRAIN STEM

1. The **locus ceruleus** is a noradrenergic nucleus found near the floor of the rostral part of the fourth ventricle, with projections throughout the brain, especially to the cortex and hippocampus. It is thought to produce a significant portion of the norepinephrine in the brain.
   a. Stimulation of the locus ceruleus in animals can produce fearful, anxiety-like behaviors.
   b. The locus ceruleus is hypothesized to play a role in anxiety and panic disorder.

2. The **raphe nucleus** is a series of nuclei in the lower midbrain and upper pons. Axon terminals from the raphe nucleus are in almost all brain regions, with probably the largest number in the hypothalamus.
   a. Cell bodies of the serotonin-containing neurons are found here.
   b. Destruction of this nucleus results in insomnia; stimulation causes somnolence.

3. The **reticular activating system** is a functional component of the **reticular formation**, a complex of cells in the brain stem. It includes centrally located areas of the brain stem from the caudal medulla to the diencephalon. It receives input from all sensory pathways.
   a. **Function.** The reticular activating system plays a central role in **cortical arousal and reception of stimuli**. It is thought to be important in sleep, attention, memory, and habituation (i.e., gradual adaptation to a stimulus).
   b. **Dysfunction.** Dysfunction of the reticular activating system is hypothesized to play a role in disorders such as akinetic mutism and generalized convulsive disorders.

E. CEREBELLUM. The classic importance of the cerebellum has been in mediating motor coordination.

III. SLEEP NEUROPHYSIOLOGY

A. SLEEP STATES. Sleep can be divided into **rapid eye movement (REM)** and **non-REM sleep**.

1. When an individual falls asleep, non-REM sleep is entered first and progresses through stages 1, 2, 3, and 4. After a period of stage 3 and 4 sleep, the stages of sleep are reversed until the individual reenters stage 2 sleep, after which REM sleep commences. REM sleep occurs about every 90 to 100 minutes; however, as the night progresses, the duration of each occurrence of REM sleep increases, and the intervals between incidences of REM sleep decrease.

2. Ideally, sleep consists of a sequence of stages 1, 2, 3, 4, 3, 2, REM, followed by repetitions of the cycle.
   a. The beginning of the second cycle occurs with stage 2 following the first REM stage.
   b. The duration of stages 3 and 4 decreases as the night progresses, and later cycles may be totally devoid of stages 3 and 4 sleep.

3. The sleep cycle varies with age.
   a. Infants spend approximately 16 hours each day asleep. This generally decreases to about 10 hours each day during childhood. The reduction of sleep time that occurs from infancy to childhood is mainly a reduction in REM sleep.
   b. Adults spend approximately 7 hours each day asleep, and the reduction in sleep time from childhood to adulthood is largely a reduction of deep, slow-wave sleep time.
   c. Geriatric sleep is normally associated with increases in stages 1 and 2 sleep and decreases in stages 3 and 4 and in REM sleep.

B. NEUROPHYSIOLOGY OF SLEEP. Sleep is thought to occur as a consequence of a gradual decrease in activity of the ascending reticular activating system and upon activation of the brain systems involved in sleep generation.

1. The system responsible for **non-REM sleep** is hypothesized to be in the **raphe nuclei**, the median forebrain area, or both.

2. **REM sleep** is thought to require active involvement of the cholinergic **gigantocellular tegmental field neurons** found in the tegmentum of the pons.
   a. It is hypothesized that the catecholaminergic neurons of the locus ceruleus and the serotonergic neurons of the raphe nuclei inhibit the neurons of the gigantocellular tegmental field.
   b. However, with low activity of the locus ceruleus and raphe nuclei, the gigantocellular tegmental field produces electrical discharges termed **pontine–geniculate–occipital (PGO) spikes**, which travel to many neurologic systems and which are believed to contribute to the generation of REM sleep. PGO spikes are probably involved in the autonomic nervous system activity seen in REM sleep and may produce the fragments of visual imagery recognized as dreams.

3. REM sleep differs physiologically from non-REM sleep in various ways.
   a. Penile erection and vaginal lubrication regularly occur during REM sleep, independently of sexual stimulation.
   b. Gastric secretion peaks during REM sleep, and at night peptic ulcer patients can secrete three to twenty times as much gastric acid as normal individuals.
   c. Heart rate and blood pressure increase and become irregular during REM sleep, and death from cardiac disorders occurs most commonly between 5 and 6 A.M. (peak REM sleep time).

C. SLEEP CHANGES ASSOCIATED WITH PSYCHIATRIC DISORDERS

1. **Major depression** is associated with increased REM sleep and decreased REM latency (latency averages 45 to 50 minutes rather than the normal 90 minutes). REM latencies after administration of acetylcholine (ACh)-like drugs have been reported to be shorter in some patients with major depression, which has been interpreted by some researchers to suggest that depression may be linked to an increased sensitivity to ACh.

2. There is no consensus as to what changes in sleep may be characteristic of **schizophrenia**. Reduced amounts of stages 2, 3, and 4 sleep have been reported in some schizophrenic patients.

3. Moderate consumption of alcohol causes early sleep onset but increased wakefulness in the second half of the night. **Alcohol intoxication** is associated with decreased REM sleep, which rebounds during alcohol withdrawal. Insomnia and sleep disturbances have been reported to persist for up to 6 months after withdrawal from alcohol.

IV. NEUROPSYCHOBIOLOGY OF LIGHT

A. **SEASONAL AFFECTIVE DISORDER.** A subtype of depression, termed seasonal affective disorder (**SAD**), has been hypothesized in which affected individuals are more depressed during months with relatively few hours of sunlight (i.e., wintertime). Bright artificial light may have an antidepressant effect in some of these individuals. The physiologic mechanism by which this reaction may occur has yet to be clarified.

B. **MELATONIN** is the major hormone produced by the pineal body. It seems to act primarily on the hypothalamus and the pituitary gland, and its actions may include the synchronization of multiple neuroendocrine rhythms. The pineal body is influenced by the amount of light seen by the eyes each day, and **light appears to inhibit melatonin production** in the brain through a complex neural pathway.

1. When exposed to bright light, some patients with depression have been reported to show a greater drop in plasma melatonin than healthy individuals.

2. The normal nighttime rise in plasma melatonin has been reported to be blunted in some patients with the melancholic subtype of depression.

V. NEUROPHYSIOLOGY OF PAIN

A. **TRANSMISSION OF PAIN.** Pain sensation is transmitted to the spinal cord via dual pathways of innervation. **A delta fibers** transmit fast, pricking, localized pain, and **C fibers** transmit slow, dull, burning pain.

1. The fast, pricking pain results in a quick reflex withdrawal from the pain stimulus. It can be accompanied by an increase in blood pressure and pulse.

2. The slow, burning pain sensation transmitted by C fibers is hypothesized by some investigators to be able to excite the reticular activating system and thus affect the entire nervous system.

B. AWARENESS OF PAIN. Pain is largely perceived in the thalamus and other subcortical centers of the brain; however, it seems to be interpreted (i.e., its site localized and its intensity and quality judged) in the cortex.

C. ENKEPHALINS AND ENDORPHINS. It has been hypothesized that some of the neurobiological systems mediating chronic pain and depression might overlap.

1. **Opiate-like substances,** called **enkephalins** and **endorphins**, exist in the brain. Basic neuroscience studies have discovered that stimulation of areas of the brain, such as the periaqueductal gray matter and the periventricular area, appear to produce analgesia sustained beyond the periods of stimulation.

2. It is not yet certain whether enkephalins and endorphins also have a part in the pathogenesis of some psychiatric disorders. Both schizophrenia and depression have been studied in relation to possible abnormalities of these endogenous brain substances.

VI. NEUROPHYSIOLOGY OF STRESS. Stress is a state of psychological or physical strain that imposes demands for internal and external adjustments.

1. **Limbic system activation by stress** causes the hypothalamus to release **corticotropin releasing factor**, which stimulates the release of **adrenocorticotropic hormone (ACTH)** from the pituitary gland, which in turn stimulates the adrenal gland to release cortisol. The limbic system commands to the hypothalamus are hypothesized to be mediated through either cholinergic or serotonergic stimulatory pathways, or both, and through adrenergic inhibitory pathways.

2. **Stress** can give rise to feelings of anxiety. Anxiety can be associated with increases in heart and respiratory rates, blood pressure, muscle tension, body oxygen consumption, as well as serum levels of lactate, cortisol, catecholamines, and cholesterol. Stress can also be associated with changes in skin conductance and decreased blood flow in and decreased temperature of the extremities, and it has been reported to be associated with decreased immune function. Anxiety is accompanied by a reduction in alpha wave abundance on the electroencephalogram (EEG).

VII. PSYCHOENDOCRINOLOGY. The cortex and limbic system seem to affect secretion of hypothalamic factors and pituitary hormones. It is hypothesized that measurable abnormalities of hypothalamic-pituitary–target endocrine gland axes possibly reflect limbic system or cortical dysfunction, or both.

Various endocrine abnormalities have been reported in patients with psychiatric illnesses; for example: Hypersecretion of cortisol has been reported in depressed patients; as many as 10% of newly admitted psychiatric patients have been reported to have abnormalities on thyroid function tests (which estimate thyroid hormone production); the basal secretion of growth hormone has been reported by some investigators to be somewhat higher in depressed individuals than in normal controls; some investigators have reported abnormalities of plasma prolactin concentration in chronic schizophrenic patients. The meaning of these associated abnormalities remains to be elucidated.

A. DEXAMETHASONE SUPPRESSION TEST

1. In a commonly described version of the dexamethasone suppression test (**DST**), the patient takes 1 mg of dexamethasone orally at 11 P.M. The serum cortisol level is measured over the next 24 hours, generally at 8 A.M., 4 P.M., and 11 P.M. The test is abnormal if the cortisol level equals or exceeds 5 μg/100 ml at any sample point; this abnormality is termed **nonsuppression**.

   a. It has been reported that about 45% to 75% of depressed patients demonstrate nonsuppression. However, a significant proportion of patients with psychiatric disorders other than depression (i.e., schizophrenia, dementia, mania, alcoholism, agoraphobia, and borderline personality disorder) also seem to have abnormal DST results.

   b. False-positive DST results have been associated with physiologic stress, uncontrolled diabetes mellitus, Cushing's disease, liver disease, acute withdrawal from alcohol and drugs, malnutrition, significant weight loss, recent surgery, and treatment with a variety of drugs, including steroids, reserpine, and anticonvulsants.

   c. False-negative results are associated with Addison's disease and corticosteroid therapy.

2. The clinical usefulness of the DST remains controversial, although the test is frequently employed as a research tool. It has been theorized that the DST may be helpful in monitoring clinical recovery of psychiatric patients. The DST should be viewed as a research tool, and routine clinical use would seem premature.

B. THYROTROPIN-RELEASING HORMONE TEST. In the most frequently described version of the thyrotropin-releasing hormone (**TRH**) test, 500 μg of TRH is given intravenously to the patient after an overnight fast. Samples of serum thyroid-stimulating hormone (TSH) are taken at baseline and at 15, 30, 60, and 90 minutes after TRH administration. In normal individuals, the level of TSH begins to rise at about 10 minutes, peaks at about 30 minutes, and then falls quickly. A blunted or decreased TSH response to TRH has been observed in about 25% of patients with major depression. These patients generally have otherwise normal thyroid function (i.e., they are not hypo- or hyperthyroid). The significance of the blunting has been debated. Like the DST, the clinical utility of the TRH test remains to be determined.

C. GROWTH HORMONE

1. Growth hormone (**GH**) response to challenge by dopamine, amphetamine, clonidine, and insulin-induced hypoglycemia has been studied. The response to provocative testing has been reported to be blunted in depressed patients.

2. Unstimulated, basal secretion of GH may be greater both in some depressed children and some depressed adults than in normal individuals.

3. It has been reported that apomorphine-induced GH responses are greater in psychotic patients with Schneiderian first-rank symptoms than in patients without first-rank symptoms or in normal controls.

4. Tests remain research tools at the present time.

D. PROLACTIN

1. Prolactin responses to TRH, L-tryptophan, and some opiates have been reported to be blunted in depressed patients.

2. Apomorphine suppression of prolactin may be greater in schizophrenic patients than in normal controls.

3. Antipsychotic medications increase levels of serum prolactin. It has been suggested that this prolactin response might be correlated with clinical response to the antipsychotic agent.

E. SUMMARY. At this time there are no clear indications for the routine use of these neuroendocrine challenge tests in clinical psychiatry. However, they remain promising research tools.

VIII. BRAIN IMAGING. Brain imaging techniques discussed below are based upon principles of neuroscience and represent powerful new research tools in psychiatry. However, the clinical applications of these approaches require extensive further investigation.

A. ELECTROENCEPHALOGRAM

1. The EEG measures electrical activity of the brain via electrodes placed in standard positions on the scalp.

2. The brain waves recorded by the EEG include:
   a. Beta waves, with frequencies over 13 Hz
   b. Alpha waves, with frequencies of 8 to 12 Hz
   c. Theta waves, with frequencies of 4 to below 8 Hz
   d. Delta waves, with frequencies less than 4 Hz

3. Perhaps the neurodiagnostic test employed most often by psychiatrists today, the EEG is used in the diagnosis of epilepsy and other neurologic disorders. The EEG pattern is evaluated for paroxysmal events such as spikes or isolated bursts of activity as well as for the presence of abnormal frequencies.

4. Schizophrenic patients as a group demonstrate more EEG abnormalities than the general population. However, there is no consensus as to any specific EEG findings that might be characteristic of schizophrenia.

B. EVOKED POTENTIALS

1. Evoked potentials are specific recordable electrical responses in the brain to discrete sensory stimuli. Ordinary EEG electrodes are placed on the scalp to measure the electrical changes. Because the evoked potentials are so small, however, they seldom can be distinguished on the record of EEG activity. Therefore, evoked responses to repetitive stimuli must be extracted ("averaged") via computer from the background activity of the EEG.

2. Common evoked potential tests include the somatosensory evoked potential (SSEP), visual evoked potential (VEP), and auditory evoked potential (AEP).

3. Evoked potentials can be of assistance in the evaluation of demylinating diseases (e.g., multiple sclerosis) and possibly in the differentiation between organic and psychogenic sensory or motor deficits.

4. Evoked potential studies can measure mental activity that occurs on the order of milliseconds.

5. Certain components of the evoked potential recording have been noted to be abnormal in some patients with serious psychiatric illness (e.g., schizophrenia) and certain organic brain disorders (e.g., Alzheimer's disease). However, there is no general agreement as to which findings might be characteristic of a specific psychiatric disorder.

C. COMPUTERIZED TOPOGRAPHIC MAPPING OF ELECTROPHYSIOLOGIC DATA

1. Electrical activity is measured by electrodes placed in standardized positions on the scalp. Large quantities of data produced by the multiple-lead EEG, as well as data produced by evoked potentials if desired, are analyzed and presented as two-dimensional color-coded brain maps.

2. Increases in EEG delta wave activity over the entire cortical surface have been observed in schizophrenic patients through the use of computerized topographic mapping.

D. COMPUTED TOMOGRAPHY. Thousands of x-ray readings are processed by computer to give a cross-sectional view of brain structure.

1. Ventricular size. Computed tomography (**CT**) has demonstrated <u>increased ventricular size in patients with schizophrenia</u> and affective disorders.
  a. In schizophrenia, large ventricles (or increased ventricle-to-brain ratios) have been reported in association with multiple previous hospitalizations, a history of persistent unemployment, and negative schizophrenic symptoms (e.g., apathy, poverty of speech, and flattened affect).
  b. The finding of large cerebral ventricles may be useful in subtyping the schizophrenic syndrome. <u>Schizophrenic patients with normal ventricles have been reported to have a better response to neuroleptic medication</u> than do those with large ventricles.

2. CT scanning might be considered for those psychiatric patients who demonstrate confusion, dementia, movement disorder or a first episode of psychosis of unknown etiology, prolonged catatonia, or a first episode of a major affective disorder or a personality change after the age of 50 years. Other neuropsychiatric studies, such as a careful neurologic examination and an EEG, would also be indicated.

E. POSITRON-EMISSION TOMOGRAPHY

1. In positron-emission tomography (**PET**), positron-emitting elements [e.g., fluorine 18 (^{18}F)] are incorporated into organic compounds (e.g., deoxyglucose) and are introduced into the body (e.g., by injection). When these compounds enter the brain, radioactive energy (gamma rays) is given off and is picked up by detectors positioned around the patient's head. The gamma rays are then analyzed and processed by a computer into an image showing distribution of the radionuclide.

2. PET provides an opportunity to study regional brain activity when the brain is at rest and during mental activity.

3. Not only have PET techniques been developed to detect differences in brain energy metabolism and blood flow, but PET also has the exciting potential to examine the functions of specific neurotransmitter systems.

4. Use of PET in psychiatry has demonstrated abnormalities of the anterior–posterior gradient of glucose utilization in certain subgroups of patients with schizophrenia and bipolar affective disorders.

F. MAGNETIC RESONANCE IMAGING

1. Magnetic resonance imaging (**MRI**) has also been termed nuclear magnetic resonance (NMR). It is an imaging system in which atomic nuclei that are exposed to a magnetic field line up in accordance with that field; when the field is removed, the nuclei return to their original status and, in so doing, emit energy. A field gradient is introduced to allow localization in three-dimensional space.

a. The magnetic field is applied to the brain, and as the field is removed, the atomic nuclei in the brain tissues release energy that is picked up by detectors placed around the head and then is compiled by a computer into an image of the brain.

b. Structures of the brain can be seen with amazing clarity with what currently appears to be limited risk (i.e., no radiation exposure).

c. In comparison to CT, MRI provides for better differentiation of gray from white matter, better displays lesions in demyelineating diseases, and usually provides a better image of the edema secondary to brain tumors. CT, however, permits better visualization of bone and small calcifications. In a number of clinical situations, MRI has revealed lesions not appreciated on CT scans.

2. Studies of MRI in psychiatric disease (e.g., schizophrenia) and neurologic disease (e.g., dementia) are currently underway. A recent report found decreased frontal lobe size as well as a smaller cerebrum and cranium in schizophrenic patients.

G. REGIONAL CEREBRAL BLOOD FLOW

1. After the inhalation or intracarotid injection of a metabolically inert radioactive substance [e.g., xenon 133 (^{133}Xe)], radiation emanating from the brain is picked up by detectors on the scalp. The procedure can be done with the subject at rest or engaging in a mental activity. In the normal brain, blood flow and cerebral metabolism are closely related. Thus, an abnormal regional cerebral blood flow (**rCBF**) can reflect abnormalities in cerebral metabolism and function.

2. Decreased rCBF to certain regions of the frontal lobe has been observed in some schizophrenic patients during cognitive activation with the Wisconsin Card-Sorting Test. Higher blood flow to the left hemisphere has been reported as well in some schizophrenic patients.

IX. OTHER PSYCHOPHYSIOLOGIC MEASUREMENTS OF SIGNIFICANCE IN PSYCHIATRY

A. EYETRACKING DYSFUNCTION. An eyetracking dysfunction is present when there is a larger than expected number of jerky movements of the eyes during eyetracking of a moving object.

1. Although measurement of eyetracking dysfunction is only a research tool at this time, it is believed that the dysfunction might represent a marker for some patients with schizophrenia. Eyetracking dysfunctions have been reported in about 50% to 60% of schizophrenic patients and in as many as 50% of their first-degree relatives.

2. They are also found in about 30% to 50% of patients with a major affective disorder but only in about 10% of their parents.

3. Eyetracking dysfunctions have been found in about 8% of the normal population.

B. ELECTRODERMAL ACTIVITY

1. Various measures of electrodermal activity (**EDA**) reflect changes in the electrical activity of the skin.
   a. The measure of skin resistance (SR) has traditionally been referred to as galvanic skin response (GSR).
   b. Measures of electrodermal response (EDR) include the skin conductance response (SCR).

2. Resistance of the skin varies with sweat gland activity: the greater the sweat gland activity, the lower the skin resistance. Sweat glands are controlled by the sympathetic nervous system so that greater sympathetic arousal results in greater sweat gland activity.

3. Fear and anger, as well as sexual, startle, and orienting responses, may produce similar EDRs.

4. Some studies have reported that subgroups of schizophrenic patients demonstrate abnormal EDRs.

C. MEASUREMENT OF 3-METHOXY-4-HYDROXYPHENYLGLYCOL

1. 3-Methoxy-4-hydroxyphenylglycol (**MHPG**) is the **major metabolite of brain norepinephrine**.

2. Some investigators have studied the utility of pretreatment urinary MHPG levels to help choose among specific antidepressants.
   a. Low MHPG levels have reportedly predicted favorable responses to more noradrenergic antidepressants such as imipramine, desipramine, and maprotiline.
   b. Study results in this area, however, have had mixed success, and routine clinical use of urinary MHPG levels seems premature.

D. LYMPHOCYTE FUNCTIONING. Reports suggest that impaired lymphocyte function may be present in depressed patients. For instance, preliminary test results suggest that patients with endogenous depression have lower isoproterenol-β-adrenergic–stimulated adenosine $3',5'$-cyclic phosphate (cAMP) levels in lymphocytes as well as lower lymphocyte mitogen responses than normal controls. The field that studies a relationship between psychiatry and immunology is called **psychoimmunology**.

E. SKIN TESTS FOR ACETYLCHOLINE RECEPTOR DENSITY. There is some evidence to suggest that there is an increased number of ACh receptors on the skin cells of some patients with affective illness. However, studies have yielded conflicting results.

    1. It is hypothesized that increased skin cell cholinergic receptor density might reflect increased brain receptors for ACh.

    2. Preliminary studies show that relatives of patients with major affective illness also may have increased skin cell ACh receptor density.

F. PHARMACOLOGIC CHALLENGE TESTS FOR ANXIETY DISORDERS

    1. Epinephrine and isoproterenol (β-adrenergic agonists), yohimbine (an α_2-adrenergic antagonist that increases noradrenergic function), and sodium lactate given intravenously reliably seem to produce anxiety and panic symptoms in susceptible individuals (i.e., in patients with anxiety and panic disorders). Oral administration of caffeine has been reported to produce greater increases in anxiety and panic symptoms in some patients with panic disorder than in normal controls. Inhalation of carbon dioxide (CO_2) is able to induce panic attacks in some panic-disordered patients.

    2. Evidence implicating the locus ceruleus in panic anxiety includes research findings suggesting that CO_2 increases the firing of the locus ceruleus (see section II D 1) and that sodium lactate infusion is known to increase cerebral CO_2.

G. POTENTIAL BIOLOGICAL MARKERS. Many other potential biological markers for psychiatric disorders are being investigated, such as measurements of cerebrospinal fluid 5-hydroxyindoleacetic acid (5-HIAA) and urinary free cortisol as well as platelet-^{3}H-imipramine binding. Besides helping to explain the neurophysiology of mental illness, some biological markers could graduate into clinical use, aiding in diagnosis and treatment evaluation.

STUDY QUESTIONS

Directions: Each question below contains five suggested answers. Choose the **one best** response to each question.

1. A patient who recently suffered a stroke has problems copying figures. When someone points to the patient's left arm and asks him who the arm belongs to, the patient responds, "I don't know; I think it might be yours." The patient most probably has sustained a stroke involving the

(A) left parietal lobe
(B) right parietal lobe
(C) left temporal lobe
(D) right temporal lobe
(E) frontal lobes

2. Deficits in recent memory function would probably be associated most with damage to the

(A) hippocampus
(B) parietal lobe
(C) temporal lobe
(D) cingulate gyrus
(E) septal area

Directions: Each question below contains four suggested answers of which **one or more** is correct. Choose the answer

A if **1, 2, and 3** are correct
B if **1 and 3** are correct
C if **2 and 4** are correct
D if **4** is correct
E if **1, 2, 3, and 4** are correct

3. Pontine–geniculate–occipital (PGO) spikes are associated with

(1) low activity of the locus ceruleus
(2) dreaming
(3) low activity of the raphe nucleus
(4) non-REM sleep

4. Established, clinically useful neurodiagnostic tests commonly used by psychiatrists include

(1) positron emission tomography (PET)
(2) electroencephalography (EEG)
(3) measurement of eyetracking dysfunction
(4) computed tomography (CT)

5. True statements about positron-emission tomography (PET) include

(1) it visualizes brain functioning at rest and during mental activity
(2) decreased utilization of glucose has been found in the frontal regions of the brain of some schizophrenic patients
(3) PET scanners can visualize some specific neurotransmitter systems
(4) it is useful in differentiating between bipolar affective disorder and schizophrenia

6. Symptoms of partial complex (psychomotor) seizures can include

(1) visual hallucinations
(2) déjà vu
(3) derealization
(4) a sense of abdominal fullness

7. True statements about the use of computed tomography (CT) in psychiatry include

(1) increased ventricular size has been demonstrated in schizophrenic patients
(2) increased ventricular size has been demonstrated in patients with affective disorders
(3) CT is useful in the evaluation of patients with confusion or dementia of unknown cause
(4) CT is a type of functional brain imaging

8. The Klüver-Bucy syndrome is associated with

(1) lesions of the parietal lobe
(2) altered sexual behavior, loss of fear, placidity, and a tendency toward oral exploration of objects
(3) hypersomnia
(4) visual agnosia

Directions: The group of questions below consists of lettered choices followed by several numbered items. For each numbered item select the **one** lettered choice with which it is **most** closely associated. Each lettered choice may be used once, more than once, or not at all.

Questions 9–13

Match each of the following characteristics of neurologic tests with the associated test.

(A) Computed tomography (CT)
(B) Positron-emission tomography (PET)
(C) Magnetic resonance imaging (MRI)
(D) Regional cerebral blood flow (rCBF)
(E) Electroencephalogram (EEG)

E   9. The neurodiagnostic test most used by psychiatrists

A   10. X-rays processed to give cross-sectional views of the brain

B   11. Injection of positron-emitting isotopes

C   12. Best differentiates gray matter from white matter

D   13. Inhalation or injection of 133 xenon (^{133}Xe)

ANSWERS AND EXPLANATIONS

1. The answer is B. (*II A 3 b*) Damage to the nondominant (usually right-sided) parietal lobe is associated with constructional apraxia (difficulty copying figures) and anosognosia (failing to recognize one's own body parts and denial of disease). The patient with anosognosia generally ignores his left side, the left side of the room, or the left side of a picture. Aphasia is associated with dominant hemisphere damage; however, the patient in the question seems able to understand questions and to communicate verbally (at least superficially).

2. The answer is A. (*II B 3*) Lesions of the limbic system include those of the hippocampus, cingulate gyrus, and septal area. Hippocampal lesions have been associated with certain memory deficits, such as an apparent loss of recent memory. While memory seems to be associated with brain structures other than the hippocampus, of the structures listed in the question, the hippocampus is the best answer.

3. The answer is A (1, 2, 3). (*III B 2 b*) During sleep, with low activity of the locus ceruleus and raphe nucleus, the cholinergic gigantocellular tegmental field neurons produce electrical discharges called pontine–geniculate–occipital (PGO) spikes. The electrical activity follows a path from the pons, to the lateral geniculate bodies, and then to the occipital cortex. PGO spikes are believed to be involved in the generation of the visual images (dreams) experienced by the sleeping individual during REM sleep.

4. The answer is C (2, 4). (*VIII; IX A*) Electroencephalography (EEG) is perhaps the neurodiagnostic test that is most used by psychiatrists today. Computed tomography (CT), while more commonly used by neurologists, has established clinical usefulness in the workup of patients with certain neuropsychiatric disorders. Because magnetic resonance imaging (MRI) at times can better detect some brain lesions not well visualized by CT, MRI might replace CT in certain clinical situations. Positron-emission tomography (PET) and the measurement of eyetracking dysfunction are primarily research tools at this time, although they currently offer many interesting clues in the quest to understand certain psychiatric disorders.

5. The answer is A (1, 2, 3). (*VIII E*) At this time, positron-emission tomography (PET) is unable to differentiate accurately between bipolar affective disorders and schizophrenia. In fact, both disorders have shown some similar findings in PET scan studies, namely, decreased utilization of glucose in frontal regions ("hypofrontality"), more recently described in the literature as abnormalities of the anterior–posterior gradient of glucose utilization. In the future, PET might be able to differentiate between some types of affective disorder and schizophrenia.

6. The answer is E (all). [*II A 2 b (2)*] Partial complex (psychomotor) seizures classically have their origin in the temporal lobe; hence, this syndrome is sometimes referred to as temporal lobe epilepsy. Hallucinations, a sense of abdominal fullness, derealization, and déjà vu are all symptoms that can be observed during a partial complex seizure. These seizures reportedly can mimic many different psychiatric disorders.

7. The answer is A (1, 2, 3). (*VIII D*) Increased ventricular size has been seen in patients with both schizophrenic and affective disorders. Computed tomography (CT) is used in the evaluation of dementia, delirium, and other organic brain disorders along with other neuropsychiatric studies. Although CT gives useful information about the structure of the brain, functioning cannot be directly evaluated by this method of brain imaging.

8. The answer is C (2, 4). [*II A 2 b (1), 3, C 3*] Destructive lesions of the temporal lobe, not the parietal lobe, are associated with symptoms of the Klüver-Bucy syndrome, which include hypersexuality, tendencies toward oral exploration of objects, loss of fear and anger, placidity, and visual agnosia. Hypersomnia is associated with the Kleine-Levin syndrome.

9–13. The answers are 9-E, 10-A, 11-B, 12-C, 13-D. (*VIII*) The neurodiagnostic test that is used most commonly by psychiatrists today is probably electroencephalography (EEG). It is used in the diagnosis of epilepsy and epileptoid-type abnormalities as well as in the workup of patients with other neurologic disorders that can have psychiatric manifestations (e.g., neoplasm, stroke, and metabolic or degenerative disease). EEG slowing (delta waves) can be seen in the awake tracing in patients with delirium and dementia.

The isotopes used in positron-emission tomography (PET) give off positrons that collide with surrounding electrons in the brain with resultant generation of gamma rays, which are picked up by detectors placed around the patient's head.

Magnetic resonance imaging (MRI) has several advantages over computed tomography (CT), including better differentiation between gray and white matter of the brain. However, CT images bone and small calcifications better than MRI. CT utilizes thousands of x-ray readings, which are processed by a computer to give a cross-sectional view of the brain. Large ventricles seen on CT have been associated with subgroups of schizophrenic and affectively disordered patients.

Regional cerebral blood flow (rCBF) is a research tool that utilizes radioactive substances such as xenon 133 (^{133} Xe). In the normal brain, blood flow (as measured by rCBF) and cerebral metabolism are closely related. Thus, problems with cerebral metabolism can be reflected by abnormalities in cerebral blood flow.

4
Behavioral Genetics

Dilip V. Jeste
James B. Lohr

I. HISTORICAL BACKGROUND. Gregor Mendel, an Augustinian monk, began studies of inheritance of garden peas in 1856. Mendel proposed that inherited traits were transmitted through inherited factors that are now called "genes" and that the results of the genetic expression could be predicted by a study of the characteristics of the parents. After Mendel read his work before the Natural Science Society in 1865, it was all but forgotten until it was rediscovered at the turn of the century after the discovery of chromosomes. In 1906, Bateson named the new science of inheritance "genetics." Three years later this science was applied to medical diseases in Garrod's book, *Inborn Errors of Metabolism*.

II. BASIC PRINCIPLES OF HUMAN GENETICS

A. GENES AND CHROMOSOMES

1. Genes
  a. Mendel's inheritable factors, which are considered to be the biological units of heredity, are called genes, a term that derives from the Greek word "**gennan**," which means "**to produce**." The concept of gene is still being modified, but basically a gene is considered to be a specific **self-reproducing segment of a chromosome responsible for a given trait or function**.
  b. Genes are composed of **deoxyribonucleic acid (DNA)**, which consists of regularly alternating chains of phosphates and deoxyribose sugars to which are attached pairs of bases. Genes are considered to be specific sequences of nucleotides within the DNA strand in a given chromosome.
  c. The particular location on a chromosome of a given gene is known as that gene's **locus**. The genes found at the same loci in a pair of chromosomes are called **alleles**.
  d. From a functional point of view, genes may be subdivided into three different types.
    (1) Structural genes code for the specific amino acid sequence in peptides and proteins.
    (2) Operator genes interact with substances known as **repressors**, and this interaction controls the activity of structural genes.
    (3) Regulator genes modulate the synthesis of repressor substances, which in turn interact with operator genes to control the activity of structural genes.

2. Chromosomes are microscopically visible structures that carry the genes arranged in a characteristic order. Chromosomes consist of linear strands of DNA and proteins called **histones**, and they occur in pairs in the nuclei of cells.
  a. In the human, there are 23 pairs of chromosomes, including 22 pairs of autosomes and 1 pair of sex chromosomes. The two chromosomes in each pair are similar in structure and position and are termed **homologous**.
  b. The sex chromosomes in males consist of one X and one Y chromosome; whereas in females, there are two X chromosomes. The **Lyon hypothesis** states that one X chromosome in the female condenses in the embryonic stage of development and appears as a **Barr body** (i.e., sex chromatin).

3. Chromosomal disorders. Some diseases have been shown to be associated with specific chromosomal abnormalities.
  a. In some cases, there is an extra chromosome, usually the result of **nondisjunction**, in which the paired chromosomes fail to separate during meiosis.
  b. In other cases, there is a **deletion**, resulting in the absence of a whole chromosome or part of it.
  c. Finally, abnormalities can occur through the process of **translocation**, in which a part of

one chromosome attaches to another, so that there is a replication of genes without an increase in chromosomal number.

d. Examples of chromosomal disorders include the following.

   (1) **Down syndrome**, or mongolism, is a condition that is associated with short stature, mental retardation, and a variety of characteristic facial abnormalities.

   (a) Usually (but not always) this is the result of **three instead of the normal two chromosomes 21 (trisomy 21)**. This type of Down syndrome is more common in the offspring of older mothers.

   (b) In some cases, Down syndrome is associated with a translocation of chromosome 21, which is attached to chromosome 15. This type of Down syndrome is less common than trisomy 21 and, unlike trisomy 21, occurs independent of the mother's age.

   (c) The two different types of Down syndrome appear identical clinically.

   (d) Other trisomy conditions also exist, including trisomy 8, 13, 14, 15, 18, and 22, all of which are associated with facial abnormalities and mental retardation.

   (2) **Klinefelter syndrome** is a condition that is characterized by a male phenotype, infertility, small testes, behavioral disturbances, and a eunuchoid appearance. It is associated with an XXY configuration of sex chromosomes, although the autosomes are normal. A Barr body is present.

   (3) **Turner syndrome** is a condition that is associated with a female phenotype, short stature, webbed neck, gonadal dysgenesis, and sterility. It is associated with a missing X chromosome (an XO genotype) and no Barr body.

   (4) **Cri du chat syndrome** is a condition that is characterized by severe mental retardation, hypertelorism, microcephaly, and a cat-like cry. It is due to a deletion of the short arm of chromosome 5.

B. DEFINITION OF COMMON TERMS

1. **Genotype and phenotype**
   a. **Genotype** refers to the **total genetic makeup** of a particular individual.
   b. **Phenotype** refers to the **observable structural and functional characteristics** resulting from the interaction of the genetic constitution of the individual with environmental influences.

2. **Genocopy and phenocopy** are terms used in reference to individuals who phenotypically resemble one another.
   a. The resemblance in genocopy is believed to be due to mimetic genes.
   b. The resemblance in phenocopy is thought to result from environmental factors.

3. **Heritability** is a measure of the degree of **influence of the genotype on the phenotype**. Thus, the heritability of a given disease is the extent (usually expressed as a percentage) to which the individual risk of acquiring that disease is due to inherited factors.
   a. Heritable conditions are **not necessarily synonymous with congenital conditions**, which are defined as those present at birth, regardless of any genetic etiology. For example, congenital hydrocephalus (which is characterized by enlargement of the head) results from a variety of causes, only some of which are genetic.
   b. On the other hand, not all heritable conditions are manifest at birth. For instance, signs of Huntington's disease (a genetically transmitted disorder) usually do not appear until the third or fourth decade of life. **Abiotrophy** refers to progressive loss of vitality of tissues associated with loss of function, and it is a term often used to describe hereditary disorders with onset late in life.
   c. The term **familial** usually refers to **conditions that aggregate in families, in which the genetic component is unknown**. Thus, there is a familial tendency toward multiple sclerosis, although no consistent genetic pattern has been discovered.

4. **Penetrance** is a measure of the **frequency** (usually expressed as a percentage) **with which a specific genetic trait appears in the phenotype of all individuals carrying the responsible gene**. For example, it appears that anyone carrying the gene for Huntington's disease manifests the disorder; therefore, the gene for Huntington's disease has complete (100%) penetrance.

5. **Expressivity** is the **degree of expression of a trait or traits** regulated by a given penetrant gene in a particular individual. The expressivity of some genes varies widely among different individuals, while other genes have relatively uniform expressivity.

6. **Homozygosity and heterozygosity**
   a. The term **homozygosity** describes the state in which an individual has inherited from both the parents identical alleles in the corresponding loci of a homologous chromosome pair.

b. In contrast, the term **heterozygosity** describes the state in which an individual has inherited two different alleles in the corresponding loci.

7. Dominance and recessivity

a. Dominant genes code for traits that can appear in heterozygotes (i.e., when the two alleles are different). Examples of **autosomal dominant transmission** include some conditions associated with mental retardation or dementia, such as:

(1) von Recklinghausen's disease (i.e., generalized neurofibromatosis, which is marked by multiple soft tumors all over the body along with areas of hyperpigmentation)

(2) Tuberous sclerosis (which is marked by tumors on the surfaces of the ventricles of the brain along with patchy sclerosis of the brain surface as well as tumors of the viscera)

(3) Huntington's disease (see section V B 1)

b. Recessive genes manifest only in homozygotes (i.e., when both alleles are the same). Examples of **autosomal recessive transmission** include:

(1) Wilson's disease

(2) Other inborn errors of metabolism, such as phenylketonuria (see section V D 3 a)

c. Most sex chromosome–linked diseases are recessive and are transmitted on the X chromosome. Typically, women are the carriers in such cases, while the disease is evident only in men.

(1) Examples include:

(a) Duchenne type muscular dystrophy (marked by progressive muscular atrophy in childhood)

(b) Hunter's mucopolysaccharidosis (marked by mental retardation, hypertelorism, dwarfism, deafness, optic atrophy, and skin lesions)

(c) Lesch-Nyhan syndrome (marked by hyperuricemia, self-mutilation, choreoathetosis, cerebral palsy, and impaired renal function)

(2) Sex-linked dominant transmission of diseases is extremely rare.

8. For some genes, the **degree of phenotypic expression** depends upon whether the individual is homozygous or heterozygous for those genes. This is called **intermediate inheritance**, and the classic example is the gene that manifests as sickle cell disease in the homozygote and as sickle cell trait in the heterozygote. The importance of intermediate inheritance in behavioral disorders is unclear.

III. METHODS OF STUDYING GENETICS. Family studies, twin studies, and adoption studies are aimed at assessing the genetic components and possible mode of inheritance of traits and diseases.

A. FAMILY STUDIES

1. Family studies assess the pattern of affliction in the relatives of an affected individual, who is called the **index case**, **propositus**, or **proband**.

a. In the absence of dominance or environmental effects, the expected correlation between two relatives reflects the average number of genes that they have in common.

b. In any disorder with an important genetic component, the incidence of that condition is significantly higher in relatives than in the general population, and it is highest in first-degree relatives (i.e., the parents, siblings, and children of the proband).

2. The family tree showing the occurrence of certain traits and diseases in different members is called the **pedigree**. By studying the pedigree, the likely mode of inheritance may be inferred.

a. For example, it is likely that a disease has an autosomal dominant pattern of inheritance in a family in which the disease is manifested in one parent and in approximately 50% of the offspring (both male and female).

b. In the case of autosomal recessive transmission, neither parent of the proband may have the disease (although both must be carriers), while approximately 25% of offspring (irrespective of gender) may suffer from the disease, 50% are carriers, and 25% do not have the responsible gene.

c. In the case of X-linked recessive transmission, females are carriers and about 50% of the males manifest the illness. (A female can inherit the disorder if her mother is a carrier and her father has the disorder.)

d. Study of pedigrees is likely to be less informative in conditions characterized by polygenic transmission or incomplete penetrance of a trait.

B. TWIN STUDIES

1. Twin studies assess the degree to which both members of a pair of twins manifest a given trait or disease. If both twins have a certain trait, they are termed **concordant** for that trait; if only one twin of the pair has the trait, the pair is said to be **discordant**.

2. Twin studies may be carried out on identical or **monozygotic twins** (who derive from the splitting of a fertilized ovum) or fraternal or **dizygotic twins** (who derive from two separate fertilized ova). The concordance rate for monozygotic twins is significantly higher than that for dizygotic twins for diseases with a strong genetic contribution.

C. ADOPTION STUDIES offer an opportunity to distinguish between genetic and environmental influences on behavior. The prevalence of specific traits or conditions in the biological versus the adoptive relatives of probands is compared. A genetic condition is characterized by a significantly higher prevalence of the condition among biological relatives when compared to adoptive relatives.

IV. GENETICS OF PSYCHIATRIC DISORDERS

A. SCHIZOPHRENIA is a severe mental illness that is marked by hallucinations (which are chiefly auditory), delusions, disorganization of thought and speech, and emotional blunting.

1. Family studies. The worldwide lifetime incidence of schizophrenia ranges from 0.35% to 2.85%, with a mean incidence of approximately 0.85%. Based upon some recent studies, the average risk for developing schizophrenia in the stepsiblings of a schizophrenic proband is about the same as that in the general population. The risk for parents is 4% to 5%. The risk for full siblings for developing schizophrenia is 7% to 8%. The children of a schizophrenic proband have a risk of 10% to 12%, but if both parents have schizophrenia, the risk for their children increases to 35% to 46%.

2. Twin studies. The concordance rate for schizophrenia is significantly higher in monozygotic twins than in dizygotic twins. Recent investigations, which have employed more conservative diagnostic criteria, have yielded somewhat lower figures for the concordance rate than studies performed before 1965. The recent figures for monozygotic twin concordance range from 35% to 58%, while figures for dizygotic twin concordance range from 9% to 26%.

3. Adoption studies. Studies comparing the prevalence of schizophrenia and related disorders in biological versus adoptive relatives of schizophrenic probands have consistently demonstrated that the prevalence is significantly higher in biological relatives in comparison to adoptive relatives.

4. Inheritance of schizophrenia
  a. All of the evidence above clearly indicates that genetic factors play a role in the development of schizophrenia. However, the exact mode of transmission is unknown, and it is apparent that there are important nongenetic or environmental contributions to the etiology.
  (1) Different investigators have proposed monogenic, digenic, and polygenic modes of transmission, but none of these proposals are consistent with all of the available data.
  (2) It is likely that schizophrenia is not a single disease but is a syndrome that comprises several subtypes, and it is likely that genetic factors may be more crucial in some subtypes than in others.
  (3) Some investigators have used the term **schizophrenia spectrum disorders** to describe conditions that are genetically related to schizophrenia but do not show the full symptom complex. Schizophrenia spectrum disorders include schizoid and schizotypal personality disorders.
  b. Exactly what is inherited in schizophrenia is not known. Some investigators have hypothesized that specific biochemical defects are transmitted. Alternatively, only the predisposition to develop schizophrenia under certain environmental situations may be transmitted.

B. AFFECTIVE DISORDERS are conditions marked by pervasive pathological changes in mood. There are two major forms. **Unipolar disorder** (sometimes called pure depressive disorder or unipolar depression) is characterized by a single episode or repeated episodes of depression, usually accompanied by sleep and appetite disturbances, feelings of guilt, and thoughts of suicide. **Bipolar disorder** (also called manic-depressive illness) is characterized by episodes of mania and depression. In a manic episode, a patient's mood is elevated, and there is often accompanying grandiosity and paranoia along with rapid thoughts and speech, impulsiveness, and poor judgment.

1. Family studies
  a. Unipolar disorder. The lifetime incidence of unipolar disorder in the general adult population is 15% to 20%. In contrast, 40% to 60% of affected individuals have a first-degree relative with an affective disorder. The morbidity risk for an affective disorder in the relatives of probands with unipolar disorder is 13% for parents, 15% for siblings, and 21% for children.

The relatives of unipolar patients are at a much higher risk of developing unipolar than bipolar illness.
  b. Bipolar disorder. The lifetime incidence of bipolar disorder in the general adult population is 1% to 2%; however, 80% to 90% of individuals with bipolar disorder will have a first-degree relative with an affective disorder. The morbidity risk for an affective disorder is 22% for parents, 25% for siblings, and 39% for children of probands. Relatives have a high risk of developing either bipolar or unipolar illness, the risk of bipolar disorder being somewhat greater. It is likely that there is more than one pattern of inheritance, at least for bipolar disorder. In some families of bipolar patients, a higher prevalence of certain X-linked markers, such as deuteranomalopia (a type of color blindness) and Xg^a blood group, indicate a possible X-linked pattern of inheritance.
  c. Family studies have not revealed a genetic link between affective disorders and schizophrenia.

2. Twin studies. Monozygotic twins reared either apart or together have a 75% rate of concordance for an affective disorder in comparison to dizygotic twins, who have a 20% concordance rate. Twin studies also reveal that twins of unipolar probands are much more likely to be unipolar than bipolar. In contrast, twins of bipolar probands may be either bipolar or unipolar (although the risk for bipolar disorder is greater than that for unipolar disorder).

3. Adoption studies. As is true with schizophrenia, the results of adoption studies of affective (especially bipolar) disorder reveal a higher prevalence of affective disorder in the biological relatives than in the adoptive relatives of an affected individual.

4. Inheritance of affective disorders. Studies strongly suggest that genetic factors contribute to the etiology of major affective disorders.
  a. Family and twin studies of bipolar disorder reveal a strong genetic component with phenotypic heterogeneity (i.e., relatives who have affective disorders may have either bipolar or unipolar disorder), whereas family and twin studies of unipolar disorder reveal a similarly strong genetic component but with much less phenotypic heterogeneity (i.e., relatives who have affective disorders usually have unipolar disorder).
  b. The exact modes of transmission are unclear. In some families of bipolar patients, there is suggestion of an X-linked mode of inheritance, but no such pattern has been observed in families of unipolar patients.
  c. Some researchers have proposed the existence of **depressive spectrum disease** on the basis of a high prevalence of alcoholism and sociopathy in male members of families of probands with major depression.

C. OTHER DISORDERS

1. Personality disorders. Personality or character disorders are conditions marked by chronic patterns of maladaptive behavior, and the patients are usually unaware of their own role in the continuing difficulties that arise.
  a. Personality disorders in general have a concordance rate that is several times higher in monozygotic than in dizygotic twins.
  b. Although it appears that a number of pathological character traits are inherited, **the most conclusive evidence of genetic transmission exists for antisocial, histrionic, schizoid, schizotypal, and obsessive-compulsive personality disorders**.
  c. In recent years, genetic investigations have revealed a probable link between schizophrenia and schizoid and schizotypal character disorders as well as between hysteria and antisocial personality disorder.

2. Obsessive-compulsive and other anxiety disorders. There is no established evidence of a strong genetic component in obsessive-compulsive disorder, and the possible genetic component in other anxiety disorders is not known.

3. Alcohol and tobacco abuse
  a. Adoption studies have indicated a genetic component in alcoholism. Twenty percent of adopted children born to alcoholic parents and only five percent of adopted children born to nonalcoholic parents were found to be alcoholic before the age of 30 years. There are also studies reporting a link among alcoholism, sociopathy, and certain forms of depressive illness.
  b. There is little evidence for a genetic component in cigarette smoking.

4. Attention deficit disorder. Twin studies have revealed a higher concordance rate among monozygotic twins than among dizygotic twins, and adoption studies have confirmed that there is likely to be a stronger genetic than environmental component to attention deficit disorder.

V. GENETICS OF NEUROLOGIC DISORDERS

A. **DEMENTIA. Alzheimer's disease** is the most common form of dementia in the United States. In some cases of Alzheimer's disease, there appears to be an autosomal dominant pattern of inheritance. In many cases, however, the evidence for genetic transmission of Alzheimer's disease is not clear; one reason is that the disease usually presents relatively late in life and many individuals die before clinical evidence of the disorder becomes apparent.

B. **MOVEMENT DISORDERS**

1. **Huntington's disease** is a condition that is characterized by progressive dementia and choreiform movements, usually beginning in the third to fifth decade of life. It has an autosomal dominant mode of inheritance with full penetrance.
   a. One interesting feature of the disorder is that the spontaneous mutation rate must be very small; in all well-documented cases of the disorder, an affected family member is consistently found.
   b. Through the use of new techniques for the identification of specific genes, the gene for Huntington's disease recently has been located on chromosome 4 (see section VII A).

2. **Parkinson's disease** is a movement disorder that usually begins in the fifth to sixth decade of life. It is characterized by hypokinesia (reduced movement), muscular rigidity, pill-rolling tremor, and loss of postural reflexes. There appears to be no major genetic component, except in certain rare cases. Twin studies have found very low concordance rates for Parkinson's disease both in monozygotic and dizygotic twins.

3. **Wilson's disease** (hepatolenticular degeneration) is a disorder of copper metabolism in which copper deposition occurs in the liver, basal ganglia, and various other areas. It is characterized by hypokinesia, dystonic movements, tremor, rigidity, and progressive dementia if it goes untreated. It has an autosomal recessive pattern of inheritance.

4. **Hallervorden-Spatz disease** is a condition marked by accumulation of iron in the basal ganglia and other areas of the brain. It presents as dystonia, rigidity, choreoathetosis, spasticity, and dementia. It has an autosomal recessive mode of inheritance.

5. **Dystonia musculorum deformans**, also called torsion dystonia, is marked by progressive dystonic movements; the usual onset is in childhood or adolescence. There are two important hereditary forms, one of which has an autosomal dominant mode of inheritance and the other, an autosomal recessive pattern. Rarely, sporadic forms of the disorder have been reported.

6. **Tourette syndrome** usually begins in childhood, and it manifests as simple and complex vocal and motor tics and, in some cases, coprolalia (compulsive uttering of obscenities). Approximately one-third of patients have a family history of the disorder, and an additional one-third have a family history of simple tics, indicating a probable genetic component. The exact mode of transmission, however, is not clear.

C. **SEIZURE DISORDERS**

1. The incidence of epilepsy is greater in relatives of patients with generalized epilepsy, especially when the epilepsy is of early onset, than it is in the general population.

2. There is an increased incidence of epileptic discharges seen on the electroencephalogram in family members of probands with a generalized seizure disorder.

3. There is an increased incidence of a family history of epilepsy in probands with post-traumatic epilepsy.

D. **MENTAL RETARDATION.** Some forms of mental retardation are associated with chromosomal abnormalities, and others show autosomal dominant, autosomal recessive, and X-linked patterns of transmission. Most cases of mental retardation, however, appear to have a pattern of inheritance in which many different genes are involved.

1. **Chromosomal abnormalities** that are involved in mental retardation occur in Down, Klinefelter, Turner, and cri du chat syndromes, among others.

2. **Autosomal dominant conditions** that are associated with mental retardation include tuberous sclerosis, von Recklinghausen's neurofibromatosis, congenital myotonia (marked by spasm and rigidity of muscles when an attempt is made to move them after rest), and some forms of muscular dystrophy.

3. **Autosomal recessive conditions** that are associated with mental retardation include inherited metabolic disorders such as phenylketonuria and Hartnup's disease.

    a. Phenylketonuria is characterized by mental retardation, fair skin, blue eyes, mild microcephaly, hyperactivity, and movement disorders. It is the result of a deficiency of hepatic phenylalanine hydroxylase. It is the most common aminoaciduria associated with mental retardation.

    b. Hartnup's disease is a condition marked by a pellagra-like rash, emotional lability, psychotic episodes, and mental retardation. It is due to dysfunction in the transport of neutral amino acids.

  4. X-linked recessive conditions that are associated with mental retardation include Duchenne type muscular dystrophy, Lesch-Nyhan syndrome, and adrenoleukodystrophy (marked by diffuse changes in the brain white matter and by pathological changes in the adrenal glands, which sometimes lead to adrenal insufficiency).

E. MULTIPLE SCLEROSIS. The risk of multiple sclerosis for first-degree relatives of probands is greater than that for the general population. However, twin studies have revealed that the concordance rates for monozygotic and dizygotic twins are equal, thus indicating that there is no major genetic component.

VI. THERAPEUTIC IMPLICATIONS

A. GENETIC COUNSELING. Tsuang (1978) and Kessler (1980) described a number of basic steps in the genetic counseling of individuals with behavioral disorders. They are as follows.

  1. Making an accurate diagnosis. This is especially important in psychiatric disorders such as schizophrenia and major affective disorders.

  2. Obtaining a family history. Much of the time, this relies on statements from family members, which can often be inaccurate, especially where behavioral disorders are involved. Written documentation and medical records should be obtained whenever possible. Also, vague terms such as "nervous breakdown" and "depression" should be investigated carefully.

  3. Estimation of recurrence risk. In some disorders in which the pattern of genetic transmission is clear, the risk of recurrence may be readily estimated. In other disorders in which the mode of inheritance is less clear (e.g., schizophrenia), it is usually better to avoid definitive statements.

  4. Psychosocial evaluation of the counselees. It is important to assess the motivation, psychological state, and the needs of the counselees in order to determine the best means of presenting information to them, as well as exactly what information to present.

  5. Assessing the risk-to-burden ratio. The counselor works with the counselees in weighing the recurrence risk against the potential burden of the disorder.

  6. Formulating a plan of action. Although, in general, the counselor needs to be relatively authoritative in this regard, he must exercise special care to take into account the wishes of the counselees.

  7. Follow-up is a very important step in genetic counseling, and it involves reassessing the information obtained earlier for accuracy and determining necessary changes in the plan of action and in the wishes of the counselee.

B. PRENATAL DIAGNOSIS

  1. It is now possible to determine early in gestation not only the gender of the child but also the presence or absence of a number of pathological conditions. This is done through **amniocentesis**, in which amniotic fluid is withdrawn from the uterus transabdominally. Many physicians advocate that pregnant women in their late thirties and older undergo routine amniocentesis.

  2. Different pathological conditions that can be detected with this technique include various chromosomal abnormalities, such as Down syndrome, as well as genetic illnesses such as Tay-Sachs disease (a sphingolipidosis characterized by progressive dementia, blindness, and paralysis).

VII. RECENT ADVANCES

A. IDENTIFICATION OF GENES

  1. Recent advances in molecular genetics have made possible the development of techniques for identifying the specific genes involved in hereditary disorders. In particular, these techniques have been used with considerable success in **Huntington's disease.**

    a. Enzymes cleave DNA at specific sites into fragments of varying lengths. These enzymes are called **"restriction" endonucleases** because they only cleave certain sections of DNA. Different individuals have different sites at which their DNA is cleaved, and these sites are inherited, just as genes are; therefore, a specific series of DNA fragments is formed for each individual.

    b. The DNA fragments are separated using gel electrophoresis. Then small segments of radioactive DNA called "probes" are generated in millions of copies when the radioactive fragments are inserted into bacterial plasmids. The probes "anneal" to specific fragments of the DNA; if they anneal to different fragments, then a **"restriction" fragment-length polymorphism (RFLP)** is said to be present.

    c. It has been estimated that the use of 200 to 300 probes would permit the entire genome to be surveyed.

  2. Because polymorphisms are very common, they are likely to be located very close to many genes of interest, and specific polymorphisms could be linked to different disorders.

    a. In the case of Huntington's disease, the DNA of many different members of two large families with the disease was studied with a number of probes. After only a dozen probes were tried, **one probe, called G8, was found to be linked to the disorder**. The marker was later discovered to be on the short arm of **chromosome 4**.

    b. Currently, investigations are underway to discover the gene product in Huntington's disease.

B. ANIMAL EXPERIMENTS

  1. Recently, techniques have been developed to breed lower mammals by brother–sister mating for many generations, leading to the establishment of strains in which all animals are genetically very similar. These are called **inbred strains**.

  2. Such strains afford the possibility of experimental manipulation of individual variables, thus allowing the study of the possible mode of inheritance of specific behavioral traits as well as responsiveness to specific neuropsychopharmacologic agents.

BIBLIOGRAPHY

Bender L: Schizophrenic spectrum disorders in the families of schizophrenic children. In *Genetic Research in Psychiatry*. Edited by Fieve RR, Rosenthal D, Brill H. Baltimore, Johns Hopkins University Press, 1975, pp 125–134

Gusella JF, Wexler NS, Conneally PM, et al: A polymorphic DNA marker genetically linked to Huntington's disease. *Nature* 306:234–238, 1983

Kaplan AR: *Human Behavior Genetics*. Springfield, Illinois, Charles C Thomas, 1976

Kessler S: The genetics of schizophrenia: a review. *Schizophr Bull* 6:404–416, 1980

Mendlewicz J, Fleiss JL, Fieve RR: Evidence of X-linkage in the transmission of manic-depressive illness. *JAMA* 222:1624–1627, 1972

Rieder RO, Gershon ES: Genetic strategies in biological psychiatry. *Arch Gen Psychiatry* 35:866–873, 1978

Schlesser MA, Altshuler KZ: The genetics of affective disorder: data, theory, and clinical applications. *Hosp Community Psychiatry* 34:415–422, 1983

Singer S: *Human Genetics: An Introduction to the Principles of Heredity*. San Franciso, WH Freeman, 1978

Tsuang MT: Genetic counseling for psychiatric patients and their families. *Am J Psychiatry* 135:1465–1475, 1978

van Valkenberg C, Lowry M, Winokur G, et al: Depression spectrum disease versus pure depressive disease: clinical, personality and course differences. *J Nerv Ment Dis* 16:341–347, 1977

Ward CD, Duvoisin RC, Ince SE, et al: Parkinson's disease in 65 pairs of twins and in a set of quadruplets. *Neurology* 33:815–824, 1983

STUDY QUESTIONS

Directions: Each question below contains five suggested answers. Choose the one **best** response to each question.

1. What percentage of offspring of a mother with Huntington's disease and a normal father is at risk for developing that disorder?

(A) 100
(B) 75
(C) 25
(D) 50, of sons only
(E) 50, of daughters only

2. Klinefelter syndrome is associated with all of the following conditions EXCEPT

(A) the presence of a Barr body
(B) female gonads
(C) 47 chromosomes
(D) nondisjunction
(E) sterility

3. The most common type of inheritance of mental retardation (i.e., an IQ below 70) is

(A) autosomal dominant
(B) autosomal recessive
(C) sex-linked recessive
(D) polygenic
(E) secondary to chromosomal abnormalities

Directions: Each question below contains four suggested answers of which **one or more** is correct. Choose the answer

A   if **1, 2, and 3** are correct
B   if **1 and 3** are correct
C   if **2 and 4** are correct
D   if **4** is correct
E   if **1, 2, 3, and 4** are correct

4. The genetic hypotheses of schizophrenia are based primarily on

(1) family risk studies
(2) twin studies
(3) adoption studies
(4) pedigree studies

5. An X-linked pattern of inheritance is associated with which of the following disorders?

(1) Schizophrenia
(2) Bipolar disorder
(3) Unipolar disorder
(4) Duchenne type muscular dystrophy

6. Multiple sclerosis has an increased familial incidence, but the concordance rates for monozygotic and dizygotic twins are equal. This suggests

(1) an autosomal recessive pattern of inheritance
(2) a significant environmental component
(3) a strong genetic component
(4) a familial component

7. Conditions that have been genetically linked to some form of depression include

(1) alcoholism
(2) cigarette smoking
(3) sociopathy
(4) epilepsy

SUMMARY OF DIRECTIONS

A	B	C	D	E
1, 2, 3 only	1, 3 only	2, 4 only	4 only	All are correct

8. True statements concerning family studies include

(1) In the absence of dominance or environmental effects, the expected correlation between two relatives reflects the average number of genes that they have in common

A (2) in any disease with a significant genetic component, the incidence of the disorder will be higher in relatives than in the general population

(3) in any disease with a significant genetic component, the incidence of the disorder will be highest in first-degree relatives

(4) it is impossible for females to develop X-linked disorders

Directions: The group of questions below consists of lettered choices followed by several numbered items. For each numbered item select the **one** lettered choice with which it is **most** closely associated. Each lettered choice may be used once, more than once, or not at all.

Questions 9–13

For each disease listed below, select its mode of inheritance.

(A) Autosomal dominant transmission
(B) Autosomal recessive transmission
(C) X-linked recessive transmission
(D) Y-linked transmission
(E) Limited genetic transmission

B 9. Wilson's disease

B 10. Phenylketonuria

A 11. Tuberous sclerosis

E 12. Parkinson's disease

B 13. Hallervorden-Spatz disease

ANSWERS AND EXPLANATIONS

1. The answer is C. (*II B 7; III A*) Huntington's disease is transmitted through an autosomal dominant gene. In the case of an affected mother and a normal father, this means that 50% of all children born to these parents will have the gene for the disease and will be at risk for developing the disorder. Since the transmission is autosomal and not sex-linked, the child's gender is not a determinant of the risk for the disease. (In the case of X-linked transmission, 50% of the sons only will be at risk.) Dominant transmission suggests that a child with the abnormal gene will have the disease (if he or she lives long enough), while a child without that gene will not have the disease. (When the transmission is recessive, 25% of the children will be at risk, 50% will be carriers, and 25% will be normal.)

2. The answer is B. [*II A 3 d (2)*] Klinefelter syndrome is characterized by an extra X chromosome (an XXY karyotype), with a total of 47 chromosomes (instead of the normal 46 with XX or XY karyotypes). Such an anomaly results from nondisjunction. The presence of two X chromosomes results in the formation of a Barr body; however, the Y chromosome is responsible for the development of male gonads. Sterility, impotence, and an increased prevalence of mental subnormality and nonspecific personality disorders are other characteristics.

3. The answer is D. (*V D*) Specific forms of mental retardation may be due to autosomal dominant (e.g., tuberous sclerosis), autosomal recessive (e.g., phenylketonuria), and sex-linked recessive (e.g., Hunter's mucopolysaccharidosis) transmission or secondary to chromosomal abnormalities (e.g., Down syndrome). The most commonly observed form of mental retardation is, however, polygenic in transmission (i.e., a number of genes contribute to the abnormality).

4. The answer is A (1, 2, 3). (*III A 2, B, C; IV A*) Genetic factors are important in the etiology of some types of schizophrenia. The exact mode of transmission is not known, although recessive and polygenic theories have been proposed. These are based on family risk studies (with a higher prevalence in first-degree relatives of a schizophrenic proband than in the general population), twin studies (with a greater prevalence in monozygotic than in dizygotic twins), and adoption studies (with a higher prevalence in biological relatives than in adoptive relatives). Pedigree studies are primarily useful in conditions that are fairly constant in their penetrance and clinical expression (e.g., Huntington's disease).

5. The answer is C (2, 4). [*II B 7 c (1) (a); IV A 4, B 4*] Duchenne type muscular dystrophy is clearly an X-linked condition, and it has been proposed that there may be X-linked transmission in some forms of bipolar (manic-depressive) disorder. No pattern suggestive of X-linked transmission has been reported for schizophrenia or unipolar disorder.

6. The answer is C (2, 4). (*V E*) The high familial incidence of multiple sclerosis suggests a familial component, but this does not necessarily mean that the component is genetic, as many factors, such as environment, can be shared in families. The fact that the concordance rates for monozygotic and dizygotic twins are equal argues against a strong genetic component, in which case the concordance rate for monozygotic twins should be much higher than that for dizygotic twins.

7. The answer is B (1, 3). (*IV C 3*) Depression, alcoholism, and sociopathy have been genetically linked in what has been termed the depression spectrum disease. This term may represent a condition that is different from other depressive disorders, as the depression occurs primarily in female members of the family whereas the alcoholism and sociopathy occur more in the male members. It is true that depressed patients may smoke cigarettes (especially if they have an agitated depression), and some patients with epilepsy (especially psychomotor epilepsy) may suffer depression. Yet, cigarette smoking has a limited genetic component to begin with, and there is no evidence of genetic linkage of epilepsy to affective disorders.

8. The answer is A (1, 2, 3). (*III A*) Females can develop X-linked disorders if their mothers are carriers and their fathers have the disorder. This is uncommon for most X-linked disorders. However, for relatively common traits such as red–green color blindness, a significant number of women may be affected.

9–13. The answers are: 9-B, 10-B, 11-A, 12-E, 13-B. (*II B 7; V B 2, 3, 4, D 3*) Tuberous sclerosis is transmitted via an autosomal dominant mode of inheritance, while phenylketonuria, Wilson's disease, and Hallervorden-Spatz disease are transmitted via an autosomal recessive mode. There is little evidence for a strong genetic component in the development of Parkinson's disease.

5
Animal Behavior
William J. Freed

I. EVOLUTION. The question of heritability of behavior first arose from the Darwinian theory of evolution by natural selection: If physical characteristics are inherited, could behavioral patterns be inherited as well?

A. BEHAVIORAL PATTERNS NOT DEPENDENT ON PRACTICE OR EXPERIENCE

1. **Invertebrates.** Many movement patterns of invertebrates appear to be fully formed without practice or experience and thus appear to be inherited.

2. **Birds.** Certain **movement patterns** are independent of their normal functional consequences. Lovebirds provide an interesting example. Some species of lovebirds transport nesting material by grasping it with their beaks, raising their back feathers, then clamping the strips of nesting material beneath their feathers. Other species carry the nesting material in their beaks. Hybrids grasp the nesting material with their beaks and raise their feathers, but they do not successfully transfer the material to the feathers, instead they carry it in their beaks. Thus, the feather-tucking movements are maintained in the hybrid animals even though they serve no functional purpose.

3. **Mammals.** Only a small part of the behavioral repertoire of mammals is inherited. For example, certain brood-rearing and display behaviors of squirrels are apparent even in animals reared in isolation.

4. **Humans.** Even the human infant has certain stereotyped movements that are independent of experience. These include lateral head movements and **Moro's reflex**, which is elicited by vestibular stimulation or stimulation of the muscles in the neck. Moro's reflex is apparently a phylogenetic remnant of the movements used by subhuman primate infants to cling to their mothers. Another example is **smiling**, which occurs even in blind infants.

B. LEARNED BEHAVIORAL PATTERNS. In higher animals, particularly in mammals, an increasingly larger part of the behavioral repertoire is learned.

1. The value of a learned or acquired behavioral repertoire is a greater **ability to adapt** to changing environmental conditions and novel situations.

2. The disadvantages of a learned behavioral repertoire include an increased period of dependency of the infant while the behavioral repertoire is acquired, a greater amount of time spent by the parents in child rearing, and a smaller number of offspring. This results in a lower reproductive rate.

II. MOTIVATION AND CONSUMMATORY BEHAVIORS

A. EATING is particularly important in the behavioral repertoire of animals, since a large part of the behavior of many animal species is devoted to the finding, acquisition, and ingestion of food.

1. Rats serve as a good species model for the study of eating behavior because of their omnivorous diet, which is similar to that of humans.
   a. When rats encounter a novel food with a salient taste, the food initially is sampled in small amounts and only later is it ingested in substantial quantities.
      (1) This phenomenon is known as **neophobia**, and it serves the adaptive value of limiting the ingestion of poisonous substances.
      (2) In experimental situations, this neophobia can be detected with flavorings such as saccharin, black walnuts, and chocolate.

(3) Neophobia helps rats to avoid many conventional poisons, making it difficult to poison the rodents.

b. Novel substances that **do** cause illness are subsequently avoided. This is known as **conditioned taste aversion.**

(1) Conditioned taste aversions are most robust when the illness follows the food ingestion by a short period of time. Nonetheless, these aversions can be detected even when the illness is delayed for many hours.

(2) In experimental situations, conditioned taste aversions are produced by first offering a novel food to the animal, which does not itself cause illness. Illness is then produced by the injection of a second, unrelated substance. This permits the properties of the illness to be manipulated independently of the food stimulus.

(a) In experimental situations, illness is frequently induced by the injection of lithium chloride.

(b) Conditioned taste aversions can also be induced by a wide range of drugs, including some that do not cause prominent illness or nausea in humans, such as amphetamines, ethanol, and barbiturates.

(c) Paradoxically, a number of potent poisons, such as certain antimetabolites, do not produce conditioned taste aversions.

(3) Thus, as demonstrated by experiments, conditioned taste aversions are produced by certain internal disturbances or visceral signs, rather than by illness or malaise per se.

c. When given access to a variety of foods, **rats are able to self-select a balanced diet**.

(1) Animals accomplish this dietary self-selection primarily by sampling foods and gradually learning to select those that maintain optimal health. Learning similar to that seen in conditioned taste aversion seems to play an important role in this behavior.

(2) Children also are able to self-select an appropriate diet under appropriate conditions. These conditions, notably, do not include the presence of highly palatable foods and sweets.

(3) When rats are given a highly palatable diet containing typical human "supermarket" foods and sweets (e.g., cookies), they become obese due to excess food consumption. This is known as **dietary obesity**.

d. Specific hunger

(1) When rats are deprived of specific nutrients, they attempt to obtain and ingest foods containing these nutrients. This is known as specific hunger.

(2) Animals show specific hunger for many nutrients, such as calcium, thiamine, and sodium.

(3) Most specific hungers appear to be learned. However, sodium-specific hunger does not have to be acquired because there are specific taste receptors for sodium. (The presence of an innate sodium-specific hunger and the presence of sodium taste receptors attest to the great importance of sodium as a nutrient.)

2. Physiologic control of eating behavior

a. The term **hunger** when applied to humans refers to an internally perceived state associated with an increased propensity to ingest food. In animals, the internally perceived state cannot be measured nor can it be shown to exist. Thus, when applied to animals, the term hunger refers to the propensity to ingest food only, not to the internal state.

b. Old theories of hunger suggested the importance of peripheral signals, now known not to be of primary importance. For example, stomach contractions were thought to be important in hunger and stomach distension in satiation. Recently, it has been found that peripheral hormones, such as the gastrointestinal peptide **cholecystokinin**, may be important in the regulation of feeding behavior.

c. Central mechanisms located largely in the hypothalamus and mediated by factors such as blood glucose concentration are of primary importance in controlling hunger. Thus, in addition to its role in other physiologic regulatory functions, **the hypothalamus has an important role in the control of hunger and eating behavior.**

(1) **Lesions of the ventromedial hypothalamus** are known to produce a syndrome of overeating and extreme obesity. These lesions do not cause a primary increase in eating but Instead cause an increase in fat deposition or an altered body weight "set point," leading to a compensatory increase in eating.

(a) Animals with such lesions are relatively inactive but are hyperreactive to sensory stimuli. Eating behavior in these animals is excessively susceptible to influence by food palatability.

(b) Similar lesions in humans (e.g., caused by tumors) also can lead to obesity.

(c) There has always been some question as to whether such lesions cause primarily a deficit in the regulation of eating or cause a complex behavioral syndrome of which overeating is only one manifestation. However, it is striking that the effects of hypothalamic lesions can be mimicked by injections of a neurotoxin called gold thioglucose, which is specifically taken up into glucose-sensitive cells in the hypothalamus, destroying those cells and leading to obesity.

(d) A milder syndrome of obesity can be produced by specific lesions of the ventral noradrenergic bundle, a norepinephrine-containing system that passes through the medial hypothalamus and is destroyed in the lesion process.

(2) Another syndrome of disordered eating behavior can be produced by **lesions of the lateral hypothalamus**, which cause anorexia.

(a) In addition to anorexia, animals with these lesions lack motor activity, lack responses to sensory stimuli, do not groom themselves, and have other behavioral abnormalities.

(b) Most aspects of this syndrome appear to be due to destruction of the ascending dopamine-containing projections from the substantia nigra to the corpus striatum.

(3) **Electrical stimulation of the lateral hypothalamus** can produce immediate vigorous eating behavior. Similar stimulation can also cause drinking behavior and other responses. Again, whether this stimulation-induced eating is caused by specific activation of an "eating circuit" has not been established conclusively. Apparently nonspecific arousal produced by mild tail-pinch (administered by a metal clamp) can induce similar eating responses, further suggesting that general arousal is involved in the response to lateral hypothalamic stimulation.

(4) Eating behavior can also be profoundly influenced by the **injection of various chemical substances into the hypothalamus**.

(a) Injection of norepinephrine into several hypothalamic nuclei increases eating behavior.

(b) Injection of several peptides into several hypothalamic nuclei decreases eating behavior.

B. DRINKING

1. Drinking behavior can be categorized into two distinctly different types on the basis of the relationship to physiologic need.

a. **Primary drinking** occurs in response to physiologic need, either because of dehydration or volume loss of fluid (hypovolemia). Primary drinking may occur in response to sweating, diuresis, blood loss, or fluid redistribution through edema.

b. **Secondary drinking** is not motivated by actual physiologic need and occurs while the animal does not have a water deficit. Secondary drinking may be associated with the ingestion of dry food or may occur because the fluid is very palatable, and for several other reasons.

2. The relative prominence of primary and secondary drinking differs among species.

a. Humans show prominent secondary drinking (e.g., ingestion of alcoholic and caffeine-containing beverages). Even in primitive societies, water is not the primary ingested beverage.

b. Rats are similar to humans in that they ingest water in excess of **minimal** physiologic needs in association with eating and only slowly make up for a water deficit.

c. Dogs, on the other hand, rapidly compensate for a water deficit through ingestion of water in a single drinking session.

3. **Primary drinking is of two distinct types**, dehydration-induced (**cellular**) and hypovolemia-induced (**extracellular**).

a. **Dehydration-induced drinking** involves cells in the preoptic area of the hypothalamus that detect a hypertonic concentration of extracellular fluid, which in turn causes osmosis of fluid from these cells.

b. **Hypovolemic drinking** occurs in response to an actual loss of body fluids, as occurs in edema and bleeding. Hypovolemia results in the release of renin, which leads to the formation of angiotensin II. To induce drinking, angiotensin II acts on the hypothalamus, the subfornical organ, and possibly several other brain areas.

4. **Oral metering**

a. In experimental situations, esophageal fistulas can be created in animals in such a way that ingested water does not reach the stomach and is not absorbed. However, the animals are able to **drink in proportion to water deficit**, even though the total amount ingested is greatly increased.

b. This occurs through oral metering. Ingested volume and cooling of the mouth are important in oral metering, as well as in the reinforcing effects of water ingestion.

c. When the oral feedback from water ingestion is bypassed, as when water is injected directly into the stomach, only the postingestion feedback from water intake remains.

5. Abnormal fluid intake

a. Rats will ingest excessively large amounts of extremely palatable solutions, such as a combination of saccharin and sucrose.

b. Rats and several other animals can be induced to drink extremely large amounts of water through a paradigm called **schedule-induced polydipsia**. When an animal is deprived of food and is given a small morsel of food once every 20 seconds to 4 minutes, it will drink extremely large amounts of water, sometimes as much as 50% of its body weight in 3 hours.

c. **The most prominent human form of abnormal drinking is alcoholism**. This is primarily related to the pharmacologic effects of alcohol, rather than to drinking behavior per se. There are certain strains of animals that ingest large amounts of alcohol voluntarily. For example, mice of the C57 strain will voluntarily consume about 90% of their fluid intake as 10% alcohol in preference to tap water.

d. Excessive water drinking is also observed in many schizophrenic patients. There is no evidence that this involves a primary regulatory abnormality but may instead be a behavioral abnormality.

C. SEXUAL AND REPRODUCTIVE BEHAVIOR

1. Stages of differentiation

a. In **early stages of development**, genetically determined males and females are outwardly similar. Both sexes pass through a stage during which they are sensitive to **hormonal stimulation**. In rats, this stage occurs around the time of birth and shortly thereafter.

(1) During this stage, if the male hormone testosterone is present, the animal will develop male characteristics and masculine behavioral patterns. If no hormonal stimulation is present, the animal will develop in a female direction. The **direction of sexual behavior** is thus determined early in development.

(2) Inappropriate sex hormones during this period may produce abnormal individuals (e.g., absence of androgens in a male will produce an individual with female external characteristics).

(3) Only external sex characteristics and behavior are influenced by sexual hormones during this stage of differentiation. For example, androgens present during the development of a female can cause male-like external sex organs and male behavior patterns to develop, but that individual will still have the internal reproductive organs of a female.

(4) This differentiating effect is seen not only for sexual behavior per se but also for other, gender-specific behavioral patterns. For example, testosterone normally stimulates fighting in male mice but does not do so in animals castrated at birth (i.e., in animals that are not differentiated males).

b. A second stage of differentiation occurs at puberty.

(1) In the rat, puberty occurs at about 2 months (about 1/20 of the life span). In the human, puberty occurs at about 13 years (about 1/6 of the life span).

(2) Although the direction of sexual behavior patterns is determined earlier, the expression of these patterns is stimulated at puberty.

(3) At puberty, sex hormones (testosterone in the male and estrogen in the female) are produced and stimulate the development of secondary sexual characteristics (e.g., deepening of the voice and development of body hair in males and enlargement of the breasts in females). In the absence of sex hormones during puberty, secondary sex characteristics and sexual behavior patterns are not expressed. For example, castration was actually employed in human males in Europe prior to the nineteenth century to produce "castrati"—undifferentiated male opera singers with clear, high-pitched voices.

c. In the **mature, differentiated individual**, sex hormones do not alter the type of sexual behavior that is exhibited, but they may enhance or inhibit the behavior. For example, human male homosexuals do not become heterosexuals when injected with testosterone but exhibit more active homosexual behavior.

2. The hypothalamus plays an important role in the control of sexual behavior.

a. Male and female sexual behavior, as well as maternal behavior (nest building), can be elicited by the stimulation of parts of the preoptic area of the hypothalamus in both male and female rats.

b. The presence of sex hormones during development influences the connections of neurons in the preoptic area of the hypothalamus, which can in turn have lasting effects on sexual behavior.

3. Integration of sexual behavior

a. Monkeys deprived of social contact during infancy do not show normal sexual behavior as adults. Humans are thought to be similarly subject to social influences (i.e., normal sexual and maternal behavior in humans is probably highly dependent upon environmental and social interactions during infancy).

  b. The control of sexual behavior by hormones is very direct and pronounced in lower animals, but, in higher animals, hormones play a less important role while neuronal, social, and environmental factors become more important. Hormonal disruption has a more pronounced effect on the sexual behavior of lower animals.

  c. Sexual behavior becomes more reflexive and stereotyped in the progression from approach and courtship through copulation. More aspects of sexual behavior are stereotyped in lower animals than in higher animals.

D. AGGRESSION

1. Aggression in animals is commonly divided into several types, depending on the eliciting stimuli. For example, the aggression elicited by pain may be quite different from the aggression exhibited by a predator in search of prey. Aggression shown by a mother protecting her young may have still different properties.

2. **Aggression can be elicited by stimulation of the hypothalamus**; for example, two types of aggression can be elicited by stimulation of the hypothalamus of the cat.

  a. Stimulation of the **medial hypothalamus** elicits an **affective attack**, a rage-like syndrome with hissing, snarling, unsheathed claws, and piloerection.

  b. Stimulation of the **lateral hypothalamus** elicits a **stalking** or **quiet biting attack**, a predatory response without the rage-like aspects. The quiet biting attack is specifically directed toward natural prey.

3. **The limbic system and aggression**

  a. Lesions of the septal area of the brain produce a temporary rage-like syndrome in rats, which subsides in several weeks. Effects of these lesions vary markedly between species, however; for example, the rage syndrome does not appear in mice, but instead a permanent flight reaction is seen. Consistent rage-like syndromes are not seen in other species, such as cats and monkeys. Thus, the septal area does not appear to have a primary role in controlling aggression.

  b. The **amygdala**, on the other hand, appears to have an **important role in aggression and emotional responses**.

   (1) Removal of the temporal lobes (including the amygdala) of rhesus monkeys produces the **Klüver-Bucy syndrome**. Animals with these lesions are very tame, do not fear natural enemies such as snakes, and also have other abnormalities such as the inability to recognize common objects, hyperactive and abnormal sexuality, and a tendency to place all objects in their mouths.

   (a) Most aspects of the Klüver-Bucy syndrome can be reproduced in animals with lesions of the amygdala.

   (b) Similar changes, particularly the taming effect, can also be produced in several other species, such as the wild Norway rat, which is normally very aggressive.

   (c) Although increased friendliness to human experimenters is always observed, animals with amygdala lesions may become more or less aggressive toward members of their own species. Inappropriate social responses are also observed.

   (2) The role of the amygdala in human aggression is controversial. In a few cases, tumors or other abnormalities of the amygdala have been identified in extremely violent patients. The amygdala has been removed in a few extremely violent human patients, although such surgery produces other changes in addition to the reduced violence.

E. SELF-STIMULATION OF THE BRAIN

1. In 1954, it was discovered that rats would return to the part of a chamber in which they received stimulation of the hypothalamus. They also found that rats would press a lever rapidly and vigorously in order to obtain stimulation of the lateral hypothalamus. This behavior is called **intracranial self-stimulation**.

  a. The most vigorous intracranial self-stimulation is obtained from areas around the lateral hypothalamus coinciding with ascending fiber systems. Reinforcing effects are also obtained from a number of other brain areas, particularly the septal area.

  b. The effects of intracranial self-stimulation may be quite dramatic. In one well-known example, a rat stimulated itself 2000 times per hour for 26 hours, slept continuously for almost a day, and then resumed the self-stimulation at the previous rate. The degree of "pleasure" involved in the stimulation cannot, however, be determined from the rate alone. Much of the rapidity and persistence of the response might simply be due to the fact that the stimulation does not satiate, as do natural rewards. Moreover, when rats are allowed to regulate the stimulus [on and off] (rather than pressing to obtain a short stimulation pulse), they will leave the stimulus on for only a few seconds and then turn it off. They do not increase the duration of the stimulation even when allowed to turn it on and off only once each day.

2. Although there has been considerable controversy concerning the relationship between self-stimulation and natural rewards, the two appear to have some similarities. A stimulus that supports self-stimulation also frequently induces eating or drinking responses. For currents that induce feeding and self-stimulation, food deprivation may facilitate self-stimulation. When animals with these electrodes are satiated, under certain conditions they will work to turn on the stimulus only if food is also present. Thus, animals may find it rewarding to self-stimulate their brain and thereby make themselves hungry, but only when they eat.

3. Brain stimulation that produces reward does not necessarily cause the sensation of eating but rather seems to cause a motivation to eat. Thus, although rewarding stimulation of the brain may not be identical to natural rewards, there does appear to be some relationship between rewards such as eating and brain stimulation.

4. Pleasurable sensations have been elicited from stimulation of the brain in human subjects, mainly in the septal area. Although pleasurable, these sensations are not overwhelming and do not seem to exceed greatly the pleasurable sensations obtainable by natural rewards.

III. LEARNING.
It is difficult to make comparisons of learning across species because of problems in equating motivation and performance. The most instructive studies are those that examine differences in types of learning among species. Some forms of learning, such as habituation, are seen in all species, from invertebrates to humans, although different mechanisms of learning may be involved. Other forms of learning, such as imprinting, are found only in some species. Generally, animals can only learn tasks that are consistent with their species-specific behavioral repertoire. For example, birds are easily conditioned to perform pecking movements but can be trained to manipulate bars and levers only with difficulty.

A. PRIMITIVE FORMS OF LEARNING

1. **Imprinting** is a very specialized form of learning that occurs only in birds and only during a short period of time after hatching. (If it does not occur within approximately 1 day after birth, it will not occur at all.) Birds learn to follow the first relatively large, moving object that they encounter; normally, birds are imprinted to follow their mothers, although they can also be imprinted to follow almost any animal, human, or even object, such as a box containing a ticking clock.

2. **Habituation and exploration**
   a. **Habituation** is a progressive decrease in the response to a stimulus produced by repeated or continued exposure to the stimulus. (Decrements in responses due to fatigue are not considered to be habituation.)
      (1) Habituation may occur for very simple, elicited responses, such as orientation toward a sound or withdrawal of the foot in response to tactile stimulation.
      (2) Habituation may also occur in more complex situations, such as the progressive decline in exploratory behavior that occurs when animals are continuously exposed to a new and unfamiliar environment. In this case, habituation involves a complex interaction between multiple stimuli and behavioral responses.
   b. Habituation and exploration are discussed together because their properties overlap. For example, an animal that hears a loud sound will turn toward the sound. The turning response is a rudimentary exploratory response. If there is no object associated with the sound, the exploratory response will quickly habituate. If there is an object, it may be explored.
      (1) Large changes in the environment elicit fear; only small changes in the environment will be explored. If large changes in the environment do not produce overtly threatening or painful stimuli, the fear too will habituate and exploration will eventually ensue.
      (2) Exploration does not satiate, as do eating, drinking, and sexual behavior. If an animal explores a novel environment, it will show renewed exploration if presented immediately with another novel environment.

B. CONDITIONING.
Incorporation of meaningful information about the environment into the behavioral repertoire of the organism occurs through conditioning. There are two main types of conditioning—classical and instrumental.

1. **Classical conditioning** concerns relationships between environmental events, and it concerns the responses that are immediately elicited by environmental events (which are usually autonomic responses).

    a. The concept of classical conditioning is derived from a paradigm devised by the Russian physiologist **Ivan Pavlov**. In his experiments, a dog was restrained and salivation was elicited by blowing meat powder into its mouth. The sound of a bell was repeatedly associated with the meat powder. At first, the bell alone did not elicit salivation, but after many associations between the bell and meat powder, it did.

    b. This paradigm involves several stimuli and responses, or reflexes.

      (1) Unconditioned stimulus (UCS) is the stimulus that elicits the response without conditioning (the meat powder).

      (2) Unconditioned reflex (UCR) is the reflex elicited by the UCS directly, without conditioning (salivation).

      (3) Conditioned stimulus (CS) is the initially neutral stimulus that is associated with the UCS during the experiment (the bell).

      (4) Conditioned reflex (CR) is the reflex elicited by the CS alone, without the UCS. Although the CR is always superficially similar to the UCR, the two are never completely identical. For example, the CR is usually weaker than the UCR.

2. Instrumental conditioning involves the relationship between specific types of behavior and environmental events and involves the behavioral responses (usually skeletomotor responses) of the organism. Behavior that is immediately elicited by environmental events is called **respondent**. Behavior that is (prior to conditioning) not elicited by a known environmental stimulus is called **operant**.

    a. The basic properties of instrumental conditioning are intuitively apparent: Instrumental conditioning is essentially **trial-and-error learning**. In simple terms, **behaviors that are rewarded will increase and behaviors that are punished will decrease**.

    b. The scientific study of instrumental conditioning was initiated by **Thorndike** and **Skinner**, whose work established a precise conceptualization of instrumental conditioning, as follows. In a specific situation, without prior experience, an animal demonstrates a more or less random sequence of behaviors. Some of these behaviors may be followed by **positive reinforcement** (i.e., reward); these behaviors are thereby **reinforced** and increase in frequency. Other behaviors may be followed by negative reinforcement (i.e., removal of positive reinforcement) or punishment and will decrease in frequency.

      (1) This conceptualization of conditioning emphasizes the fact the behavior is **controlled by its consequences**. Stimuli are thus characterized as reinforcing. The behavior of an animal is not characterized in terms of the subjective experience of the animal, which cannot be measured objectively.

      (2) Through many conditioning experiences, involving the acquisition of food, avoidance of threatening situations, and so on, enduring changes in the behavioral repertoire of an animal (or of a human) may take place. Conditioning of this kind dominates human learning. In animal experiments, positive reinforcement usually consists of food or other tangible stimuli. In humans, it is apparent that reinforcement may be much more subjective; praise and other social stimuli as well as secondary reinforcement (reinforcement established through association with prior reinforcement) become extremely important.

    c. Two types of experimental paradigms are most often employed for the study of instrumental conditioning.

      (1) In **maze-learning paradigms**, animals are required to learn complex behavioral responses involving locomotion and spatial relationships. Representative mazes include the following.

        (a) Early mazes (such as the Lashley type 3 maze and the Warner and Warden multiple T maze) employed successive left-right choices or successive choices between alternative alleyways.

        (b) A recent type of maze is the radial arm maze, devised by D. Olton. This consists of a central hub with a number of radiating alleyways (usually eight) with food reinforcements at the end of each alleyway. Animals are allowed exactly eight trips down alleyways, and, in order to obtain the maximal amount of food, they must remember which alleyways they have already visited. Rats are able to perform this task very well and orient themselves by external cues in the testing room. They do not, surprisingly, learn to visit each alleyway in a clockwise or counterclockwise sequence, nor do they leave scent deposits in each alleyway that they visit.

        (c) Another frequently employed maze is the Morris water maze. Rats must swim to find a submerged platform on which to rest. The platform is placed just beneath the surface of the water in a large tank, and the water is made opaque by adding powdered milk.

      (2) Operant conditioning involves a behavioral response that is very simple in and of itself (such as the pressing of a bar by a rat). The **rate of the behavior**, however, is modulated as a consequence of reinforcement. Operant conditioning tasks usually involve the adaptation of animals to various **schedules of reinforcement**, which reinforce the responses of animals in various patterns.

(a) In continuous reinforcement (CRF), every response is reinforced.

(b) In fixed ratio (FR), a fixed proportion of responses is reinforced (e.g., in a FR 4 schedule, every fourth response is reinforced).

(c) In variable ratio (VR), a variable proportion of responses is reinforced (e.g., in a VR 4 schedule, reinforcement is random so that an average of one of every four responses is reinforced).

(d) In fixed interval (FI), the first response after a fixed interval of time is reinforced [e.g., for an interval of 1 minute (FI 1 min), no responses are reinforced; the first response occurring after 1 minute is reinforced, and then another interval is started].

(e) In variable interval (VI), the first response after a variable interval is reinforced. The length of the interval is varied randomly around a mean length of time; thus, the animal cannot predict when reinforcement will occur.

(f) In differential reinforcement of low rates (DRL), animals are reinforced after a fixed interval of time, providing no responses have taken place in the interim.

(g) In extinction (EXT), no responses are reinforced.

3. **Special forms of conditioning.** Classical conditioning typically involves autonomic responses, or responses that are elicited by the environment, whereas instrumental conditioning typically involves skeletomotor responses, or responses that are not elicited by an environmental stimulus. There are, however, unusual forms of conditioning that do not fit neatly into either category.

a. **Autoshaping.** Certain skeletomotor responses can be elicited by reinforcement and are, therefore, susceptible to conditioning by classical paradigms.

(1) An experiment using pigeons demonstrates that if the availability of food is signaled by a lighted key and the key is illuminated just **before** the food is available, pecking of the key will be elicited by the light, even though the pecking does not cause the food to be delivered.

(2) Autoshaping occurs for responses closely associated with the reinforcement being used; for example, pecking is reinforced by food in the pigeon and rooting is reinforced by food in the pig.

b. **Biofeedback**

(1) Certain autonomic responses can be brought under voluntary control providing they are monitored mechanically and feedback is given to the subject on the responses to be conditioned.

(2) A human subject, for example, may be asked to attempt to modulate the temperature of his middle finger. When the capillaries at the extremities constrict, the temperature of the extremities drops. Relaxation causes dilation of the capillaries, and the extremities become warmer. When biofeedback is used to monitor the temperature of the middle finger, a device is attached to the finger and the temperature of the finger is displayed on a meter, so that the subject is made aware of his response.

(3) Evidence of biofeedback conditioning in animals is inconclusive, although in humans there is excellent evidence that such conditioning can take place and that an individual can control to a degree various autonomic processes.

IV. BEHAVIOR IN CONFLICT SITUATIONS.
In their natural environment, it is common for animals to be faced with alternatives among various motivating factors—different consummatory objects, such as food, water, and sexual partners, or fear and pain-provoking stimuli. Conflict is present when alternatives exist.

A. **CLASSIFICATION OF CONFLICT SITUATIONS.** Conflict situations are typically classified as approach–approach, approach–avoidance, or avoidance–avoidance, depending on the prevailing behavioral alternatives.

1. **Approach–approach conflict** describes a situation involving two incompatible approach responses, such as the presence of more than one food source, sexual partner, and so forth.

2. **Approach–avoidance conflict** describes a situation involving incompatible approach and avoidance responses. For example, an animal may find a food source that is in an open area susceptible to predators.

3. **Avoidance–avoidance conflict** describes a situation involving two incompatible avoidance responses. For example, an animal may be confronted with a choice between an uncomfortably cold area and an area open to predators.

B. BEHAVIORS EXHIBITED IN CONFLICT SITUATIONS

1. **Suppression of lower priority responses.** In most conflict situations, one of the alternatives has a lower priority, and that alternative is suppressed to allow for expression of the higher priority response. For example, certain birds may spend about 30% of the day grooming and resting in the summer, but in the winter, when food is more scarce, the birds spend 90% of the day feeding, leaving less time for these other activities.

2. Animals may also show preparatory movements, which consist of components of one of the alternative behaviors; or they may alternate between initiating the alternative behaviors; or they may compromise by demonstrating behavior that contains components of the alternatives.

3. A very interesting type of behavior that often occurs in birds (and sometimes in other animals) in conflict situations is **displacement behavior**, or displacement activities. Displacement behavior occurs when animals are somehow prevented from continuing or executing a prominent behavior, such as aggression, sexual behavior, or feeding. The prominent behavior may be suppressed, for example, by the sudden appearance of a competitor. In these situations, the animals may suddenly begin to exhibit apparently irrelevant behaviors, such as grooming or pecking at the ground.

C. SCHEDULE-INDUCED BEHAVIORS

1. Schedule-induced polydipsia (see section II B 5 b) may be an experimental analogy of displacement behavior.

2. Behaviors other than drinking, such as aggression, may also be elicited by intermittent delivery of small food pellets (schedule-induced aggression).

D. RESPONSE-SUPPRESSION PARADIGMS. These experiments employ a motivator such as food but require the animal to endure a threatening or painful situation to obtain the food.

1. In the **Geller-Seifter Conflict Test**, animals are trained to press a lever to obtain food, but only some of the lever presses are rewarded with food. During some periods, all lever presses are rewarded, but the animals are also shocked each time they press the lever. A light signals the shock periods, and lever pressing normally is suppressed. This test has proved to be a very useful **method of testing antianxiety agents**. Drugs such as the benzodiazepines, which reduce anxiety in humans, increase lever pressing during the shock periods of this test.

2. Based on this principle, several other tests for antianxiety agents have also been developed. In these tests, animals must enter a large, brightly lit area in order to obtain food, or they are allowed to explore a brightly lit section of a testing enclosure. Antianxiety agents reduce the reluctance of animals to enter such threatening areas. Such situations are, at least at face value, analogous to anxiety-provoking situations, such as agoraphobia (fear of open spaces), which affect humans.

E. CONDITIONED NEUROSES (experimental neuroses)

1. When an animal is tested by means of discrimination tests (e.g., when an animal is required to discriminate between two different but similar tones) and when the discrimination is gradually made more difficult, at some point the animal may begin to show inappropriate behavior. These responses have been called **experimental conditioned neuroses**.

2. These behaviors were originally observed in an experiment by a student of Pavlov. In the experiment, dogs were trained to discriminate between a circle and an ellipse, and the ellipse was gradually made more and more like a circle. At some point (when the ratio between the length of the axis was 9:8), the discrimination broke down and the dogs began to show violent and emotional behaviors in the testing situation. The inappropriate responses persisted during continuing testing.

3. Similar responses have been observed in sheep, goats, cats, rats, and monkeys.

4. Conditioned neuroses are most likely to develop when:
   a. Strong motivators (such as shock) are used
   b. Positive and negative stimuli are alternated without repetition
   c. Stimuli are presented rapidly

F. LEARNED HELPLESSNESS

1. Learned helplessness is a term used to describe a paradigm developed in dogs by M.E.P.

Seligman, in which the avoidance of shock becomes impaired in animals due to their prior exposure to unavoidable shock.

    a. Dogs are given inescapable shock and later are compared to dogs that have received shock from which they could escape or no shock at all. In a different testing situation, in which the animals can escape from the shock, animals that had previously received inescapable shock passively accept the shock and do not learn to escape.

    b. This behavior is attributed to the animals forming an expectation that they will be unable to control the outcome of subsequent situations.

2. Learned helplessness occurs in fish, rats, cats, dogs, monkeys, and also in humans in analogous situations.

3. Learned helpless animals show reduced aggression, weight loss and anorexia, and deficits in social and sexual behavior in addition to the deficits in shock avoidance. It can be prevented by prior exposure to escapable shock, particularly when the prior exposure occurs in infancy. It can be cured by forcing the animals to escape from the shock.

4. Learned helplessness has been suggested as an animal model of depression.

STUDY QUESTIONS

Directions: Each question below contains five suggested answers. Choose the **one best** response to each question.

1. Which of the following classes is most highly dependent upon inherited (i.e., unlearned) behavioral patterns?

(A) Birds
(B) Mammals
(C) Reptiles
(D) Insects
(E) Fish

2. Neophobia refers to

(A) avoidance of novel foods
(B) avoidance of unfamiliar places
(C) avoidance of newborn offspring
(D) fear of open, brightly lit spaces
(E) fear of sexual behavior

3. What part of the brain is most important in the control of hunger?

(A) Hypothalamus
(B) Cerebellum
(C) Red nucleus
(D) Hippocampus
(E) Amygdala

4. Which of the following conditions induces hypovolemic drinking?

(A) Edema
(B) Alcoholism
(C) Sweating
(D) Eating of dry foods
(E) Schedule-induced polydipsia

5. Testosterone can increase all of the following types of behavior EXCEPT

(A) aggression
(B) eating behavior
(C) male sexual behavior
(D) female sexual behavior
(E) homosexual behavior

6. Stimulation of what part of the brain elicits rage (an affective attack)?

(A) Lateral hypothalamus
(B) Medial hypothalamus
(C) Thalamus
(D) Substantia nigra
(E) Septum

7. True statements concerning self-stimulation include all of the following EXCEPT

(A) stimulation that elicits self-stimulation also may elicit feeding behavior
(B) stimulation that elicits self-stimulation also may elicit drinking behavior
(C) stimulation that elicits self-stimulation also may elicit an affective attack
(D) food deprivation may facilitate self-stimulation
(E) animals may self-stimulate their brains only if food is present

8. All of the following behaviors can be elicited by stimulation of the hypothalamus EXCEPT

(A) eating
(B) imprinting
(C) sexual behavior
(D) aggression
(E) drinking

9. Animal conflict studies serve as models for the study of all of the following mental disorders EXCEPT

(A) neurosis
(B) anxiety
(C) schizophrenia
(D) agoraphobia
(E) depression

10. Advertising in which an attractive couple is shown smoking cigarettes employs which of the following learning principles?

(A) Biofeedback
(B) Autoshaping
(C) Imprinting
(D) Classical conditioning
(E) Operant conditioning

11. Intracranial self-stimulation is readily obtained from the

(A) hippocampus
(B) septum
(C) amygdala
(D) corpus callosum
(E) thalamus

Directions: The question below contains four suggested answers of which **one or more** is correct. Choose the answer

A   if **1, 2, and 3** are correct
B   if **1 and 3** are correct
C   if **2 and 4** are correct
D   if **4** is correct
E   if **1, 2, 3, and 4** are correct

12. Rats are not easily poisoned because they

(1) avoid novel foods
(2) vomit poisons very rapidly
(3) develop conditioned taste aversions to poisonous foods
(4) are immune or resistant to most poisons

ANSWERS AND EXPLANATIONS

1. The answer is D. (*I A*) Insects and other invertebrates are highly dependent upon inherited behavior patterns. Invertebrates have very little ability to alter their behavioral repertoire in response to changes in environmental conditions. Increasingly higher animals have more and more ability to learn new behavioral patterns. Mammals are particularly able to learn and, therefore, are able to adapt behaviorally to changing environmental conditions.

2. The answer is A. (*II A 1 a*) The general meaning of neophobia is a fear of new things or novelty. In animal behavior, neophobia specifically refers to avoidance of novel foods. This is an adaptive response that serves to protect against poisoning. Animals will generally sample very small amounts of novel foods and gradually will increase the amounts that they eat if they do not become ill.

3. The answer is A. (*II A 2 c*) The hypothalamus is important in the control of hunger as well as drinking and many other visceral and homeostatic functions. The cerebellum and red nucleus are involved primarily in the control of motor function. The hippocampus is thought to be important in memory and learning. The amygdala has been discussed as important in aggression and emotional responses.

4. The answer is E. (*II B 1 a*) Hypovolemic drinking takes place in response to a physiologic need. It is a form of primary drinking that occurs when there is a loss of body fluids, which may result from edema or bleeding. This is distinct from dehydration, which may be induced (e.g., by sweating).

5. The answer is B. (*II C, D*) Testosterone can increase male, female, and homosexual forms of sexual behavior. When administered during adulthood, testosterone does not change the type but merely stimulates the predominant form of sexual behavior. Testosterone also can increase other forms of male-associated behavior (such as aggression) when administered during development. However, eating behavior is not particularly associated with testosterone administration.

6. The answer is B. (*II D 2 a*) Stimulation of the medial hypothalamus of a cat elicits a rage-like response, whereas stimulation of the lateral hypothalamus elicits a quiet, biting attack, which is directed toward prey.

7. The answer is C. (*II E 2, 3*) Eating and drinking behavior are sometimes elicited by currents that elicit self-stimulation of the brain. Food deprivation can facilitate self-stimulation. Under certain conditions, animals may work to turn on electrical brain stimulation only if food is also present. An affective attack is elicited from the medial hypothalamus, where self-stimulation is not obtained.

8. The answer is B. (*III A 1*) Imprinting is a form of learning observed in young birds, and it cannot be elicited by brain stimulation in the hypothalamus. Imprinting is the learning by birds to follow almost any moving animal or other object encountered soon after birth. Birds are most readily "imprinted" to follow large objects and objects that make noise. Usually, this is the mother.

9. The answer is C. (*IV D, E, F*) Conflict paradigms for conditioned neuroses have been developed, based on an experiment originally performed by Pavlov, and conflict paradigms for the study of anxiety as well as agoraphobia have been developed, based on the Geller-Seifter conflict test. The learned helplessness paradigm serves as an animal model of depression. Schizophrenia, however, is a complex disorder that is not modeled by any behavioral conflict paradigm.

10. The answer is D. (*III B 1*) Classical conditioning is a method of eliciting a response (usually autonomic) to a neutral stimulus through pairing the neutral stimulus with one that normally elicits the desired response. Advertising showing an attractive couple attempts to form an association between the attractive couple and the product, so that responses to the attractive features of the couple become associated with the product.

11. The answer is B. (*II E*) Intracranial self-stimulation is readily obtained from the septum of rats. In humans, stimulation of the septum can also have pleasurable effects, although not of an overwhelming nature. Vigorous self-stimulation is also obtained from the hypothalamus. Animals will self-stimulate most rapidly when the hypothalamus is involved, but the degree of "pleasure" derived from the stimulation cannot be derived from the rapidity of the behavior alone.

12. The answer is B (1, 3). (*II A 1 a, b*) Survival in animals depends upon the finding, acquisition, and ingestion of food. Rats avoid novel foods, eating only small amounts of foods that are unfamiliar. If they become ill after eating a small amount of a poisonous food, they develop a conditioned taste aversion to that food and do not eat any more of it.

6

Theories of the Mind

Jerry M. Wiener

I. PSYCHOANALYTIC–PSYCHODYNAMIC THEORY

A. DEFINITION. The psychoanalytic theory is a theory of the mind and personality development that is centrally based on the concept of **conflict** among forces within the mind (i.e., **intrapsychic conflict**).

1. The theory originated in the early 1890s, and its origins and development have been uniquely identified with **Freud** (1856–1939). Subsequently, it has been revised and elaborated.

2. Originally it was proposed to explain neurotic symptoms (e.g., phobias, hysteria, obsessions, and compulsions), which are due to intrapsychic conflict [e.g., a sexual drive (or wish) versus the force of conscience or morality, resulting in a compromise solution].

3. Gradually it expanded to become a general theory of both normal and abnormal development and personality formation.

4. The term **psychoanalysis** is used to refer to both:
   a. A method of **treatment** of mental disorders
   b. A method or technique for learning about mental processes (i.e., **research**)

B. BASIC CONCEPTS

1. The **unconscious mental process**
   a. It is theorized that much of mental activity (e.g., that of drives, wishes, defenses, and conscience) occurs outside of awareness.
   b. However, unconscious mental activity influences conscious thought and behavior, although it is not available to voluntary recall.
   c. This unconscious process represents thoughts, wishes, urges, impulses, feelings, and fantasies that, were they to come to awareness or be acted on, would be considered **unacceptable** or in some way **dangerous**.
   d. Also considered to be unconscious are parts of the personality such as:
      (1) The conscience (e.g., an unexplained feeling of guilt or shame or one that is out of proportion to the identified cause)
      (2) The defenses [e.g., rationalization; see section I B 5 b (7)]
      (3) Some automatic behavior (e.g., being able to drive home from work without "thinking" about it)

2. **Psychic determinism**
   a. The concept of psychic determinism is that **all mental activity is meaningful and purposeful** and is connected with previous life experiences, albeit often unconsciously so.
   b. Consequently, no mental activity (and, therefore, no behavior) is random, accidental, or meaningless.

3. **Instinct (drive)**
   a. Drive is the **motivation** that is behind mental activity and action.
   b. The psychological manifestations of drives are experienced as urges, wishes, and fantasies.
   c. There are two major categories of drives:
      (1) Sexual drive (libido)
      (2) Aggressive drive
   d. Drives press toward gratification and discharge. In the infant and young child, this action is more direct and overt, then gradually it conforms more with parental, societal, and cultural standards (see section I B 4).

4. The **psychosexual stages of development** comprise a gradual, sequential process in the development of the sexual drive (instinct) from infancy (infantile sexuality) to adulthood (genital sexuality), reflecting maturation of the body and nervous system on the one hand and interpersonal experience on the other.
   a. The **oral stage** (birth to 1½ years). Primary drive satisfaction is achieved by sucking, feeding, and chewing behaviors.
   b. The **anal stage** (1½ to 3 years). The primary (not the exclusive) focus of pleasure and interaction shifts to the anal zone and to activities of expulsion and retention (both anal and urinary), followed by the acquisition of voluntary control.
   c. The **phallic (oedipal) stage** (approximately 3 to 6 years)
      (1) The focus shifts to the genitals as the primary source of interest, pleasure, and organization of wishes. This is manifested by masturbation, curiosity, and exhibitionism.
      (2) The **Oedipus complex** is experienced in the interaction with and wishes directed toward the parents. The child increasingly wishes to have an exclusive (quasiadult) relationship with the opposite-sex parent but also wishes to preserve a positive relationship with the parent of the same sex.
      (3) This complex of feelings leads to **oedipal conflict**, which is a fear that the same-sex parent will be displeased and angry with the child for his rivalrous wishes and will retaliate. This in turn leads to fear of bodily damage in the boy (castration anxiety) and fear of loss of love in the girl.
      (4) The conflict is resolved by relinquishing the rivalrous "sexual" wishes and maintaining the original relationship with the parent of the opposite sex by choosing to be like the father (boy) or the mother (girl) when grown-up.
   d. **Latency** (approximately 6 to 12 years)
      (1) This is the period between resolution of the oedipal conflict and the onset of biological and psychological puberty.
      (2) The primary interests turn to peers and school, with socialization and acquisition of knowledge and skills.
   e. The **genital stage** (puberty to adulthood)
      (1) This is the only psychosexual stage with explicit neuroendocrine and maturational components.
      (2) Ideally the drives, aims, and objects of previous psychosexual stages are integrated into primary genital sexuality, with the previous stages now active as part of foreplay rather than forming the primary sexual aim.

5. **Defenses**
   a. **Definition.** Defenses are mental (psychological) operations that function outside of awareness (unconsciously) **to ward off anxiety** and maintain a sense of safety, well-being, and self-esteem.
      (1) Defenses emerge, along with maturation, in a developmental sequence.
      (2) They may emerge episodically (e.g., as in a transient regression) or become habitual and operate as a part of the particular personality (e.g., rationalization, intellectualization, or compulsiveness). They may become fixed as part of a symptom formation, as in a phobia.
   b. **Classification** (in order from least mature to most mature)
      (1) **Denial** is blocking from awareness (or acceptance) information or perceptions that seem to be unacceptable.
      (2) **Projection** is the assignment of an unacceptable inner impulse, feeling, or both (e.g., anger) to another person or agency (e.g., it is not I who am angry, but you who are angry at me). An individual can also project his own sexual feelings to another as "bad."
      (3) **Splitting** is a way of maintaining a perception of self and others as either all good or all bad.
      (4) **Repression** is a dominant and important intrapsychic defense that operates to keep unconscious any unacceptable urges, thoughts, wishes, and feelings.
      (5) In a **reaction formation** only one intensified side of an attitude or relationship is allowed into awareness. This may be experienced, for example, as a harsh morality, self-righteousness, exaggerated affection or generosity, or self-sacrifice.
      (6) **Isolation of affect** maintains the separation of a thought from its otherwise unacceptable or painful feeling (e.g., speaking calmly of what otherwise would be a painful, humiliating, or frightening experience). The affect may also be thought of as repressed.
      (7) **Rationalization** is substituting acceptable or even admirable motives for attitudes or behavior related to more self-serving or otherwise unacceptable motives.
      (8) **Intellectualization**, a common defense in our culture, involves addressing an issue that would be painful or threatening by understanding or explaining it intellectually (e.g.,

parents of a child with a serious or fatal illness learn all of the details about the illness to ward off feelings of helplessness and hopelessness).

(9) **Undoing** involves a thought or action that "magically" neutralizes (or "undoes") harm or consequence related to an unconscious wish. Undoing is a defense found in ritualistic and superstitious behaviors such as knocking on wood, throwing salt over one's shoulder, and avoiding the path of a black cat.

(10) **Regression** is a special case, as much a process as a defense, and can be more or less adaptive. It is the return to or revival of earlier forms of behavior or thought in response to a current stress or threat. This is very common in younger children, and is seen in a return to thumb sucking or immature speech following the birth of a sibling.

  6. Structural theory of mental functioning. A theoretical model of the mind, the structural model organizes mental processes and behavior according to function, and it groups related functions together. The groups are referred to as the "structures" of **id**, **ego**, and **superego**.

    a. Id is the **psychic representation of drives** (wishes), which are largely unconscious, particularly sexual and aggressive infantile and childhood drives. Examples include sucking drives, anal retentive drives, and sadistic and destructive drives.

    b. Ego is a group of functions that provide for **adaptation** to the demands of the drives and to the requirements of external reality. Functions may be classified as primarily maturational (i.e., biological or genetic) or primarily developmental in origin.

      (1) Maturational functions include:
        (a) Motor activity
        (b) Sensory function
        (c) Language
        (d) Cognition and memory
      (2) Developmental functions include:
        (a) Defenses and signal anxiety
        (b) Reality testing
        (c) Object relationships
        (d) Sexual development
        (e) Identity
        (f) Overall integration of personality

    c. Superego represents:
      (1) Judgment, self-criticism, and conscience, which are affectively regulated by guilt (what one should not think, feel, or do)
      (2) Aspirations and values to live up to, the "ego-ideal" component of the superego, affectively regulated by shame
      (3) Conscience and the ego-ideal, which develop by the movement of prohibitions, permissions, expectations, and values from external authority (parents) to an internal agency

C. PERSPECTIVES OF PSYCHOANALYTIC THEORY

  1. Genetic
    a. All mental activity (both conscious and unconscious) and behavior are related to all earlier development and experience.
    b. Earlier forms of thinking, wishing, and coping remain available for reemergence (e.g., as in regression).

  2. Dynamic
    a. All behavior expresses a compromise of conflicts among internal, intrapsychic forces.
    b. These forces include biological drives, defenses, affects, conscience, values, and perceptions of self and others.
    c. These forces are largely unconscious.

  3. Economic
    a. There are psychological energies, analogous to physical energy, that originate in biological instinctual drives.
    b. Energies that are derived from sexual and aggressive drives are subject to processes of damming up, transformation, and discharge. For example, biting may be the direct discharge of an oral aggressive drive. Biting or the wish to bite may be inhibited by fear of punishment, the energy dammed up and transformed, resulting perhaps in a symptom such as tooth grinding or an aversion to eating certain foods.

  4. Structural
    a. Mental activity and behavior is grouped by function into stable and enduring structures.
    b. These structures are the id, ego, and superego.

5. Adaptive
   a. Psychological processes and mental development begin from behavior that is genetically programmed to provide for adaptation to the environment (e.g., grasping, sucking, head-turning, and eye-following).
   b. Subsequently, all behavior represents some aspect of adaptation to reality.

D. PSYCHOANALYSIS AS TREATMENT

1. Major characteristic
   a. **Free association.** The patient is instructed to say whatever comes to mind, no matter how insignificant, embarrassing, or irrelevant it may seem. (The reporting of and then the free association to **dreams** is also emphasized.)
   b. The **rationale** rests upon the assumption that the content, plus its associated affect, is significant in and of itself or represents an evasion of or defense against significant content, affect, or both.
   c. Anything that interferes with free association is considered **resistance** and is itself examined for its meaning.

2. Conditions for treatment
   a. The **frequency** of treatment is variable but is usually four or five times per week, in order to establish continuity, to focus on intrapsychic rather than external events, and to enable a full analytic process.
   b. The **length** of treatment must of necessity be considered open-ended, but it usually is thought of in terms of 3 or 4 years.
   c. **Stipulations**
      (1) The patient lies on the couch, facing away from the analyst. The rationale for this position is to minimize external cues and stimuli, especially the facial expressions and body language of the analyst, and to enable both patient and analyst to be as relaxed as possible.
      (2) The patient is responsible for the fee and for missed sessions unless previous arrangements have been made. Any deviation from this understanding and obligation is subject to examination and analysis.

3. Transference and countertransference
   a. **Transference.** The attitudes, feelings, thoughts, and wishes that involve important figures in the past (e.g., parents) are unconsciously reenacted with individuals in the present. In analysis, this process in the patient progressively focuses onto the person of the analyst and is subjected to analysis.
   b. **Countertransference.** This is the same process as transference, but it occurs on the part of the analyst toward the person of the patient. One important reason why one's personal analysis is considered essential to be an analyst is to minimize the influence of countertransference.

4. Techniques
   a. **Clarification** involves obtaining further associations and information about issues and relationships (i.e., connecting the present to the past).
   b. **Confrontation** is pointing out the operation of defenses, resistance, and other unconscious influences on behavior by identifying connections, continuities, inconsistencies, and so forth.
   c. **Interpretation** is a construction to the patient of the unconscious wishes and thoughts and their associated affects as they have been gradually revealed through clarification and confrontation.

5. Defense analysis and working through
   a. **Defense analysis** is based on the rationale that intrapsychic conflict is most apparent through the operation of the ego's defenses, and as the nature and operation of these defenses are repeatedly identified, the conflicts and unconscious wishes will emerge.
   b. **Working through.** This term is used to refer to the process of resolving issues of conflict once their unconscious components have been identified. Working through requires repeated examination of all connections in and ramifications of the personality structure.

II. LEARNING THEORY (BEHAVIORISM)

A. DEFINITION. All behaviors and personality development represent the acquisition and organization (i.e., the learning) of reactions, responses, and patterns. These originate in and are governed by principles of learning that are subject primarily to environmental influences.

   1. The learning theory is particularly associated with the work of **Pavlov** (the conditioned reflex

or **classical conditioning**), **Watson** (behaviorism), and **Thorndike** and **Skinner** [reward and punishment paradigms or **operant conditioning**] (see section II C).

2. Although internal motivations such as hunger and thirst are acknowledged, the focus is on **external events** in determining, maintaining, or eliminating a behavior.

3. What cannot be observed and therefore described and measured is considered unimportant. Such concepts as the unconscious, intrapsychic conflict, and the "disease" or medical model are considered unnecessary, inappropriate, or both.

4. Maladaptive behaviors such as phobias and aggression are "learned" in the same way as adaptive or "normal" behaviors.

B. BASIC CONCEPTS

1. **Learning** is the acquisition, modification, and elimination of behaviors and response patterns occurring in association with environmental conditions. It is the establishment of a connection between a stimulus and a response where no connection existed before.

2. **Stimulus** is a cue, and literally anything, any internal or external event, may act as a stimulus.

3. **Response** is the behavior occurring in association with a stimulus. Responses may be motoric, cognitive, affective, or imaginal.

4. **Motivation** may be provided by innate or primary **needs** (e.g., hunger) provoking the organism to action or may be in the form of **learned motives**. Learned motives are behaviors that were **rewarded** by a reduction in painful tension and are then repeated and refined throughout the life cycle. These include the need for praise and approval as well as dependent behavior.

5. **Reward, reinforcement, and punishment**
   a. **Reward**
      (1) **Primary rewards** satisfy the primary needs of hunger, thirst, and warmth. (The classification of sexuality and human contact is not as clear-cut, but they are considered to be primary needs.)
      (2) **Learned rewards** gratify a **motive** (not a primary need). The rewards may include dependency, power, control, or praise.
   c. **Reinforcement** is a concept similar to that of reward. An association will be established between a stimulus and a response when a primary need or learned motive is gratified. For example, when a child is hungry, he is given food (a primary need is met by a primary reward). The reward **reinforces** the behavior used to indicate or communicate the need. If the child is also given praise for eating, the praise becomes a learned reward and secondary reinforcer.
      (1) **Continuous reinforcement** (presented after **every response**) eventually loses its reward value, and the behavior is **extinguished**.
      (2) **Fixed-ratio reinforcement** (presented after every second or every third response) is better than continuous reinforcement.
      (3) **Variable, intermittent, and unpredictable reinforcement** establishes the strongest, most persistent learning (i.e., the repetition of the behavior). The Las Vegas slot machine is the classic example.
   d. **Punishment** is an aversive, painful, or frustrating event **as defined by the subject** and involves withholding a positive response or reward. Disapproval or criticism may be painful or it may be reinforcing by providing attention. Punishment may eliminate a behavior or simply suppress the behavior.

6. **Stimulus generalization** is a response learned in one situation (e.g., a fear of dogs) that has a tendency to occur in other similar situations (e.g., a fear, then, of all furry or four-footed animals).
   a. The similarity may be determined by a concrete resemblance in size (all small animals), color (all brown animals), shape, and so forth. Generalizations of this type are particularly common in young children.
   b. Similarity may be established by **language**—the most common basis for generalization in humans. For example, the term "dog" might at first stand for only one particular four-footed aminal, then for all four-footed animals, and finally for one class of four-footed animals. This last step is **discriminated generalization**.

7. **Extinction.** A previously learned behavior disappears if the reward is withheld so that the behavior is not reinforced or if the reward is continuous and thereby loses its reinforcing quality.

C. TYPES OF LEARNING

1. **Classical conditioning** [Pavlov and Watson] (see Chapter 5, section III B)
   a. **Definition.** Classical conditioning elicits an inherent (reflex) "nonlearned" behavior (e.g., salivation) in response to a learned stimulus (e.g., a bell or buzzer).
   b. The **unconditioned stimulus** for the inherent behavior of salivation is food, and if each time food is presented a buzzer also sounds, the animal will begin to salivate at the sound of a buzzer.
   c. Any inherent behavior, including fear or anxiety, can be conditioned to appear in response to a learned stimulus.

2. **Operant conditioning** (Skinner and others)
   a. **Definition.** Operant conditioning elicits a new, noninherent or nonreflex behavior in response to a stimulus acting as a reward or as a punishment.
   b. It is a method of shaping or eliciting any desired behavior or extinguishing any undesired behavior by using the principle that **behavior is a function of its consequences**. If a behavior is followed by a rewarding consequence (e.g., attention, praise, or success), that behavior will be reinforced and therefore repeated. Vice versa, if the consequence is aversive or nonrewarding, the behavior will not be repeated (it will be extinguished).
   c. The focus of classical operant conditioning is entirely on **observable behavior** in terms of stimulus and response. Any intervening variables (motivational state, ideation, or fantasy) are largely ignored.
   d. For example, a child's temper tantrum (stimulus) is followed by parental attention, gratification, or both (response), which are rewarding to the child and therefore reinforce the behavior. Ignoring the tantrum or isolating the child for a while is a change in the response, which removes the reinforcement and extinguishes the behavior.

3. **Cognitive–behavioral learning** (Bandura)
   a. By the 1970s, it began to be recognized that there were intervening variables between stimulus and response and that most important behaviors were more complex units.
   b. In order to understand, predict, and influence behavior better, account must be taken of ideation, imagery, and meaning.

4. **Observational and imitational learning** is a further elaboration on the learning theory that tries to take into account the observation that behavioral changes can take place on the basis of observing another's behavior or imitating another's behavior without any external, descriptively observable, reward. This theory introduces the clearly nonoperant (i.e., nonobservable) concept of enhanced self-esteem or an enhanced sense of mastery as the reward or reinforcer.

D. TREATMENT TECHNIQUES.
The treatment techniques related to the learning theory are discussed below in order from the most behaviorally objective to the most subjective.

1. **Aversive conditioning.** An unwanted behavior (such as drinking alcohol) is paired with a noxious or painful stimulus (an electric shock), leading to aversion for alcohol. This conditioning can be extended to the thought of alcohol, the smell of alcohol, and so on.

2. **Positive reinforcement and extinction.** A desired behavior (either spontaneously occurring or taught) is rewarded immediately, at first consistently and then intermittently, and conversely with undesirable behavior.

3. **Systematic desensitization** (Wolpe). This technique is applied especially in the attempt to eliminate phobic behaviors (such as irrational fear and avoidance). In relevant cases, avoidance reduces or eliminates the anxiety and is, therefore, positively reinforcing in a self-defeating way. The task is to **desensitize** the individual to the situation.
   a. The individual is taught how to relax completely, in that relaxation is the opposite of anxiety.
   b. While the individual is relaxed, the sensitized (anxiety-provoking) stimulus is gradually introduced by gradients, so that the link between the stimulus and the anxiety is gradually weakened.
   c. The sensitized stimulus can be introduced by having the individual imagine the anxiety-provoking situation while completely relaxed before the actual stimulus is introduced.

4. **Modeling** is learning new behaviors and overcoming inhibitions to desired behavior by observing someone else carry out the behavior or by imagining others or oneself carrying out the behavior (which is very similar to desensitization). Assertiveness training is a variant of this approach.

III. COGNITIVE THEORY

A. **DEFINITION.** Cognitive theory was developed primarily by the Swiss epistemologist **Jean Piaget** and is based on a combination of naturalistic observation, experiment, and inference.

  1. It is a theoretical framework for understanding **intellectual** (cognitive) **development** from birth through adolescence and maturity.

  2. It describes an **invariable set of stages and sequences, each one building on the former.**

B. **BASIC CONCEPTS**

  1. There are **two classes of reflexes**. The infant is born with:
     a. Classic reflexes
        (1) These inherent reflexes reflect neurologic maturation.
        (2) They are **fixed stimulus–response pathways** that are not significantly altered or influenced by experience.
        (3) Examples of classic reflexes include the Babinski reflex, the knee jerk, the triceps reflex, and cranial nerve reflexes.
     b. Innate reflex patterns (reflex schema)
        (1) These reflex patterns exist at birth, although they require stimulation for activation and stabilization.
        (2) Interactions between the infant and the environment are mediated by the reflex patterns, which are progressively modified as a result of experience (learning) and, with modification, create new possibilities for environmental interaction.
        (3) They provide basic behavioral units for more complex behaviors.
        (4) They are the **foundation for the sensorimotor stage of development** (see section III C 1).
        (5) Examples of innate reflex patterns include the sucking reflex, the grasping reflex, eye-following, and smiling.

  2. **Two basic processes** characterize all interactions between the organism and the environment. These are **assimilation** and **accommodation**.
     a. Assimilation
        (1) External stimuli are registered (experienced) and incorporated into existing reflex patterns (the reflex schema).
        (2) The biological analogy is of aliment taken in and **transformed to conform** to the organism's metabolism rather than altering that metabolism (e.g., as a toxin or poison might do).
        (3) Cognitively, the infant or child incorporates an experience or perception into an already existing understanding or schema.
        (4) Examples
           (a) The infant **assimilates** the nipple into the inborn reflex schema of **sucking** or assimilates an object placed in the palm into the reflex schema of **grasping**.
           (b) At a higher level, by assimilation, the child retains a preexisting comprehension even in the presence of a new or different (albeit similar) perception. For example, if flying objects equal birds, an airplane is identified as a bird, and the concept is assimilated into the preexisting schema.
     b. Accommodation
        (1) A reflex, reflex schema, or conceptual understanding is changed by experience to "fit" the new perception.
        (2) This results in progressive modification of reflex systems to form new behavioral units.
        (3) Examples
           (a) Sucking behavior is repetitively **activated** and modified into different kinds (patterns) of sucking for different objects [e.g., the breast (nutritive) or a pacifier (nonnutritive)].
           (b) Eye-following and smiling reflex patterns are initially activated by a broad range of stimuli, and the infant progressively discriminates the meaningful objects, particularly the mother's voice and face.

  3. **Adaptation** is the result of the **interaction of assimilation and accommodation.**
     a. Reflex behavior "readiness" plus the appropriate environmental stimulation guarantees a progressive interweaving of maturation and experience.
     b. Each interaction involving varying degrees of assimilation and accommodation progresses to an **equilibrium**.
     c. Equilibrium, reestablished by **assimilation and accommodation**, becomes **adaptation**.

4. Origin of action, or **motivation**
   a. The stimulus for an action comes from any **change in the** state of the **organism** (e.g., hunger itself will activate sucking and crying behaviors), a **change in the** state of the **environment, or both**.
   b. This establishes a **disequilibrium** in the reflex schema or, later, in the cognitive system.
   c. Equilibrium is reestablished by assimilation and accommodation.
   d. Reflex systems or schemata are initially preprogrammed to be activated by only appropriate stimulus sets; for example, a nipple does not activate the grasping reflex, a rattle does not activate the sucking schema, and so forth.

C. STAGES OF COGNITIVE DEVELOPMENT

1. Sensorimotor stage. The first 1½ to 2 years of life is divided into **six periods** or substages. These substages occur in an **invariable sequence** of emerging intellectual capacities, reflecting an inexorable and logical progression.
   a. Birth to 1 month is a period of reflex operations.
      (1) There is the exercise, consolidation, and early differentiation of innate reflex patterns, which are survival-oriented.
      (2) These reflex patterns include sucking, grasping, crying, eye-following, and smiling.
      (3) Accommodation occurs to objects without the assumption of any actual awareness (or "knowing") of the objects, thus "reflex."
   b. Two to five months is a period of primary circular reactions.
      (1) Reflex patterns begin to be activated and coordinated with each other.
      (2) If an infant has both his hand and an object in view at the same time, he will grab at what he sees (**coordinating grabbing and seeing**).
      (3) An object is not acted on or searched for if it is not directly available as a sensory stimulus [i.e., objects (including persons) do not have an independent existence].
   c. Five to nine months is a period of secondary circular reactions.
      (1) This is the beginning of intentional activity and interest in the results of that activity (e.g., causing an object to move or swing and then repeating that action on other objects).
      (2) The infant gradually learns the difference between an action and the object, so that objects begin to have a separate existence.
      (3) Truly **imitative behavior** begins.
   d. Nine months to one year is a period of coordination of schemata.
      (1) Means-to-ends behavior begins. The infant will repeat an action to achieve a previously experienced result.
      (2) He demonstrates the capacity to **keep in mind a sense** (or representation) **of an object**, even if it is not directly providing a sensory stimulus.
      (3) Objects have now acquired an independent existence and independent properties.
   e. One year to eighteen months is a period of tertiary circular reactions.
      (1) There is progressive differentiation of objects as independent and, therefore, separate from the self.
      (2) The capacity begins to evolve for concept formation—thinking "about" an action and then acting.
      (3) Therefore, the image or idea of an object or behavior can be held in mind.
      (4) This is the period when language begins. Words represent things.
   f. Eighteen months to two years is the time of invention of new means.
      (1) The capacity evolves for true mental representation of objects; for example, a child will look for an object where it might be, rather than only where it was last seen.
      (2) A clear separation of external events and objects from the self has been achieved. There is now a sense or an image of the self.
      (3) The stage is set for intelligent, conceptual **thought**.

2. Conceptual–representational stage. The age of 2 years to maturity is divided into four periods.
   a. Two to four years is the preoperational period.
      (1) There is expansion (by maturation plus learning) of symbolic capacity and representational thought.
      (2) **Thinking** now serves the purpose that direct action on objects did in an earlier stage. Learning can occur by considering an action and its consequences rather than by the action itself.
   b. Four to seven years is characterized by intuitive thought.
      (1) There is an increasing capacity for **symbolic thought**.
      (2) The child comprehends classes of objects and **classification by similarities and differences** (e.g., how an orange and apple are alike and different: At age 4 the child may say that they are both round, but by age 7 he may say that they are both fruit).

       (3) The child is able to intuit; that is, he can arrive at correct answers without necessarily being able to explain why or how.
- c. **Seven to eleven years** is a time of **concrete operations**. The child acquires **three important capacities for logical thought**.
  - (1) **Reversibility** (e.g., the reciprocal relationship between square and square root, between vapor and water)
  - (2) **Conservation** (e.g., the child sees a round object flattened yet realizes that it is still the same quantity, even though the dimensions are changed; similarly, **changes in** color, location, or other **characteristics do not change the nature or identity of an object**)
  - (3) **Rules of logic** [e.g., the child understands "greater than" and "less than" and understands (not intuits) classification by similarities and differences—albeit, he still requires observation of the objects and cannot yet classify them in a purely mental operation]
- d. **Adolescence to maturity** is characterized by **formal operations**.
  - (1) The individual can reason and arrive at conclusions without the presence of concrete objects and so is **capable of purely abstract, symbolic thought**.
  - (2) The adolescent can conceptualize the past, present, and future as a continuum and consider what might be possible.
  - (3) The individual can conceptualize the meaning of death and the finiteness of existence in final, mature terms. The adolescent so becomes capable of both logical planning about the future and philosophical thought about the meaning of life and about values and ideals.

IV. PSYCHOSOCIAL THEORY

- **A. DEFINITION.** The psychosocial theory is a broad but systematic framework for understanding the patterns and sequences of psychological and social development.
  1. Analogous to embryogenesis, there is an underlying **basic plan for development that sequentially unfolds**.
  2. Different elements of the personality emerge as primary at different times.
  3. This concept is most identified with **Erikson**, who was originally trained as a teacher in the Montessori method.

- **B. BASIC CONCEPTS**
  1. **Stages.** There are **eight stages in the life cycle**, from birth through old age.
     - a. The stages sequentially unfold as an interaction between maturation and unique individual experience.
     - b. Each stage is characterized by a major **developmental task requiring active confrontation and successful resolution**.
  2. **Zone.** For the early developmental stages, there is a primary zone (or part of the body) around which major social interactions occur.
  3. **Mode.** For each zone, there is a primary mode by which transactions take place (e.g., the **oral zone** is characterized by taking in and spitting out modes; the **anal zone** by holding on and letting go modes, and so on).
  4. **Crisis and resolution.** Each stage contains a central combined psychological and social developmental task. Confronting this task is the "crisis" of each stage; its particular resolution determines the nature and resolution of the next stage.

- **C. PSYCHOSOCIAL STAGES AND DEVELOPMENTAL TASKS**
  1. **Oral–sensory stage: birth to 1 year—trust versus mistrust**
     - a. The **mouth is the dominant zone**, although taking in also occurs through seeing, hearing, touching, and grasping.
     - b. The **dominant modes** are **taking in**, feeling stimulated, and feeling filled and satisfied.
     - c. Consistent experience and stimulation via parenting is the condition for developing a sense of **basic trust versus** a sense of **mistrust** by the end of the first year.
  2. **Muscular–anal stage: 1 to 3 years—autonomy versus shame and doubt**
     - a. The **anal zone** is considered to be the somatic model, with maturational acquisition of voluntary sphincter control at about 18 months. More broadly, there is general neuromuscular maturation and increasing motor autonomy, including walking, balance, and language.
     - b. The **dominant** (not exclusive) **mode** is **holding on** and **letting go**.

    c. The child must come to terms with internal drives and the capacity for independence and exploration and with external control and authority.

    d. The child emerges with a healthy sense of **autonomy** and acceptance of limits **versus** control by **shame and doubt**.

3. Locomotor–genital stage: 3 to 6 years—initiative versus guilt

    a. The **genital (phallic) zone** is considered to be the somatic model, around which emerge active, inquisitive, competitive, and comparing behaviors. The aim of these behaviors, especially, is to be like the parents.

    b. The **dominant modes** of behavior in this stage are **intrusive** (phallic) **and competitive** for the boy, **inclusive and competitive** for the girl.

    c. The crisis of this stage is conflict between aggressive, risk-taking, exuberant, competitive behavior, referred to as **initiative**, and the fear of punishment and retaliation internalized as an excessive and inhibiting sense of **guilt**.

4. Latency: 6 to 12 years—industry versus inferiority

    a. There is no dominant somatic zone or mode per se. **Development shifts from** a predominantly **self-centered and intrafamilial focus to** the larger world of formal schooling, other adults, and **peers**.

    b. The child must blend competition with cooperation and aggressiveness with acceptance by the group.

    c. The acquisition of societally valued knowledge and skills by externally (or objectively) measured learning, achievement, and mastery becomes most important.

    d. The outcome is either a realistically based and rewarded sense of **industry** (the sense that one is competent and "can do") or a sense of **inferiority** (a sense of failure and incompetence).

5. Adolescence: 12 to 18 or 20 years—identity versus role diffusion

    a. This stage of development is marked by the dramatic neuroendocrine and physical changes initiated by puberty.

    b. There is a continuation, and at the same time, upheaval, of the previously established sense of self, with the experience of intense new feelings and sexual impulses, a new body image, and strivings for independence.

    c. As adolescence progresses, the individual must consolidate old and new developments into a new sense of identity, including sexual identity and preparation for intimacy, vocational identity, and his role within the family and within the peer group.

    d. The alternative to **identity consolidation** is **role diffusion** (or **role confusion**), which may be based on failure to master earlier stages, uncertain sexual identity, or excessive dependency interfering with healthy independence.

6. Young adulthood: 20 to 30 years—intimacy versus isolation

    a. Independence from the parents is consolidated during young adulthood.

    b. Vocational goals are established as is the **capacity for** both sexual and social **intimacy**. The capacity for intimacy is built on a sufficiently firm sense of basic trust, autonomy, initiative, and, especially, identity, which has developed from previous stages. The alternative is withdrawal, fear of commitment, and an excessive need for control, leading to **emotional isolation**.

7. Adulthood: 30 to 65 years—generativity versus self-absorption or stagnation

    a. For most, adulthood is characterized by the establishment of a family with children, and the role of the individual as a parent emerges.

    b. Abilities and achievements in career and avocation mature.

    c. There is recognition and acceptance that all options are no longer open and that choices are limited, and there is acknowledgment that a balance exists between wish and reality, satisfaction and disappointment.

    d. **The challenge is to maintain a sense of generativity**—a continued sense of productivity and satisfaction with oneself and a sense of responsibility and transmitting that responsibility to the next generation.

    e. This is in contrast to an attempt to preserve or restore an illusion of still being young (**self-absorption**), the inability to let children grow up and become independent, or a sense of emptiness and **stagnation**.

8. Maturity: 65 years and older—ego integrity versus despair

    a. Maturity is a period of **biological decline**, although **with great individual variation**. There are **gradual** decrements in strength, energy, tolerance to stress, and physical health.

    b. For most, maturity is a period that involves retirement, a change in economic circumstances, **the loss of loved ones**, and the realization of one's own mortality. At the same time, many individuals call on physical and emotional reserves to adapt to change, to decline, and especially to loss.

c. Ego integrity involves a sense of pride or satisfaction in one's past and in one's family (children and grandchildren), a sense of mellowness, perspective, equanimity, and wisdom about life and the life cycle.

d. The alternative is **despair**—the depression, lack of self-regard, futility or worthlessness (often confused with organic mental changes or senility) associated with an increase in alcoholism, physical illness, and, in men, suicide.

STUDY QUESTIONS

Directions: Each question below contains five suggested answers. Choose the **one best** response to each question.

1. Defenses have all of the following characteristics EXCEPT

(A) they are unconscious psychological mechanisms

(B) they emerge in a developmental sequence from less to more mature

(C) they play a role in most anxiety disorders

(D) they are observed primarily in patients with psychiatric disorders

(E) they may be episodic or habitual

2. Innate reflex patterns form a basic concept of cognitive developmental theory. All of the following descriptions of innate reflex patterns are accurate EXCEPT

(A) they exist at or shortly after birth

(B) they require stimulation for activation and stabilization

(C) they represent the foundation for the sensorimotor stage of development

(D) they include sucking, grasping, and eye-following

(E) they operate as relatively fixed stimulus–response pathways

3. Which of the following characteristics describes the psychosocial stage of ego integrity versus despair?

(A) The developmental crisis of midlife

(B) A time of generally rapid and consistent decline in tolerance to stress, in physical abilities, and in intellectual capacity

(C) A clash between honesty, values, and ethics and angry hopelessness

(D) Reaffirmation of parenthood and transmitting values to children

(E) None of the above

4. Developmentally based ego functions include all of the following EXCEPT

(A) object relationships

(B) reality testing

(C) signal anxiety

(D) speech and language

(E) defenses

Directions: Each question below contains four suggested answers of which **one or more** is correct. Choose the answer

A if **1, 2, and 3** are correct
B if **1 and 3** are correct
C if **2 and 4** are correct
D if **4** is correct
E if **1, 2, 3, and 4** are correct

5. The stage of intimacy versus isolation has which of the following characteristics?

(1) It is associated chronologically with mid-adolescence

(2) The capacity to establish close interpersonal relationships is developed

(3) If this stage is not successfully resolved, it will lead to a sense of role diffusion and a confused sense of identity

(4) It is followed by the stage of generativity versus stagnation

6. As an explanation for behavior, traditional learning theory can be described as proposing that

(1) behavior is best understood as an interaction between external events and inner subjective states

(2) maladaptive behaviors are "learned" in the same way (or by the same rules) as adaptive behaviors

(3) all needs that motivate behavior are learned through experience

(4) all behavior is responsive to and modifiable by external events

7. A professional toastmaster becomes terrified of speaking in public. He cancels his speaking engagements, fearing forgetting and embarrassment. He seeks treatment and is first taught how to relax completely and then while relaxed to imagine going to a luncheon, then sitting on the platform, then rising to introduce guests, and so forth. Statements that can be made about this situation include

(1) the patient stopping his speaking activities acts as a positive reinforcement
(2) the purpose of the relaxation part of the therapy is to divert the patient so that he will accept the instructions
(3) this overall approach is known as systematic desensitization
(4) this approach combines aversive conditioning and positive reinforcement

8. The latency stage of development in psychosocial theory can be described as

(1) the stage of industry versus inferiority
(2) somatically involved with "letting go"
(3) a time of acquisition of culturally valued knowledge and skills
(4) the focus shifting from socialization with peers to working out intrafamilial relationships

9. The structural model is a concept in psychoanalytic theory that refers to

(1) both conscious and unconscious activities within the mind
(2) the organization of mental functions that are related to each other
(3) the terms ego, superego, and id
(4) the organization of instinctual drives by their aims and objects

Directions: The group of questions below consists of lettered choices followed by several numbered items. For each numbered item select the **one** lettered choice with which it is **most** closely associated. Each lettered choice may be used once, more than once, or not at all.

Questions 10–14

For each of the definitions listed below, select the defense mechanism being described.

(A) Denial
(B) Isolation of affect
(C) Rationalization
(D) Reaction formation
(E) Repression

10. The unconscious exclusion from awareness of urges, thoughts, wishes, or feelings

11. The development of an attitude opposite the attitude in the unconscious to avoid awareness of the unacceptable feeling

12. The distortion of external reality by altering perception

13. The intrapsychic separation of a thought from its otherwise unacceptable or painful feeling

14. The substitution of an acceptable motive to conceal one that is less acceptable

ANSWERS AND EXPLANATIONS

1. The answer is D. (*I B 5*) Defenses are, by definition, unconscious mechanisms, and they function to ward off anxiety and to maintain a sense of well-being. They operate in all individuals and are as much a part of healthy or normal personalities as they are of disordered personalities. They emerge in a developmental sequence from less to more mature and are considered to be an essential component of symptom formation.

2. The answer is E. (*III B 1*) There are two types of reflexes identified in cognitive developmental theory: classic reflexes and innate reflex patterns. Classic reflexes are relatively fixed stimulus–response pathways that involve neurologic maturation, and they are relatively unable to be modified by experience or learning. Examples include the Babinski reflex, the knee jerk, the triceps reflex, and cranial nerve reflexes. Innate reflex patterns, on the other hand, form the basis for initial interactions with the environment and are significantly modified by experience and learning.

3. The answer is E. (*IV C 7–8*) The stage of ego integrity versus despair is associated with older age and maturity, not with midlife (generativity). This is a time of gradual and very variable decrements in physiologic and intellectual status. It is a time of satisfaction with one's life and family versus a sense of failure, futility, and lack of pride (despair). Reaffirmation of self and transmitting values to the next generation is characteristic of the previous stage of generativity.

4. The answer is D. (*I B 6*) Developmentally based ego functions are individually shaped (learned) out of the combination of maturation and experience. Maturational function, such as sensory development, proceeds in a relatively similar fashion for each individual, but reality testing combines sensory experience, memory, perception, and personal experience, especially with the parents. Speech and language are maturationally based and are dependent primarily on neurologic integrity.

5. The answer is C (2, 4). (*IV C 6*) The stage of intimacy versus isolation is associated chronologically with young adulthood, occurring after the stage of identity formation associated with adolescence. The major task during this stage is development and consolidation of the capacity to establish close or intimate relationships. The stage of intimacy versus isolation precedes the adult stage, in which generativity is the major task.

6. The answer is C (2, 4). (*II A*) Traditional learning theory (classical and operant conditioning) emphasizes observable and quantifiable behavior and the external response contingencies that influence that behavior. Inner subjective states are considered to be unimportant or irrelevant in this stimulus–response paradigm. Learning theory recognizes two classes of needs: primary needs such as hunger, thirst, and sex, which are innate and not learned, and learned needs such as those for attention, praise, control, and dependency.

7. The answer is B (1, 3). (*II D 3*) When the toastmaster stopped his speaking activities, he relieved his anxiety, which allowed him to feel better. Therefore, stopping his speaking activities is a positive reinforcement to his phobic avoidance. The purpose of the relaxation training is to induce a state that is the opposite of and incompatible with anxiety, and in that state the patient is to imagine, in gradients, the situation associated with his anxiety. Aversive conditioning is the association of a painful stimulus with the undesirable behavior and does not apply in this situation.

8. The answer is B (1, 3). (*IV C 4*) The latency stage of psychosocial development (age 6 to 12 years) is described by Erikson as the stage of industry versus inferiority. The stage follows those of the major developmental tasks associated with the oral, anal, and phallic zones, but it is not identified with a dominant somatic zone itself. The child's focus shifts from intrafamilial relationships to the extrafamilial world of school, peers, and other adults (e.g., teachers).

9. The answer is A (1, 2, 3). (*I B 6*) Structural theory organizes the functions of the mind into ego, superego, and id as related activities that are reasonably stable over time. The ego is thought of as the executive, adaptive functions, the superego as the functions of conscience and ego-ideal (the ideal self), and the id as the source of drives and needs, the objects of which would be part of ego functions. Activities of the ego and superego include both conscious and unconscious components.

10–14. The answers are: 10-E, 11-D, 12-A, 13-B, 14-C. (*I B 5*) Repression is an automatic, unconscious defense whereby unacceptable urges, thoughts, wishes, or feelings are kept from awareness.

Reaction formation is the development of the opposite of an unconscious attitude in order to avoid awareness of the unacceptable attitude or interest. For example, excessive affection may be felt toward someone who is very hostile.

Denial, the act of blocking from awareness unacceptable information or perceptions, is considered to be a primitive or immature defense mechanism because it involves a distortion of reality.

Isolation of affect is the unconscious separation of thought from its otherwise painful feeling. Either the feeling and thought are excluded from the awareness or the feeling may be attributed to a different thought altogether.

Rationalization is the substitution of an acceptable motive for attitudes or behavior for an unacceptable motive.

7
The Life Cycle
James H. Egan

I. DEFINITION OF TERMS

A. **THE LIFE CYCLE** is best understood within the context of the biopsychosocial model (see Chapter 11, section I C), which proposes that all behavior can be viewed as an interaction among biological, psychological, and sociocultural variables.

B. **GROWTH** refers to an increase in physical size.

C. **MATURATION** is the biologically based, phylogenetically determined, sequential unfolding of forms and functions (e.g., motor and sensory functions, language, and cognition).

D. **DEVELOPMENT** can be defined as the acquisition of capacities and functions that evolve through experiences in one's environment as these experiences influence elements provided by maturation.

II. INFANCY TO TODDLER

A. BIOLOGICAL FACTORS

1. **Prenatal and postnatal influences**
   a. **Genetic factors** play a prominent role in determining the biological potential of a fetus. The process of development is a sequential unfolding of events that is genetically determined, as are certain disorders and conditions.
      (1) In roughly 40% of children with an attention deficit disorder (ADD), hereditary factors are the basis for the disorder.
      (2) Other common genetically determined conditions include Down syndrome (trisomy 21), Klinefelter syndrome (XXY), and the fragile X syndrome.
   b. **Response to sensory stimulation** in utero has been demonstrated by fetal monitoring. The fetus responds to stimuli with certain reflex patterns such as sucking and kicking, indicating that conditioned learning may actually begin in utero.
   c. **Sex and survival factors.** There are roughly 160 male conceptions for each 100 female conceptions; however, at birth there is only a very small excess of males to females. Thus, from a significant excess of male conceptions, one-third do not eventuate in live births. While the exact reasons for these findings presently are not understood, certain facts are clear.
      (1) Some of the males who survive are at considerable risk for some degree of brain dysfunction.
      (2) Approximately 5% of middle-class males and 10% of lower-class males will have ADD. The male-to-female ratio is roughly 10:1.
   d. **Gestational age and weight at birth** are predictors of outcome. It is now clear that infants with a low weight for gestational date fare worse than infants who are the expected weight for gestational age. The implication is of inadequate fetal nutrition in utero that could be due to poor maternal health and nutrition or inadequate placental functioning.
   e. **Perinatal factors** might compromise the biological endowment in a variety of ways. Among these are low birth weight premature infants, low weight for date infants, postmaturity, eclampsia, or serious dystocia.

2. **Neonatal capacities**
   a. At birth, the infant is preadapted to be cared for by the mother by the presence of **attachment behaviors**. Initial attachment behaviors (e.g., crying and clinging) increase the likelihood of maternal care and assist the infant in attaching to the mother.

b. The neonate possesses a number of innate, simple reflexes.

(1) Moro's reflex, or **startle reflex**, involves the flexion of the extremities as a response to sudden stimulation. Similar reflexes include an innate pupillary reflex to light stimulation by closing the eyelids.

(2) The **palmar grasp reflex** is less adaptive, involving the infant's reaction to a finger placed in his palm by a contraction, grasping, and clinging response.

(3) The **rooting and sucking reflexes** both aid in the feeding of the infant. The rooting reflex is the response of the infant to a stroke of the cheek by turning toward the touch. If something is placed into the infant's mouth, he will respond by sucking it.

(4) The **Babinski reflex** is normal in neonates, involving the hyperextension and spreading apart of the toes in response to stroking the sole of the foot. The normal adult response to this stimulus is a closing down of the toes; the Babinski reflex in an adult is an indicator of neurologic damage.

3. The motor, vocal, and sensory development sequences of the infant are listed in Table 7-1.

4. Cognitive maturation. By age 18 to 24 months, the child is capable of elementary trial-and-error reasoning. For example, the child will attempt to place a square object into the square opening of a form box after trying to insert it into the circular or triangular opening.

B. PSYCHOLOGICAL AND SOCIAL DEVELOPMENT

1. The **principal psychological** task of the first year of life is the formation of an **intimate differentiated attachment** to the mother or caregiver. This process is impeded, for example, when there is a multiplicity of caretakers, as occurs in institutionally reared children or when the mother is emotionally unavailable due, for example, to depression or serious deficits in her own early development. Failure on the part of the infant to develop this specific early attachment may result in later defects in the capacity for empathy and for close, warm, reciprocal relationships.

2. The **smile** develops from an innate reflex response at birth ("endogenous smiling") to a response to the form of a face at age 8 weeks ("exogenous smiling") to a preferential social smile specifically in response to the mother's face at 12 to 16 weeks. This social smile is an early marker of the beginning development of a specific, differentiated relationship, as are the

Table 7-1. Development Sequences

Development	Age	Description
Motor	1 month	Lifting the head up from the prone position
	2 months	Lifting the chest up from the prone position
	4 months	Sitting with support
	7 months	Sitting without support
	8 months	Standing without support
	10 months	Creeping
	11 months	Walking when led by the hand
	13 months	Climbing stairs
	15 months	Adept at independent locomotion
Vocal	At birth	Crying
	6–8 weeks	Cooing, the precursor to later babble and speech
	2 months	Development of 7 phonemes*
	6 months	Development of 12 phonemes
	12 months	Development of 18 phonemes; words like "mama" and "dada" emerge
	18 months	50 words
	3 years	Excess of 100 words
	4 years	Style of adult language is established
Sensory	At birth	Infant can discriminate sound and visually follow a light; capacity for visual fixation within several hours after birth
	10 days	Infants can respond differentially to the smell of mother versus nonmother
	4 months	Infant can fully accommodate visually; visual fixation is increased if the pattern is complex and especially if it resembles the human face

*There are 35 phonemes (distinct sounds) in adult American speech.

preferential vocalization, visual pursuit, and anticipatory gesturing of the 5-month-old infant in the presence of the mother.

3. **Stranger anxiety**, commencing when the infant is between age 7 and 9 months, is yet another marker of the attachment process, in which the infant becomes observably distressed when presented with the face of an individual who is not the mother. In addition to reacting to the presence of someone other than the mother, the infant is reacting to the mother's absence.
   a. The appearance of stranger anxiety suggests that the infant now has the beginning cognitive capacity to maintain or recall a mental picture (representation) of the mother (or others), even when she is not present. The capacity to maintain representations in the absence of current stimuli is called **object permanence**.
   b. **Anaclitic depression** is the name given by Spitz to the reaction of apathy, emotional withdrawal, and a falling developmental quotient that occurs in the infant if separated from the mother when he is between 6 and 12 months of age.

4. Margaret Mahler has proposed a useful description of the sequential development of **object relations** within the framework of psychoanalytic theory.
   a. From 0 to 1 month is a period of relatively little self-aware interaction with the environment and is referred to as the stage of **"normal autism."**
   b. From 2 to 4 months is a period of **symbiotic development** between the mother and infant, referring to the inference of a sense of "oneness" and mutuality between them before there is any sense that infant and mother are separate individuals.
   c. From 5 to 9 months is a period of **differentiation**, a dim but increasing sense of awareness of the mother as a separate entity. One frequently sees what is called a "customs inspection" of the mother as the child explores and examines her eyes, mouth, and nose and pulls at her hair.
   d. From 10 to 16 months is the **practicing phase**—locomotion permits the child to move away from the mother and then come back to her as a home base for emotional refueling. During this time, the toddler is relatively unaware of the dangers of physical injury and moves about with exuberance.
   e. From 18 to 36 months is the **rapprochement subphase**. It is inferred that during this time the child's sense of invulnerability and omnipotence is undercut by the increasing recognition that the mother is not and will not always be there to protect and nurture him.
      (1) **Separation anxiety** reaches its peak at 18 months. The rapprochement crisis is manifested by anxiety and staying close to or clinging to the mother (shadowing and darting away).
      (2) As the psychological separation of mother and child is accomplished, the child develops a sense of being a distinct entity. This is the achievement of **individuation**.

5. When a child between the ages of 12 and 30 months is subject to maternal deprivation or separation, a sequence of protest, despair, and detachment is the hallmark of the child's reaction.
   a. First, the child protests (e.g., crying, fretting, and irritability) the mother's absence for 1 or 2 days.
   b. The child then appears subdued and quietly depressed (i.e., demonstrating despair).
   c. If the mother and child are not united in 3 to 4 weeks, the child becomes **detached**.

6. Further aspects of psychological development between age 18 months and 3 years include the following.
   a. **Play**
      (1) Initially, play has a **compensatory or self-soothing function** that provides for tension reduction and pleasure. From this evolves the pleasure of playing as **a way of mastering functions**. The 9-month-old infant plays "peekaboo" and later "hide-and-seek" as a means of mastering the anxiety associated with separation and loss. The 18-month-old child will "play" for hours practicing going up or down stairs.
      (2) **Doll play** is very common in the toddler. The child feeds and takes care of the dolls as he has seen the mother and father do for him. Such **dramatic play** is conspicuous in the toddler as the child puts on the parents' clothing and pretends to be "grown up" and plays house with other children. At other times the child simply pretends to be doing what the parents do (e.g., bathing, shaving, cooking, and cutting the grass).
   b. **Autonomy and self-awareness**
      (1) Between 18 and 36 months the child increasingly attempts to separate psychologically from the mother.
         (a) As a means of achieving a greater sense of autonomy, the child frequently manifests noncompliant behaviors, and resists parental authority. Saying "no" or "I'll do it my way" enhances a subjective sense of power and autonomy in the toddler.
         (b) Virtually all aspects of life may be invaded by this process, including refusal to eat,

sleep, or eliminate at parental request. Collectively these conflicts are referred to as "**the terrible twos**." When these conflicts are severe, disorders of conduct, sleeping, eating, or eliminating may develop.

(2) By 18 months of age, a relatively stable **core gender identity** (i.e., the sense of being a boy or girl) is established through experiences and expectations of what is masculine and what is feminine. Between 18 and 36 months, there is an increasing sense of self as a separate individual within the confines of the family and social world.

C. SOCIOCULTURAL FACTORS

1. Many powerful economic and sociocultural forces influence and shape the developmental process. It is well-known, for example, that the rate of **psychiatric disorders** is roughly twice as high in inner cities as it is in rural areas.

2. Similarly, the frequency of **ADD** is twice as high in low-income families as it is in middle-class families. This most likely reflects differences in the prenatal nutritional status of the mothers and differences in the quality of obstetrical care.

3. There is an increased risk of **obstetrical complications** in very young, often poor, mothers as well as in "the elderly primagravida," who is often in the upper middle class. The inverse relationship between social class and reproductive complications has been demonstrated by Pasamanick and Knoblock.

4. **Psychosocial, or sociocultural, retardation** is a term applied to the deficient language, speech, and cognitive skills associated with a relative deficiency in early adequate stimulation, occurring more often in those from the lower socioeconomic class.

5. For a different perspective, it is instructive to look at two prominent developmental experiences in infancy and early childhood from the vantage point of social class.
   a. In terms of oral training (i.e., weaning from breast or bottle to cup), there are significant class differences. Typically, the middle-class infant is weaned at about 1 year of age, while many lower-class children still have bottles at 3 to 4 years of age.
   b. In regard to anal (toilet) training, the differences along class lines are equally striking. Most middle-class children go through toilet training between 18 months and 3 years of age, while many children from disadvantaged homes have completed bowel training by 14 months of age.

III. CHILDHOOD.
The years in a child's life from age 3 years to puberty are a period of major change, with a shift of emphasis from a central focus on the child's relationship with the mother, to the child's relationship with both parents, to socialization with the child's peers.

A. BIOLOGICAL AND MATURATIONAL FACTORS

1. **Physical growth**
   a. At age 3 years, the average boy is 38 inches tall and weighs 33 pounds; the average girl at this age is 37 inches tall and weighs 32 pounds.
   b. At age 6 years, the average child is 46 inches tall and weighs 48 pounds, and the brain has reached 90% of its adult weight.
   c. At age 9 years, the average child is about 55 inches tall.

2. **Motor development**
   a. At age 2 years, a child can reproduce a circle; at 3 years, a cross; at 5 years, a square, and at 7 years, a diamond.
   b. At age 3 years, a child can walk up stairs unaided, stand on one foot, and build a tower of nine or ten cubes.

3. **Speech and language development** proceeds at a prodigious rate. Between ages 3 and 5 years, the average child learns two new words per day.

4. **Cognitive maturation** continues from the sensory motor stage involving object permanence (see section II B 3 a, 4) to involve two further stages during childhood: the preoperational and concrete operational stages.
   a. **The preoperational stage** (age 2 to 7 years) is marked by a transition from a focus on action and sensation to that of thought. Several characteristics distinguish this cognitive stage.
      (1) **Symbolic function** first appears in this stage, with a child learning that words are symbols and objects are symbols (e.g., the word "doll" is a symbol for the object that is a doll, and the object that is a doll is a symbol for a baby).
      (2) **Egocentrism** is a feature of the preoperational stage whereby the child is unable to put himself in the place of someone else. A facet of egocentrism is that children can con-

ceive of a thing only occupying one class at a time (e.g., the child learns to group objects by color or shape, but not by both).

(3) Animism is a belief by the child that every moving object is alive and has emotional feelings and thoughts, including such objects as feces, which has implications for toilet training children at this age (i.e., a child may not want to give up something he perceives as alive inside him).

(4) Artificialism is a belief whereby the preoperational child believes that all things are made by humans and for humans, with everything having a specific use. Children can perform certain types of reasoning only with visual, not verbal, representation. In addition, children believe that all questions have answers, and that adults know those answers.

(5) Preoperational children do not have any concept of the ability to **conserve**; that is, the child can comprehend only one property or one dimension of an object at a time. If an object changes in shape, such as Piaget's classic example of clay, the child cannot comprehend that the object "conserves" its original mass or volume.

(6) The preoperational child is unable to distinguish between **physical** and **psychological causality**; thus, a child may believe that an illness is punishment for having done or thought something wrong.

b. The concrete operational stage (age 7 to 11 years) is marked by the ability of the child to learn and master many of the characteristics of the preoperational stage.

(1) The capacity for **reversibility** is understood by the concrete operational child. As a result of learning that processes can be reversed mentally, the child can now grasp the concept of conservation (e.g., understanding volume and mass).

(2) The child is now able to put himself in the place of someone else. In addition, the child can comprehend multiple classifications, as well as two or more classes occurring simultaneously. As a result, the child can order objects serially along a dimension, such as increasing size from smallest to largest.

B. PSYCHOLOGICAL AND SOCIAL DEVELOPMENT

1. Psychosexual development

a. Following the establishment of an emotionally positive attachment, a sense of autonomy, and a sense of self, the child enters the **phallic (oedipal) stage** (age 3 to 6 years) of development, characterized by the **Oedipus complex** (see Chapter 6, section I B 4 c).

(1) The phallic stage is marked by a primary interest in the genitals as the focus of pleasure and concern as manifested by masturbation, exhibitionism, and curiosity.

(2) The **Oedipus complex involves the triadic relationship among the father, mother, and child** in which the child typically wishes to have sole possession of the parent of the opposite sex.

(3) As a consequence, this complex of feelings leads to **oedipal conflict**, in which the child feels intense rivalry with the parent of the same sex and fears retaliation, usually in terms of bodily damage. This fear in the boy is called **castration anxiety**. In the girl, the fear is often loss of love.

(4) Under the impetus of this anxiety, the Oedipus complex passes at about age 6 years. The child relinquishes the desire for the parent of the opposite sex and resolves to grow up to be like the parent of the same sex. The child also identifies with the authority of the parent, with the consequent development of an internalized conscience (or **superego**).

b. Latency is the psychoanalytic term applied to the period between the resolution of the oedipal conflict and the onset of puberty.

(1) It is a period characterized by a strict conscience and strong defenses such as reaction formation (as in "I hate girls"), identification (as in superheroes), and displacement (as in competition through involvement on a Little League team instead of with the father).

(2) Fantasies during latency are common. In the "family romance" fantasy the child imagines that he is not the product of his own (devalued) parents, but that his "real" parents are ideal, rich, and powerful. The fantasy of an "imaginary companion" may be an individual or animal or a twin who provides companionship, love, and attention.

2. Play is an important part of the young child's world.

a. At about age 3 to 4 years, **role play** becomes quite prominent, with the child usually preferring to be a powerful adult or ironically the feared monster of his nightmares or fantasies. This kind of play can be seen as a type of mastery.

b. When observing young children at play in a group, one is impressed at the degree to which each child functions in a manner that is essentially autonomous. This is called **parallel play**. Subsequently the child develops the capacity for interactional, or reciprocal, activity that is called **cooperative play**.

    c. The young school-aged child usually engages in group games ranging from hide-and-seek and cowboys and indians to board games or playing on an athletic team. These activities provide bodily mastery, self-confidence, and an expanded opportunity for peer relationships, as well as providing an opportunity for sublimated competitiveness. In addition, these activities provide opportunities to experience and hopefully resolve anxieties concerning winning and losing.

3. Social development
    a. At age 3 years, nursery school, day-care experiences, play groups, and birthday parties help the preschool child to expand his social development and enlarge the universe of people important to him.
    b. Entry into school continues this in a profound and dramatic way.
      (1) The child's social world is enlarged with the consequent impact of peer relationships ("best friends") and entry into group relationships, especially of the same sex.
      (2) In addition, school is the societally prescribed experience that prepares the young ultimately to fulfill their roles as adults.

IV. ADOLESCENCE

A. BIOLOGICAL FACTORS

1. Puberty is the name given to the biological changes that occur in early adolescence, which include the sexual changes of genital enlargement, pubic and axillary hair, breast development and menarche in girls, and semen production in boys. Puberty generally occurs between ages 10½ and 12½ years for girls and between ages 12 and 14½ years for boys. Although biologically based, these phenomena have profound psychological consequences.

2. Cognitive development reaches its final stage, the **formal operational stage** (age 11 years and older).
    a. Most adolescents attain the capacity for **abstract and propositional thinking** about multiple variables, are capable of looking at a problem from multiple points of view, and can analyze each variable independently and as part of a whole. For example, the adolescent can look at 20 different chairs and see the aspect of how they are all alike. At the same time, he can distinguish the ways in which each chair is different.
    b. In addition, abstract concepts of truth or virtue are subject to discussion and analysis.
    c. Egocentrism changes in form, with the adolescent believing that he is the center of attention and constantly under observation by others.

B. PSYCHOLOGICAL FACTORS

1. Developmental tasks
    a. Psychological separation from one's parents is a life-long process, but there is often a resurgence of struggles for autonomy in early adolescence. These struggles frequently present as parent–adolescent conflicts over grooming, household chores, homework, and choice of friends. A serious and pathological example of the conflict over dependency versus autonomy is seen in the discord over eating in anorexia nervosa.
    b. The consolidation of one's sense of self is a major developmental task during adolescence. Erikson has referred to this process as the formation of **ego identity**. As a part of this process the adolescent's sense of the ideal self undergoes considerable modification. This change frequently reflects values acquired from one's peers and is often at variance with the parental ideals. Frequently this leads to conflict between the adolescent and his parents. The result is an emergence of the adolescent as distinct and thus separate from his parents.
    c. The development of the capacity for love relationships outside of the family is an important aspect of late adolescence. It usually begins with dating or crushes in midadolescence and progresses toward more mature love relationships by late adolescence.
    d. Control of impulses, especially sexual and aggressive ones, is an important milestone of a healthy adolescence. Severe over- or undercontrol of sexual and aggressive impulses generally reflects a disturbance in one or all of the preceding developmental tasks.

2. Adolescent turmoil. It was once commonly thought that extreme behavioral and emotional shifts reflect the normal tumult of adolescence. Thus, suicide attempts, sexual promiscuity, substance abuse, and academic failure could be understood as essentially a reaction to the process of adolescence and were called **adolescent turmoil** or an **adjustment reaction to adolescence**. Empiric studies of normal adolescents, however, did not support this view. Normal adolescents, in general, do not show serious emotional or behavioral changes, and these behaviors are now better understood as evidence of moderate to severe disorders.

C. SOCIOCULTURAL FACTORS

1. To a very large degree, adolescence as a developmental stage is socioculturally determined. In general, the more highly developed (industrialized) a culture is, the longer the adolescence.

2. In underdeveloped cultures, the young person at or around the time of puberty begins to join the adults of the same sex in performing those tasks that the culture assigns to them. Thus, entry into the adult world begins quite early. Marriage and procreation tend to follow shortly thereafter, so that by 14 to 15 years of age, most young people have entered the world of the adult. There is very little in the way of a true adolescence as it is understood in the United States.

3. Social class significantly determines the nature of middle and late adolescence. In lower-class families, formal education frequently ends with graduation from high school or, in some instances, earlier. Young people from these backgrounds rather regularly join the work force by 16, 17, or 18 years of age. Marriage and child rearing are frequently undertaken at the same time. Persons from the middle and upper-middle classes generally anticipate formal post secondary education. For them, adolescence is prolonged until 22, 25, or even 26 years of age. Some authorities have called this extended period of dependence on the family of origin the stage of **youth**.

V. ADULTHOOD

A. EARLY ADULTHOOD is considered as age 20 to 40 years.

1. **Biological factors.** During this time, the body reaches its physical, reproductive, and cognitive peaks. Adult development is not as concerned with the acquisition of new capacities as it is with the use to which available capacities are put.

2. **Psychological factors.** The principal developmental tasks of this stage include the following.
   a. **Development of the capacity for intimacy** in a loving, sexually satisfying relationship. From this emerges the hallmark of this adult phase, namely parenthood. Parenthood is dramatically different at 25 years of age than at 55 or 65 years of age. Parenthood involves the reactivation of prior conflicts and dynamics from one's family of origin. Issues of autonomy and dependency as well as triangular oedipal themes reemerge.
      (1) Parenthood as a developmental phase permanently alters the life of the individual and also the structure of the marital relationship. Children provide parents with an opportunity to resolve some lingering conflicts from their own childhoods. Parenthood permits people to provide alternative experiences for their own children, with whom they can then identify, thereby healing some wounds, hurts, or frustrations. This is commonly reflected when the child is given the piano or tennis lessons that the parent never received.
      (2) Healthy families are those who are able to adjust continuously to the shifting demands of an ever-changing family. The children of effective parents are able to develop and emerge from the family with surprisingly little strife. These families are characterized by parents who convey a clear set of expectations to the children and who thereby demonstrate that the parents (not the children) are flexibly in charge of the family.
      (3) Separation and divorce are increasingly common in many American families. People who come from families of divorce are much more likely to divorce than those who have not. People who lack psychological flexibility in the give-and-take of marriage may find the strains of marriage and parenthood too overwhelming and thus need to separate or divorce.
   b. **Career.** For men and increasingly for women, adult identity is influenced by the work one does. The competing demands for time and energy among the roles of parent, spouse, and worker are frequently a source of stress at this stage of development.

3. **Sociocultural factors.** Social class plays a pivotal role in the structure of adult development.
   a. Offspring of middle- and upper-class families tend to postpone marriage and parenthood, while continuing education for a number of years (e.g., the study of medicine).
   b. In lower-class families, formal education frequently ends with high school, whereupon the adolescent begins his vocational life. The responsibilities of marriage and parenthood may be undertaken shortly thereafter.

B. MIDDLE ADULTHOOD spans from age 40 to 60 years.

1. **Biological factors.** The aging process plays a major role in shaping the psychological develop-

ment of middle adulthood. Aspects of illness and dying begin to emerge as inescapable and inevitable facets of this phase of the life cycle.

   a. The onset of menopause, occurring between the ages of 40 and 53 years, marks the end of the reproductive life of women as ovarian function is lost and menstruation ceases.

   (1) Symptoms may include irregular bleeding, vasomotor imbalances ("hot flashes"), and sweats, with decreases in estrogen secretion and changes in organic and metabolic functions.

   (2) Hormone replacement therapy is controversial in the treatment of postmenopausal women. While its benefits include relief of symptoms of vaginal atrophy and vasomotor imbalances as well as retardation of bone loss, its hazards include an increased risk of uterine endometrial carcinoma.

   (3) While menopause is a biological event, the most frequent effects are psychological. Confronted with the end of their reproductive life, women may experience periods of anxiety and depression as they appraise prior and future stages of their lives and examine life choices that they have made.

   b. In men, there is no specific biological equivalent to menopause. Hormone levels in men only slightly decrease during middle adulthood. Declining muscle strength and endurance can be preserved with regular exercise.

2. Psychological factors

   a. The **midlife crisis** refers to a dramatic change in commitment to career and spouse, and it is generally accompanied by self-doubt, stress, anxiety, agitation, or depression. Causes of midlife crisis include debilitating personal illness, death of a spouse, the responsibility of caring for an elderly parent, job loss or lack of career advancement, or dependent adult children.

   b. A less severe form is the "**midlife transition**," which occurs in 80% of individuals in their forties. A discrepancy between life aspirations and expectations (e.g., career and family) and actual events, coupled with the sense of the finiteness of time, serve to generate the midlife crisis or transition.

   c. Relationships with children change. The growth of one's children into autonomous adults requires the relinquishment of control over them, which may cause a sense of impotence or powerlessness and consequent resentment.

   d. This stage of life frequently requires that one also deal with the declining health and the death of one's own parents. Subtle or abrupt changes accompany the increasing awareness of and perhaps the first personal contact with death, including fears regarding one's own death. Time becomes viewed more in terms of how much is left as opposed to the time since birth.

   e. Pleasure is also derived from being in the middle generation. As children become autonomous, parenting responsibilities may diminish, allowing more or new commitment to marital and other relationships. Advantages of wisdom, experience, rank, and even power are appreciated more fully.

VI. LATER ADULTHOOD AND OLD AGE is considered as age 60 years and over.

A. BIOLOGICAL FACTORS. Gradually diminishing physical and cognitive capacities combine with the increased likelihood of acute and chronic illness as individuals enter late adulthood and face old age. The degree of these occurrences, however, is not necessarily uniform.

1. The **pathological process of aging** is influenced by numerous factors (e.g., genetics, nutrition, and environmental conditions) that produce physical changes, including the following.

   a. Loss of tissue elasticity is most commonly manifested as wrinkling of the skin.

   b. Postural changes related to loss of elasticity and bone loss may become pronounced as bones become brittle and actual shrinking in height occurs.

   c. Deficits in auditory and visual capacities often become prominent due to neural and non-neural changes. Compensation for such losses is possible to varying degrees.

2. Cognitive capacities such as recall and new learning may be diminished; however, not every individual demonstrates appreciable loss of mental ability. Diminutions may be affected by level of intelligence, lack of motivation, disuse, or disease but not necessarily by brain function failure.

3. While there is a **general decline in physical function**, physical incapacitation is not an inevitable consequence of aging. For example, the frequency and intensity of sexual activity in men and women diminish with age, but interest and participation in sexual activity continue in individuals even in their nineties.

B. PSYCHOLOGICAL FACTORS

1. **Retirement** is a nodal point in development, a time when an individual may feel that he is of no use anymore. Frequently, a reduction in income occurs with retirement, with increased anxiety about paying for future medical or nursing care.

2. With the prospect of dying increasingly becoming a reality, individuals are confronted with an appraisal of the life that they have lived. If they feel that they have lived a good moral life, they may emerge from that appraisal with a reaffirming sense of integrity. On the other hand, a negative evaluation may result in despair (Erikson).

3. With better medical care, individuals are living longer, healthier, and more productive lives than in the past. Older men are generally married, whereas the majority of older women are widows due to the higher death and remarriage rate for men. Interestingly, only 20% of older individuals will ever require institutional care, despite a frequent concern of the elderly that they will become dependent or senile.

C. SOCIOCULTURAL FACTORS.
An increasing percentage of the population is 65 years and older. As the postwar baby boom generation reaches retirement, over 20% of the total population will be older than age 65.

1. Erikson refers to the last stage of psychosocial development in the life cycle as **ego identity versus despair**. Ego identity is maintained if the life one has lived and continues to live is viewed as satisfying and fulfilling. Individuals who fail to achieve a final integration of the choices and events in their lives will suffer from despair.

2. The traditional youth-oriented society is becoming increasingly old-age conscious. Senior citizens' groups have brought political and social issues to the attention of the public in combating prejudicial and stereotypical attitudes about old age.

3. As older individuals enjoy healthier, longer lives, the retirement years may be the most pleasurable and rewarding of the life cycle if not complicated by poverty, illness, or unresolved loneliness.

VII. DEATH AND DYING

A. CHILD'S PERSPECTIVE

1. A child's response to death is based on his level of awareness. An awareness of the meaning of death becomes more concrete with developing comprehension abilities.
   a. Children younger than age 5 years tend to view death as abandonment. When they do think about death, they fail to appreciate its finality and irreversibility. They may be heard to say, "When grandma comes back to life. . ." or "When grandma comes to visit. . ." even when told explicitly about her death. For these reasons they are not able to mourn fully important individuals in their lives.
   b. By middle childhood, a more realistic view of death begins to emerge, with children understanding the finality of the event.
      (1) The anxiety at this point about death concerns not only the loss of (separation from) loved ones but also fears of mutilation (castration anxiety) and suffering and pain.
      (2) Because of the egocentric thinking of children, they tend to feel guilty and to view themselves as responsible for their own or others' illness and death. Frequently, the illness or death is viewed as a punishment for having been bad.
   c. By adolescence comes an adult cognitive view of death and with it a clear understanding of its irreversibility. In addition, there is a capacity to mourn, especially by midadolescence.
      (1) Adolescents with chronic physical illnesses such as cystic fibrosis are regularly confronted with the death of their similarly affected peers, and thus precociously develop a sense of the finiteness of life, often living their lives while waiting for the final stage of their own illness.
      (2) With a decrease in the egocentricity of their thinking and a diminished tendency to view their illness or death as justified or deserved, adolescents experience alternations of resentment and despair as they struggle to accept their own death.

2. **Parental response to a child's death.** A child's death is surely one of the most devastating experiences that could befall any parent. If the death is not a sudden one, there is a tendency for the parents unconsciously to undergo **anticipatory mourning**, resulting in the gradual relinquishment of strong emotional ties to the child. The results of this can be very hurtful to the child and parent alike.

    a. Because of the parental disengagement, the child senses less emotional involvement by the parents and thus experiences the dreaded sense of abandonment, even though the parents may be physically in attendance. Often the relationship becomes bland and lacking in intensity as the parents try not to let the child see them "upset." An emotional barrier is erected, the talk is superficial, and the subject most on the child's and parents' minds becomes taboo.

    b. When the child dies, the parents may feel guilty that they are not more upset by the child's death or that they are relieved to have the ordeal over. Unless properly counseled, they may think of themselves as callous or nonloving when in fact they have already grieved, albeit unconsciously and in advance.

B. ADULT'S PERSPECTIVE

1. Adults tend to be anxious about their own death because of a dread of being separated from their loved ones, concern about pain and suffering, and because of the narcissistic injury associated with the end of existence. There is a sense of having not left an indelible mark on the world that will assure "perpetual existence" and thus avoid nothingness.

2. According to the investigations of Elisabeth Kübler-Ross, the dying patient experiences five stages before death occurs.

    a. The stage of **denial** is often expressed by the patient who, when told of his impending death, responds in terms such as: "No, it's not true; it can't be me."

    b. The stage of **anger** that follows is expressed as rage, bitterness, or as more subtle, intense feelings: "Why me? What have I done to deserve this?"

    c. The stage of **bargaining** is characterized by a search for meaning in life and often by a return to religious institutions. This stage is often marked by a belief that some magical power will intervene.

    d. The stage of **depression** involves two phases of grieving.

        (1) Preparatory grief is often demonstrated by emotional detachment and a relinquishing of social and family bonds and responsibilities.

        (2) Final grief involves a patient's preoccupation with his own death, marked by reflections about existence and life.

    e. The stage of **acceptance** can be manifested as emotional detachment or neutrality or as a calm, even euphoric, state of being.

C. PHYSICIAN RESPONSE. There are several common responses observed in physicians who care for dying patients.

1. One is the sense of **failure**. In spite of rationally knowing otherwise, many physicians harbor a belief that if they had tried harder perhaps the outcome would have been different.

2. A common difficulty for the physician occurs when the patient reminds him of a loved one, whether it be a child, spouse, friend, parent, or fellow physician. These circumstances make enormous additional **emotional demands** on the physician.

STUDY QUESTIONS

Directions: Each question below contains four suggested answers of which **one or more** is correct. Choose the answer

    A   if **1, 2, and 3** are correct
    B   if **1 and 3** are correct
    C   if **2 and 4** are correct
    D   if **4** is correct
    E   if **1, 2, 3, and 4** are correct

1. Attainment of urinary continence can be described as

(1) a maturational process
(2) due to growth
(3) reflecting ontogenetic factors
(4) a developmental process

2. The family romance is a common fantasy that is characterized by its

(1) reflection of adolescent infatuation
(2) oedipal nature
(3) occurrence in late adulthood
(4) occurrence in school-age children

Directions: The group of questions below consists of lettered choices followed by several numbered items. For each numbered item select the **one** lettered choice with which it is **most** closely associated. Each lettered choice may be used once, more than once, or not at all.

Questions 3–7

For each definition below, select the aspect of psychological development that it defines.

(A) Individuation
(B) Intimate differentiated attachment
(C) Object permanence
(D) Practicing phase
(E) Rapprochement crisis

3. A process of differentiation through which the child develops an entity distinct from that of the mother

4. The principal psychological task of the first year of life

5. Development of locomotion, which allows exploration of a greater segment of the environment and return to the mother for emotional reinforcement

6. A period marked by excessive shadowing and moving away

7. Development of a mental representation of things and people

ANSWERS AND EXPLANATIONS

1. The answer is D (4). (*I C D*) Maturation is the biologically based, phylogenetically based, sequential unfolding of functions. When these are combined with experience, resulting in new, learned behaviors, the process is referred to as development. Thus, myelinization that permits toilet training to proceed is a maturational step. The process of achieving continence is a learned, developmental process.

2. The answer is D (4). [*III B 1 b (2)*] Latency is a period of psychosocial development that extends from the end of the oedipal period to the beginning of puberty. Fantasies are common in latency-aged children. The "family romance" fantasy arises with the child's disillusionment with his real parents. He then imagines ideal parents who are rich and powerful and who are maybe even royalty.

3–7. The answers are: 3-A, 4-B, 5-D, 6-E, 7-C. [*II B 1, 3 a, 4 d, e (2)*] Individuation is a term that describes the psychological separation of mother and child. It is the process of molding an individual personality.

Intimate differentiated attachment is the foremost psychological task of the first year of life, in which the infant forms a bond to the mother (or primary caregiver). Formation of this attachment is essential to the development of future intimate relationships.

Object permanence is the infant's capacity to maintain the mental representation of the mother, even when she is not present. This allows the infant to recognize that a stranger is not the mother. Thus, the stranger represents the mother's absence, which creates stranger anxiety.

The practicing phase is associated with walking, and it is the time when the toddler is literally practicing his walking skills. Locomotion permits exploration of the environment, with movement away from the mother and back to her for encouragement and emotional support.

During the rapprochement subphase, the child becomes aware of the separateness of the mother, and that awareness can become acute. Reactions to the separation can be intense. The child follows the mother carefully (shadowing) or runs away from her (darting away), reflecting the toddler's tendencies toward reunion and separation, respectively.

8

Clinical Assessment

Joan K. Barber
Robert L. Jenkins

I. INTRODUCTION. The **mental status examination (MSE)** and **psychometric evaluation** (which is also known as **psychological testing**) are systematic methods for the evaluation of behavioral, emotional, and cognitive processes. Both are important in understanding a patient's current mental status.

The MSE and psychometric evaluation are always used in conjunction with a complete **medical history** (data on autonomic nervous system activity, sleep, food intake, medications, and drug use); a complete **physical examination**, with emphasis on autonomic hyperactivity (i.e., tachycardia, fever, hypertension, skin color and temperature, and restlessness); a **neurologic examination**; and various **laboratory and x-ray studies**. In this context, the MSE is part of the broader psychiatric examination, and psychometric evaluation is part of the broader perspective of psychological assessment.

There is overlap in item content. Some items of the MSE are similar and occasionally identical to those of the psychometric evaluation. Items of the MSE are especially relevant to medical and psychiatric diagnosis, whereas the content of the psychometric evaluation may or may not have obvious medical or psychiatric relevance, and complex interpretation may be necessary to arrive at a conclusion.

A. THE MENTAL STATUS EXAMINATION is a survey examination for use in the emergency room, at the bedside, or in the office. It is vital to a complete neurologic or psychiatric examination, especially for assessment of the following conditions:

1. Baseline performance and to monitor the progress of patients with acute or fluctuating changes in mental state

2. Changes in cognition and emotion in patients with head trauma, neurologic disorder, or systemic illness

3. All psychiatric patients with acute onset of symptoms

4. All psychotic states

5. Vague somatic complaints that are difficult to substantiate by physical or neurologic examination

B. PSYCHOMETRIC EVALUATION is an examination consisting of one or more psychological tests that are administered under highly standardized and replicable conditions. It can be viewed as an **extension of the psychiatric and neurologic evaluation**, particularly of the MSE, and it provides for a more detailed and in-depth analysis of the patient's state. Two types of psychometric evaluation are distinguished: The "psychological" addresses intellectual and personality factors; the "neuropsychological" focuses on understanding the patient's difficulties in terms of brain–behavior relationships. A psychometric evaluation should be considered under the following circumstances:

1. To obtain more detailed information about behavioral, cognitive, and emotional functioning for descriptive, diagnostic, prognostic, or management purposes

2. For any psychiatric patient in whom diagnosis or for whom the important situational or intrapsychic issues are not reasonably clear

3. For any patient with significant brain injury (e.g., to assist in rehabilitation planning)

4. To evaluate vague complaints difficult to substantiate by traditional neurologic or psychiatric examination so as to delineate organic dysfunction from functional impairment

5. To determine a baseline level of functioning in order to monitor future improvement or deterioration

6. To assess patient change in behavioral, cognitive, or emotional functioning for cases in which there is associated litigation

7. For patients about whom there are questions regarding behavioral functioning (e.g., impulse control, motivation, and social maturity), cognitive ability (e.g., intellectual functioning, academic achievement, and neurobehavioral impairment), vocational issues (e.g., career decisions and vocational rehabilitation), or emotional and personality factors (e.g., psychological conflicts and dynamics, suicide potential, reality testing, interpersonal skills and style, and general stability)

II. THE MENTAL STATUS EXAMINATION

Mental Status Examination Score Sheet

Check or circle appropriate answer
0 = normal   1 = mild-to-moderate impairment   2 = severe impairment

I. Level of consciousness

Alert	yes____	no____
Lethargic (somnolent)	yes____	no____
Stuporous	yes____	no____
Comatose	yes____	no____
Alternating	yes____	no____

II. Attention, vigilance

A. Clinical assessment

Attention	0	1	2
Concentration	0	1	2

B. Formal testing
- Digits forward____
- Digits backward____
- Continuous performance task   0 1 2

III. Behavioral observations

A. Appearance

Clothing	0	1	2
Grooming	0	1	2

B. Motor activity

Increased	0	1	2
Decreased	0	1	2
Tics	0	1	2
Repetitive acts	0	1	2
Other (specify)	0	1	2

C. Facial expression

Angry	0	1	2
Happy	0	1	2
Sad	0	1	2
Anxious	0	1	2
Inappropriate to verbal content	0	1	2

D. Mood/affect

Angry	0	1	2
Sad	0	1	2
Apathetic	0	1	2
Fluctuating	0	1	2
Happy	0	1	2

Inappropriate to verbal content	0	1	2
Fearful	0	1	2
Anxious	0	1	2

E. Interview behavior

Cooperative	yes____	no____	
Angry outbursts	0	1	2
Impulsive	0	1	2
Irritable	0	1	2
Passive	0	1	2
Demanding	0	1	2
Negativistic	0	1	2
Evasive	0	1	2
Apathetic	0	1	2
Withdrawn	0	1	2
Silly	0	1	2
Helpless	0	1	2
Unconcerned	0	1	2
Euphoric	0	1	2

IV. Speech, language, thought, memory

A. Handedness L____ R____ mixed____

B. Language comprehension

Oral	0	1	2
Reading	0	1	2

C. Spontaneous speech

Rate increased	0	1	2
Rate decreased	0	1	2
Muteness	0	1	2
Dysarthria	0	1	2
Dysprosody	0	1	2
Aphasia	0	1	2

D. Writing

Dictation	0	1	2
Self-originated	0	1	2
Dyspraxia	0	1	2

E. Thought

1. Form

Reduced content	0	1	2
Incomplete sentences	0	1	2

A. GENERAL CONSIDERATIONS

1. Patients who are at high risk for acute disturbances in behavior and psychological function include:
   a. Older patients
   b. Patients with metabolic and endocrine disorders
   c. Patients in intensive care and postsurgical settings (especially patients who have had extracorporeal circulation)
   d. Cardiac patients; patients with hypoxia
   e. Patients who have been on medication affecting central nervous system function

2. The MSE is organized upon a "staircase" schema that is hierarchical, moving upward from the brain stem to the prefrontal cortex, and going from the lowest (arousal) to the highest (executive) level of mental activity (Fig. 8-1). Dysfunction of the lower two levels of the staircase

---

Mental Status Examination Score Sheet (cont.)

Circumstantiality	0 1 2	
Derailment	0 1 2	
Tangentiality	0 1 2	
Flight of ideas	0 1 2	
Clang associations	0 1 2	
Confabulation	0 1 2	
Neologisms	0 1 2	
Echolalia	0 1 2	
Perseveration	0 1 2	
Word salad	0 1 2	

2. Content
   Illusions   0 1 2
   Delusions   0 1 2
   Hallucinations
      Auditory   0 1 2
      Visual   0 1 2
      Olfactory   0 1 2
      Tactile   0 1 2
   Assaultive thoughts   0 1 2
   Homicidal ideas   0 1 2
   Homicidal plans   0 1 2
   Feelings of
      hopelessness   0 1 2
   Feelings of
      worthlessness   0 1 2
   Feelings of guilt   0 1 2
   Suicidal thoughts   0 1 2
   Suicidal plans   0 1 2
   Obsessions   0 1 2
   Phobias   0 1 2
   Sexual themes   0 1 2
   Somatic
      preoccupations   0 1 2
   Religiosity   0 1 2
   Other   0 1 2

F. Memory
   Sensorium—orientation to:
      Time   yes____ no____
      Place   yes____ no____

      Situation   yes____ no____
      Person   yes____ no____

   Short-term memory
      Recall of last few days   0 1 2
      Four words   0 1 2
      Retelling story   0 1 2

Remote memory
   Details of medical
      history   0 1 2
   Significant anniver-
      saries/birthdays   0 1 2
   Naming of presidents in
      patient's lifetime   0 1 2

V. **Problem solving, learned material**
   Constructional ability   0 1 2
   Calculations   0 1 2
   Fund of information   0 1 2

VI. **Abstract thinking, conceptual ability**
   Judgment and insight
      Similarities   0 1 2
      Proverbs   0 1 2
      Abstract thinking   0 1 2
      Conceptual ability   0 1 2
      Social awareness   0 1 2
   Understand need for
      hospitalization   0 1 2
   Understand degree of
      illness   0 1 2
   Understand need for help   0 1 2

VII. **Summary of positive findings**
   A. History

   B. Mental status examination

   C. Physical examination

   D. Neurologic examination

   E. Laboratory

VIII. **Differential diagnosis**
   Axis I   _____
   Axis II   _____
   Axis III   _____
   Axis IV   _____
   Axis V   _____

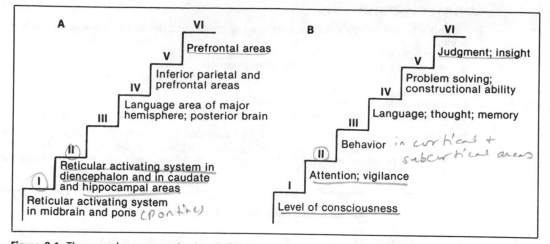

Figure 8-1. The mental status examination (MSE) "staircase" schema, which is ranked upward from the lowest (arousal) to the highest (executive) level of mental activity. The *roman numerals* on the staircase refer to sections numbered similarly on the MSE score sheet. Behavior is based on the function of many cortical and subcortical areas; only rarely does specific behavior have a precise location (e.g., *A*, level III).

is always reflected in the testing of the higher areas [e.g., poor concentration invariably produces deficits in short-term memory; severe distractibility and inattentiveness frequently produce flight of ideas (see section II E 2 a (6)); subalert states may be accompanied by changes in thought form (derailment, tangentiality) (see section II E 2 a (3), (4)) and thought content (illusions, hallucinations)]. Behavior is based on the functioning of many cortical and subcortical areas; only rarely can a specific behavior be precisely localized within the nervous system.

B. LEVEL I—LEVEL OF CONSCIOUSNESS (Fig. 8-2)

1. The **brain site** affected is the pontine and midbrain **reticular activating system (RAS)**.

2. The **causes** of reduced consciousness are 70% metabolic and 12% subtentorial. Rarely, there is widespread cortical damage (e.g., due to carbon monoxide poisoning).

3. **Assessment** involves clinical evaluation only.
   a. **Alert.** The patient is defined as awake, aware, interacting, and responsive to stimuli. This state is **not** the same as being attentive.
   b. **Lethargic.** The patient can be roused but does not maintain arousal.
   c. **Stuporous.** The patient can be roused slightly with intense stimulation.
   d. **Comatose.** The patient cannot be roused, even with the most painful stimuli.

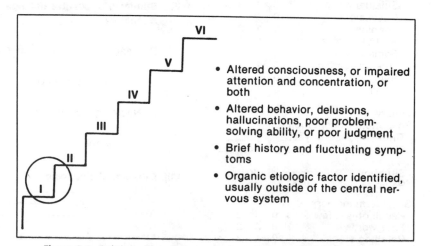

Figure 8-2. Delirium. The *circle* marks the primary area of dysfunction.

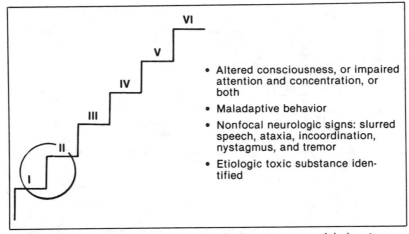

Figure 8-3. Intoxication. The *circle* marks the primary area of dysfunction.

C. **LEVEL II—ATTENTION AND VIGILANCE (CONCENTRATION)** [Figs. 8-3, 8-4, 8-5]. **Attention** is the capacity to focus on a single stimulus and to screen out irrelevant stimuli. **Vigilance (concentration)** is the ability to focus attention over a more extended period of time.

1. The **brain sites** affected include the RAS, the RAS–thalamic projection system, the reticulocortical and corticoretiular connections, and the RAS hippocampal and caudate areas. The development of these areas is complete about the time of puberty.

2. The **causes** of reduced concentration include metabolic disorders, intoxications, withdrawal syndromes, infections, hypoxia, postoperative states, electrolyte imbalance, attention deficit disorders, severe depression, preoccupation with hallucinatory experiences, and severe anxiety.

3. **Assessment**
   a. **Clinical assessment** consists of noting the patient's ability to be task-oriented while obtaining the history and conducting the examination. Distractibility is observed when the patient's attention wanders from one stimulus to another.
   b. **Digit span** (forward and reversed) **measures attention of less than 10-second duration**.
      (1) Numbers should be intoned, without inflection, at approximately one per second; numbers should be read from a prepared list to ensure smooth delivery of difficult sequences.

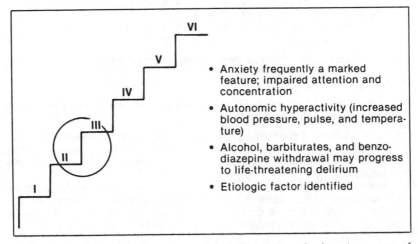

Figure 8-4. Withdrawal (substance specificity). The *circle* marks the primary area of dysfunction.

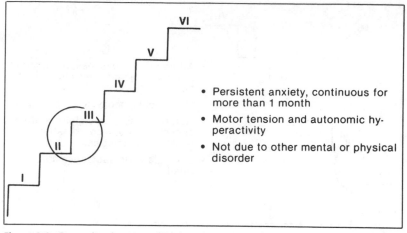

- Persistent anxiety, continuous for more than 1 month
- Motor tension and autonomic hyperactivity
- Not due to other mental or physical disorder

Figure 8-5. Generalized anxiety disorder. The *circle* marks the primary area of dysfunction.

(2) The same numbers may be used for digits reversed (the patient is asked to reverse the sequence of the numbers read aloud). The ability to reverse digits requires more concentration than forward repetition. Patients who do poorly on this usually also do poorly on vigilance or continuous performance testing (CPT; see section II C 3 c).

37
416
5318
26593
614783
9362514

(3) If a patient's clinical progress is followed by repetition of this test, the numbers should be changed daily.

c. **Auditory vigilance** is measured by CPT. This test **measures concentration of approximately 1-minute duration**.

(1) The patient is asked to tap with his finger or a pencil whenever he hears an "A" read aloud from a list of random letters. The letters should be read aloud by the examiner in an uninflected, monotonous delivery, at about one per second.

L P T E A A I C T
D A L A A N I A B
F S A M R C O A D
P A K L A Y J Y O
E A B A A E F M U
S A H E V A R A T

(2) **Scoring.** No errors should be made by a normal adult.

D. LEVEL III—BEHAVIOR (Figs. 8-6, 8-7)

1. **Brain sites.** Behavior has roots in many cortical and subcortical areas (e.g., the limbic system, the prefrontal area, the caudate area).

2. **Clinical assessment.** Observations of a patient's mood, facial expression, clothing, and ability to relate to the examiner are usually very helpful in establishing a diagnosis. Observations are clustered into **appearance**, **motor activity**, **facial expression**, **mood and affect**, and **interview behavior**.

a. Observations about **appearance** and grooming are valuable in the diagnosis of almost all clinical syndromes. Notable is the sometimes bizarre dress of patients with schizophrenia and mania, the seductive dress of an individual with a histrionic personality disorder, or the soiled and stained clothing of demented and intoxicated patients.

b. **Motor activity**

(1) Increased activity is seen in patients with agitated depressions, mania, some attention deficit disorders, and often in patients with delirium.

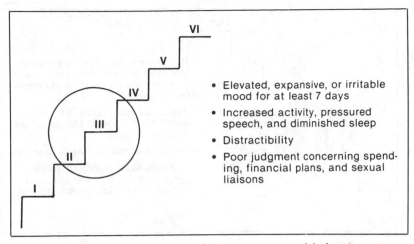

Figure 8-6. Mania. The *circle* marks the primary area of dysfunction.

(2) Reduced activity is seen in patients with depression, catatonia, some frontal lobe syndromes, parkinsonian-like states, or delirium.

(3) Tics are simple motor actions involving a few muscle groups (e.g., blinking and grimacing).

(4) Repetitive acts are complex movements involving entire limbs, or a limb and the head (e.g., a movement resembling haircombing).

c. Facial expression. Patients with little or no facial expression may be depressed, have a neurologic syndrome (e.g., Parkinson's disease or a minor hemisphere stroke), or have a drug-induced parkinsonian-like syndrome.

d. Mood and affect. Affect is the immediate overt expression of an emotional state; mood reflects the more sustained or underlying emotion.

$$\frac{\text{affect}}{\text{mood}} = \frac{\text{moment}}{\text{hour}}$$

Significant findings here are suggestive of an affective disorder (i.e., depression, mania, or hypomania). The absence of facial expression may make diagnosis more difficult, but the mood of a patient is usually transmitted despite this.

e. Interview behavior. At times, striking changes occur even in short interviews; irritability, demanding behavior, anger, and euphoria may all be seen in a manic patient. Helplessness and demanding behavior are frequently signals of underlying personality disorders.

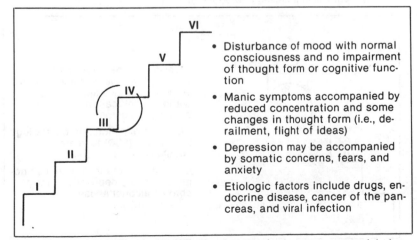

Figure 8-7. Organic affective disorder. The *circle* marks the primary area of dysfunction.

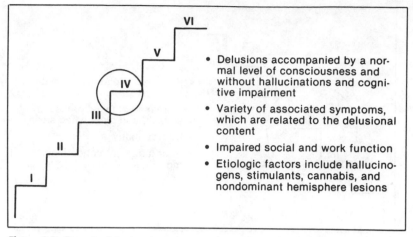

Figure 8-8. Organic delusional syndrome. The *circle* marks the primary area of dysfunction.

E. **LEVEL IV—LANGUAGE, THOUGHT, AND MEMORY** (Figs. 8-8, 8-9, 8-10, 8-11)

1. **Language**
   a. **Brain sites** assessed are those of the language areas of the major (usually left) hemisphere. These include the sensory cortices, the secondary and tertiary association areas of the inferior parietal lobe, the subcortical pathways to frontal and prefrontal areas, and pathways from the prefrontal area to the motor cortex involved with speech (Broca's area).
   b. **Causes of impairment**
      (1) **Structural brain disease** in one or more areas [e.g., a vascular lesion in Broca's area, producing impaired motor output of speech; a diencephalic–hippocampal lesion, producing an anterograde amnesia (such as Korsakoff's psychosis)]
      (2) **Delirium** (or intoxication or withdrawal delirium), producing serious deficits in attention, with subsequent abnormalities in rate of speech, thought form (derailment or flight of ideas), and memory (failure of short-term memory secondary to loss of concentration)
      (3) **Abnormalities in neurotransmission**, as occur in affective disorders and schizophrenia
      (4) **Metabolic disorders**, producing syndromes in which thought form and content are abnormal (e.g., myxedema madness and manic-like syndromes seen in hypercortisolism)
   c. **Assessment**
      (1) **Handedness**
         (a) Knowledge of handedness is important in studying any patient with difficulty in understanding spoken or written language or who has difficulty speaking. The patient (or the patient's family) is asked which hand is used in writing, eating, throwing a ball, dealing cards, and so forth.

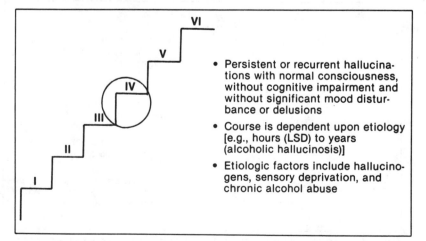

Figure 8-9. Organic hallucinosis. The *circle* marks the primary area of dysfunction.

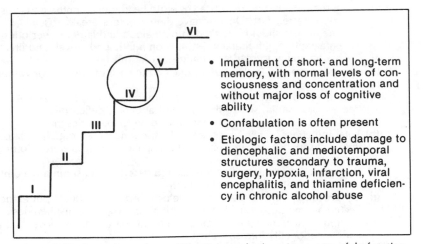

Figure 8-10. Amnestic syndrome. The *circle* marks the primary area of dysfunction.

   (b) Hemispheric dominance is associated with contralateral hand preference. Most individuals (even the left-handed) have their critical language function in the left hemisphere. Patients with mixed dominance are assumed to have more bilateral language representation, and they have better recoveries after strokes involving the language areas.
 (2) Language comprehension
   (a) Brain sites. Lesions in the left temporal perisylvian region cause loss of ability to understand spoken or written language; rarely, the ability to read is preserved.
   (b) Causes. The most common causes of these aphasias are vascular lesions of the middle cerebral artery and its branches.
   (c) Testing. If in the course of taking the medical history, the examiner finds that a supposed English-speaking patient does not understand what is asked or said, a full aphasia screening is required. Patients with "fluent aphasias" (while the patient still has unimpaired speech production mechanisms, his utterances are mixtures of words or phrases that carry no meaning) may be mistaken for psychotic patients with severe degrees of derailment, tangentiality, or flight of ideas. The patient may be tested for understanding comments.
      (i) A patient should be asked to carry out a series of increasingly difficult commands (e.g., show me your nose, your hand, your ankle, shoulder blade, brow). To guard against the patient being apractic (i.e., unable to act on command despite intact receptive and motor capacity) and hence unable to carry out motor commands, another series of simple to complex questions should be

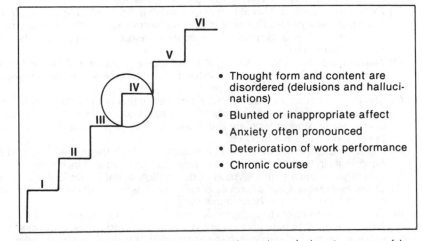

Figure 8-11. Chronic paranoid schizophrenia. The *circle* marks the primary area of dysfunction.

asked, which require only a yes or no head movement (e.g., Is this a hotel? Did you eat breakfast? Do you have dinner before breakfast?).

(ii) The patient should be asked to read aloud and later answer questions about a paragraph-length literacy test. It is on a fifth-grade level, and literacy is judged by the ability to read and understand at this level.

(3) **Spontaneous speech.** Evaluation is done on the basis of observations alone; no special testing is required.

    (a) **Changes in the rate of speech** are common in many psychiatric disorders (e.g., in depression, mania, schizophrenia, and attention deficit disorders). Specific structural lesions causing these changes have never been described.

    (b) Total **muteness** is seen in some psychiatric syndromes (e.g., in catatonia and elective mutism) but not in aphasia. Even patients with severe motor aphasia can phonate some sounds.

    (c) **Dysarthria** is a nonspecific term used to describe and summarize difficulties in articulation, intonation, and phonation.

    (d) **Dysprosody** refers to the loss of melodic aspects of speech; utterances are uninflected and monotonous. Patients with minor (right) hemisphere lesions, involving an area corresponding to Broca's area in the left brain, may lose their ability to **encode** emotionality into speech.

(4) **Writing.** (Evaluation of writing ability may be omitted if there is no concern about a possibility of aphasia.) Writing deficits are most often associated with frontal lesions.

    (a) The inability to write to dictation (with no paresis of the arm or hand) is called **agraphia**. It can be produced by posterior perisylvian lesions, but it is rarely found alone; the inability to write is usually associated with other aphasias. Writing samples of aphasic patients are often characterized by spelling and grammatical errors.

    (b) **Dysgraphia** is a term used to describe the faulty production of letters and words. It is seen in many situations including a child learning to write, children with learning disorders, and patients with delirium and dementia.

    (c) **Testing.** The patient should be asked to write a sentence to dictation and to originate a written sentence of his own.

2. **Thought.** The examiner, in listening to a patient, judges not only **what** is said (**content**) but also **how** it is said (**form**). Combinations may be found of both form and content disorders. When disorders of both are present, the patient is generally identified or judged to be psychotic. Delirious and intoxicated patients frequently have delusions and hallucinations that usually are not accompanied by a thought form disorder.

  a. **Thought form.** Form disorders are found in many severely disturbed psychiatric patients. The disorders listed below as yet have not been found to be associated with lesions of specific higher cortical areas.

    (1) **Reduced content** describes a poverty of ideas often associated with vague, repetitive, overly abstract speech, which contains little information. It is usually adequate in amount and has no syntactical or vocabulary errors. It is sometimes called "empty philosophizing."

    (2) **Circumstantiality** describes speech in which there are delays in reaching the point because of unnecessary detail and parenthetical speech.

    (3) **Derailment** refers to shifts in thinking in which the patient's ideas move from one unrelated topic to another. The patient does not seem aware of the incongruity of the juxtaposed ideas. This is also called **loosening of associations** and is to be distinguished from circumstantiality.

    (4) **Tangentiality** refers to loosening of associations or derailment that occurs in response to the examiner's question. Shifts in topic at first may be related but progressively move further away from the starting topic.

    (5) **Blocking** describes a sudden cessation of speech that is voluntarily explained by the patient as having occurred because the thought was lost or because his mind became blank. Many patients who are distracted by inner perceptual disturbances (hallucinations) appear to have blocked.

    (6) **Flight of ideas** is a type of speech pattern in which there is accelerated speech and rapid shifts in topic. Speech may become disorganized and incoherent. Syntax and vocabulary are usually intact. Another description might be rapid derailment.

    (7) **Clang associations** are a form of derailment in which shifts in topic are based on the sound of words rather than the meaning.

    (8) **Confabulation** refers to apparent fabrication of facts or events to fill gaps in memory. This is common in patients with organic amnestic syndromes (e.g., Korsakoff's psychosis), but it is not ordinarily seen in patients with the amnesia associated with dementia.

    (9) **Neologisms** are new words—inventions by the patient or distortions of standard words (e.g., "the grass is grumps").

(10) Echolalia describes the echoing of words or phrases of others. It is often associated with perseverative repetition of the same words. It is common in children with developmental language disorder, in individuals with transcortical aphasias, and, more rarely, in schizophrenic patients.

(11) Perseveration describes persistent repetition of words and phrases. It is found in patients with developmental language disorder, organic syndromes, and, more rarely, schizophrenia.

(12) Word salad is a form of severely disorganized speech in which syntax is lost and vocabulary use is idiosyncratic. It is now believed to be caused most often by a fluent aphasic process.

b. Thought content. Thought content disorders are commonly seen in many medical, neurologic, and psychiatric syndromes. A content disorder alone would be unlikely in patients with schizophrenia or mania.

(1) An **illusion** is a misperception of a real external stimulus, (e.g., the moving shadow of a tree on a bedroom wall appears to be a figure outside the window). Illusions are frequently seen in delirium and dementia.

(2) A **delusion** is a false personal belief based on an incorrect interpretation of reality (e.g., the telephone ringing only once becomes absolute documentation of a CIA plot against the patient). Delusions are common in many clinical situations; schizophrenic patients tend to have more organized and fixed types of delusions (e.g., the patient's thoughts are being controlled; his thoughts are being broadcast via television) than do delirious patients, whose delusions tend to be more fleeting and frequently based on illusions or hallucinations.

(3) Hallucinations are found in patients with psychoses of multiple origins, from intoxications and delirium to dementia. The type and nature of the misperception has been said to suggest the type of underlying pathology (e.g., auditory hallucinations are more characteristic of schizophrenia; tactile hallucinations are more characteristic of a withdrawal delirium), but exceptions to the rule are very common. Types of hallucinations include the following.

   (a) Auditory hallucinations are usually experienced as a human voice or voices; other sounds may be less frequently reported. Patients with complex partial seizures (temporal lobe epilepsy) may report a variety of simple or complex sounds or music.

   (b) Visual hallucinations are usually of focused images such as a human form, objects, and, less commonly, lights. These can be reported in all psychotic states.

   (c) Olfactory hallucinations involve a sense of smell, and frequently the odors reported are unpleasant (e.g., burning rubber). These are frequently reported by patients with complex partial seizures (temporal lobe epilepsy) and often are accompanied by gustatory hallucinations.

   (d) Gustatory hallucinations are usually perceptions of an unpleasant taste.

   (e) Tactile (haptic) hallucinations involve the sense of touch on or under the skin. Formication is a sense of something crawling or creeping; it is most often experienced by individuals in alcohol withdrawal delirium and in the recovery stages from cocaine intoxication.

(4) Assaultive thoughts are wishes or intentions to harm an individual or, less commonly, an institution or organization.

(5) Homicidal thoughts are wishes or intentions to kill another person or persons. These may be vague and poorly formulated thoughts or may be an impulsive, momentary wish.

(6) Homicidal plans suggest that the intention or wish to kill has been crystallized into a potentially real threat. In several states, it is a law that mental health personnel report to potential victims the possibility of an assaultive or murderous attack; they must also take the necessary steps to arrange an involuntary hospitalization for the patient.

(7) Feelings of hopelessness are encountered in a variety of clinical situations, most often accompanying a depression or grief reaction.

(8) Feelings of worthlessness are also common. Sometimes they appear to be merely a bid for reassurance, but, more seriously, they are an invariable companion of severe depression.

(9) Feelings of guilt vary from regret over mild social solecisms to a sense of overwhelming culpability, which is frequently found in patients with serious depression.

(10) Suicidal thoughts vary from the statement, "I wish I was dead," of a student overwhelmed with work to that of a patient who is voicing death as the only way to end psychic pain or to reunite with a dead, longed-for loved one. It is important to distinguish between the ominous need to end pain and the manipulative and angry suicidal thoughts of a jilted lover or of a teenager whose parents are insufficiently understanding.

(11) Suicidal plans must be asked about if intentions or wishes to die are exposed. It is extremely important to check the probability of a plan succeeding (e.g., if the patient says that he might shoot himself, are there guns at home? If the patient says that he will overdose on sleeping pills, are there pills in the medicine cabinet?). Dangerousness to self is a reason for involuntary hospitalization in all states; if the examiner believes that a suicide plan exists, the necessary legal steps should be taken for hospitalization.

(12) Obsessions are recurrent, persistent ideas, images, or impulses that are not experienced as being produced voluntarily but as being invading thoughts (i.e., they are ego-dystonic). Obsessions are seen in both psychotic and nonpsychotic states, including obsessive-compulsive disorder, eating disorders, schizophrenia, and depression.

(13) Phobias are irrational, persistent fears of an object, activity, or situation that produce a wish to avoid the fear-producing stimulus. Closeness to the stimulus causes increased feelings of anxiety and overactivity of the autonomic nervous system.

(14) Sexual concerns are demonstrated by a large variety of patients. There may be real concerns or concerns in the form of obsessions (e.g., the penis becoming smaller), delusions (e.g., the most powerful penis in the world), or phobias (e.g., the vagina having teeth).

(15) Somatic preoccupations are seen in patients in all branches of medicine, often appropriately related but, more commonly, unrelated to any underlying pathologic processes. These may be part of the symptomatology of anxiety disorders, somatoform disorders, factitious disorders, psychoses, and so forth.

(16) Religiosity refers to a preoccupation with religious themes that is well beyond the usual. The preoccupation may achieve the level of delusion ("I am God") or may be an obsession, a conviction of guilt and worthlessness, and so forth. Religiosity is found in many psychiatric illnesses.

3. Memory

a. Brain sites. Although some neuroanatomic structures have been identified with memory, the process is far from clarified. Tests of attention (digit span; see section II C 3 b) measure immediate recall, which some authorities classify as a memory function per se. However, the RAS and the primary auditory cortex play a major role in this function, and it is safer to conceive of the digit span test as one only of attention. Limbic structures are involved in long-term storage and retrieval of recent information. The hippocampus, mamillary bodies, and dorsal medial nuclei of the thalamus are essential subcortical links in storage and retrieval of verbal and nonverbal memories. Memory traces are presumed to reside in the neocortex, although clearly many subcortical structures are necessary in the total memory process.

b. Assessment

(1) Sensorium

(a) While many MSEs start with orientation questions, questions about time, place, situation, and person are essentially tests of awareness and memory. Failure to answer some or all of these questions usually indicates an "organic" syndrome. The important question of whether the memory failure stems from a dementing process (top of the staircase; see Fig. 8-1) or a delirium (bottom of the staircase; see Fig. 8-1) is usually not addressed. It is critical to further evaluation and treatment to know whether a disoriented patient has **must-treat delirium** or is demented. In most instances, performance on digit span and the CPT clarifies this differential (most demented patients continue to perform well in tests of attention until late in the course of the disease).

(b) Valid **memory testing** requires a patient to be attentive, to be capable of cooperating with the examiner, and to have no deficits that impair comprehension of task requirements.

(i) Time orientation is checked by asking the day, month, year, time of day, and season of the year.

(ii) For assessment of **place** orientation, the examiner asks for the name of the hospital. When the patient is uncertain, the examiner may provide alternatives (e.g., Is this a hotel, school, or hospital?).

(iii) The patient is asked about the **situation** that he is in (i.e., Why are you here today?).

(iv) Orientation for **person** is rarely lost; however, in the absence of a medical history or upon findings suggestive of serious central nervous system pathology, the possibility of psychogenic amnesia or a fugue state exists.

(2) Short-term memory testing requires the patient to retain new information for a minimum of 5 minutes. This necessitates that the patient be able to concentrate, recognize and register the information, and retain and then retrieve the information upon questioning.

(a) Accurate recall of the last 24 hours may require the presence of a relative or friend for corroboration, but it gives a good estimate of the patient's ability to input new information.

(b) Formal testing can be done by asking the patient to learn new material such as four words that are diverse semantically and phonetically or by telling a story that the patient is asked to repeat. The **four words** could be: shovel; yellow; anger; sofa. The patient is asked to repeat these three times (in order to check attention and concentration) and is told that in 5 minutes he will be asked to say them again.

(c) Scoring. A normal adult will recall all four words; recall of two or less indicates a serious difficulty in short-term memory.

(3) Remote memory testing. Difficulties in this area are usually first detected while taking the medical history. Documentation of the degree of loss can be made by asking the patient to recall important people and events in his lifetime (e.g., presidents, wars) and by asking for important family dates and anniversaries if the family is available to verify accuracy. Patients rarely forget their own, their parents', or their siblings' birthdays; wedding anniversaries and children's birthdays are more often remembered by women.

F. LEVEL V—CONSTRUCTIONAL ABILITY, CALCULATIONS, AND LEARNED MATERIAL (Fig. 8-12)

1. **Brain sites.** Many brain areas (i.e., the parietal lobe, the language area, and the frontal and prefrontal lobes) are evaluated at this level. Failures in tasks do not have specific localizing significance. If a patient performs well on all of these tasks, the examiner may have some confidence in the integrity of many neural structures and their connecting pathways.

2. **Assessment**
   a. **Constructional (graphomotor) ability** is the capacity to copy or draw two- or three-dimensional shapes or designs. This is a complex task involving visual, perceptual, and analytical functions of the occipital and parietal lobes and the motor planning and action of the prefrontal and frontal lobes. Although both hemispheres are involved in the task, damage to the right (minor) parietal lobe produces severer impairment in performance.

   (1) The patient is asked to copy simple two- and three-dimensional objects and shapes such as a cube and a flower in a pot.

   (2) Scoring is 0 for perfect or near-perfect reproductions; 1 for minimal distortions or rotations; 2 for moderately distorted or rotated designs and loss of third dimension.

   (3) This is an excellent screening test because a good performance indicates the integrity of many neural structures. In the early stage of a dementia (e.g., in Alzheimer's disease), the test is usually performed poorly.

   b. **Calculations** measure the ability of a patient to perform mental arithmetic. Performance in normal individuals is highly correlated to intelligence and education, so that poor performance must be evaluated with these factors in mind.

   (1) Impaired performance may occur with lesions in one or both hemispheres; lesions of the major hemisphere usually produce more impairment than similar lesions of the minor side. Diminished attention and concentration clearly impair performance, and testing becomes valueless. Anxiety may also be a major reason for poor performance.

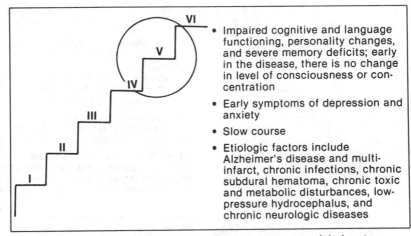

Figure 8-12. Dementia. The *circle* marks the primary area of dysfunction.

(2) Testing
  (a) Simple mental arithmetic
    (i) The test begins with single-digit addition and subtraction and proceeds to multiple-number addition and subtraction.
    (ii) Scoring is dependent on intellectual and academic level.
  (b) Serial subtraction
    (i) The patient is asked to subtract 7 from 100 and to continue subtracting 7 from the remainder, giving only the answer. Serial 3 subtraction may be used if the patient does not succeed with 7.
    (ii) Scoring. A normal adult should have no difficulty with this task.
  c. Learned material. Questions tap the patient's store of knowledge or general information. Intelligence and schooling influence the patient's responses, so the patient's background must enter into the interpretation of answers. Sample questions may include: "How many minutes are in an hour?"; "What is the function of the kidneys?"; "How many miles lie between San Francisco and New York?".

G. LEVEL VI—ABSTRACT THINKING, CONCEPTUAL ABILITY, JUDGMENT, AND INSIGHT (Fig. 8-13). This level of the MSE measures the higher aspects of cortical function, the so-called **executive ability**.

1. Abstract thinking
  a. Similarities is a measure of an individual's verbal abstract ability to analyze and describe relationships among words, objects, and ideas.
    (1) Failure to give appropriate abstract responses suggests some deficits in higher cortical function or, in many psychiatric disorders, deficits possibly secondary to a progressive brain disease. Parietal (major hemisphere) lobe damage may also cause a loss in abstract reasoning as well as in calculating ability.
    (2) Assessment. Testing is conducted by asking the patient to explain how word pairs are alike (e.g., turnip and cauliflower; chair and table; painting and symphony; horse and grapefruit).
    (3) Scoring is 0 for the best abstract answer; 1 for indicating properties of both items that are similar or shared; 2 for a response that describes properties of only one of the pair, or generalizations that do not apply.
  b. The **interpretation of proverbs** is highly dependent on the patient's cultural, intellectual, and educational background. Many well-educated young adults are unfamiliar with proverbs, so interpretation of responses in this section of the examination must be done with care. In general, the ability to generate an abstract response is dependent on an intact fund of general information and the ability to apply the generalities to information with which one may not be familiar.
    (1) Brain sites. The brain sites that are involved in this skill are presumed to be primarily the prefrontal and frontal cortices. Language processing skills must be intact (see section II E 1).
    (2) Assessment. The examiner should ask the patient to explain the following proverbs: "Rome wasn't built in a day"; "A bird in the hand is worth two in the bush"; "Birds of

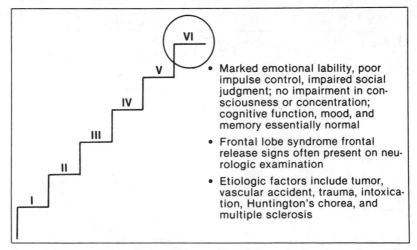

Figure 8-13. Organic personality syndrome. The *circle* marks the primary area of dysfunction.

a feather flock together''; ''A rolling stone gathers no moss''; ''An apple falls near its tree.''

    (3) Scoring

        (a) A normal individual with an average education would be able to score at least a ''1''.

        (b) For example: ''Rome wasn't built in a day'': 0 for the most abstract response—''It takes time to do things well''; 1 for a partial abstract response—''Don't do things too fast''; 2 for a concrete response—''It took a long time to build Rome.''

2. Conceptual ability

  a. Brain sites. Conceptual ability is the product of an intact brain. Damage to the prefrontal cortex, however, can destroy this capacity. Lesions limited to only the prefrontal area can leave the remainder of cognitive and language skills intact. Some forms of frontal lobe disease (e.g., deep medial and supraorbital disease) produce a syndrome of apathy, withdrawal, and indifference.

  b. Assessment

    (1) Overall conceptual ability can be hard to appraise. One method of testing is to have the patient solve unfamiliar and complex verbal problems. Completion of a series of numbers, letters, or words (presented visually in written form) is a more formal assessment.

    (2) The patient is asked to complete the following sequences. (The correct answers follow in parentheses.)

        (a) A   C   E   G   ___   (I)

        (b) 1   4   7   10   ___   (13)

        (c) AZ BY CX D   ___   (W)

        (d) 1   4   10 22   ___   (46)

        (e) Hydrangea   763047168

              Jewel   49823

              Hat   ___   (three-digit numeral)

  c. Scoring. Most patients will be able to do half of these examples; lesser scores suggest some impaired function in verbal reasoning ability.

3. Judgment can be measured informally when listening to the patient's account of his illness and problems. Any delusional patient has impaired judgment. **Social awareness** refers to the patient's ability to understand conventional responses to social situations (e.g., what do you do if you smell smoke in a theater? if you find a wallet in the street? if the car behind you follows too closely?).

III. THE PSYCHOMETRIC EVALUATION

A. DEFINITION. Psychometric evaluation is a set of test techniques by which a sample of behavior is elicited, observed, recorded, analyzed, and interpreted.

B. INTERFACE WITH PSYCHIATRIC EVALUATION. The psychometric evaluation is an extension of the information gathered by the MSE and is complementary to the overall psychiatric evaluation. It may reduce the time needed to obtain information, access psychological information unavailable through history taking and interviewing, provide an additional source of information to contribute to the differential diagnosis, facilitate an understanding of the patient, and address specific questions raised by the psychiatric evaluation.

C. PURPOSES OF THE PSYCHOMETRIC EVALUATION

1. To **provide descriptive information** about an individual

2. To enhance the understanding of an individual's **psychological dynamics**

3. To examine areas of behavioral, cognitive, and emotional functioning to assist in **establishing the diagnosis**

4. To assist in **making decisions** about specific issues (e.g., competency, academic placement, occupational choice)

5. To assist in **treatment** and **discharge planning**

6. To **establish baseline performance** levels for monitoring change

7. For **prognostic and predictive** purposes

8. To evaluate changes in **brain–behavior relationships** (i.e., to evaluate neuropsychological functioning)

D. **PRINCIPLES OF PSYCHOMETRIC EVALUATION.** Three very important principles of psychometric measurement in general, and of any psychological test in particular, are **standardization**, **reliability**, and **validity**.

1. **Standardization** refers to collecting normative data from a group of individuals representative of the population using exactly the same materials and methods of administration under controlled environmental conditions. The standardization sample should be of adequate size and representation so that the group norms can be used as a comparison for clinical inference. The procedures for any test must be replicable and specified in detail such that every individual examined is subject to exactly the same stimuli, treatment, and conditions.

2. **Reliability** refers to the consistency and accuracy of a test, and it is a reflection of both true variance and error variance. Perfect reliability is highly improbable since human traits are not necessarily stable (true variance) and factors unrelated or unintentionally related to the traits being measured also affect performance (error variance or noise). Reliability is expressed as a type of correlation coefficient. Reliability coefficients of .80 to .90 or above are generally considered adequate for clinical uses, while those of .70 or above may be meaningful for research purposes. There are three main types of reliability.
   a. **Test–retest reliability** reflects the stability of a test over time. It addresses the degree to which a test would yield the same score on two or more successive administrations. This type of reliability should be demonstrated when the traits and characteristics being measured are stable.
   b. **Alternate-form reliability** refers to the degree to which two tests, designed to measure the same variables, would yield similar scores. It is used to establish the consistency and equivalence of multiple forms of the same test.
   c. **Intratest reliability** includes split-half reliability and internal consistency reliability. These measure the reliability of one or more segments of a test against the reliability of the test as a whole or against that of other segments of the test.

3. The **validity** of a test addresses the issue of whether the test measures what it is intended to measure. **Establishing validity is the most important aspect of test development**. Tests can be well standardized and highly reliable, but without demonstrated validity, the results may be meaningless. There are three important categories of validity.
   a. **Criterion-based or empirical validity** is determined by correlating scores on the test in question with an outside measure known to represent accurately the variable that the test is intended to measure. Methods for determining criterion-based validity are very important and are most commonly employed in developing diagnostic and prognostic test instruments. There are two types of criterion-based or empirical validity.
      (1) **Predictive validity** is assessed by correlating scores on the test in question with some criterion that is achieved and measured at a future time (e.g., determining the predictive validity of the MCATS by correlating it with later performance in medical school).
      (2) **Concurrent validity** refers to the association of test performance with an existing criterion (e.g., determining the concurrent validity of a National Board examination by correlating the scores achieved with current performance in medical school).
   b. **Construct validity** involves determining the parameters of the variables that are to be assessed by the test in question. Establishing construct validity is a complex task of determining the component meanings of the variables measured.
   c. **Content validity** refers to the determination by experts that a test covers the major content areas of the variables to be measured. This is a more subjective process than that employed in establishing other types of validity. A similar type of validity is known as **face validity**, which determines if the item content appears to measure what it is believed to measure. In this case, the judgment is made by the test user or consumer rather than by the experts who establish content validity.

E. **TYPES OF PSYCHOLOGICAL TESTS.** Psychological tests differ in the nature of the information obtained (the focus of the test) and in the processes of the assessment procedure.

1. **Nature of information obtained and focus of the test**
   a. Tests of **intellectual functioning** and **academic achievement** are the most common. Both types fall under the more general category of **tests of cognitive ability**.
   b. Tests assessing **personality** reveal information that may be descriptive of the individual or of his ongoing personality dynamics and functioning.
   c. **Vocational tests** assess interests, attitudes, and aptitudes in the context of a more general understanding of the individual to assist in making vocational decisions.
   d. **Neuropsychological tests** assess brain–behavior relationships.
   e. **Behavioral assessment** refers to assessment techniques that minimize inference and have particular emphasis on observable, quantifiable measures. This is a newly developing area

of assessment that addresses both the content of the assessment (i.e., the nature of information to be obtained) as well as the process by which information is collected.

2. Process of the assessment procedure

    a. Individual versus group tests. Some tests can be administered to more than 1 person at a time, and these are referred to as group tests. These tests are time efficient but can be less informative in understanding the individual. Individually administered tests, while time inefficient, yield better understanding of the individual patient.

    b. Objective versus projective tests

        (1) Objective tests are highly standardized for administration, scoring, and interpretation and are usually highly structured in format. Clearly identifiable correct answers exist. True–false and multiple choice test formats are frequently referred to as objective because all response possibilities are obvious and scorers can agree on the result.

        (2) In contrast, **projective tests** are less structured and allow greater leeway for the expression of individuality and important individual dynamics. These tests are based on the **projective hypothesis** that suggests that, given less structure and more ambiguous stimuli to which to respond, an individual will impose internal structure to interpret the stimuli and in the process will reveal (project) unconscious issues and aspects of his personality and cognitive style. Projective tests have been criticized for their lack of objectivity and reliability, but recently great effort, spearheaded by John Exner, has gone into increasing the objectivity of the most famous projective test, the **Rorschach**, without compromising the advantages of its projective format.

    c. Potential ability versus typical performance. Tests for measuring potential focus on obtaining an individual's maximum performance, while tests of typical performance address not what the individual can do but what he typically does. Tests of potential ability often measure cognitive capacities or specific aptitudes and abilities, while those of typical performance most often address aspects of personality, cognitive style, and observable behaviors.

F. MAJOR PSYCHOLOGICAL TESTS

    1. Tests of intellectual ability. Intelligence is an abstract concept seen operationally as a composite of general and specific cognitively mediated abilities important to adaptive interaction with one's physical, social, and psychological environment. Such abilities include the capacity to acquire, store, access, and manipulate information; the ability to learn from experience; insight; abstract reasoning; the capacity to adapt to new situations; and the ability to focus and sustain direction in activities. Measured intelligence tends to be quite stable after adolescence, and test–retest reliabilities are quite high, even in young children. However, **IQ is not static** and may change considerably in children over a period of years.

    a. The Wechsler Scales. Intelligence scales developed by David Wechsler are the tests in most common use today.

        (1) The Wechsler Adult Intelligence Scale-Revised (WAIS-R). (This is the most recent version of the test, which was restandardized in 1981.) The WAIS-R is used to test individuals from 16 years of age, and norms are available to the age of 74 years.

            (a) Uses. The WAIS-R is the standard test of intellectual functioning used to assess current functioning and capacities and the potential for adaptive behavior. The test is for educational planning, placement and remediation, vocational or career counseling, personnel selection, and psychodiagnostic purposes, and it is used in the evaluation of personality functioning.

            (b) Content. The WAIS-R consists of 11 subtests constituting **verbal and performance sections**. Six subtests are concerned with verbal information and reasoning abilities, auditory attention, and memory, and five **performance subtests** address perceptual accuracy, organization, and perceptual–manipulatory skill. A list of individual subtests with their general meanings is in Table 8-1.

            (c) Reliability and validity. Standardization of the WAIS-R is excellent. Table 8-1 presents reliability estimates. Internal consistency reliability is very good and generally yields coefficients exceeding .80 for individual subtests and .90 for the summary IQ measures. Test–retest reliability is similarly high. Criterion validity is fairly well established in studies assessing the relationship of WAIS-R to other existing criteria of adaptive behaviors (e.g., educational achievement, documented brain dysfunction, independent diagnosis of mental retardation).

            (d) Interpretation. Specific interpretations are rarely made on the basis of one score or one response. Instead, responses on a test such as the WAIS-R or on a WAIS-R subtest are compared for consistency with responses on other tests included in a psychological test battery. For example, a diagnosis of mental retardation is not based

Table 8-1. Coefficients of Reliability and Interpretation of the WAIS-R*

	Test–Retest Reliability[†]	Internal Consistency Reliability[†]	Correlation with Full-Scale Score[†]	Interpretation
Verbal subtests				
Information	.91	.89	.76	Twenty-nine questions tap general fund of information and past learning
Digit span	.86	.83	.58	Tests auditory attention and immediate memory for digits forward and backward
Vocabulary	.92	.96	.81	Assesses depth and breadth of vocabulary by asking for definitions of 35 words
Arithmetic	.85	.84	.72	Assesses immediate memory, freedom from distractibility, and mental arithmetic reasoning
Comprehension	.81	.84	.74	Sixteen questions address understanding of common sense information and practical problem solving
Similarities	.84	.84	.75	Evaluates ability to see relationships between objects or concepts
Performance subtests				
Picture completion	.88	.81	.67	Assesses ability to detect logical inconsistencies in pictures of familiar objects
Picture arrangement	.73	.74	.61	Requires evaluation of subtle social cues in a series of stimuli and organization of them into a meaningful story
Block design	.86	.87	.68	Tests visual capacity to analyze abstract designs and requires spatial–constructional ability in reconstructing the designs using blocks
Object assembly	.70	.68	.57	Taps perceptual organization and manipulation of puzzle-like pieces into familiar but initially unknown objects
Digit symbol	.84	.82	.57	A clerical-like task of psychomotor coordination requiring rapid copying of symbols
Verbal IQ	.96	.97	.95	Verbal information, reasoning, and freedom from distractibility
Performance IQ	.90	.93	.91	Perceptual organization and psychomotor manipulatory ability
Full-scale IQ	.96	.97	. . .	Summary score reflecting the overall adaptive functioning of the individual

Note.—Adapted from Wechsler D: *Wechsler Adult Intelligence Scale-Revised*. San Antonio, The Psychological Corporation, 1981, Tables 10, 11, and 16, pp 30, 32, and 46.
*WAIS-R = Wechsler Adult Intelligence Scale-Revised.
[†]Reliability coefficients of .80 to .90 or above are generally considered adequate for clinical uses, while those of .70 or above may be meaningful for research purposes.

on an IQ score alone. Other indices such as social adaptive functioning and life skills are considered as well.

    (i) **Verbal, performance, and full-scale IQ measures are derived** from the scaled scores of the subtests. These are then represented on a standard scale with a theoretical mean of 100 and a standard deviation of 15. IQ ranges and the corresponding percentiles are listed in Table 8-2. The disparity between verbal and performance IQ is evaluated. Usually differences greater than 15 points, depending on the direction of the difference, may reflect academic achievement, socioenvironmental factors, type of psychopathology, learning disabilities, or lateralized brain dysfunction.

    (ii) **For interpretation of individual subtests, age-appropriate scaled scores** are used.

    (iii) **Inter- and intrasubtest variability is examined** to determine an individual's relative strengths and weaknesses and his limits and consistency in performance. The type of variability observed may relate to the individual's adaptive skills, underlying personality, and emotional factors or to particular types and loci of brain dysfunction.

    (iv) **Individual responses are examined.** Verbal subtests are particularly prone to elicit unique, unusual, and idiosyncratic responses. These may reveal much about thought process and thought content. Responses and performance on subtests requiring a high degree of perceptual accuracy point to the individual's capacity to organize his world and maintain contact with reality. Unusual and bizarre responses to performance subtest items are often suggestive of a major psychiatric disturbance.

  (2) **The Wechsler Intelligence Scale for Children-Revised (WISC-R).** The WISC-R is intended for use with children ranging from 6 to 16 years of age. The WISC-R contains the 11 subtests of the WAIS-R but with age-appropriate items and an additional optional Mazes subtest requiring visual spatial planning and problem solving. Reliability and validity are comparable to the WAIS-R, and principles of interpretation are similar.

  (3) The **Wechsler Preschool and Primary Scale of Intelligence (WPPSI)** was developed for use with children of ages 4 through 6½ years. It contains 11 subtests, for which there is some item overlap on verbal subtests with the WISC-R. Several subtests are substantially different in item content. Reliabilities are comparable to the WISC-R. The validity is good, although somewhat variable and not as impressive as that for the WISC-R or the Stanford-Binet Scale.

b. The **Stanford-Binet Scale** is a current version of the original Binet Scale, which was developed in 1905 and which is generally acknowledged as the first formal test of intelligence.

  (1) **Uses.** The Stanford-Binet Scale is used with individuals of ages 2 through 18 years. It is most useful with the very young (6 years and under), the very impaired, and the very bright. Portions of the Stanford-Binet Scale are occasionally used in the evaluation of impaired adults. This test is used to assess giftedness and address educational placement issues, and it is used as a test of general intellectual ability.

  (2) **Content.** The Stanford-Binet Scale comprises 142 brief tests, sampling a wide variety of skills including language, problem solving, arithmetic, manual manipulation, reasoning, and logic. Content is arranged in age-appropriate levels.

  (3) **Reliability and validity.** Reliability studies of the current Stanford-Binet Scale are few, but those reported give reliability coefficients of .90 or above. Criterion validity studies have yielded significant but moderate coefficients, generally ranging from .50 to .90. The Stanford-Binet Scale correlates quite highly with the WAIS (a previous version of the WAIS-R), although there may be substantial differences between mean IQ scores.

Table 8-2. IQ Ranges and Theoretical Percentile Distribution

IQ	Descriptor	Approximate Percentage and Percentile Range of Persons Included
≥ 130	Very superior	2% (98–100)
120–129	Superior	7% (91–98)
110–119	High average	16% (75–90)
90–109	Average	50% (25–75)
80–89	Low average	16% (10–25)
70–79	Borderline	7% (2–9)
< 70	Mentally retarded	2% (0–2)

Note.—Adapted from Wechsler D: *Wechsler Adult Intelligence Scale-Revised.* San Antonio, The Psychological Corporation, 1981, Table 9, p 28.

(4) **Interpretation.** Both quantitative and qualitative methods of interpretation are used. The deviation IQ, similar to the WAIS-R IQ, is the most general score. Strengths and weaknesses in particular skill areas can be evaluated by using the standard deviations associated with those skill areas as a guide to relative performance. The test primarily measures the verbal abilities of older children and adolescents, while substantial portions of the tests are nonverbal for younger children.

2. **Achievement tests.** Measurement of achievement is the evaluation of mastered information and skills that have been part of specific instruction. Tests of achievement, therefore, do not necessarily assess aptitude or future performance. These tests are used widely in the educational system but also are useful in counseling and industry and may be included as part of psychological and neuropsychological test batteries.

   a. **Wide-Range Achievement Test (WRAT)**
      (1) **Uses.** The WRAT provides an estimate of achievement in three academic areas: reading, written spelling, and arithmetic. It is often used as part of psychological, neuropsychological, and psychoeducational test batteries to assess achievement or competence in these basic academically acquired skills.
      (2) **Content.** This test, individually administered, is available for ages 5 through 11 years (level 1) and for ages 12 through 75 years (level 2). The test is comprised of three subtests: reading (letter reading and word recognition and pronunciation), spelling (copying, name writing, and written spelling), and arithmetic (counting, number recognition, and mathematical computation).
      (3) **Reliability and validity.** Estimates show internal consistency reliability to be very good, with coefficients generally above .90. Test–retest reliability follows a similar pattern, with most coefficients above .90. Concurrent validity studies yield moderate correlations (.60 to .90) between WRAT scores and scores on other well-standardized achievement tests. Content validity is the basis on which this and other types of achievement tests are developed and is thus presumed to be excellent.
      (4) **Interpretation.** Norms are available for 28 age groups ranging from 5 to 75 years. Subtest scores can be translated into grade equivalents, percentile rank, and standard scores using the same scale as the WAIS-R.

   b. **Other popular achievement tests** include the **Iowa Tests of Educational Development**, the **Stanford Achievement Test**, the **California Achievement Tests**, and the **Peabody Individual Achievement Test**. Many, but not all, achievement tests can be given in a group format. Standardization of achievement tests is usually very good, reliability is high, and the validity acceptable.

3. **Tests of personality functioning**
   a. The **Minnesota Multiphasic Personality Inventory (MMPI)** is a widely used objective, self-report test that was developed originally in 1940 to obtain diagnostic and clinical information on psychiatric and medical patients.
      (1) **Uses.** The MMPI is the most used, and sometimes abused, personality test. It is employed for both clinical and research purposes and often serves as the criterion against which other personality tests are compared. A limited sampling of its varied uses includes diagnosis, assessment of response to treatment and treatment outcome, forensic evaluation, and general assessment of personality functioning. The MMPI is frequently utilized to substantiate issues of malingering and in evaluating psychological determinants of patients with chronic pain.
      (2) **Content.** The MMPI consists of 550 statements to which the respondent answers true or false. The responses are scored along 10 primary clinical dimensions and 3 validity scales reflecting information about the response style (Table 8-3). Additionally, many new scales have been developed based on recombinations of the original items. Several of the most popular are the anxiety scale, the repression scale, and the MacAndrew alcoholism scale. The test is available in either group or individual format and in its complete form takes about 75 minutes to complete. Several short forms of the test are also available.
      (3) **Reliability and validity.** Reliability and validity of the MMPI involve complex issues because of the characteristics measured, the type of items used, and the methods by which these items are included and the scales are constructed. Reliability estimates have not, surprisingly, been variable and modest. The test has, however, been extensively validated using empirical and construct validation methods. The validity of several short forms of the MMPI that are available is not well established.
      (4) **Interpretation**
         (a) Demographic factors of age, socioeconomic status, and education are considered, as they may affect interpretation.
         (b) Raw scores on each scale are transformed to T scores, with a mean of 50 and a stan-

Table 8-3. The Minnesota Multiphasic Personality Inventory (MMPI)

Scale	Abbreviation	Number	Interpretation of Scale Elevation*
Validity			
Lie scale	L	. . .	Denial of common faults and shortcomings; naive defensiveness
Frequency scale	F	. . .	Endorsement of rare or statistically unusual items; faking bad; cry for help
Correction scale	K	. . .	Denial of inadequacy; sophisticated defensiveness
Clinical			
Hypochondriasis	Hs	1	Degree of concern about somatic functioning
Depression	D	2	Cognitive, emotional, behavioral, and physiological correlates of depression
Hysteria	Hy	3	Denial; high need for affection; somatization; egocentric, manipulative, demanding traits
Psychopathic deviate	Pd	4	Impulsiveness; low frustration tolerance and poor social adjustment; authority problems
Masculinity–femininity	M–F	5	Suggestive of a pattern of interest and attitudes more typical of the opposite sex
Paranoia	Pa	6	Suspiciousness; hypersensitivity; rigidity; possible delusions
Psychasthenia	Pt	7	Anxiety, worry, fears, and self-doubt; personal distress
Schizophrenia	Sc	8	Social and emotional alienation; unusual and idiosyncratic thoughts; bizarre experiences; possible hallucinations
Mania	Ma	9	Ineffective hyperactivity; agitation; restlessness; irritability; no tolerance for delay; expansiveness
Social introversion	Si	0	Shyness; withdrawal; social ineptness; social anxiety

*Interpretations given here are extreme simplifications of possible interpretations that can be associated with a significant scale elevation.

dard deviation of 10. Scores falling at least 2 standard deviations from the mean (i.e., 70 or greater) are considered to be clinically significant, although scores deviating less than 2 standard deviations (particularly for scores below the mean) may also influence the interpretation of the results. Every score, whether elevated or not, may serve to enrich the interpretation of the overall profile configuration.

   (c) The pattern of scores on the validity scales is analyzed to assess response characteristics such as defensiveness, exaggeration of symptoms, and comprehension of the test items.

   (d) Elevations on clinical scales are identified, and the configuration of the profile is compared with established profile patterns, referred to as code types.

b. **Rorschach Inkblot Test.** The Rorschach technique is regarded as the major projective test of personality assessment. Originally developed around 1920 by a psychiatrist, Hermann Rorschach, the test has been the subject of several thousand publications.

   (1) **Uses.** The Rorschach is used to assess personality dynamics and organization as well as cognitive style. The responses reveal information about thought processes, perceptual organization, reality testing, unconscious needs, conflicts and dynamics, interpersonal style, coping mechanisms, affective responses, degree of self-focus, as well as other specific aspects of personality organization. More recent studies show this technique to hold promise for evaluation of suicide potential. The Rorschach is usually included in any thorough assessment of personality functioning. It serves to acquire information, which may be unavailable or would take a great deal of time to acquire by other means, for purposes of understanding, prediction, and diagnosis.

(2) Content. The Rorschach consists of 10 cards (plates), each containing a bilaterally symmetrical inkblot design. Five of the cards contain designs of black, white, and intermediate achromatic shades, and five cards have designs entailing some color. Cards are presented individually with simple instructions such as, "What might this be?" The patient is given a chance to respond to all 10 inkblots in the **performance proper**. Afterwards, the examiner conducts the **inquiry**, during which the inkblots are reviewed and the patient is asked to describe more of what he has seen, so as to help the examiner see and understand the percepts as the patient has. The performance proper and, to a somewhat lesser extent, the inquiry are conducted in such a way that unnecessary structure and influence are not imposed on the patient's responses.

(3) Reliability and validity. Despite extensive clinical use and research, adequate reliability and validity have not been demonstrated until relatively recently. Lately, John Exner worked intensively on what is probably the most comprehensive, psychometrically oriented Rorschach system to be developed. The **Exner method** is fast becoming the predominant method of Rorschach being taught and utilized. Studies using this technique indicate test–retest and inter-rater reliability to be acceptable.

(4) Interpretation. Common to all Rorschach methods is **quantitative scoring** of several basic response characteristics. These include scoring for number of responses, location of responses, and response determinants including form level and quality, movement, color usage, shading, and texture. **Reaction times** are noted, and responses are also evaluated for content categories and whether or not the response is a popular percept. Basic scoring categories and their meaning are presented in Table 8-4. Interpretation, however, relies most heavily on quantitative indices or formulas that combine and compare the basic scoring categories. Such indices lead to a much more detailed, integrated, and dynamic understanding of the individual's ways of responding. Following quantitative analysis, most clinicians analyze the responses for repetitive content and themes, unusual responses and logic, and the sequential characteristics of both the process and content of responses.

c. Thematic Apperception Test (TAT). The TAT was developed in the early 1940s by Henry Murray as a way to evaluate drives, emotions, sentiments, and conflicts of which an individual may be unaware. This is a projective test, but the stimuli have somewhat greater structure than those of the Rorschach test.

(1) Uses. The TAT is used in the assessment of personality functioning. The test is used more to assess the content of personality rather than the process. The TAT is useful in

Table 8-4. Major Scoring Categories of the Rorschach Test

Category	Meaning
Location of response	Responses are scored as to whether the percept encompasses the whole blot, large details, small details, or white spaces. Location provides information on how an individual approaches the world intellectually (e.g., whether by attempting to organize various elements into a whole or by focusing on the practical or even the unusual details).
Movement	Movement is subdivided into major categories of human movement, animal movement, and inanimate movement. Movement responses are associated with inner fantasy and impulses and imagination.
Form	A score is given to responses determined only by shape. Form relates to the perceptual and intellectual control of the individual. Interpretation is importantly modified by form quality and the percentage of form responses.
Color	Responses determined by chromatic and achromatic characteristics are scored taking into account the degree to which form is also present. Responses with color determinants reflect the emotional responsiveness to and control of the individual over outside stimulation.
Shading	Percepts involving shading as primary determinants are felt to address awareness and ways of dealing with affectional needs.
Form dimension	These are responses for which the perception of depth, distance, or dimension has been an important characteristic. These responses relate to an individual's awareness of and handling of anxiety.

addressing core issues, needs, conflicts, motivational characteristics, aspects of inter-personal functioning, and the ability to employ fantasy and imagination. The results are interpreted in the context of a comprehensive psychological test battery.

   (2) Content. The TAT consists of 30 cards depicting 1 or more persons, whose activities and feelings, as well as the tone and context of the situation, are ambiguous. The stimuli on the cards have been found to address certain types of characteristic issues (e.g., father–son relationships, suicidal thoughts), and the specific cards used are often chosen for an individual on this basis. Typically 10 to 20 cards are presented. The patient is asked to make up a story about each picture, describing what is happening, what led up to the situation, what the characters are thinking and feeling, and how the story turns out.

   (3) Reliability and validity. Because of the nature of the test materials and the possible range of patient responses, reliability studies are very difficult and are not necessarily appropriate. Some studies have demonstrated satisfactory inter-rater reliability, but many clinicians do not use a formal rating system, and subjective judgment is utilized. More problematic is a lack of demonstrated agreement on the specific interpretation of scores. Assessment of validity is similarly problematic. Like the Rorschach test, however, despite questionable reliability, the TAT in the context of a more complete psychometric assessment adds considerably to the clinical understanding of the patient.

   (4) Interpretation. Although several scoring and interpretive systems exist, most clinicians employ a qualitative method. Generally, an attempt is made to single out the character in the card with whom the patient identifies (the hero) and then evaluate the story in terms of a list of needs (internal determinants) or pressures (environmental determinants) that influence behavior. Consistent themes are identified, and responses may be further analyzed sequentially or individually.

 d. Sentence Completion Tests (also known as Incomplete Sentences)

   (1) Uses. These tests provide an economical means of surveying a patient's thoughts, feelings, motivations, and behavior along a number of important psychological dimensions.

   (2) Content. Many forms of these tests are available. The tests usually contain 50 or more sentence stems, which the patient is asked to complete with the first thing that comes to his mind. Items elicit responses that relate to fears, desires, fantasies, aspirations, relationships, self-concept, frustrations, attitudes, and so forth. The task has obvious structure but contains projective elements as well.

   (3) Interpretation. Although some scoring guidelines exist, interpretation is usually based on a simple inspection of the items, and the results of the test are used to flesh out other clinical and test data. The answers are often taken at face value, but they may also serve as a focal point for further discussion and clarification in an interview format.

 e. Projective drawings. This test category includes a variety of tests including Draw-a-Person, House-Tree-Person, Draw-a-Family, and Kinetic Family Drawings.

   (1) Uses. These types of procedures are used more to assess personality adjustment than aspects of intelligence.

   (2) Content. In each task, the patient is instructed to make one or more drawings.

   (3) Reliability and validity are questionable; however, projective drawings continue to be widely used as one component of personality assessment.

   (4) Interpretation. Standard guidelines are available for drawing interpretations, and they take into account such characteristics as quality, size, placement, organization, symmetry, erasures, detail, transparencies, distortions, omissions, perspective, shading, and specific emphasis. The results are considered as symbolic representations of the more unconscious aspects of a patient's psychological structure and functioning; hence, these are considered to be projective tests.

 f. Other tests of personality functioning are often employed in medical settings for research and clinical purposes.

   (1) The **Symptom Checklist-90** is a 90-item questionnaire, which can be completed in 15 to 30 minutes. It yields information concerning several clinical dimensions, including somatic concerns, obsessive–compulsiveness, interpersonal sensitivity, depression, anxiety, phobic anxiety, hostility, paranoid ideation, and psychoticism; it also provides a global severity index. Norms are available for both inpatient and outpatient groups.

   (2) The **Millon Clinical Multiaxial Inventory**, developed in 1976, was standardized on individuals seeking treatment in mental health systems. The results are interpreted along clinical characteristics closely relating to the personality disorders.

   (3) The **Beck Depression Inventory** is a widely used screening device for the assessment of the behavioral, cognitive, affective, and physiological components of depression.

   (4) The **Sixteen Personality Factor Inventory** is a 182-item questionnaire that is an objective test, and it can be administered in a group or individual format. Interpretation may emphasize clinical aspects, career development considerations, and marital issues. The test is oriented toward nonpathological aspects of personality functioning.

(5) The **California Psychological Inventory** is another self-administered objective questionnaire that can be given individually or to a group. The 468 items assess stable personality traits relating to behavior, feelings, and attitudes in the context of social, ethical, and family considerations. The emphasis on interpretation lies in the individuality of normal personality adjustment, not in personality pathology.

4. **Vocational tests** are used infrequently in medical settings, so only brief mention of the most popular tests of vocational interest follows.

    a. The **Strong-Campbell Interest Inventory**, along with other vocational tests of aptitude and ability, is used in career counseling.

    b. Kuder Interest Inventories. Several forms of the Kuder scales are available, with versions appropriate for a wide variety of age groups. Information is yielded on general interest areas and on interest areas that are analogous to various occupations.

5. **Neuropsychological assessment.** The evaluation of brain injury and dysfunction in humans through the use of psychological tests has become an increasingly sophisticated and practical speciality of psychology. The neuropsychological evaluation may entail a comprehensive or a fairly specific assessment of cognitive, emotional, and adaptive behaviors using standardized tests that have demonstrated sensitivity to the condition of the brain. The tests provide diagnostic, descriptive, and prognostic information and entail no risk. The major approaches to assessment have been through the use of standardized batteries [e.g., the Halstead-Reitan Neuropsychological Test Battery (HRB)] or groups of tests assembled to meet the needs of a particular patient. The information gained from the neuropsychological assessment may add considerable depth to significant findings observed on the MSE. The neuropsychological evaluation often reveals important but subtle changes in cognitive and emotional spheres, even before they can be detected by the MSE.

    a. The **Halstead-Reitan Neuropsychological Test Battery.** The HRB originated in the work of Ward Halstead in the 1940s, and it was largely developed and researched by Halstead's student Ralph Reitan beginning in the 1950s. It is available in forms for younger children, older children, and adults.

        (1) Uses. The bulk of the extensive research for this battery addresses questions of the presence, absence, and localization of **brain dysfunction**. Prognostic and rehabilitative statements are often made on the basis of the HRB and other supplementary neuropsychological tests.

        (2) Content. The HRB proper contains five tests; however, the battery is almost always supplemented by other tests. Table 8-5 describes the core tests of the HRB. Administration of an entire comprehensive battery may take 5 to 8 hours, depending on the patient.

        (3) Reliability and validity. Extensive cross-validation studies have substantiated the empirical (both predictive and concurrent) and construct validity of this battery as related to the presence and localization of brain dysfunction. Research has been neither consistent nor impressive regarding discrimination between brain dysfunctional patients and those with chronic psychiatric disorders. The accuracy of comprehensive test batteries such as the HRB in discriminating normal individuals from those who are organically impaired is approximately 90%. Discrimination between brain dysfunctional individuals and general psychiatric patients is about 70% accurate. Several studies demonstrate adequate reliability of the battery, although this has not been a strong focus of the research on the HRB.

        (4) Interpretation. The results of the HRB are interpreted using four methods of inference.

            (a) The five primary tests of the HRB are used to calculate an **impairment index**, reflecting the degree of overall impairment in neuropsychological functioning.

            (b) Secondly, test results are analyzed for differences that occur between task performances carried out by the left and right sides of the body (e.g., use of the right or left hand on the tactual performance test).

            (c) Thirdly, the pattern of results is inspected for consistencies in level impairment and impairments on tasks of a specific sensory–motor modality, those utilizing specific cognitive abilities, and those known to be mediated by particular brain regions.

            (d) Finally, the results are analyzed for pathognomonic signs—those signs that, when present, are indicators of brain dysfunction (e.g., aphasic errors).

    b. The **Luria Nebraska Neuropsychological Battery** was developed by Charles Golden and colleagues in the mid-1970s, based on the theory and clinical technique of the late A.R. Luria, a Russian neuropsychologist. It is a promising assessment tool that is clinically useful, although not fully accepted for routine assessment. Both adult and child versions are available.

(1) **Uses.** The test is particularly useful in the evaluation of low-functioning and markedly impaired individuals and in planning rehabilitation.

(2) **Content.** The battery consists of 269 individual items; it takes approximately 2½ hours to administer. The items are grouped into 11 scales relating to motor functions, rhythm

Table 8-5. Halstead-Reitan Neuropsychological Test Battery (HRB)*

Test	Description
Primary	
Category test	This is test of abstract and conceptual reasoning and concept learning. It consists of 208 visually presented stimuli organized into 7 subtests. It is the most sensitive measure in the HRB of the effects of brain dysfunction.
Tactual performance test	Patients while blindfolded place 10 geometric forms into a formboard, first with the dominant hand, then with the nondominant hand, and with both hands on a third trial. The patient draws from memory a diagram of the board and blocks. The task requires tactual spatial analysis, constructional ability, novel problem solving, and cognitive visualization. It is very sensitive to general brain dysfunction and is the best measure of lateralized cortical dysfunction in the HRB. Measures of time, memory, and proper location of drawn figures contribute to the impairment index.
Seashore rhythm test	This test consists of pairs of sequentially presented rhythmic patterns for which the patient indicates whether the patterns in each pair are the same or different. It requires auditory attention and tracking and nonverbal auditory discrimination.
Speech sounds perception test	Nonsense words presented from an audiotape are matched to their printed representation. Perception and matching phonemes and graphemes are required.
Finger oscillation test	As a measure of fine motor control and speech, the patient taps a key on 5 consecutive 10-second trials with the index finger of the dominant and nondominant hands.
Impairment index	This consists of the percentage of 7 measures from the aforementioned tests falling in the impaired range. An index of .5 or greater indicates neuropsychological impairment.
Ancillary	
Trail-making test	Part A consists of 25 circles randomly distributed on the paper and numbered 1 to 25. Patients draw lines connecting them in numerical sequence. Part B consists of circles with either numbers or letters, which the patient connects in sequence while alternating between numbers and letters. Part A requires visual searching, motor speed, and simple sequence planning. Part B additionally requires flexibility in thinking.
Aphasia screening test	This consists of a brief task sampling expressive and receptive language capacity and language-mediated skills. Clear-cut deficits are considered to be pathognomonic of brain dysfunction.
Sensory perceptual examination	This includes tasks of bilateral simultaneous stimulation in visual, auditory and tactile modalities, finger localization, fingertip number writing, and tactile form recognition. Visual field confrontation is also included.
Lateral dominance examination	This provides measures of hand, eye, and foot dominance. A formal test of ocular dominance is included, and the strength of grip for each hand is measured with a hand dynamometer.

*Primary and frequently used ancillary tests.

and acousticomotor functions, tactile functions, visual–spatial ability, receptive speech, expressive speech, writing, reading skills, arithmetic ability, memory, and intellectual processes. Three additional scales are the pathognomonic scale (consisting of items most sensitive to brain dysfunction) and right and left hemisphere scales.

(3) Reliability and validity. Test–retest reliability is adequate, and coefficients range from .78 to .96 for the individual scales. Acceptable validity has been found in terms of accuracy at discriminating among brain dysfunctional, psychiatric, and control patients. Construct validity is not well demonstrated, and the procedure has received considerable criticism and remains controversial on this basis and other methodological shortcomings.

(4) Interpretation. Items scored are tallied on their respective scales and then are plotted on a T-score distribution. The resulting profile is much like that of the MMPI. The number of scales falling 1 and 2 standard deviations above the baseline (adjusted for age and education) are noted to determine the likely presence or absence of brain dysfunction. The pattern of elevations, along with special localization scales, are utilized to specify location. A qualitative analysis of performance on items falling within descriptive factor scales (subcomponents of the major scales that have been identified through factor analysis) is then performed to enhance the understanding of specific strengths and weaknesses.

c. Individualized neuropsychological batteries. Most neuropsychologists use a basic battery of tests on most patients and then select additional tests based on individualized criteria. This method allows for general assessment of a wide range of cognitive processes, elaborating on the standard MSE and permitting an in-depth exploration of particular referral questions. All batteries should include measures to assess attention, concentration, memory, language, spatial analytic and spatial manipulatory ability, practical and abstract problem solving, conceptual ability, and flexibility in thinking.

d. Other popular neuropsychological tests

(1) The **Bender Visual Motor Gestalt Test** consists of nine designs that are presented individually to the patient and are copied by him one at a time. Some examiners follow this initial test with a recall trial, in which the patient draws as many designs as he can from memory. This task has been used almost universally as a screen for "organicity" (i.e., brain dysfunction) as part of standard psychological test batteries. Although it is fairly insensitive in this respect, when combined with the Canter Background Interference procedure, the Bender Gestalt becomes a reasonably powerful neuropsychological screening instrument. Qualitative analysis of the drawings may reveal information about localization of dysfunction.

(2) The **Benton Visual Retention Test** is another spatial constructional graphomotor task that can be used in a format addressing copying ability or immediate and short-term recall. It consists of 10 designs with alternate forms that the patient draws from copy or from memory.

(3) The **California Verbal Learning Test** is a repeated-trial word-learning task that is useful for assessing the rate of learning, immediate and short-term memory, learning strategies, and interference effects.

(4) The **Ravens Progressive Matrices.** This test primarily requires visual–spatial analysis and spatial conceptualization. Available in several levels of difficulty, the basic task is to complete an incomplete design sequence by choosing the correct one from an array of designs.

(5) The **Shipley Hartford Institute of Living Scale.** This test consists of two subtests: The first is a multiple choice vocabulary task, and the second is a verbal abstract reasoning task involving interpolative and extrapolative thinking. The purpose of the test is to assess the disparity between vocabulary (which is considered relatively resistant to brain dysfunction) and abstract reasoning (which is sensitive to brain dysfunction).

(6) The **Wechsler Memory Scale** is a widely used memory test that assesses recall of current and past information, orientation, attention, concentration, memory for story content, memory for designs, and associative learning. This test is often modified to yield estimates of immediate recall and 30-minute delayed recall of stories and designs. The test yields a memory quotient very similar to the IQ, and when used with the delayed recall trials, **impairment indices** of immediate memory, recent memory, and forgetting can be derived.

(7) The **Wisconsin Card Sorting Test** involves abstract and conceptual reasoning, flexibility in thinking, and learning to learn. The patient must learn to sort cards into categories of color, form, and number, learning these concepts and shifting categories when appropriate on the basis of feedback about whether any particular response is right or wrong. This task is thought to be one of the better methods to assess frontal lobe functioning.

G. ANALYSIS AND INTEGRATION OF TEST RESULTS

1. A single score or result on a psychological or neuropsychological test is rarely considered in isolation. Rather, test data are examined for patterns and are considered in the context of other test data as well as in the context of the individual's behavior and history.

2. Psychological tests emphasize personality adjustment and pathology, thought processes and content, as well as general style. Neuropsychological tests emphasize the assessment of cognitive-mediated abilities. Together, they provide an in-depth extended mental status.

3. Factors such as race, age, intelligence, education, and current circumstances (e.g., occupation, living arrangements) are considered as part of the interpretive process.

H. REPORTING OF TEST INFORMATION

1. While the administration and scoring of psychological tests may be performed by a trained technician (psychometrist), the interpretation, integration, and reporting of the information is the responsibility of a clinical psychologist.

2. A written summary of the assessment should be generated. Reports may be very specific or broad, depending on how concisely the referral source poses the questions to be addressed (referral questions should be as specific as possible).

   a. Reports should contain basic identifying information, a clear statement of the purpose of the examination, pertinent background information, a list of procedures utilized, and a description of the tested individual's status and behavior during the examination.

   b. Psychologists differ widely in the presentation of results, some listing scores, others discussing performance on tests and test items, and some providing only interpretation. It is preferable that information be presented in such a way that any interpretation can be related to the data contained in the report or that the basis of the interpretation would be clear to another clinical psychologist.

   c. Test reports are often concluded with a section variously entitled "Summary," "Assessment," or "Impression." This section should contain a clear response to the referral question, based upon data presented or referred to earlier in the report. Any recommendations are usually outlined at this point.

BIBLIOGRAPHY

Adams RL, Jenkins RL: Basic principles of the neuropsychological examination. In *Clinical Practice of Psychology*. Edited by Walker CE. New York, Pergamon, 1981

Buros OK: *The Eighth Mental Measurements Yearbook*. Highland Park, N.J., Gryphon Press, 1978

Exner JE: *The Rorschach. A Comprehensive System*, vols 1, 2, 3. New York, John Wiley, 1974, 1978, 1982

Goldstein G, Hersen M (eds): *Handbook of Psychological Assessment*. New York, Pergamon, 1984

Groth-Marnat G: *Handbook of Psychological Assessment*. New York, Van Nostrand, 1984

Jastak S, Wilkinson GS: *Wide Range Achievement Test Administration Manual*. Wilmington, Del., Jastak Assessment Systems, 1984

Lachar D: *The MMPI: Clinical Assessment and Automated Interpretation*. Los Angeles, Western Psychological Services, 1974

Leigh H, Reiser M: *The Patient*. New York, Plenum Press, 1980

Luria AR: *Higher Cortical Functions in Man*. New York, Basic Books, 1966

Marks P, Seeman W, Haller DL: *The Actuarial Use of MMPI with Adolescents and Adults*. Baltimore, Williams and Wilkins, 1975

Plum F, Posner JB: *The Diagnosis of Stupor and Coma*, 3rd ed. Philadelphia, Davis, 1982

Sattler JM: *Assessment of Children's Intelligence and Special Abilities*. Boston, Allyn and Bacon, 1982

Strub RL, Black FW: *The Mental Status Examination in Neurology*. Philadelphia, Davis, 1985

Wechsler D: *Wechsler Adult Intelligence Scale-Revised*. New York, Psychological Corporation, 1981

Zimmerman IL, Woo-Sam JM: *Clinical Interpretation of the Wechsler Adult Intelligence Scale*. New York, Grune and Stratton, 1973

STUDY QUESTIONS

Directions: Each question below contains five suggested answers. Choose the **one best** response to each question.

1. A young woman with hallucinations and frightening delusions is seen in the emergency room. On examination, she is found to be drowsy with severe impairment of short-term memory. The physician's next step should be to

(A) look up causes of memory impairment
(B) order a urine toxicology screening
(C) prescribe a stimulant drug
(D) admit the patient to the psychiatric ward
(E) order skull x-rays

2. The accuracy of neuropsychological test batteries in differentiating organically impaired individuals from individuals with psychiatric disorders is approximately

(A) 100%
(B) 85%
(C) 70%
(D) 50%
(E) 35%

Directions: The question below contains four suggested answers of which **one or more** is correct. Choose the answer

A if **1, 2, and 3** are correct
B if **1 and 3** are correct
C if **2 and 4** are correct
D if **4** is correct
E if **1, 2, 3, and 4** are correct

3. Findings consistent with the diagnosis of dementia in an older patient include

(1) disinhibited behavior (loss of appropriate social conduct)
(2) normal concentration with zero out of four words recalled after 5 minutes
(3) poor design reproduction
(4) hallucinations

Directions: The groups of questions below consist of lettered choices followed by several numbered items. For each numbered item select the **one** lettered choice with which it is **most** closely associated. Each lettered choice may be used once, more than once, or not at all.

Questions 4–8

For each area of the brain listed below, select the most appropriate test for functional evaluation. (The patient's language function is assumed to be normal.)

(A) Recall of four items after 5 minutes
(B) Repetition of digits, forward and reversed
(C) Interpretation of proverbs
(D) Serial 7's subtraction
(E) Copying simple shapes and objects

4. Visual cortex; visual association areas of parietal lobe; motor areas of frontal lobe

5. Pontine and midbrain reticular activating system (RAS)

6. Prefrontal cortex

7. Left hippocampus and temporal lobe

8. RAS; left parietal lobe; hippocampus and other cortical and subcortical memory areas

Questions 9–12

For each of the following case studies, select the test that would provide the most pertinent information.

(A) Minnesota Multiphasic Personality Inventory (MMPI)
(B) Wechsler Adult Intelligence Scale-Revised (WAIS-R)
(C) Projective drawings
(D) Rorschach Inkblot Technique
(E) Halstead-Reitan Battery (HRB)

9. An 18-year-old man is considering applying to college for the upcoming year. Having a very weak record of academic performance, he is urged by his parents to see the family physician for guidance. According to the family, the young man is outgoing, levelheaded, happy, and well adjusted. He has not had any behavioral or emotional difficulties in the past. The family physician consults with a psychologist and recommends psychological assessment. Which test results are of most interest to the physician?

10. A 50-year-old executive experienced a brief episode of mild, right-sided paresthesia and left-sided headache of about a 12-hour duration. One week later, he went to his physician, at the advice of a colleague, because of forgetfulness, decreased understanding of complex spoken information, and difficulty in organizing his activities. The results of which test are most pertinent?

11. A young man with narcissistic personality disorder has been in insight-oriented psychotherapy for 1 year. The psychiatrist feels that there has been little or no progress in therapy for several months. Which test would most likely reveal personality dynamics that might be helpful in understanding the therapeutic impasse?

12. A 40-year-old man sees his physician 4 months after he was involved in a minor automobile accident. The patient complains dramatically of constant neck pain, a labile mood, bizarre sensations, and an inability to work. The patient has filed suit for damages and suffering against the other driver. Laboratory and x-ray studies and physical examination have not revealed any cause, and appropriate medications have been tried but with no effect. Which test may be particularly informative?

ANSWERS AND EXPLANATIONS

1. The answer is B. *(Figs. 8-2, 8-3)* The most significant observation in the vignette is that the patient is drowsy. Alterations in the level of consciousness, reduced levels of attention and concentration, and psychotic symptoms suggest a delirium or intoxication. Impairment of consciousness (which is a brain stem function) can produce a variety of findings at higher cognitive levels, so that the memory disturbance and changes in thought content are secondary to the underlying problem. Schizophrenia does not cause impairment in consciousness. The most frequent cause of a syndrome such as that described above is drug intoxication, and urine screening would be the preferred next step.

2. The answer is C. *[III F 5 a (1) (3)]* Comprehensive neuropsychological test batteries such as the Halstead-Reitan Battery (HRB) have only moderate capacity (HRB's accuracy rate is placed at about 70%) to discriminate between brain dysfunctional individuals and individuals with psychiatric disorders. However, they provide highly accurate, but not perfect, differentiation of normal individuals from brain dysfunctional individuals. The evaluation of brain injury and dysfunction through the use of these tests has become a sophisticated and practical specialty of psychology—prognostic and rehabilitative judgments are often based on the results of HRB and other neuropsychological tests.

3. The answer is A (1, 2, 3). *[II C 2, E 3 b (1), (2), F 2 a; Fig. 8-12]* Early symptoms of dementia are gradual loss of social skills as well as the more obvious loss in short-term memory. Normal ability on tests of concentration are the rule in early dementing illness. Design copying is a sensitive test of cortical integrity and ability and may be lost very early in a patient with Alzheimer's disease because of widespread damage. Patients with poor memory often appear to be paranoid as they accuse others of stealing when they cannot find their possessions; however, hallucinations are a rarity, especially early in the course of dementia.

4–8. The answers are: 4-E, 5-B, 6-C, 7-A, 8-D. *[II C 3 b (2), E 1 a, 3 b (2) (b), F 2 a, b, G 1 b (1)]* Short-term memory is dependent upon an ability to concentrate. Information for short-term memory is stored in the hippocampus and temporal lobe. Digit repetition measures attention and requires an intact reticular activating system (RAS) in the pons and midbrain. (Rare deep medial frontal lobe lesions can cause indifference and inattention.) Interpretation of proverbs requires the use of brain areas where the highest cortical function appears to be located. The analytic and conceptual skills are largely based in the prefrontal cortex.

The copying of a design requires many areas of the brain—namely, the visual or occipital cortex, the parietal association areas, and the prefrontal and frontal cortices. Damage to the right parietal lobe results in greater impairment in this task than a similar lesion on the left side. A good performance indicates integrity of many neural structures; hence, this test is a good screening method. Poor performance requires appraisal of each area involved (e.g., is the problem related to poor motor control of writing? is there a problem in the analysis of the design?).

While serial 7's subtraction is used by some as a test of concentration (i.e., a test of brain stem RAS integrity), this utilization is an underestimate of the complexity of the task. The ability to calculate is highly dependent upon intelligence and education; therefore, the task is calling upon brain areas other than the RAS—namely, calculating abilities in the left parietal lobe and recall of mathematical facts in memory storage areas.

9–12. The answers are: 9-B, 10-B, 11-D, 12-A. *[I B 4, 7; III F 1 a (1), 2 a, 3 a (1), b, 4 c, 5 a]* Although the consulting psychologist would probably administer a battery of psychological tests to evaluate a range of factors of influence on past and future academic performance, in the absence of obvious difficulties, the physician would be most interested in tests of intellectual and academic achievement. The Wechsler Adult Intelligence Scale-Revised (WAIS-R) is the test of intelligence that is used most often, and the test results serve as an indicator of potential and correlate highly with academic performance. Results from the Wide-Range Achievement Test (WRAT) would also be pertinent. The WRAT provides a check for the level of mastery of basic skills such as spelling, arithmetic, and reading.

Right-sided paresthesia and left-sided headache are suggestive of lateralized neurologic events, and subsequent changes in mental status warrant a full neurologic workup, including neuropsychological evaluation. The Halstead-Reitan Battery (HRB) is the only comprehensive neuropsychological evaluation technique listed. Such an evaluation can provide a detailed assessment of cognitive functioning in relation to brain functioning.

The Rorschach Inkblot Technique is based on the hypothesis that individuals will respond to the ambiguous and unstructured test materials in ways that project unconscious dynamics, current forces, drives, and motivations. Drawings alone, while perhaps helpful in this situation, are not likely to reveal information of a specific nature that would be directly related to the referral question.

The Minnesota Multiphasic Personality Inventory (MMPI) in this instance is likely to divulge important information about the individual's general response style and tendency to exaggerate symptoms. The MMPI has been used extensively with pain patients and may provide considerable insight into psychological characteristics that often accompany psychogenic pain.

9

Clinical Syndromes and Psychopathology

Marc Hertzman

I. THE NATURE OF PSYCHIATRIC ILLNESS

A. PSYCHOPATHOLOGY IS A DISEASE STATE, and it can be recognized as such in much the same way that physiopathology is recognized.

1. Psychopathologic dysfunction has a cluster of **signs and symptoms** that can be readily recognized by trained, independent observers. As a disease, psychopathology takes a **recognizable course**.

2. An individual's illness cannot be classified as ''organic'' or ''inorganic'' any more simply than the individual can be divided into body and psyche. Physical illness and mental illness overlap, and the boundaries become more indistinct when a disease state such as schizophrenia or an organic brain syndrome exhibits its somatic symptoms. Disease weakens the performance of an essential function. Definitive laboratory tests may not exist for psychiatric disorders, and the etiology may not , in some cases, be known; however, this does not argue against the acknowledgment of a process as a disease. (For example, tuberculosis and syphilis both were widely recognized before laboratory tests were developed and before their respective etiologies were defined, and today, in both instances, central nervous system findings that mimic psychopathologic signs and symptoms may be the sole indicators of disease.)

3. The psychiatric symptoms reported by patients can often lead to an accurate diagnosis of psychological disease more readily than common diagnostic studies such as chest x-rays can pinpoint physical disease.

4. Psychiatric illnesses often respond to well-defined biological and psychological treatments, which may be curative or palliative.

B. PSYCHOPATHOLOGIC THEORIES

1. **Psychological theory.** Sigmund Freud demonstrated that **conscious thought and behavior are often discordant**. He explained this discrepancy by postulating a structural model of mental functioning, which encompasses the id, the ego, and the superego.
   a. The **id** comprises basic instincts, drives, impulses, and wishes, which are **unconscious**.
   b. The id is normally overridden by the **ego**, which serves a function of **control**. The ego mediates between the individual and reality.
   c. The **superego** embodies the **ego-ideal**, which comprises internal standards and ideals. The superego represents **conscience**.

2. The **biological theory** of psychopathology is based on the assumption that emotion, mood, and behavior can be influenced by a pathophysiologic dysfunction that affects the central nervous system. It can then be assumed that the dysfunction can be corrected through pharmacologic manipulation. The psychological effects of hashish and cocaine were studied in the nineteenth century, and the effects of drugs such as amphetamine and lysergic acid diethylamide (LSD) were studied in the first half of the twentieth century; however, the beginning of modern psychopharmacology was the discovery in 1952 that chlorpromazine significantly ameliorates the acute symptoms of schizophrenia. This discovery hastened the formulation of biological theories of psychopathology.

3. The **psychosocial–family systems theory** explains the origin and maintenance of psychopathology from early in life as the fundamental characteristic of a stable system that functions to resist change. Psychiatric symptoms are an adaptive response to family miscommunications and unusual behavior. In order for psychological growth to occur in individuals, entrenched interactions within the family must be disrupted.

C. DEFENSE MECHANISMS

1. Psychodynamic theory postulates that **psychiatric signs and symptoms are significantly the result of failure of psychological defenses to function effectively**.

2. A defense mechanism is an unconscious, intrapsychic process by which anxiety is diminished (see Chapter 6, section I B 5). Defense mechanisms include:
   a. Denial
   b. Projection
   c. Splitting
   d. Repression
   e. Reaction formation
   f. Isolation of affect
   g. Rationalization
   h. Intellectualization
   i. Undoing
   j. Regression

3. **Defense mechanisms are not diagnostic by themselves**, but they do tend to cluster in psychiatric syndromes, and modern psychiatric diagnosis is made by searching for clusters of signs and symptoms.

D. THE BIOPSYCHOSOCIAL MODEL OF PSYCHIATRIC ILLNESS

1. A psychiatric diagnosis presumes the assessment of a patient's **predisposing biological characteristics**, such as a family history of similar illness. It presumes the assessment of **social factors**, such as home, work, and school. **Psychological signs and symptoms** are equally considered.

2. The third edition of the *Diagnostic and Statistical Manual of Mental Disorders* (DSM III)* uses a multiaxial method for the assessment of mental disorders. It attempts to determine the resources and susceptibilities of the psychiatric patient to ensure that information pertinent to the diagnosis and to predicting the prognosis is evaluated. Five axes are used: Axes I, II, and III are diagnostic; IV and V are prognostic in intent.
   a. **Axis I** comprises the acute diagnosis (clinical syndromes).
   b. **Axis II** comprises characterological and conduct disorders.
   c. **Axis III** comprises contributing physical disorders.
   d. **Axis IV** rates the pyschosocial stressors.
   e. **Axis V** rates the level of function.

II. ORGANIC BRAIN SYNDROMES

A. DEFINITION

1. **Organic brain syndrome** is a general term for a known or presumed biological illness that alters brain function. It may result in cognitive, affective, or behavioral signs and symptoms.

2. The designation **delirium** is reserved for **acute** organic brain syndromes, which are often but not exclusively associated with fever, a hypermetabolic state, or drug withdrawal. A common laboratory finding in delirium is a normal or fast electroencephalogram (EEG) in the face of grossly impaired cognition, as evidenced by altered attention and the results of vigilance testing.

B. INCIDENCE AND PREVALENCE

1. The **incidence** of organic brain syndromes among hospitalized medical and surgical patients is about 10%.

2. The **prevalence** among psychiatric patients is about 20%.

C. DIAGNOSIS. Because an organic brain syndrome can be life-threatening and because it is possible that the process is reversible, an accurate diagnosis is essential.

1. **Signs and symptoms**
   a. Clouding of consciousness
   b. Alteration in concentration ability or vigilance
   c. Decrement in cognition

---

*Diagnostic and Statistical Manual of Mental Disorders, 3rd ed. Washington, D.C., American Psychiatric Association, 1980.

       d. Change in behavior or mood
       e. Hallucinations, delusions, or both, of any kind

  2. Differential diagnosis
      a. The isolation of a particular etiology among the known causes of organic brain syndrome is based upon a complete neurologic examination, including:
         (1) Clinical findings
         (2) Specific laboratory tests:
            (a) Complete blood count
            (b) Urinalysis
            (c) Blood chemistry determinations
            (d) Computed axial tomography (CAT) scan
      b. Organic brain syndromes must be differentiated from the major psychiatric disorders with psychosis (see section III). This can be done by:
         (1) Ruling out known causes of organic brain syndromes
         (2) Looking for history, signs, and symptoms of:
            (a) Mania
            (b) Serious depression
            (c) Schizophrenic disorders

D. TREATMENT

  1. Treatment of an organic brain syndrome usually requires removal of the causative agent, an antidote for the causative agent, or both.

  2. Treatment is supportive, reassuring, but not intrusive. In most organically induced psychoses, frequent reorientation to time, place, and person is helpful.

  3. Major tranquilizers may be useful.

III. SCHIZOPHRENIA

A. DEFINITION

  1. The diagnosis of a psychosis such as schizophrenia implies a deficiency in reality testing, which is usually overt.

  2. The term schizophrenia refers to a group of mental disorders that are characterized by disturbances in behavior, language, thought form and content, and affect.

B. HISTORY

  1. Emil Kraepelin defined **dementia praecox** as a thought disorder of adolescence, which gradually leads to functional deterioration (differentiating it from manic-depressive psychosis).

  2. Eugene Bleuler introduced the concept of the "four A's"
      a. Autism (preoccupation with self)
      b. Affect (blunted or inappropriate external expression of feelings)
      c. Association (loosening of associations or incoherence)
      d. Ambivalence (uncertainty, erraticism, or unpredictability)

C. ETIOLOGIC THEORIES

  1. Psychological. It has been theorized by some authorities (including Freud) that schizophrenia is the **outcome of very early adverse experiences**, including:
      a. Extreme deprivation of nurturance during the first year (the oral period) of life
      b. Parental schizophrenia and maternal depression, which are associated with later development of the disorder

  2. Biological
      a. Current evidence demonstrates that the schizophrenic disorders are a result **of neurotransmitter dysfunction**, including:
         (1) Striatal dopamine deficiency, with or without gamma-aminobutyric acid (GABA) or acetylcholine (ACh) derangements
         (2) Overactivity of dopamine in the limbic system
      b. A consistent finding associated with a deteriorating course in schizophrenia is the presence of **dilated ventricles on CAT scan.**
      c. Studies of monozygotic twins show a high concordance rate for schizophrenia; this rate is essentially the same for monozygotic twins who are reared apart from birth and for those who are raised together.

3. Social. Communication theorists believe that schizophrenia may occur in susceptible adolescents from backgrounds in which **intrafamilial communications** are notably:
   a. Highly critical
   b. Filled with negative emotional content

D. TYPES OF SCHIZOPHRENIC DISORDERS

1. **Disorganized** type, characterized by:
   a. Frequent incoherence
   b. Absence of systematized delusions
   c. Unusual affect

2. **Catatonic** type, recognized by:
   a. Catatonic stupor, muteness, or rigidity
   b. Aimless and stereotyped excitement or bizarre posturing

3. **Paranoid** type, characterized by:
   a. Persecutory or grandiose delusions
   b. Jealous delusions
   c. Hallucinations with persecutory or grandiose content

E. DIAGNOSIS

1. **Diagnostic criteria**
   a. Evidence of a thought disorder, including:
      (1) Bizarre, persecutory, or nonpersecutory **delusions**
      (2) Auditory or other types of **hallucinations**
      (3) Illogical thinking
      (4) Disturbed affect
      (5) Bizarre behavior
   b. Deteriorated functioning in work, social relationships, and self-care over at least a 6-month period
   c. Manic and depressive syndromes, if present, developing **after** the onset of schizophrenic symptoms, or of brief duration
   d. Onset before the age of 45 years
   e. Symptomatology not due to other organic mental disorders or to mental retardation

2. **Differential diagnosis**
   a. Patients with the cardinal symptoms of schizophrenia that have lasted less than 6 months are diagnosed as having either a **brief reactive psychosis** (if the disturbance lasts approximately 1 week) or a **schizophreniform disorder** (if the disturbance lasts more than 2 weeks but less than 6 months).
   b. Manic-depressive illness, manic type, may have symptomatology that is similar to that of schizophrenia. However, the affective symptoms either began before the symptoms of thought disorder occurred or they are more prominent than those of thought disorder.
   c. Schizoaffective illness is a psychotic disorder in which symptoms of both schizophrenia and a major affective illness are present, but neither set of symptoms is obviously predominant.
   d. An **organic delirium** must always be considered in the differential diagnosis of schizophrenia. It may coexist with a schizophrenic disorder, or it may be the result of alcohol or other drug abuse, which is more common in schizophrenics than in the general population.

F. TREATMENT

1. Psychotherapy alone has not been demonstrated to be of value in psychotic illnesses. However, **supportive psychotherapy** is an essential element of a comprehensive treatment, and **family therapy** may be very helpful.

2. **Neuroleptic medication** (e.g., haloperidol and chlorpromazine) is the most effective form of treatment of schizophrenia. Important common **side effects** include anticholinergic and extrapyramidal, Parkinson-like effects.

G. PROGNOSIS. Although schizophrenia is usually a serious and progressive disorder with remissions and relapses, the majority of patients are able to function in the community with sustained treatment and support services.

IV. MAJOR AFFECTIVE DISORDERS

A. BIPOLAR (MANIC-DEPRESSIVE) DISORDER

1. Etiologic theories
   a. Strong evidence exists for a **genetic predisposition** in families with histories of bipolar disorders.
   b. Dynamic theory postulates that mania is a defense against strong depressive emotions. It is suggested that **constant conflict**, which is resolved only partially, is responsible for the swings between mania and depression.

2. Incidence and prevalence
   a. The incidence of new cases of bipolar disorder is 0.3% per year.
   b. The disease is more common in certain ethnic groups, notably Jewish. Individuals in the middle- and upper-socioeconomic strata are also affected more often than those in the lower classes.

3. Diagnosis
   a. The diagnosis of bipolar disorder rests upon the occurrence of a manic episode at some time in life. Any major depressive disorder may later prove to be an episode of bipolar illness if mania occurs eventually. **A manic episode is characterized by:**
      (1) Unusual activity, talkativeness, or racing thoughts
      (2) Decreased sleep or easy distractibility
      (3) Excessive and inappropriate activities that are potentially self-damaging (e.g., shopping sprees; promiscuity)
   b. Differential diagnosis
      (1) The **schizophrenic disorders** must be excluded before bipolar illness is diagnosed, or the manic symptoms must have occurred before the schizophrenic disturbance or must be more prominent.
      (2) Single manic episodes may be indistinguishable from schizophrenia or **schizoaffective or paranoid disorder**; however, a history of multiple manic episodes is diagnostic of bipolar disorder.
      (3) Known causes of **manic-like syndromes** are many, including:
         (a) Drugs, such as amphetamines, alcohol, and steroids
         (b) Tumors
         (c) Endocrine disorders, such as thyrotoxicosis

4. Treatment
   a. Lithium carbonate decreases the incidence and severity of both manic and depressive episodes, thus lengthening symptom-free intervals.
   b. Carbamazepine (an anticonvulsant) may also be effective.
   c. Major tranquilizers (e.g., haloperidol and chlorpromazine) may be required to control the acute symptoms of mania, before lithium begins to work (as with other antidepressants, therapeutic effectiveness is not reached for several weeks).

B. UNIPOLAR DISORDER (MAJOR DEPRESSION)

1. Etiologic theories
   a. Psychological theories postulate that depression is due to the loss of an important individual, object, or source of security, and often unacceptable rage at that loss is redirected (retroflexed) upon one's self.
   b. Biological theories focus upon neurotransmitter dysfunction. Levels of **norepinephrine** and **serotonin** are decreased in depressed individuals.

2. The **incidence** in the general population is 3.5%.

3. Differential diagnosis
   a. Depression may be the presenting symptom of medical illness, including:
      (1) Infections
      (2) Cancer
      (3) Heart disease
   b. Prescribed medications and recreational drugs may cause or exacerbate depression. These include antihypertensive agents such as reserpine, corticosteroids (particularly if they are withdrawn too quickly), as well as alcohol, opioids, and other drugs of abuse.

4. Treatment includes both biological and psychological interventions.
   a. Tricyclic antidepressants are effective and safe, although relief of the depression is not immediate.
   b. Monoamine oxidase (MAO) inhibitors are relatively safe and are second-line drugs for the treatment of depression; they are used to treat individuals who do not respond to tricyclic agents.
   c. Electroconvulsive therapy (ECT) is fast, effective, and safe. Patients are given anesthesia,

and muscle relaxation (to prevent fractures) is achieved via the administration of succinylcholine.
d. Psychotherapy is effective by itself or with medication.

V. SOMATOFORM AND RELATED DISORDERS. Somatoform and related disorders are characterized by signs and symptoms of anxiety, which the patient attributes to physical illness.

A. TYPES OF SOMATOFORM DISORDERS

1. **Somatization disorder (hysteria)** begins early in life, generally in adolescence. There are numerous, changing, and inconsistent physical complaints of several years duration and for which no consistent physical disease pattern can be found. The symptoms are multiple and pervasive, and a wide variety of body systems are affected, including the cardiopulmonary and gastrointestinal. Psychosexual and conversion symptoms also arise.

2. **Conversion disorder** is characterized by a circumscribed set of signs and symptoms, such as paralysis or failure of sight or hearing, for which there is no known medical basis. The symptoms cannot be explained by anatomical or neurologic organization. They can be directly related to a psychological conflict and are not under the conscious control of the patient.

3. **Psychogenic pain disorder** is characterized by chronic pain syndromes in which the pain cannot be attributed to any known physical disease, does not follow anatomical patterns, or is out of proportion to the cause. The pain leads to some significant impairment in life function. There are usually identifiable contributing psychological conflicts, and often there is abuse of prescribed and nonprescription pain medications.

B. TREATMENT

1. **Psychological treatment** is generally supportive and attempts to promote more functional social skills.

2. Although there is no specific biological treatment, **withdrawal of unnecessary medications** may be required.

VI. ANXIETY DISORDERS

A. DEFINITION. These disorders, formerly classifed as "neuroses," are characterized by defensive (unconscious) symptom formation in response to stress in the absence of psychosis.

B. TYPES OF ANXIETY DISORDERS

1. **Phobic disorder**
   a. Description
   (1) Phobias are characterized by specific avoidance of objects, activities, or situations because of irrational fears.
   (2) Common examples include:
      (a) Agoraphobia (fear of open or unfamiliar places)
      (b) Acrophobia (fear of heights)
      (c) Social phobia (fear of scrutiny by or shameful behavior before others)
   b. Treatment
   (1) Psychological treatment is by means of **behavioral therapy**, such as desensitization (gradual reexposure to the anxiety-provoking stimulus).
   (2) Some phobias may respond to tricyclic antidepressants.
   (3) Psychodynamic psychotherapy is often recommended.

2. **Generalized anxiety disorder**
   a. Description. This is a chronic (over 6-months duration), persistent, and pervasive anxiety, mainly manifested by:
   (1) Motor tension
   (2) Sympathetic and parasympathetic symptoms, such as sweating, dizziness, and a dry mouth
   (3) Apprehension
   (4) Vigilance and scanning (e.g., edginess, irritability, and easy distractibility)
   (5) Insomnia, restless sleep, and fatigue
   b. The **diagnosis** is made when symptoms from three out of the first four categories listed above are present, and there is no stressor evident. The anxiety must be clearly distinguishable from the patient's usual state (e.g., psychotic or depressed).
   c. Treatment
   (1) Psychotherapy or behavior modification is often helpful.

(2) Minor tranquilizers, such as diazepam, may modify symptoms at their worst.
3. Panic disorder
  a. Description. A panic disorder is characterized by the sudden, discrete, and repeated onset of a cluster of severe anxiety symptoms, without an obvious phobic stimulus. The symptoms include the following. (Diagnosis requires the presence of at least four of these symptoms.)*
    (1) Dyspnea
    (2) Palpitations
    (3) Chest pain
    (4) Choking sensations
    (5) Dizziness or vertigo
    (6) Feelings of unreality
    (7) Paresthesias
    (8) Hot and cold flashes
    (9) Sweating
    (10) Fainting
    (11) Trembling or shaking
  b. Differential diagnosis. For the diagnosis of a panic disorder, phobias cannot be associated. The panic disorder cannot be due to a physical disorder, withdrawal of drugs, or another psychiatric illness.
  c. Treatment
    (1) Minor tranquilizers or tricyclic antidepressants may be helpful.
    (2) Psychodynamic and cognitive–behavioral psychotherapies are recommended.

VII. SUBSTANCE ABUSE

A. DEFINITIONS
  1. Abuse is the use of any drug, including alcohol, that results in physical, social, or psychological dysfunction.

  2. Dependence is the use of any drug that results in:
    a. Tolerance (i.e., the need to increase dosage over time in order to achieve the same effects)
    b. Withdrawal symptoms, including:
      (1) Elevated pulse, temperature, or blood pressure
      (2) Jitters, shakiness, or irritability
      (3) Changes of perception, hallucinations (including visual and tactile), or delusions

B. TYPES OF SUBSTANCE ABUSE
  1. Alcohol abuse and dependence
    a. Signs and symptoms
      (1) Denial of a problem in the face of clear dysfunction associated with alcohol intake
      (2) Concern with control ("I can stop whenever I want to")
      (3) Family or work (or school) problems
      (4) Unexplained accidents such as falls and work injuries
      (5) Automobile and pedestrian accidents
    b. Alcohol abuse often presents as a latent diagnosis of another psychiatric problem, especially depression and anxiety.
    c. It often is accompanied by abuse of and dependence on other drugs, such as minor tranquilizers (e.g., benzodiazepines).

  2. Opioid abuse and dependence
    a. Signs and symptoms
      (1) Complaints of illnesses that require pain medication (e.g., back pain)
      (2) A feeling on the part of the physician that he is being manipulated
      (3) Use of multiple drugs prescribed by many physicians
      (4) Physical stigmata, such as scars and "track" marks and collapse of veins
    b. Opioid abuse may accompany other psychiatric disorders, especially depression and anxiety.
    c. It often is accompanied by the abuse of and dependence on other drugs, such as cannabis, minor tranquilizers, alcohol, and hallucinogens.

---

*This information is taken from the *Diagnostic and Statistical Manual of Mental Disorders*, 3rd ed. Washington, D.C., American Psychiatric Association, 1980.

3. Minor tranquilizer, barbiturate, and cannabis abuse and dependence
  a. **Signs and symptoms**
   (1) Subjective experience of anxiety or depression, which is self-medicated
   (2) Gradual increase in dosage
   (3) Insomnia
   (4) Objective appearance of sleepiness
  b. Abuse often is associated with that of other drugs, especially alcohol, with which these drugs may induce cross-tolerance.

4. Hallucinogen abuse
  a. **Signs and symptoms**
   (1) Hallucinations, including visual and tactile
   (2) Bizarre behavior, including aggressive and hypersexual behavior
   (3) Altered mood and depressed cognition
  b. Hallucinogen intoxication causes psychiatric symptoms, especially psychotic symptoms of schizophrenia and mania as well as depression and anxiety.

C. TREATMENT

1. **Elimination of the drugs of abuse** is the first objective. Detoxification generally requires days to several weeks.
   a. Drug substitution is occasionally necessary. Longer-acting drugs may be substituted for shorter-acting drugs to ameliorate withdrawal symptoms (e.g., chlordiazepoxide can be substituted for alcohol and methadone for opioids).
   b. Doses of the original drug generally may be reduced by 50% each day; however, barbiturates must be tapered by no more than 10% each day because of the danger of withdrawal convulsions.
   c. Hallucinogen withdrawal is treated symptomatically.
   d. Disulfiram is a useful aversive drug for the treatment of alcoholism.

2. The patient and family should be engaged in definitive alcohol or drug abuse treatment immediately.
   a. Alcoholics Anonymous, Narcotics Anonymous, and other self-help groups are helpful but of themselves are not sufficient for most abusers.
   b. Family treatment is highly desirable.

VIII. PERSONALITY DISORDERS

A. DEFINITION.
A personality disorder is a chronic or lifelong pattern of behavior that is characterized by a group of traits that are:

1. Severely dysfunctional in terms of interpersonal relationships

2. Usually more troublesome to others than to the affected individual

3. Relatively stable over time

B. MAJOR TYPES OF PERSONALITY DISORDERS

1. **Personality disorders in which fear of others predominates**
   a. **Paranoid personality disorder** is characterized by:
    (1) Suspiciousness and mistrust
    (2) Avoidance of accepting blame
    (3) Hypervigilance
    (4) The absence of clear delusions (e.g., as are present in schizophrenia, paranoid type)
   b. **Schizotypal personality disorder** is characterized by psychotic-like symptoms, such as:
    (1) Illusions
    (2) Odd forms of communication (e.g., tangential speech)
    (3) Ideas of reference
    (4) Magical thinking
    (5) Suspiciousness, social isolation, or social hypersensitivity

    like schizophrenic ←

   c. **Avoidant personality disorder** is characterized by symptoms of isolation and withdrawal; however, the affected individual really does desire acceptance and will respond to strong encouragement.
   d. **Schizoid personality disorder** is similar to avoidant personality disorder, but there is no desire for intimacy. The disorder is characterized by:
    (1) Lack of desire for social involvement
    (2) Indifference to praise, encouragement, and criticism

2. Personality disorders in which self-preoccupation predominates
   a. Antisocial personality disorder is characterized by:
      (1) A cluster of "acting out," deviant behaviors beginning in childhood, including:
         (a) Aggressive acts, such as lying, stealing, and property destruction
         (b) Poor academic performance
         (c) Drinking, drug abuse, or aggressive sexual behavior
      (2) Continuing acting out as an adult, with similar criminal and aggressive behavior
      (3) Marked difficulty with intimacy
   b. Borderline personality disorder is characterized by a cluster of unstable and impulsive behaviors, including:
      (1) Self-damaging and self-defeating acts, ranging from suicide attempts to drug abuse
      (2) Unstable interpersonal relationships
      (3) Marked shifts in mood that are brief in duration
      (4) Identity disturbances, such as a confused self-image or sexual identity
      (5) Feelings of emptiness and difficulty tolerating being alone
   c. Narcissistic personality disorder is characterized by:
      (1) Grandiosity and a preoccupation with fantasies about power, beauty, and so forth
      (2) A need for constant attention and admiration
      (3) Markedly negative or empty feelings toward the criticism of others
      (4) Disturbed interpersonal relationships, exemplified by:
         (a) Feelings of entitlement
         (b) Taking advantage of others
         (c) Alternations between overidealization and devaluation of others
         (d) Inability to empathize with the needs of others

3. Disorders of containment of aggression
   a. Obsessive-compulsive personality disorder is characterized by:
      (1) Restricted ability to be warm and tender
      (2) Perfectionism and demands for it in others
      (3) Dedication to work and accomplishment on one hand but indecisiveness on the other
   b. Passive-aggressive personality disorder is characterized by:
      (1) Resistance to demands for performance by failing to do things, forgetting, and so forth
      (2) Resultant ineffectiveness in social and work spheres
      (3) Failure to capitalize upon opportunities to be assertive or effective

C. TREATMENT. Acute episodes of psychiatric disorders (e.g., affective and anxiety disorders) superimposed on personality disorders may require treatment. However, underlying personality disorders are **resistant to treatment**, although they may respond to psychotherapy prolonged over a number of years.

STUDY QUESTIONS

Directions: Each question below contains five suggested answers. Choose the **one best** response to each question.

1. A 72-year-old woman enters the hospital. She has lost 15 pounds and says she has no interest in eating. Her physical examination and laboratory findings are normal. She has been awakening at 5 A.M. for several months and cannot fall back to sleep. She says she has been feeling anxious and helpless since her husband died 3 years ago. A reasonable medication to prescribe for her would be

(A) haloperidol
(B) a tricyclic antidepressant
(C) a minor tranquilizer
(D) chlorpromazine
(E) a β-blocking agent

2. Intensive individual psychotherapy may be effective for which of the following disorders?

(A) Major affective disorder, manic type
(B) Alcohol-induced delirium
(C) Antisocial personality disorder
(D) Opioid dependence
(E) Major affective disorder, depressed type

3. Which of the following personality disorders is characterized by odd forms of communication, ideas of reference, illusions, and other psychotic-like thinking, which may make it difficult to distinguish from schizophrenia?

(A) Paranoid
(B) Borderline
(C) Schizotypal
(D) Schizoid
(E) Obsessive-compulsive

Directions: Each question below contains four suggested answers of which **one or more** is correct. Choose the answer

A   if **1, 2, and 3** are correct
B   if **1 and 3** are correct
C   if **2 and 4** are correct
D   if **4** is correct
E   if **1, 2, 3, and 4** are correct

4. Disorders of cognition and the inability to carry out logical operations occur in which of the following disorders?

(1) Schizophrenia
(2) Manic-depressive illness
(3) Organic brain syndromes
(4) Anxiety disorders

5. A 34-year-old woman comes to the emergency room complaining of "depression." On examination she is unable to concentrate well enough to finish a straightforward thinking task. She constantly looks around to see who is entering the room, and she is startled by ordinary noises. The most probable diagnosis includes

(1) an organic brain syndrome
(2) depression
(3) drug ingestion
(4) anxiety disorder

Directions: The group of questions below consists of lettered choices followed by several numbered items. For each numbered item select the **one** lettered choice with which it is **most** closely associated. Each lettered choice may be used once, more than once, or not at all.

Questions 6–10

For each case history described below, select the appropriate diagnosis.

(A) Narcissistic personality disorder
(B) Phencyclidene (PCP) ingestion
(C) Schizophrenia
(D) Borderline personality disorder
(E) Bipolar illness

6. Over the past year, Andrew, age 17, has retreated more and more often to his room. He has few friends and never calls anyone. His school performance has deteriorated during this time. His mother finds pieces of paper in his trash can with unintelligible poems on them.

7. Margot is brought to the hospital by her husband after she had run through the family bank account by making lengthy long-distance telephone calls and by purchasing jewelry and designer clothing.

8. George is indignant when his graduate school thesis committee refuses to approve his project. "They're just jealous of me because they know I'll be the most brilliant anthropologist in history." This is the attitude he has had all of his life.

9. Sharon's life has always been chaotic. She is frequently fighting and breaking up with her friends. On occasion, she has attempted suicide in an effort to get her boyfriends to return. Last year she contracted gonorrhea and delayed getting medical help.

10. Jean and a friend are discussing a party that they attended several nights before. Her friend tells Jean that she behaved in a bizarre and even threatening manner at the party, in a way that was totally uncharacteristic. Jean is used to smoking marijuana, but she remembers nothing of the party after smoking one joint.

ANSWERS AND EXPLANATIONS

1. The answer is B. (*IV B 4 a*) A tricyclic antidepressant is an acceptable first choice as an antidepressant agent, particularly for an elderly individual with a normal cardiovascular system. Newer "minor" tranquilizers (e.g., benzodiazepines) are sometimes prescribed for agitated depression; however, they are not licensed by the Food and Drug Administration for this use, and their employment for this purpose is not consensually established. This patient has a broad spectrum of depressive symptoms, and a sleep disorder is better treated by treatment of the underlying illness. Haloperidol and chlorpromazine are antipsychotics, and the patient has no indications of psychosis, delirium, or dementia.

2. The answer is E. (*II D 2; III F 1; IV A 4, B 4; VII B 2, C; VIII C*) A patient with a major depression may respond quite well to psychotherapy, as either the single mode of treatment or in conjunction with medication. Patients with delirium and psychoses such as mania require supportive treatment. Individuals with antisocial personality disorder respond poorly, if at all, to intensive individual psychotherapy, which is true of a number of the other personality disorders. The treatment approach to patients who are dependent on opioids involves withdrawal via drug substitution and support within a therapeutic community of other addicts; for the most part, individual psychotherapy has not been successful.

3. The answer is C. (*VIII B 1 a, b, d, 2 b, 3 a*) The psychotic-like symptoms of schizotypal personality disorder are difficult to distinguish from the symptoms of schizophrenia. The distinction is the limited nature of schizotypal symptoms and their stability. Therefore, they contribute only indirectly to the decrement in social functioning. Paranoid personality disorder is precluded by psychotic symptoms, as is obsessive-compulsive personality disorder. The schizoid individual actively avoids other people but does not exhibit psychotic symptoms.

4. The answer is A (1, 2, 3). (*II A 1, C; III A 1, 2; IV A 3*) Difficulties in logical thought, intellectual operations, abstraction, and the like are the hallmarks of schizophrenia and organic mental disorders, especially those associated with significant delirium or dementia. However, manic psychoses also often are characterized by a thought disorder, which may persist even when the manic episode improves.

5. The answer is B (1, 3). (*II A 2, C; VII B*) The patient has deficits in attention, is hypervigilant, and is easily distracted. These symptoms are all signs of an organic brain syndrome. None of them is common in depression or anxiety alone. Drug ingestion is a possible cause of an acute organic brain syndrome.

6–10. The answers are: 6-C, 7-E, 8-A, 9-D, 10-B. (*III A 1, E; IV A 3 a; VII B 3, 4; VIII B 2 b, c*) Andrew's deterioration in performance, his social withdrawal, and his apparent difficulties in cognition have lasted longer than 6 months. These symptoms as well as his age indicate a diagnosis of schizophrenia.

Spending sprees and grandiosity that extend to energetic, dysfunctional actions are characteristic of manic episodes. Although acute states such as these can be present in patients with narcissistic personality disorder, they are usually of brief duration.

The type of reaction to major disappointments that is exhibited by George is typical of individuals with narcissistic personality disorders. These individuals are given to a sense of self-importance and entitlement. Fantasies concerning success and infinite capabilities are also characteristic.

"Stable instability" is characteristic of borderline personality disorder. It is evidenced by instability of interpersonal relationships (i.e., difficult relationships punctuated by anger, threats, and even suicidal manipulations). It is associated with fluctuating moods and potentially self-damaging acts.

Jean is amnestic in regard to her behavior. Phencyclidine (PCP) is often inhaled by smoking marijuana laced with the drug and, therefore, can be taken unknowingly.

10
Human Sexuality
Robert L. Hendren

I. SEXUALITY THROUGHOUT THE LIFE CYCLE. Sex is a natural function in all life forms and is influenced by biological, psychological, and social factors in primates. Expression of sexuality begins at conception and continues throughout the life cycle.

A. PRENATAL PERIOD

1. **Chromosomal sex** is determined at the moment of conception. In normal development, the the **XX (female)** or **XY (male) chromosomes** determine whether the **undifferentiated fetal gonads become ovaries or testes by 5 to 6 weeks** of fetal life. The secretions of the male testes, the fetal androgens, determine male fetal development. Without these secretions, the fetus develops as a female. **Biological sex is fairly well determined by 12 weeks** of fetal life.

2. Just before or soon after birth, the **presence or absence of testosterone** influences the hypothalamus in a process referred to as **sex-typing** the brain.
   a. The brain that is influenced by testosterone develops the male, or acyclic, pattern for gonadotropin release.
   b. A cyclic pattern of gonadotropin release is established in the female-typed brain.

3. Rare conditions can cause the **development of ambiguous genitals** or genitals that are incongruous with genetic sex.
   a. **Syndromes**
      (1) The **androgen-insensitivity syndrome** (testicular feminization syndrome) results in a genetic male born with incompletely developed male genitalia or with normal external female genitalia.
      (2) The **adrenogenital syndrome** results from elevated levels of androgens that produce an enlarged clitoris or normal-appearing penis and scrotal sac in a genetic female.
   b. **Surgery for sexual reassignment** in children with ambiguous genitalia should take place by at least **18 months of age** in an attempt to limit difficulties in establishing gender identity.

B. INFANCY PERIOD

1. **General considerations**
   a. Being touched and held in a trustable, comfortable manner are important aspects of early sensual experiences.
   b. Male infants are capable of having an erection, and females have the potential for lubrication and orgasm.
   c. Differences in responses and adaptation to the environment exist between males and females from birth onward.

2. **Gender identity**
   a. Behavioral differences between males and females are influenced biologically by the effect of hormones on sex-typing and by the hemispheric specialization of the brain.
   b. Psychological and social influences include parental, familial, and cultural values.
   c. All of these factors affect the formation of **gender identity**, which **is the infant's sense of being masculine or feminine.**
   d. **Sex assignment**, (i.e., the sex assigned by the external genitalia) **and child rearing are the crucial variables** in determining gender identity or gender role.

C. CHILDHOOD

1. **General considerations**
   a. As the infant becomes a toddler (at about the age of 1 to 2 years), **a core gender identity** is

established. By 2½ years of age, normal children have established their gender, can categorize men and women by gender, and have some awareness of anatomical differences.
- **b.** The preschool child often identifies with the same-sex parental figure and forms attachments to the opposite-sex parental figure. During this time, children may engage in sexual play and exploration of their own bodies (masturbation) and those of their friends.
- **c.** Three- to six-year-old children begin to form theories about sex. For example, they often believe that conception occurs through the act of swallowing; that delivery of the baby is through the anus or the navel; and that sexual intercourse between the mother and father is an act of violence.
- **d.** Children continue to be interested in sex and sexual behavior throughout childhood, although the intensity of this curiosity usually diminishes as the child enters school.

2. **Gender identity disorders** become evident during the preschool years through the child's dress, play, and mannerisms. Abnormal attitudes of the parents and certain external stresses contribute to sexual identity problems. Males are at a much greater risk for gender identity disorders than are females.

D. ADOLESCENCE

1. **Profound changes occur** in the sexual anatomy and physiology **during puberty**.
   - **a.** In **girls**, budding of the breasts and growth of pubic hair occur at about 10 to 11 years of age (the range is from 8 to 13 years), while menstruation usually occurs between 11 and 13 years of age.
   - **b.** In **boys**, testicular enlargement and growth of pubic hair occur between 12 and 16 years of age, with ejaculation and enlargement of the penis occurring between 13 and 17 years.

2. Changing secondary sexual characteristics have a powerful influence on how the adolescent feels about himself or herself both intrapersonally and interpersonally.

3. Many new and sometimes poorly understood sexual events occur during adolescence, including menstruation, nocturnal emissions (wet dreams), conflicts about masturbation, sexual relationships, pregnancy, and childbirth.

E. YOUNG ADULTHOOD

1. **One of the tasks of young adulthood is developing intimacy** in relationships rather than existing in isolation.

2. Nonmarital sexual activity is prevalent during this period, especially since the 1970s. While this allows more freedom, it may lead to anxiety, guilt, and concerns about sexual performance.

F. ADULTHOOD

1. For many, adulthood involves deepening of intimacy in marriage and the parenting of children. Expressions of sexuality change as each partner copes with these events and the aging of the body. Sexual problems may emerge as a result of poor communication between partners, with resultant sexual dysfunction, boredom, stereotypic behavior, and dissatisfaction. Monotony, feelings of being taken for granted, concerns with career, illness in either partner, and overindulgence in food and drink all interfere with sexual activity in both men and women.

2. As **women** age, estrogen levels decrease and **menopause** occurs. This generally happens early in the sixth decade and results in **changes in estrogen-dependent tissue** such as the breasts and vagina. There may also be emotional symptoms. Vaginal lubrication often decreases, and the vaginal vault expands less with sexual arousal. With age, changes are noted in the uterus, labia majora and minora, and in the size of the clitoris. The orgasmic phase becomes shorter, uterine contractions may become spastic and painful, and there is a more rapid resolution phase.

3. In **men**, sexual responsiveness is influenced by biological and emotional factors in middle age. Physiologic changes include delay in attaining an erection as well as an erection that is less full. The feeling of ejaculatory inevitability may vary, and the explosive force decreases as does the volume of seminal fluid. Resolution is quickened, and the erection is lost more rapidly. The refractory period is longer. Ejaculatory control improves, but the desire for ejaculation may decrease.

4. **Sexual interest and activity persist but decline** throughout adulthood and older age (most noticeably between 46 and 55 years of age). The extent to which this happens depends on earlier levels of sexual interest and activity. Men report greater interest and activity than do women.

G. OLDER AGE

1. Changes in estrogen and androgen-dependent tissue and organs continue in older age. The physiologic changes that affect the sexual response cycle continue to progress as well.

2. The frequency of intercourse and masturbation decreases over the life cycle, and although interest and activity remain fairly consistent with earlier levels, they are related to the quality of health and the availability of a partner. Cessation of intercourse is most often attributed to poor health or sexual dysfunction of the man.

II. THE SEXUAL RESPONSE CYCLE

A. FOUR PHASES OF PHYSIOLOGIC CHANGE that occur in the sexual response cycle are described by Masters and Johnson and other researchers. The primary change in all phases **involve vasoconstriction and myotonia.**

1. **Excitement phase**
   a. In the **woman**, pelvic congestion and myotonia result in the clitoris enlarging and becoming more sensitive. The inner two-thirds of the vagina "balloons" in length and width, and sweating (transudate production) of the vagina occurs, producing lubrication. The labia majora thickens and moves away from the introitus. Nipples become erect and more sensitive; breast size increases. There is some voluntary and involuntary muscle tensing of the lower abdominal and pubococcygeal region. The heart rate and blood pressure increase as the sexual excitement increases.
   b. In the **man**, there is penile tumescence and erection, which may be partially lost and regained in this phase. Tensing and thickening of the scrotal sac occurs with elevation of both testes as the spermatic cord shortens. Nipple erection may occur as well as tensing of the abdominal and pelvic muscles. Heart rate and blood pressure also increase.

2. **Plateau phase**
   a. In the **woman**, the clitoris retracts against the anterior body of the symphysis pubis underneath the clitoral hood. Vasoconstriction of the outer third of the vagina and labia minora results in increased size of this tissue; this is referred to as the orgasmic platform. The uterus becomes fully elevated, and the cervix elevates, producing a tenting effect of the vagina. The labia minora changes in color from bright red to a deep wine, which is indicative of impending orgasm. Bartholin's glands release a few drops of mucoid secretions. The sex flush, a maculopapular rash, may spread over the abdomen and chest at this time or in the excitement phase.
   b. In the **man**, the penis increases in circumference at the coronal ridge and the testes increase in size and elevate further; this is indicative of impending ejaculation. Cowper's glands release a few drops of mucoid secretions, which may have a few active spermatozoa. The sex flush may also appear over the man during this phase.

3. **Orgasmic phase**
   a. In the **woman**, contractions in the orgasmic platform occur with increasing intervals and decreasing intensity. The musculature of the pelvic floor contracts, forcing blood out of the area; this may be one factor responsible for orgasm. Contractions of the uterus begin at the fundus and spread downward. The intensity of these contractions parallels the intensity of the orgasm. The rectal sphincter may contract, and the pulse rate and blood pressure increase further. Orgasmic expulsions of lubricating secretions may be triggered by stimulation of the Gräfenberg spot on the anterior vaginal wall. Both vaginal and clitoral orgasms have been described.
   b. In the **man**, contractions of the prostate, vasa efferentia of the testes, the epididymis, vas deferens (and seminal vesicles), and urethra propel seminal and prostatic fluids to the exterior while the bladder sphincter closes. Involuntary contractions may occur as well as contractions of the anal sphincter. Heart and respiration rates increase with a more pronounced increase in blood pressure in the man than in the woman.

4. **Resolution phase**
   a. In the **woman**, the clitoris quickly returns to its normal position with more gradual detumescence. The vaginal walls and orgasmic platform lose their vasocongestion as do the labia majora and minora. The uterus returns to its normal position, and the cervix descends to the seminal basin in the dorsal area of the vagina. Because the vasocongestion and myotonia subside less quickly in women than in men, the clitoral and perineal tissues are sensitive enough to respond almost immediately to continued stimulation.
   b. In the **man**, there is a rapid loss of vasoconstriction in the penis with a resulting decrease in size and a slower involution to preexcitement levels. The testes descend, and the scrotum relaxes. The refractory time varies from less than 10 minutes to 45 minutes and increases with age.

B. PHYSIOLOGIC ASPECTS OF THE SEXUAL RESPONSE CYCLE

1. Prior to the excitement phase there is an **appetite, or desire phase**, which appears to be mediated by the limbic and hypothalamic system, with connections to the pleasure and pain centers of the brain.
   a. Testosterone is important in mediating sexual desire in both men and women. Luteinizing hormone may also be important. Serotonin seems to act as an inhibitor to the sexual centers of the brain, while dopamine seems to act as a stimulant.
   b. The connections between the areas of the brain that are responsible for sexual excitement and areas that govern other emotional responses (e.g., depression, anger, and happiness) can affect sexual responses. This effect may be responsible for sexual dysfunction that seems beyond the individual's conscious control.

2. Vasoconstriction in the excitement phase of the sexual response cycle is governed largely by the parasympathetic nervous system, which accounts for the loss of erection with an intense sympathetic response such as fear or anxiety.

III. INFLUENCES ON SEXUAL EXPRESSION

A. **SOCIOCULTURAL FACTORS** that affect sexual expression include the customs, traditions, and attitudes of the family and the society in which an individual lives.

1. The **culture** in which an individual is raised or currently lives determines to a large extent how sexuality is expressed. This includes areas such as the boundary between what is considered to be sexual and what is not; the purpose of sex (i.e., whether sex is only for procreation or if it may be enjoyed at other times); the role of the woman and the man; the acceptance of nonmarital sex; sexual positions, foreplay, and duration; and the way in which sexual feelings are communicated.

2. The **sexual values of the family** may reflect the cultural values or may be in conflict with them. Parents who have moved from one culture to another or who have differing cultural values may create conflicts about sexual expression not only between themselves but also in their children.

3. The **culture surrounding a particular race** may also affect sexual behavior (i.e., within the United States, several studies have demonstrated that blacks have a more permissive attitude toward sexuality than whites).

4. **Social class** differences regarding sex have also been demonstrated. A study of lower-class families in which the marital relationship had a high degree of role segregation revealed less frequent and less satisfying sexual expression than occurred in middle-class families in which the roles were more jointly organized.

5. **Religious teachings** vary from viewing sexuality as part of human relationships, to sex for procreation only, to sexual enjoyment as a sign of wickedness. Religious training early in life may continue to influence sexual behavior at a later age, even if the religious beliefs of the individual may have changed.

B. PSYCHOLOGICAL FACTORS

1. **Early experiences** with intimacy, sexuality, trust, and guilt exert continued influence upon the individual through both conscious and unconscious attitudes.

2. **Early sexual traumas** occurring within and outside of the family provide a continuing source of anxiety and guilt later in life. Examples include incest, sexual abuse, sexual awkwardness due to lack of knowledge and experience, and impulsive "acting out."

IV. SEXUAL VARIATIONS.
The delivery of health care to individuals who engage in variations of sexual expression is contingent upon the unprejudiced and sensitive attitude of the health care provider. It is important that the health care provider be aware of variations in the presentation of sexually transmitted diseases.

A. **HOMOSEXUALITY** involves the erotic attraction between individuals of the same sex who view this attraction as congruous with their biological sex. The term **bisexual** is used to describe individuals who experience erotic arousal toward or relate sexually to both sexes.

1. Approximately 5% of all males and 2% of all females are reported to be homosexual. This may represent underreporting, however.

2. There is some disagreement about whether homosexuality per se is an illness. Until 1973, the

American Psychiatric Association diagnosed homosexuality as a mental illness. Since then, however, only ego-dystonic homosexuality (in which the individual feels conflict about being homosexual, wants to change sexual orientation, or both) is considered to be a diagnostic category.

3. **Suggested etiologies** include biological, psychological, and social causes.
    a. Predisposing biological factors include hormonal and chromosomal variations. The only demonstrated factor is a lower level of androgen in some homosexual men.
    b. The family pattern of a domineering, protective mother and a hostile, weak, or detached father has been found in some, but not all, male homosexuals.
    c. Social exposure to homosexuality, especially at a young age, has been suggested as an etiology based on learned behavior. However, exposure alone does not predict homosexuality. Furthermore, sexual experimentation with a partner of the same sex, especially during childhood and adolescence, does not classify an individual as homosexual.

B. **TRANSSEXUALISM** is a disorder of gender identity. It is characterized by a belief on the part of affected individuals that they belong to the opposite sex. There may be crossdressing, not for sexual gratification, but because transsexuals may be uncomfortable in the clothing of their biological sex. Sexual relationships may be conducted with either sex.

1. The **incidence** of transsexualism in the United States has been estimated at 1 in 20,000 to 1 in 40,000 for males and much less for females.

2. **Etiology.** As with homosexuality, there is no clear etiology. Identity confusion is usually noticed between 18 and 36 months of age.

3. Many transsexuals of both sexes seek sexual reassignment. This involves hormonal reassignment, surgical reassignment, or both and should be performed only after careful evaluation and screening.

C. **TRANSVESTISM** is a paraphiliac disorder, and it is characterized by the need on the part of the affected individual to crossdress for sexual gratification, pleasure, or both. Crossdressing is done by both homosexual and heterosexual men.

V. SEXUAL DYSFUNCTION

A. **GENERAL CONSIDERATIONS.** Sexual dysfunctions are classified as **primary**, in that they are present throughout the individual's life, or **secondary**, in that they are acquired after a period of normal functioning. In most instances, there is **a disturbance in both the subjective sense of pleasure or desire and in the objective performance**.

1. In diagnosing sexual dysfunction, the clinician must take into account frequency of occurrence, chronicity, subjective distress, and effects on other areas of functioning.

2. Sexual dysfunction may be generalized or situational, total or partial, and while it generally occurs during sexual activity with a partner, it may occur during masturbation.

B. **CLASSIFICATION.** Sexual dysfunctions are classified according to the stage in the sexual response cycle in which they occur.

1. **Inhibited sexual desire** involves a low level of interest or aversion in the man or woman.
    a. **Primary low level of interest** is usually associated with early or adolescent experiences that result in a failure to learn the script for sexual response. This can include severe medical problems or disruption in the parent–child bond.
    b. **Secondary low level of interest** can result from physical factors such as fatigue, substance abuse, pain, and medication. Other factors include depression, reaction to the partner's loss of interest, medical conditions in the partner, and age.
    c. **Sexual aversion** is much more common in women than in men and is associated with a fear response to the sexual act. There is often a reluctance to begin a sexual encounter, but this may be followed by excitement and orgasm once the initial reluctance is overcome. Often there is a history of frightening or painful experiences associated with sexuality.

2. **Inhibited sexual excitement** has also been termed frigidity or impotence.
    a. The time for erection or lubrication may take 15 to 30 seconds in younger individuals; in those past the age of 60, it might take 1 to 3 minutes.
    b. In **women**, inhibited sexual excitement is almost always associated with distractibility. This leads to failure to be aroused and results in a lack or loss of lubrication. Side effects of medication and age need to be ruled out as etiologic factors.

    c. In **men**, impotence can result from performance anxiety, phobias or panic disorders, situational stresses such as fatigue or alcohol, and depression. Biological etiologies, such as diabetes, and medication side effects need to be ruled out.

  3. Orgasmic phase dysfunctions include inhibited orgasm in women and premature ejaculation and ejaculatory incompetence in men.

    a. Inhibited female orgasm may be primary or secondary.

      (1) Reasons for primary inhibited orgasm include fear of letting go stemming from conflicts in early experience or lack of knowledge.

      (2) Reasons for secondary inhibited orgasm include pain, depression, fatigue, illness, substance abuse, medication, and an impaired relationship with the sexual partner.

      (3) The Hite report (1981) found that two-thirds of the women studied needed stimulation beyond what they were receiving to achieve orgasm.

    b. Premature ejaculation is a more common dysfunction in men than is ejaculatory incompetence.

      (1) Etiologic factors in premature ejaculation include anxiety, phobic states, conditioning from previous episodes of premature ejaculation, abstinence, and extremely erotic stimuli.

      (2) Etiologic factors in **ejaculatory inhibition** or **incompetence** include "spectatoring," in which the individual observes himself in the sexual act rather than fully experiencing it, and difficulty in letting go both sexually and with other feelings. Biological factors, medications such as sympathetic blocking agents, repeated catheterization, and prostatectomy can also cause ejaculatory inhibition.

      (3) Both premature ejaculation and ejaculatory inhibition can be associated with erectile dysfunction.

C. VAGINISMUS AND DYSPAREUNIA are other factors that can cause sexual dysfunction.

  1. Functional vaginismus is an involuntary tensing of the muscles at the vaginal opening, especially at the time of penetration.

    a. Etiologic factors include childhood injury to the urogenital region, a feeling of discomfort with the genital region, conflicts about sexuality, and conflicts about relationships with men. The most common cause, however, is vaginitis.

    b. Vaginismus often occurs during the pelvic examination, which can help confirm the diagnosis.

  2. Functional dyspareunia is intercourse associated with recurrent and persistent genital pain in either the man or woman. Physical causes such as insufficient lubrication and vaginismus need to be ruled out in order to make the diagnosis.

D. TREATMENT. The treatment of sexual dysfunction begins with a complete history of the problem.

  1. Physical causes for the dysfunction **should be treated**. If the etiology is not physical or the physical cause cannot be treated, a complete explanation should be given to the patient.

  2. Education and counseling by the primary care physician can relieve many cases of sexual dysfunction.

  3. Referral to a specialist may be indicated when the sexual dysfunction is symptomatic of more deep-seated pathology.

VI. SEXUALITY IN MEDICAL PRACTICE

A. SEXUAL HISTORY. Taking the sexual history of the patient should be **a routine part of every review of systems**. The manner in which this is done may vary according to the patient's age and social background as well as the reason for seeking medical help. It should not be avoided because of the practitioner's discomfort with sexuality. Studies have shown that only 10% of patients will initiate a discussion of sexual functioning, but 50% will discuss their sexual functioning if asked.

  1. A method that uses the **chronology of sexuality** throughout the life cycle is often less threatening to the patient, provides a better understanding of sexual functioning, and implies that sexuality is a natural function.

  2. If sexual dysfunction is present, the history should include a description of the problem and the meaning of the problem to the individual.

B. SEXUALITY DURING PREGNANCY AND LACTATION

1. Bodily changes, societal expectations, personal feelings about pregnancy, and fear of harming the fetus are major factors affecting eroticism and the **frequency of sexual intercourse** for both men and women during pregnancy. Wide variation in frequency is reported.
   a. There is **a decrease in sexual interest and frequency throughout pregnancy**, especially for nulliparous women. Some studies report an increase in sexual awareness and performance in the second trimester in comparison with the first and third trimesters.
   b. The frequency of sexual intercourse, masturbation, and orgasm before pregnancy is directly related to the frequency during pregnancy.
   c. There are few reasons that contraindicate sexual activity during pregnancy. If abstinence is necessary, a clear explanation of the reason should be given.
   d. Both men and women may experience conflict concerning the coexistence of motherhood and sexuality, which can interfere with sexuality during pregnancy and afterward.

2. In the **postpartum period**, most couples resume sexual relations within 6 weeks.
   a. Many women report increased sexual desire in the postpartum period, but most often there is a decreased frequency of intercourse often due to pain and fatigue.
   b. Sexual activity usually returns to near prepregancy levels by the first year postpartum.

3. Sexual stimulation during breast feeding is reported by many nursing mothers. This may result in conflictual feelings.

C. CARDIOVASCULAR DISEASE AND SEXUALITY

1. Myocardial infarction can often result in decreased self-esteem of the patient, concerns about impotence, and, in general, **a decrease in the frequency of sexual intercourse**.
   a. Myocardial infarction occurs occasionally during intercourse as a result of the physical and emotional stress of unusual circumstances such as an extramarital affair, inebriation, an "unsafe" place, or an atypical means of sexual intimacy.
   b. It is not unusual for cardiac patients to experience cardiovascular symptoms during intercourse.
   c. The most common reasons for a decrease in the frequency of intercourse after a myocardial infarction are psychological.

2. There is greater return to normal sexual activity after a myocardial infarction in patients who receive **exercise training and education**. It is important to include the spouse of the patient in educational programs since the spouse often has concerns that interfere with the recovery of sexual activity.

D. SEXUALITY AND CHRONIC ILLNESS

1. **General considerations.** Chronic illness affects the patient's self-esteem, sexual functioning, and marital relationship. Therefore, the attitude of the health care provider toward sexuality is an important factor in the sexual adjustment of both patient and spouse.
   a. The sick role (see Chapter 12, "The Physician–Patient Relationship," section II B) places the patient in a dependent position, which may lead to regressive behavior.
   b. Certain disease processes interfere with the physiologic functioning necessary for sexual response. These include malaise, anxiety, and depression. The effect of medications necessary to treat the disease can also affect sexual response.
   c. The sexual roles of each partner are often altered as a result of illness, and the healthier partner assumes a more nurturing role. The partners may also be physically separated as a result of the illness and hospitalization.

2. **Chronic renal failure** results in a high incidence of sexual dysfunction, especially in those patients with untreated uremia, those undergoing dialysis, and those who have undergone renal transplantation.

3. **Diabetes** results in a high incidence of sexual dysfunction, which increases with the duration of the disease. Organic causes are not always etiologic. Impaired self-esteem and fears of impotence should be considered along with organic etiologies. Diabetic men can experience transient periods of organically based erectile dysfunction, and diabetic women can experience problems with arousal and vaginal lubrication, which may be complicated by vaginitis.

4. The sexual functioning of patients with physical illnesses such as arthritis, cerebral vascular accident, and spinal cord injury should be determined. Developmentally disabled adolescents should also be evaluated for sexual dysfunction.

E. DRUGS THAT AFFECT SEXUAL FUNCTIONING. Over 6% of the population abuse alcohol and other drugs.

  1. Alcohol. Small amounts of alcohol may enhance sexual desire by decreasing inhibitions, but large amounts cause significant dysfunction in both men and women.

  a. Alcohol interferes with sexual functioning due to its depressant effect on the central nervous system. Also, diseases related to alcoholism and psychological disorders exacerbated by alcohol abuse can cause sexual dysfunction even after cessation of drinking. Irreversible sexual dysfunction can result from chronic abuse. Other individuals may recover sexual functioning completely after a period of abstinence.

  b. The most common sexual dysfunctions of alcoholic women are inhibited desire, dyspareunia, and orgasmic dysfunction. In alcoholic men, the most common sexual dysfunctions are inhibited desire, erectile dysfunction, and delayed orgasm or ejaculation.

  2. Recreational drugs, often used initially to enhance sexuality, can cause sexual dysfunction with regular use.

  a. Marijuana (cannabis). There is a higher incidence of decreased libido and impaired potency among cannabis users than among nonusers. Chronic use has been shown to decrease plasma testosterone levels, sperm count, and sperm motility in men.

  b. Chronic **cocaine** use has been shown to decrease sexual functioning and interest.

  c. Narcotic addiction has been shown to result in nonemissive erections and impotence in men and amenorrhea, infertility, reduced libido, and spontaneous abortions in women.

  d. Amphetamines may help increase physical performance initially, but with larger doses, there is loss of interest in and withdrawal from sexual activity.

  e. Barbiturates may lower sexual inhibitions; however, in larger doses they depress sexual performance.

  3. Many **prescription drugs** also impair sexual functioning.

  a. Antihypertensive drugs that act by blocking sympathetic nervous system functioning can cause sexual dysfunctions. These include such drugs as methyldopa (Aldomet), reserpine (Serpasil), and trimethaphan (Arfonad). Other antihypertensive agents that are known to interfere with sexual functioning include chlorothiazide (Diuril) and spironolactone (Aldactone).

  b. Antidepressant drugs may interfere with sexual functioning. Among the tricyclic antidepressants, the anticholinergic effects are primarily responsible for the sexual dysfunction. Monoamine oxidase (MAO) inhibitors interfere with sexual functioning due to their tendency to block peripheral ganglionic nerve transmission. Lithium carbonate has also been reported to interfere with sexual functioning.

  c. Antihistamines, with continuous use, may interfere with sexual activity due to anticholinergic effects and blockade of parasympathetic nerve impulses.

  d. Antispasmodic agents may interfere with sexual functioning through ganglionic blockade.

  e. Neuroleptic medication can result in decreased sexual interest and performance in some individuals. Thioridizine (Mellaril) can cause retrograde ejaculation.

  f. Sedative–hypnotic drugs, in small doses, may improve sexual functioning in anxious individuals, but chronic use often results in impaired performance.

BIBLIOGRAPHY

Diagnostic and Statistical Manual of Mental Disorders, 3rd ed. Washington, D.C., American Psychiatric Association, 1980

Gees J, Heiman J, Leitenberg H: *Human Sexuality*. Englewood Cliffs, N.J., Prentice-Hall, 1984

Kaplan H: *The New Sex Therapy: Active Treatment of Sexual Dysfunctions*. New York, Brunner/Mazel, 1974

Kolodny RC, Masters WH, Johnson VE: *Textbook of Sexual Medicine*. Boston, Little, Brown, 1979

Masters WH, Johnson VE: *Human Sexual Inadequacy*. Boston, Little, Brown, 1970

Masters WH, Johnson VE: *Human Sexual Response*. Boston, Little, Brown, 1966

Woods NF (ed): *Human Sexuality in Health and Illness*. St. Louis, CV Mosby, 1984

STUDY QUESTIONS

Directions: Each question below contains five suggested answers. Choose the **one best** response to each question.

1. The androgen-insensitivity syndrome results in

(A) a genetic female born with an enlarged clitoris or a normal-looking penis and scrotal sac
(B) a genetic male born with female genitalia
(C) a genetic male born with incompletely developed or absent male genitalia
(D) an XXY chromosomal pattern
(E) an XYY chromosomal pattern

2. At what age is gender identity established?

(A) The first year of life
(B) Years 1 to 3
(C) Years 3 to 5
(D) Years 5 to 7
(E) Years 11 to 13

3. The concept of ego-dystonic homosexuality is best characterized by individuals who

(A) feel erotic attraction to people of the same sex and who view this attraction as congruous with their own biological sex
(B) believe that they are in the body of the wrong biological sex
(C) dress as members of the opposite sex
(D) feel erotic attraction to people of the same sex and feel conflict about this attraction
(E) feel erotic attraction toward others of the same sex but who have had only heterosexual relationships

4. What is the most common cause of vaginismus?

(A) Childhood injury to the urogenital region
(B) A feeling of discomfort with the genital region
(C) Conflicts about sexuality
(D) Insufficient lubrication
(E) Vaginitis

5. All of the following statements about the influence of cardiovascular disease upon sexuality are true EXCEPT

(A) some patients have impaired sexual functioning following a myocardial infarction
(B) myocardial infarctions that occur during intercourse are often associated with unusual and stressful circumstances
(C) the most common reason for decreased frequency of intercourse after a myocardial infarction is anginal pain associated with intercourse
(D) there is a higher incidence of return to normal sexual activity by patients who receive exercise training and education than by those who are not involved in such programs
(E) the spouse of a patient who has had a myocardial infarction needs to be involved in educational programs as his or her fears can interfere with resumption of sexual activity

Directions: Each question below contains four suggested answers of which **one or more** is correct. Choose the answer

A   if **1, 2, and 3** are correct
B   if **1 and 3** are correct
C   if **2 and 4** are correct
D   if **4** is correct
E   if **1, 2, 3, and 4** are correct

6. True statements about the sexual response cycle include

(1) testosterone secretion is important in the sexual cycles of both men and women
(2) the limbic and hypothalamic systems have important connections to sexual centers of the brain
(3) dopamine seems to act as a stimulant to the sexual centers of the brain
(4) the vasocongestion that occurs in the excitement phase is largely a sympathetic response

7. The sexual response of infants involves the potential for

(1) erection in the male
(2) orgasm in the female
(3) lubrication in the female
(4) ejaculation in the male

8. True statements about puberty include

(1) budding of the breasts and growth of pubic hair occur prior to the onset of menstruation
(2) testicular enlargement and growth of pubic hair occur before enlargement of the penis and the capability of ejaculation
(3) in most cases pubertal changes occur in girls before they do in boys
(4) the anatomical and physiologic changes that occur during puberty generally have little effect on healthy adolescents

9. Sexuality in middle age is characterized by

(1) a decrease in vaginal lubrication and in the duration of orgasm following menopause
(2) a noticeable decline in sexual interest and activity with increasing age in both men and women
(3) a delay in attaining an erection and a longer refractory period
(4) loss of ejaculatory control with increasing age

10. Sexuality during pregnancy can be characterized by

(1) a decrease in sexual interest and frequency for most women
(2) the continuing possibility of harming the fetus
(3) levels of sexual activity directly related to prepregnancy levels
(4) prepregnancy levels of sexual activity resumed within the first few weeks postpartum for most couples

11. Medications that interfere with sexual functioning include

(1) antihypertensives
(2) antispasmodics
(3) antidepressants
(4) antihistamines

12. Chronic marijuana use has been found to be associated with which of the following sexual dysfunctions?

(1) Decreased plasma testosterone levels
(2) Decreased libido
(3) Decreased sperm count and mobility
(4) Impaired potency

ANSWERS AND EXPLANATIONS

1. The answer is C. (*I A 3*) The release of androgen determines if male genitalia will develop. In the androgen-insensitivity syndrome (testicular feminization syndrome), a genetic male fails to develop fully male external genitalia due to hypothalamic insensitivity to androgen. The infant has a normal XY chromosomal pattern.

2. The answer is B. (*I B 2*) The biological determination of sex occurs before birth; however, gender identity is influenced by social and cultural factors, and it should be established by 1 to 3 years of age. By 2½ years of age, children can categorize people by sex and recognize their own sex. Gender identity disorders become evident in the preschool years.

3. The answer is D. (*IV A 2*) Ego-dystonic homosexuality is characterized by individuals who feel erotic attraction to people of the same sex yet feel conflict about this attraction. Individuals who have not engaged in a homosexual relationship but who have an erotic attraction to people of the same sex are not necessarily ego-dystonic about homosexuality. Ego-syntonic homosexuality is characterized by individuals who are erotically attracted to people of the same sex and who view this as congruous with their own sex. Transsexual individuals are those who believe that they are in the body of the wrong biological sex. Transvestism describes the behavior of individuals who dress as members of the opposite sex. Transsexuality and transvestism may occur in an individual with a homosexual or heterosexual orientation.

4. The answer is E. (*V C*) Although childhood injury to the urogenital region, a feeling of discomfort with the genital region, and conflicts about sexuality all can cause vaginismus, the most common cause is vaginitis. A lack of lubrication can cause dyspareunia but does not in itself cause the involuntary tensing of the muscles of the vaginal opening.

5. The answer is C. (*VI C 1*) The most common reasons for a decreased frequency of sexual intercourse after a myocardial infarction are psychological. Patients who have had a myocardial infarction can have decreased self-esteem and concerns about impotence. The stress associated with an unusual circumstance (e.g., an atypical sexual activity, inebriation, or a new sexual partner) is often responsible for myocardial infarction during intercourse. Exercise and educational programs have been effective in helping cardiac patients resume a normal life, but the involvement of the spouse in these programs is important.

6. The answer is A (1, 2, 3). (*II B*) Testosterone is important in mediating sexual desire in both men and women. The limbic and hypothalamic systems mediate the appetite or desire phase of the sexual cycle through pleasure and pain centers in the brain. Research has demonstrated that serotonin has an inhibiting effect on sexual centers of the brain while dopamine has a stimulating effect. The vasoconstriction and congestion in the excitement phase is governed largely by the parasympathetic nervous system.

7. The answer is A (1, 2, 3). (*I B 1 b*) At the time of birth, the male infant is capable of having an erection, and it is not unusual for an erection to be present at the time of delivery. Also from the time of birth, the female infant is capable of lubrication and orgasm. The ability of the male to ejaculate does not develop until puberty.

8. The answer is A (1, 2, 3). (*I D*) In girls, the budding of the breasts and growth of pubic hair occur at about 10 to 11 years of age, while menarche usually occurs between 11 and 13 years of age. In boys, testicular enlargement and growth of pubic hair occur between 12 and 16 years of age, and ejaculation occurs between 13 and 18 years of age. Emerging secondary sexual characteristics have a profound interpersonal and intrapersonal influence on all adolescents.

9. The answer is B (1, 3). (*I F*) Menopause occurs early in the sixth decade of life in most women and results in changes in estrogen-dependent tissues. There is often a decrease in vaginal lubrication, and the orgasmic phase becomes shorter. In men, physiologic changes include delay in attaining an erection, an erection that is less full, and a longer refractory period. Sexual interest and activity in middle age are related to earlier levels of interest and activity. While frequency may decrease somewhat, interest and enjoyment continue in individuals who enjoyed sexual relationships prior to middle age.

10. The answer is B (1, 3). (*VI B*) Sexual interest and activity are reported to decrease during pregnancy for most women. However, the level of activity and interest is directly related to that before pregnancy. There are few reasons to avoid sexual activity during pregnancy as harm to the fetus is only possible just prior to delivery. Most couples report resumption of sexual activity within 6 weeks postpartum and a return to near normal levels by the first year postpartum.

11. The answer is E (all). *(VI E 3)* Antihypertensive medications that act by blocking sympathetic nervous system functioning can cause sexual dysfunction. Ganglionic blockade is often responsible for the sexual dysfunction associated with medications, including antispasmodics. The anticholinergic side effects of antidepressants and antihistamines can interfere with sexual potency.

12. The answer is E (all). *(VI E 2 a)* Although data on the harmful effects of cannabis abuse is conflicting, decreased plasma levels of testosterone, decreased libido, decreased sperm count and mobility, and impaired potency all have been found in chronic users of marijuana.

11
Social and Family Behavior
Frederick S. Wamboldt

I. GENERAL SYSTEMS THEORY

A. INTRODUCTION. A system is a unit that functions as such due to the interdependence of its parts. The general systems theory is a **holistic model** that was developed by a number of biological and physical scientists to explain how a wide variety of systems function as wholes. The general systems theory emphasizes the embedment of phenomena in their environment; this can be compared to the **reductionistic model**, which considers phenomena as isolated events.

The general systems theory has proven useful for the study of family and social behavior, and it has particular relevance for important health issues related to behavior.

B. SYSTEM. A system is a set of **interrelated elements** that function as a whole (e.g., the immune system, solar system, family system, and international political system). Systems can be characterized by their structure, organization, and environmental context. They are dynamic entities and hence potentially subject to **disintegration**.

1. Structure. The elements, or components, of a system and the relationships among them at any given time define the structure of the system.

    a. Recurrent structure. Certain relationships among elements of the system may occur with such regularity that the structure of the system is **predictable**. Recurrent structure is characteristic of a system at **equilibrium**. Examples include the following.

        (1) A **boundary** is a recurrent, interactive relationship between the elements of a system and the system's environment. The recurrent relationship between the body's dermis and vascular components in maintaining the epidermal boundary can be compared to to the interactions within a family that determine what constitutes information that should or should not be told to outsiders.

        (2) A **bond** or **alliance** is a recurrent, interactive, relationship among elements of a system.

        (3) Emergent properties. Some relationships or interactions among elements in a system can generate new properties within the system.

            (a) As depth perception is an emergent property involving the interaction between the two separate retinal images in the visual system, so "personality attributes," such as dependency and hatred, can be seen as emerging from and being maintained within certain relationships.

            (b) If the relationship changes, the emergent property may disappear. Consider the shift in American public opinion of the Red Chinese from untrustworthy enemies to industrious people after Nixon's visits in the 1970s.

    b. Novel structure. Unpredictable or novel structures arise in a system attempting to adapt to stress. Such novel structures may become recurrent structures if they successfully allow the system to adapt and regain equilibrium, or they may be simply transient structures that will fail.

2. Organization of a system involves those relationships among components that are required for a system to retain its **identity** or membership within a specific class. The organization of any given system usually allows a variety of potential structures and hence significant ability to adapt.

    a. For example, there are a number of possible structures that water can assume in adapting to stress while retaining its organization: ice, liquid, and vapor.

    b. Similarly, a family that regards itself as "close-knit" may be unable to master the developmental task of a child separating to go to school, especially if additional stress is incumbent (e.g., if the father works two jobs due to financial hardship). The child, by refusing to go to school and staying home, can be seen as helping the family reaffirm the identity that arises from its organization (i.e., "we are close-knit and stay together").

3. **Environment.** Living systems exist within an environment, or context, and are continually adjusting their structure to conserve their organization in the face of stresses, demands, or perturbations of the environment. These adaptive adjustments involve some combination of:

   a. **Morphostasis**, or homeostasis, in which the system attempts to maintain the original structure to the maximal degree [e.g., the negative feedback effects of plasma cortisol on the hypothalamic–pituitary axis, which result in the return of cellular activity to the steady state prior to the release of corticotropin releasing factor–adrenocorticotropic hormone (CRF–ACTH)]

   b. **Morphogenesis**, in which the system undergoes maximal change or innovation in structure (e.g., consider the transition of water from liquid to gas in response to the perturbation of heat)

4. **Disintegration.** If a system is not able to adapt successfully (i.e., conserve its organization in the face of environmental stress), it disintegrates.

   a. For example, passage of sufficient electric current through an atmosphere of hydrogen and oxygen molecules disintegrates the systems of hydrogen and oxygen molecules, which reorganize as water molecules.

   b. Similarly, some families cannot successfully adapt to the demands of their environments and, therefore, fragment, with their members winding up in foster homes, halfway houses, and other institutions.

C. **THE BIOPSYCHOSOCIAL MODEL** was proposed by Engel as an alternative model for medical science. It is based on general systems theory.

1. The **biomedical model** is currently the dominant model in medicine. It is both **reductionistic** (i.e., an effort is made to explain all complex phenomena in the language of molecular biology) and **dualistic** (i.e., somatic variables are given priority while psychosocial variables are typically ignored). While this model has served medical science admirably as a heuristic guide, its major faults are its neglect of certain dimensions of human experience and its inability to answer many important medical questions. For example, why would a woman wait until a breast lump has reached massive proportions, perhaps even is eroding the skin, before consulting her physician?

2. The **biopsychosocial model** proposes that to understand human illness adequately, a physician must consider as relevant influences not only biomedical data but also **interpersonal behavior** (e.g., an individual who is used to being in charge may have difficulty assuming the role of patient), the patient's **family** (e.g., family interventions have been able to lower serum blood sugar in adolescents with diabetes mellitus and reduce psychotic recurrences in young adults with schizophrenia), and the larger **social groups** of which the patient is a member.

II. INTERPERSONAL BEHAVIOR

A. **UNITS OF INTERACTION.** Social behavior can be viewed as being composed of discrete units of interaction that occur between **dyads** (e.g., a unit may be the entire speech of one speaker until someone else begins speaking or a complete thought in which a single message is given to another individual, which may or may not be followed by another message).

B. **DIMENSIONS OF INTERPERSONAL BEHAVIOR.** Models exist for classifying the units of interpersonal behavior into categories of **interpersonal postures**. These models typically involve the following three dimensions (Fig. 11-1).

1. **Focus** (see the *other* and *self surfaces* in Fig. 11-1). It should be determined if in any specific unit the individual is initiating an action toward the other individual (**focus on other**) or responding to an action from the other (**focus on self**).

2. **Interdependence** (see the *vertical axes* in Fig. 11-1). It should be determined to what degree the action represents an attempt to control or influence (**focus on other**) versus an offer for autonomy (**focus on other**) or represents submission (**focus on self**) versus an assertion of independence (**focus on self**).

3. **Affiliation** (see the *horizontal axes* in Fig. 11-1). It should be determined to what degree the action of the individual represents hostility toward another (**focus on other**) versus friendliness (**focus on other**) or withdrawal protesting a hostile act (**focus on self**) versus approach enjoying a friendly act (**focus on self**).

C. **DYADIC INTERACTION IS INEVITABLE. One cannot** *not* **interact or behave.** Even a response of total silence is an interpersonal posture (e.g., see Fig. 11-1: *ignoring and neglecting* or *walling off and avoiding*).

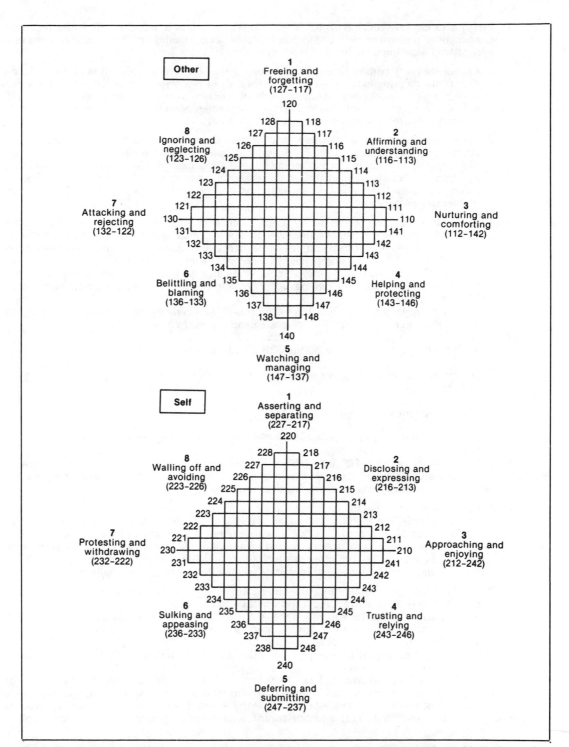

Figure 11-1. Cluster version of interpersonal surfaces of Benjamin's structural analysis of social behavior model (SASB). Benjamin's model allows classification of all behaviors in terms of three dimensions: **focus** on *other* or *self* (*surfaces*); degree of **friendliness** (*horizontal axis*); and degree of **interdependence** (*vertical axis*). The cluster version presents eight groups of behaviors per surface and is a condensation of the full SASB model, which describes thirty-six behaviors per surface. For example, cluster 5 from the focus on *other* surface (*watching and managing*) contains five closely related behaviors from the full model (137: *intrude, block, restrict*; 138: *enforce conformity*; 140: *manage, control*; 148: *specify what is best*; 147: *benevolently monitor, remind*). [Adapted from Benjamin LS: Principles of prediction using structural analysis of social behavior (SASB). In *Personality and the Prediction of Behavior*. Edited by Zucker RA, Aronoff J, Rabin AJ. New York, Academic Press, 1984.]

D. PATTERNS OF DYADIC INTERACTION. Dyadic interaction tends to stabilize into recurrent, characteristic patterns or cycles of interpersonal behavior. Pairings of interpersonal postures of particular clinical importance have been described.

1. **Complementary postures** are pairings involving similar degrees of affiliation and interdependence but differing focus [e.g., an **enmeshed dyad** prototypically includes one individual with prominent controlling behavior (high interdependence; focus on other) and one individual with prominent submissive behavior (high interdependence; focus on self)]. Complementary postures tend to be quite **stable** over time.

2. **Symmetrical postures** are pairings involving similar degrees of affiliation and interdependence as well as the same focus. For example, a **power struggle** involves two individuals with high controlling behavior [high interdependence; focus on other] (see Fig. 11-1: *watching and managing* or *belittling and blaming*). Symmetrical postures tend to be quite **unstable**, resulting in interactions of escalating intensity, and over time typically move toward complementary postures.

3. **Antithetical postures** often can be useful to change the posture of a dyadic partner. Antithetical posturing involves responding with a posture that differs in focus and is directly opposite in degrees of affiliation and interdependence from the partner's previous message. For example, the parent who complains, "Come on, Doctor, you've been poking my daughter with needles for days and she looks sicker; when are you going to do something right?" (see Fig. 11-1: *belittling and blaming*) may react better to the physician who responds with the **antithetical statement**:
   a. "I'm disappointed too; I was hoping for more, but I certainly want to keep trying to help you daughter." (See Fig. 11-1: *disclosing and expressing*.)

   Than to the physician who responds with a **symmetrical**:

   b. "Well, you know, you have not done much of value either!" (See Fig. 11-1: *belittling and blaming*.)

   Or a **complementary response**:

   c. "You're right, I need to try harder." (See Fig. 11-1: *sulking and appeasing*.)

E. INTERACTION IN LARGER GROUPS. As individuals are added to a group, the number of dyads increases geometrically and, hence, the social interaction becomes more complex and difficult to examine. Two points are worth mentioning.

1. **Coreceivers**, or a relevant audience, may exist for any seemingly dyadic interaction. For example, consider the attending physician on a surgery service, who while on rounds rather relentlessly "grills" one medical student, whose father is a prominent local physician and the attending physician's golf partner. **Superceding the dyadic message** in this case **is the message to the coreceivers** (the other medical students on the service), "Even though I am his father's friend, I will be fair to you in that he will not be treated preferentially on this service."

2. **Triads or triangles** are inherently **unstable** during interaction and characteristically evolve into one closely aligned dyad and a more distant third person.
   a. **Rigid triangles** are those in which the alignment among the individuals does not vary over time. Such triangles are frequently observed in dysfunctional interaction.
   b. Two specific types have been described.
      (1) In the **scapegoating triangle**, the individual in the distant position is blamed or attacked as the source of the group's problems.
      (2) In the **inverted power hierarchy triangle**, one individual (of power level X) allies with another (of power level Y) vis-à-vis a third (of power level X). For example, families in which parent–child incest occurs often have a rigid cross-generation alliance, involving a "parentified child" and one parent, with the other parent taking a childlike role.

III. LARGE GROUP BEHAVIOR. Individuals and families invariably are embedded deeply in a series of increasingly larger and more diverse groups; for example, neighborhoods, religious congregations, ethnic groups, towns, and nations all have important effects on people's behavior, including their interactions with medical personnel. These effects can be categorized as involving the **framing and coordination of normative behavior** and the **provision of alternative social support**.

A. SOCIAL COORDINATION OF BEHAVIOR. Social existence requires orderly procedures to make interpersonal behavior predictable and to channel adaptive responses to the environment.

1. **Cultural aspects of coordination.** Culture includes the collective set of beliefs, values, and norms used by members of a large group to give understanding and purpose to their lives. Culture involves as well the roles, rituals, and conventions that the members of the group employ to order their social interactions. The presence of a culturally bound rule can often be inferred by the unexpected behavior exhibited by the member of another culture when such a rule has been unwittingly broken. The following cultural concepts are especially important in medical settings.

   a. The **ease of communication** between two individuals is directly related to their degree of cultural similarity.

   b. **Explanatory models.** Individuals living within different cultures may have varying conceptions of how events, including medical illness, occur. For example, when ill, they may have differing views concerning:

      (1) What constitutes a symptom or disease

      (2) The interpretation and presumed causes of disease

      (3) The classification of symptoms into syndromes

      (4) What is acceptable treatment

      (5) What role a physician should play in treatment

   c. **Cultural relativism** is a doctrine that asserts that the cultural values and customs of any given group are best examined in the context of that particular group and should be judged primarily in regard to their utility within that group. **Ethnocentrism** is a term describing the common tendency to view one's own culture as superior and differing cultures as inferior.

   d. **Socialization** is the process through which cultural beliefs and practices are passed on. This learning occurs primarily during childhood via:

      (1) **Modeling**—learning based on observation (see Chapter 6, section II D 4)

      (2) **Operant conditioning**—learning based on manipulation of reward and punishment [see Chapter 5, section III B 2 c (2), and Chapter 6, section II C 2]

   e. **Consensual component of reality.** Cultural beliefs and practices are dependent on the continuing consensual validation of members of the culture. While in most cases the consensual validation is so automatic that it goes unnoticed, in some situations it is much more prominent. For example, one could consider the medical examination of an individual's genitals by a physician of the opposite sex. Both physician and patient need to cooperate actively to maintain the reality that, "This is a medical procedure and hence okay."

2. **Structural aspects of coordination.** The cultural beliefs and practices of any given group are concreted over time as social realities, and these social structures have significant inertia to change. Consider the consistent correlation of an increased incidence of perinatal complications associated with lower socioeconomic status. This finding in part appears to be attributable to the structurally based limited availability of medical care to poorer people, since when good prenatal care has been equally available, no difference between socioeconomic classes in perinatal complications has been found.

B. **SOCIAL SUPPORT SYSTEMS.** Individuals form networks of attachments that seek to promote adaptation to or mastery of the difficult life events that occur to members of the group. While typically an individual's social support system includes family members, a viable network can be maintained with an assortment of nonrelatives, especially those who share similar cultural beliefs and practices.

The **mediating and buffering role** that social support systems can play in the medical care of an individual is drawing increasing attention. Effective social support systems have been shown to:

1. Promote adherence to medical regimens

2. Enhance the effectiveness of medical treatment (e.g., effective social support systems have been found to reduce steroid doses required under stress in adult asthmatics and to reduce the complications of pregnancy in women judged to be at high risk)

3. Protect against depression and other psychological problems in the face of adverse life events

4. Promote the return to normal growth and stability after severe medical illness (e.g., the degree of effectiveness of a family's social support system can predict the development of a crisis in families who have experienced the death of a child from cystic fibrosis)

IV. **FAMILY BEHAVIOR.** The family in which an individual grows up, combined with the family created through marriage, usually provides the most influential and intense interpersonal relationships likely to be experienced in life. Findings from many different disciplines point to the central role played by family relationships in the health of its members. Nonetheless, the American family is currently in a state of flux. At this time, there exists a broader array of "family" situations than ever before.

A. DEFINITIONS OF FAMILY

1. Structural

    a. Extended family. The United States Census Bureau defines the family as any group of individuals related by blood, marriage, or adoption. The emphasis is on the **legitimacy of the connection among family members**. This connection is often of significant interest to physicians (e.g., in genetic counseling).

    b. In a **nuclear family**, the family members not only have legitimate connections but also live together in one household.

    c. A **family of orientation**, or family of origin, is the nuclear family in which an individual has (or had) the status of child.

    d. A **family of procreation** is the nuclear family in which an individual has the status of parent.

2. Functional. A family is a psychosocial system consisting of an adult and one or more individuals (children or adults or both) in which there is a commitment to mutual need fulfillment and nurturance. This definition, by emphasizing **normative functions (i.e., need fulfillment and nurturance)**, is virtually identical to the concept of a social support system.

3. Interactional. The family is a group of intimates, related by strong reciprocal affections and loyalties, with a history and a future, who share a sense of home. The emphasis in this definition is on the **affective bonds** that arise out of recurrent interaction.

B. DEMOGRAPHICS AND CURRENT TRENDS

1. The majority (90%) of the United States population lives with relatives.

2. Marriage remains extremely popular (95% of the population marries at some time; 80% of those who divorce remarry). Married individuals are found consistently to be in better health than single individuals of similar age. Marriage most likely fosters better health by:

    a. Providing a more stable life-style

    b. Increasing everyday social contact and decreasing loneliness

    c. Allowing individuals to develop a consensus of the world

    d. Providing a forum to discuss problems and receive feedback

3. The **number of children** born to married couples is declining. The number of families that remain childless is increasing (currently 10% to 15% of all couples, with half actively making this decision and half simply postponing pregnancy too long).

4. The **divorce rate** remains high, yet it may have leveled off (currently it is projected that 40% of new marriages will end in divorce, with about half of these occurring during the first several years of marriage). Risk factors for divorce include:

    a. Short courtship

    b. Marriage at a young age

    c. Premarital pregnancy

    d. Persistent parental opposition to the marriage

    e. Limited social support system

    f. Extreme difference in socioeconomic background

5. The number of **single-parent families** is increasing rapidly and now comprises about 20% of families; 90% of these are headed by women.

    a. Although aggressive and delinquent behavior is increased in children whose parents have divorced (although not in children whose parents have died), this effect appears to be caused by ongoing parental discord and not divorce per se, as it is seen in families with high parental discord whether or not divorce has occurred.

    b. Single-parent families typically have less social support, more limited financial resources, and decreased ability to adapt to parental illness, and, accordingly, they are considered to be a higher health risk.

6. Working parents. Currently 40% of all children under the age of 18 years live in families in which both parents work outside the home. Only 20% of children live in families in which the father is the sole family wage earner.

7. The number of individuals living in **alternative family situations** continues to increase, but dyadic situations (e.g., heterosexual cohabitation and nonintimate rent-sharing arrangements) have been responsible for this rise, with larger, communal-living situations showing marked decline.

8. Extended family interactions. The geographic distance between extended family members continues to increase, but there is little evidence that the affectional and psychological distance has also increased; in fact, interaction among extended family members remains high (e.g., as evidenced by telephone calls and holiday visits). The extended family continues to serve as the major source of support during major life transitions and crises.

9. Family violence includes child, spouse, and parent abuse and incest. The rate of physical violence in families is increasing (currently 5% to 10% of families have an abused member; 25% of all murders occur among family members). It is unclear whether this rise is due to an actual increase in violent behavior or to improved case detection and reporting. Family violence frequently occurs with neglect (either in the absence of care or in poorly timed care).

Most abusers do not have a history of psychiatric problems, although a history of violent acts is relevant. Individuals who are likely to abuse family members often have:
  a. A history of abuse or deprivation as a child (80% of abusers have experienced abuse); however, not all individuals who have been abused abuse others
  b. Severe social and economic stress
  c. A poor social support system
  d. Stressful interactions with the abused individual (e.g., 25% of premature infants are abused, as opposed to 8% of full-term infants; premature infants may be more difficult and demanding and, accordingly, create more stress for their parents)

C. THE FAMILY LIFE CYCLE is a normative model of family life, which postulates that families face specific tasks at different stages of development. While healthy families do differ, the life cycle model can be of use to the clinician in deciding what are likely to be relevant events in the lives of his patients.

1. Stage I: formation of a new family. This stage extends from the time that two individuals get together as a seriously attached couple until the birth of their first child. The major tasks include:
  a. Making the transition from life as single adults to that of a dyad, creating a satisfactory mix of intimacy and individual autonomy
  b. Establishing working marital roles
  c. Restructuring relationships with both families of orientation

2. Stage II: child rearing. This stage of family development has several substages.
  a. Stage IIa: preschool age. The preschool stage extends from the birth of the first child until that child enters school. Major tasks include:
    (1) Dealing with the intense physiologic and psychological dependence of young children
    (2) Renegotiating the balance of intra- versus extrafamily responsibilities (e.g., careers and child-care arrangements)
    (3) Blending the role of intimate partner with that of parent
    (4) Renegotiating the relationship with the families of orientation (grandparents may expect greater involvement once grandchildren are present)
  b. Stage IIb: primary school age. Major tasks include:
    (1) Managing the tension that results from a family member entering and interacting with the larger social system (this becomes more problematic the more the family culture differs from the prevailing system; accordingly, minority and immigrant families may have an especially difficult time)
    (2) Maintaining satisfying marital life given the lack of privacy of this primarily child-centered period
  c. Stage IIc: adolescence. The major task is fostering the development of identity and independence of the child, while maintaining concern for his well-being.

3. Stage III: child launching. This is the stage during which the children leave home. Major tasks include:
  a. Transferring increasing freedom and responsibility to the young adult
  b. Maintaining a supportive home base for the children
  c. Reestablishing individual interests and careers
  d. Reexamining the marital relationship
  e. Coping with the decline, increasing dependency, and eventual death of the grandparents

4. Stage IV: return of independence. This stage and stage V usually account for well over half of the duration of a family's life. Major tasks include:
  a. Rebuilding the marital relationship now that the nest is empty
  b. Continuing involvement with individual interests and careers
  c. Maintaining ties with the extended family in the older and younger generations

5. Stage V: dissolution of the family. Major tasks include:
  a. Maintaining integrity in the face of one's own decline and that of one's spouse
  b. Planning for the dispersion of the family estate

D. CRISIS AND THE FAMILY LIFE CYCLE. A crisis is any event, personal or interpersonal, within or outside of the family, that requires an adaptive response from the family. Crises increase the stress within the family and, if not mastered, can lead to a decline in the family's health. **Adequate family functioning** requires that these stresses be **recognized** and **validated** by the family as potential problems and subsequently **mastered** either by the family itself or through the assistance of members of the family's social support system.

1. **Normative crises** include the developmental events given central status in the family life cycle model, such as marriage, birth of children, children entering school, and so forth. Although these events regularly occur in most families, they mark important transitions in family life and are considered crises in that they require adaptive responses from the family.

2. **Paranormative crises** involve events that occur frequently but generally catch families by surprise. It is these crises that make any family's life cycle distinctive. Examples include miscarriage, separation and divorce, as well as the illness, disability, or death of a family member.
    a. In over 50% of families, at least one family member will develop a diagnosable mental illness at some point in the family's development.
    b. More of these individuals will be treated by primary care physicians than by psychiatrists or other mental health professionals.

E. FAMILY THERAPY. Despite the diversity of existing family therapies and their use for many different types of clinical problems, outcome studies uniformly find family therapy to be very effective. Family therapies can be roughly divided into three schools.

1. **Behavioral–psychoeducational approaches** involve a number of similar methods, all drawing heavily from the principles of social learning theory (see Chapter 6, section II B), which emphasize that **interpersonal behavior is controlled, maintained, and shaped by the reinforcement properties of current environmental events** and hence is changed best through the manipulation of these events. Treatment usually involves some combination of the following:
    a. Identification of dysfunctional behavior
    b. Training family members in the principles of social learning theory
    c. Communication training
    d. Problem-solving training
    e. Contingency contracting (i.e., "If you do. . ., I will do. . .")

2. **Structural and strategic approaches.** These independently developed methods borrow concepts from general systems theory and view all problems as arising out of dysfunctional attempts by the family to adapt to its current life context. Some methods emphasize **structure** (i.e., the alliances, coalitions, and hierarchies in the family), while others focus upon **process** (i.e., the family's rules for communication and its circuits of interaction). Structural and strategic therapists typically use many types of interventions, including behavioral techniques. They are especially renowned for use of **cognitive reframing techniques and paradoxical interventions**. (Strategic/systemic therapists claim that such techniques are quite potent—like all potent therapeutic agents in medicine, such as strong drugs and sharp scalpels, these techniques are best used only by trained professionals.)
    a. The technique of **cognitive reframing** assumes that the understanding or view that a family has of their problem can interfere with the family resolving their problem. Typically such views are highly negatively charged; for example, "Our family would be perfectly alright if it wasn't for our daughter, Mary, who has spent all her time recently moping and crying." By suggesting another explanation that also fits the "facts," the therapist attempts to open other avenues for the family's recovery. For example, "Maybe Mary is remembering Grandma Jean for all of you. After her death last year you all got back to business as usual pretty quickly. Mary might be taking care of some unfinished business for the family."
    b. **Paradoxical interventions** are counterintuitive suggestions that are based on the assumption that recurrent problem interactions are to some degree complex interpersonal reflexes that once triggered run their course. Frequently the therapist "prescribes the patient's symptom," as a way to change the interactional context enough to inhibit the reflex from activating as readily. For example, a therapist urges a couple who entered marital therapy with a chief complaint of frequent arguments to be sure to have at least one argument before their next therapy session, even if it means pretending to provoke the other so that they will have some "fresh data" to talk about. The therapist is hoping that by instructing the couple to argue the reflex to quarrel will be inhibited, perhaps due to each person considering, "Is he/she really trying to pick a fight with me, or just following the doctor's orders?"

3. **Intergenerational–experiential approaches** are a loose collection of diverse approaches that

tend to view dysfunctional behavior as resulting from family developmental fixation (e.g., insufficient differentiation from or excessive obligation toward the families of orientation). Symptoms appear when some new developmentally related stress (e.g., the first child goes to school or a parent falls ill), cannot be mastered adequately due to the family's developmental fixation. The therapist's interpersonal skill in inducing a healing, emotional experience is seen as the major determinant in the outcome. Techniques used include:

a. Evaluating detailed extended family histories
b. Clarifying transgenerational patterns
c. Facilitating communication
d. Elaborating the family's myth or identity
e. Modeling play and fantasy experiences

BIBLIOGRAPHY

Benjamin LS: Principles of prediction using structural analysis of social behavior (SASB). In *Personality and the Prediction of Behavior*. Edited by Zucker RA, Aronoff J, Rabin AJ. New York, Academic Press, 1984

Engel GL: The need for a new medical model: a challenge for biomedicine. *Science* 196:129–136, 1977

Engel GL: The clinical application of the biopsychosocial model. *Am J Psychiatry* 137:535–544, 1980

Medalie JH (ed): *Family Medicine: Principles and Applications.* Baltimore, Williams and Wilkins, 1978

Parke R (ed): *The Family: Review of Child Development Research*, vol 7. Chicago, The University of Chicago Press, 1984

Taylor RB (ed): *Family Medicine: Principles and Practice*, 2nd ed. New York, Springer-Verlag, 1983

von Bertalanffy L: *General Systems Theory*. New York, George Braziller, 1968

Wamboldt FS, Wamboldt MZ, Gurman AS: Marital and family therapy research: the meaning for the clinician. In *Integrating Research and Clinical Practice, The Family Therapy Collections*, vol 15. Edited by Andreozzi LL, Levant RF. Rockville, Md., Aspen Systems, 1985

STUDY QUESTIONS

Directions: Each question below contains five suggested answers. Choose the **one best** response to each question.

1. All of the following are viewed as processes of adaptation in general systems theory EXCEPT

(A) morphostasis
(B) morphogenesis
(C) random chance
(D) novel structure formation
(E) negative feedback

2. All of the following statements are consistent with the doctrine of cultural relativism EXCEPT

(A) an individual's beliefs should be evaluated primarily in regard to their utility within the culture to which he belongs
(B) a member of a foreign culture may have valid reasons for not complying with the requests of his American physician
(C) when all of the facts are considered, some cultures actually do have better medical practices than others
(D) important values and beliefs are passed from one generation to the next through the process of socialization
(E) it may be more work for a physician to provide satisfactory care to a patient from a different culture

Directions: Each question below contains four suggested answers of which **one or more** is correct. Choose the answer

A if **1, 2, and 3** are correct
B if **1 and 3** are correct
C if **2 and 4** are correct
D if **4** is correct
E if **1, 2, 3, and 4** are correct

Questions 3–5

A young couple returns to the physician's office 2 months after the birth of their first child. Although the wife has healed promptly after delivery and is interested in resuming sexual relations, her husband has recently been unable to sustain an erection. The husband assures the physician that this had not been a problem before their baby was born.

3. According to the family life cycle model, appropriate tasks for a couple at this stage of development include

(1) blending the roles of intimate partner and parent
(2) renegotiating who does what chores around the house
(3) dealing with the physical and emotional demands of young children
(4) distancing themselves from their own parents

The physician reassures them that their problem is really quite common, suggests some ways for them to "restart sexually," and asks them to return in 1 month for follow-up. Surprisingly, they are not better. The husband says that he just cannot stand the thought of "making love to a mother" and tells the physician that he was often beaten severely as a child by his mother.

4. Which of the following conditions would further increase the physician's concern that this man may abuse a family member?

(1) The couple has few friends in town
(2) The baby was born 1 month premature
(3) He is finishing graduate school and interviewing for jobs
(4) He has seen a psychiatrist in the past for depression

The physician refers them to a family therapist in his health maintenance organization (HMO). He has worked with the therapist before, and he knows that he was trained in an intergenerational–experiential approach to family therapy. The man returns to the clinic 1 year later for an employment physical. He states that he and his wife had a good experience, seeing the therapist 20 times, and he is pleased to report that he is "back to normal."

5. He is likely to report that the therapy included

(1) exploration of their family histories
(2) discussion of cross-generational triangles
(3) a search for family developmental fixation
(4) strong emotional experiences

6. The family of a patient with diabetes mellitus may influence the course of this individual's disease in which of the following ways?

(1) By influencing the emotional climate in which the patient lives
(2) By influencing when the patient defines himself as "sick enough" to consult a physician
(3) By influencing how friendly the patient is with nonfamily members, including the physician
(4) By promoting the patient's compliance with treatment

E

7. Increasing demographic trends of family life in the United States include the

(1) number of children born per couple
(2) percentage of the population that eventually marries
(3) importance of extended family members as sources of social support
(4) number of childless married couples

D

ANSWERS AND EXPLANATIONS

1. The answer is C. (*I B 3*) Adaptation is a response of a system to environmental stress or perturbation. While random chance could be seen as influencing the stresses or perturbations that the environment presents to a system, the processes of adaptation are seen as governed by the organization of the system and hence are never random.

2. The answer is C. (*III A 1 b, c, d*) Cultural relativism is a doctrine that asserts that the cultural values and customs of any given group are best examined within the context of that particular group and primarily in regard to their utility for that group. The continuity of cultural beliefs is in part due to the process of socialization. While the proponents of the doctrine of cultural relativism would agree that it may be more difficult to communicate with or understand the members of a different culture, they would not agree that cultural practices, including medical care, can be judged in terms of better or worse.

3. The answer is A (1, 2, 3). (*IV C 2 a, D 1, 2*) The preschool substage begins with the birth of the first child. During this time the couple is likely to be attempting to cope with the responsibility of their baby and deciding how best to integrate this responsibility with the other demands in their lives. It is a difficult time to distance oneself from one's parents in that grandparents usually expect greater involvement in their own children's lives once grandchildren are present. ("I had all that work with you, now it's my turn to enjoy a baby.")

4. The answer is A (1, 2, 3). (*IV B 9*) Family violence includes child, spouse, and parent abuse as well as parent–child incest. The issue of family violence frequently goes unnoticed unless the physician retains a high degree of suspicion. While considerable overlap exists between abusive and nonabusive individuals, abusers frequently have been abused as children, are experiencing current social or economic stress, and have limited social support systems. Of premature infants, 25% are abused (as opposed to 8% of term babies), perhaps because premature infants are more stressful to care for. Most abusers do **not** have a history of psychiatric treatment.

5. The answer is E (all). (*IV E 1, 3*) The intergenerational–experiential approach to family therapy is actually a loose collection of diverse approaches, with families seen by therapists who are, among others, psychoanalytically oriented therapists, gestalt therapists, client-centered therapists, and existential therapists. In general, the approaches view symptomatic behavior as arising due to a family's inability to resolve current life stresses in the face of prior family-level developmental failure. A major goal of therapy is to induce a healing, affective experience by detailing extended family history, clarifying transgenerational patterns, facilitating family communication, elaborating the family's myth–identity, and modeling play–fantasy experiences.

6. The answer is E (all). [*I C 2; III A 1 b (1), B 1, 2; IV*] Families provide their members with some of the most influential and intense relationships that the individuals are likely to experience in life. Family experience can influence how one orients himself toward the world at large—how one makes sense of life events, what one expects of oneself and others, and how one interacts with others. Additionally family-level variables, including the family's emotional climate, have been shown to have measurable effects on the course of an assortment of different disease processes (e.g., blood sugar levels in juvenile diabetic patients, survival in renal dialysis patients, and rate of psychotic recurrence in schizophrenic individuals).

7. The answer is D (4). (*IV B 2, 3, 5, 8*) Demographic trends currently suggest that the American family is in a state of flux. Whether these changes represent crisis or progress is a widely debated contemporary issue; however, it is certain that the diverse ramifications of our culture's evolution are likely to be important in the future practice of medicine. Married couples are having fewer children, and due to intention or postponing pregnancy too long, more couples are remaining childless.

12
The Physician–Patient Relationship

Bernard L. Frankel

I. INTRODUCTION

A. The physician–patient relationship is a two-person social system, which is determined by the expectation that particular roles will be assumed by both physician and patient and by their individual personalities. It transcends the traditional "bedside manner," which is the physician's personal style and only one part of the relationship.

B. The physician provides **emotional support** and **legitimizes illness**; both functions contribute significantly to the effectiveness of active treatment or, conversely in a poor relationship, significantly compromise the effectiveness of any treatment. The relationship is an important mediator of the therapeutic effect of every treatment program (the so-called **placebo** or nonspecific effect).

II. THE SICK ROLE

A. SOCIETAL EXPECTATIONS OR "GROUND RULES." Society assigns a specific role to the ill person by virtue of his being ill. According to sociologist Talcott Parsons there are **four key aspects to the sick role**.

1. **The sick person is exempt from normal social-role responsibilities**. This "right" of the sick person must be legitimized, usually by the physician, in order to prevent abuse (malingering).

2. **The sick person is not to blame for his illness**. He cannot get well by "pulling himself together." His condition requires that he be taken care of.

3. **The sick person is obliged to want to get well**. Being ill should be seen by the patient as an undesirable and unfortunate condition, and he should be highly motivated to get out of the sick role.

4. **The sick person is obliged to seek technically competent help**. He usually contacts a physician, with whom he is expected to cooperate in the process of attempting to recover from his illness.

B. PERFORMANCE OF THE SICK ROLE. How an individual actually behaves when he becomes sick is influenced by several factors.

1. **Economic**
   a. **Individuals who are financially hard pressed** might be reluctant to assume the sick role because of loss of income, resulting in greater economic stress.
   b. **Individuals who are injured on the job** may intensify and prolong the sick role as long as secure income and exemption from work result from continuation of the illness.
   c. **Students and those individuals embarking upon careers** might be disinclined to assume the sick role because of the interruption in achieving academic or career objectives.

2. **Personal experiences.** Exposure to individuals who have benefited from being sick may influence an individual to seek at opportune times the exemptions and secondary gains inherent in the sick role.

3. **Society's view of a particular illness** may affect an individual's motivation in assuming the sick role. He may be reluctant to do so because stigmatized illnesses such as venereal disease and drug addiction often connote personal responsibility.

4. Psychological factors
  a. The personality types (habitual patterns of thought, behavior, and feelings) **of individuals** are loosely defined categories that are useful in the context of medical care for understanding the very important influence of personality on the perception and performance of the sick role. The following eight types are often encountered.
  (1) Dependent, demanding individuals want (need) a lot of reassurance and special attention from physicians and nurses. They tend to become overly dependent upon them, making frequent, inappropriate, urgent calls.
    (a) These patients feel resentful and rejected when their demands are not fully met and may consider their illness to be a result of lack of concern and protection by others.
    (b) They may be perceived as "enjoying" their sickness.
  (2) Orderly, controlling individuals want (need) very much to control the external as well as their internal environment, probably in part due to a great fear of losing control and of being helpless.
    (a) They generally experience illness with little evidence of an emotional reaction and describe their symptoms thoroughly, precisely, and dispassionately.
    (b) These patients are usually quite sensitive about punctuality and attention to detail.
    (c) They may feel very threatened by the control that physicians assume over their lives and bodies in order to diagnose and treat them.
  (3) Dramatizing, emotional individuals have an underlying need for reassurance that they are still attractive and desirable and will not be abandoned, even when ill.
    (a) They relate their histories in an impressionistic and diffuse rather than precise manner and are often experienced as charming, fun to talk with, amusing, and as having a dramatic flair.
    (b) They often behave in a covertly (and sometimes overtly) seductive way toward their physicians.
  (4) Long-suffering, self-sacrificing individuals have generally endured protracted pain and suffering, with the current sickness being yet another episode in a long succession of unpleasant events.
    (a) These patients communicate in a complaining or wailing style about their bad luck, disasters, and disappointments in the efforts of their physicians to the extent that they appear to be exhibiting their misfortunes.
    (b) Intense, underlying guilt feelings typically are the source of the pain and suffering that these patients experience and use (often unconsciously) to maintain interpersonal relationships.
  (5) Guarded, suspicious individuals are hypervigilant and overly concerned about being harmed, exploited, and criticized.
    (a) They are apt to misinterpret the physician's statements and actions (especially if these statements and actions are ambiguous) along ominous or threatening lines, and they have marked difficulties in trusting physicians sufficiently to cooperate fully with them.
    (b) These patients tend to blame others for their illness.
  (6) Superior, special individuals behave like VIPs (even if they are not) in their snobbishness, self-confidence, arrogance, and even grandiosity. They need to see themselves as being invulnerable and perfect.
    (a) These patients are often overtly proud of their bodies, physical abilities, and occupational achievements.
    (b) They tend to seek the most eminent physicians and prestigious medical centers and often look for shortcomings in their physicians, as if to maintain a sense of superiority over them.
  (7) Aloof, seclusive individuals are shy, remote, detached, and clearly prefer solitary pursuits.
    (a) Through emotional noninvolvement, they appear to be unconcerned about symptoms and procedures that normally arouse anxiety.
    (b) They want to maintain privacy and often delay seeing a physician because of their aversion to the close interpersonal contact necessitated by medical care.
  (8) Impulsive individuals have a low frustration threshold, and, being unable to delay gratification, demand immediate relief from their symptoms, no matter how minor.
    (a) These patients repeatedly do things that they do not "mean to do," without deliberation.
    (b) They are prone to act out aggressively (e.g., by cursing the physician or kicking a piece of equipment) when frustrated and tend to be perceived by their physicians as deficient and childish and are thus disliked.
  b. The **personal meaning of illness** is a second category of psychological factors that may influence the behavior of a patient. Feeling constrained and threatened by his disorder,

especially when it is serious or chronic, and markedly affected by his personality type, the sick individual typically searches for a personal meaning for the illness. He may view or interpret his illness as:

(1) A challenge to be met or an obstacle to be overcome

(2) Evidence of an inherent weakness

(3) An enemy threatening to destroy him

(4) A punishment for past transgressions (often of a sexual nature)

(5) A strategy to cope with life's demands (e.g., the use of illness to obtain disability benefits)

(6) A relief or reprieve from societal responsibilities or expectations (e.g., exemption from the draft)

(7) An overwhelming irreplaceable loss or irreparable damage

(8) A positive experience that aids in the appreciation of the meaning of life and provides other aesthetic values

   c. The **method of coping with illness** reflects both the personality type of the patient and his personal interpretation of the illness. It encompasses the individual's characteristic ways of perceiving, thinking, problem solving, and acting when ill.

      (1) Cognitive responses to illness

         (a) Minimization refers to the tendency to ignore, deny, or rationalize the personal significance of one's illness. It includes the delusional denial of illness, the selective misinterpretation of facts, as well as reasonable doubting.

         (b) Vigilant focusing is a brisk response to perceived danger signals and an ongoing effort to reduce ambiguity and uncertainty about all aspects of the illness. It encompasses hypervigilance, exaggeration of all threats to bodily integrity, obsessional gathering and arranging of pieces of medical information, anxious rumination, as well as rational planning based on the realistic recognition of the bodily threats and changes in life-style that are inherent in disease.

      (2) Behavioral responses to illness

         (a) Tackling is characterized by an active attitude toward the challenges and tasks posed by the illness or disability (e.g., an individual uses a diseased part of his body as though it were intact).

         (b) Capitulation is characterized by passivity and either withdrawal from or dependent clinging to others in times of illness. (It is not to be confused with willing acceptance of periods of relative inactivity in the service of recovery.)

         (c) Avoidance pertains to active attempts to escape from the exigencies of the illness ("flights into health"). It is typically associated with marked minimization or denial of the illness. Social interactions with others generally remain unchanged.

C. EXCEPTIONS TO THE SICK ROLE CONCEPT

1. Incurable illnesses necessitate adjustment and adaptation rather than motivation to get well.

2. Minor illnesses by definition necessitate neither exemption from normal social roles nor contact with a physician.

3. Legitimate sick roles, such as some physical handicaps, do not necessitate exemption from usual responsibilities, continuing attention by a physician, or a motivation to recover.

III. THE ROLE OF THE PHYSICIAN

A. SOCIETAL EXPECTATIONS. Parsons has similarly described **five key aspects to the physician's role**.

1. Technical competence. The physician is expected to acquire and maintain a high level of knowledge of up-to-date technical skills in the science of medicine.

2. Medical role "universalism"

   a. Becoming a physician is available to anyone meeting the performance criteria.

   b. The physician renders professional services to any individual, not just to friends and relatives.

3. Functional specificity

   a. Specificity of competence. The physician is expected to use only the skills and practice areas of medicine only in which he is competent and not treat patients who require skills or knowledge that he does not have.

   b. Specificity of the scope of concern. The physician is expected to practice his skills **only for the purpose of medical care**. The patient is not to be exploited by the physician.

4. **Affective neutrality.** The physician is expected to strive for and maintain objectivity in relating to patients and not become emotionally involved (as manifested by, for example, erotic arousal or personal friendship). His attitude should be one of professional concern and compassion. He should strive to treat his patients equally whether he likes them personally or not.

5. **Collectivity orientation.** The physician is expected to subordinate his own personal gains to the patient's welfare in order to facilitate the development of trust. Bargaining over fees, advertising, and refusing "poor–credit-risk" patients are practices that are traditionally proscribed in protecting and upholding this expectation.

B. **PATIENT EXPECTATIONS.** In addition to the five factors discussed above, the patient has specific **clinical expectations** of the physician.

1. **Relief from distress** typically is the highest priority. Regardless of the underlying disease, the patient, hoping for relief, expects the physician to **attend to his symptoms**.

2. **An unhurried setting and atmosphere** is to be created by the physician wherein the patient can tell his "story"; be informed about the physician's findings, diagnoses, and treatment options; and ask questions.

3. Rather than be abandoned, the patient expects the physician to "always be my doctor" and to be there at least to **comfort** him when cure of disease or relief of symptoms is not feasible.

C. **PHYSICIAN EXPECTATIONS.** Every physician seems to have vague but very firm ideas concerning the behavior of a patient. This belief system is immensely powerful, and it influences practically every detail of the physician's interaction with his patients.

1. **A patient is perceived as "good"** when he:
   a. Is seen to be suffering legitimately from or is significantly distressed by his symptoms rather than presenting with a minor or trivial complaint
   b. Presents with objective signs and symptoms of a treatable disease process
   c. Cooperates in the treatment process (e.g., by obeying orders and asking few questions)
   d. Does not make any emotional demands on the physician (e.g., by not displaying excessive emotion)
   e. Displays gratitude for the physician's efforts upon recovery or relief

2. **Blaming the patient** is typical when these five conditions are not fulfilled, and problems develop, even though such problems may stem from the physician's:
   a. **Failure to communicate effectively** his expectations of the patient and his attitudes about how he practices medicine
   b. **Deficiency in technical skills**, knowledge, or judgment

D. **PROFESSIONAL DEVELOPMENTAL ISSUES.** Described here are five issues that must be confronted in the development of the physician. How they are resolved significantly affects the physician's role in the physician–patient relationship.

1. **Balancing objectivity and empathy**
   a. In assessment of the patient, **objectivity** (at one end of the spectrum) is characterized by cool evenhandedness in eliciting and weighing information.
   b. **Empathy** (at the other end) employs transient yet strong identification with the patient's feelings in order to obtain data.
   c. Good medical practice depends on using both objective and empathic modes of gathering information in order to arrive at an integrated and thorough understanding of the person, his behavior during illness, and his disease.

2. **Nurturance and executive necessity**
   a. **Nurturance** refers to taking care of others.
   b. **Executive necessity** refers to the physician's being responsible, decisive, and active; willing to be in charge; knowing that he will inflict pain in order to produce cure or relief; and knowing that he will work on another person's body.
   c. Good medical practice must integrate the two.

3. **The wish for omnipotence and omniscience and the toleration of uncertainty**. The physician must first recognize his wish to gain power over disease and death through knowing everything, and then he must control that wish by learning to tolerate and work with the **uncertainty that is always present in every clinical situation**.

4. **Formation of a professional ego-ideal** involves interweaving the three developmental stages discussed above.

    a. This process is dependent upon the physician's expectations of himself as a professional and upon an internal ideal of that profession.

    b. The ego-ideal provides a substrate for what the physician-trainee feels that he should become in order to remain internally satisfied and socially and professionally valued.

5. Maturation of a professional operational identity. The effective resolution and integration of the developmental stages and long-standing individual personality and behavioral styles allow the establishment and maintenance of a physician identity that is resilient enough to support a daily work load involving the stress of constant contact with disease, illness behavior, pain, suffering, death, and uncertainty.

6. Personality factors significantly affect the development of the physician. Most prevalent among medical students is the obsessive–compulsive (orderly, controlling) personality style, which typically pushes the developmental balance in the direction of:

    a. Excessive objectivity at the expense of empathy

    b. Excessive decisiveness and "doing to" at the expense of "taking care of"

    c. Excessive striving for omnipotence and omniscience at the expense of the toleration of uncertainty

IV. MODELS OF THE PHYSICIAN–PATIENT RELATIONSHIP. The four models described have their prototypes in the developmental stages of the relationship between parents and children.

A. ACTIVITY–PASSIVITY MODEL. The oldest conceptual model is based on one person's influencing another in such a way and under such conditions that the individual acted upon is unable to contribute actively or is considered to be inanimate. The prototype is that of the **parent–infant relationship**.

  1. Task definition. The physician determines and defines the illness, which the patient neither perceives nor understands. The physician selects the treatment, applies it, and determines its success without the patient's awareness or active involvement.

  2. Roles and role images

    a. The physician perceives himself as a self-sufficient (with respect to the patient) technical expert and perceives the patient as a complex, biological system.

    b. The physician interacts often with colleagues but rarely with the patient.

    c. If he perceives the physician at all, the patient sees only his external ministrations and has no conception of his evaluation, strategy, or outlook. Thus **the patient takes almost no part in his own treatment**.

  3. Tacit understandings and behavior codes

    a. The physician has full license from the outset to evaluate the patient and institute and stop any treatment.

    b. The patient does not have to know what his evaluation is, what treatment is in progress, when it will end, or why.

  4. Gratifications

    a. The physician may satisfy his own needs for technical understanding and mastery of complex and essentially mechanical or inanimate principles and devices.

    b. The patient's most elemental dependency needs are satisfied. He is relieved of anxiety arising from the uncertainty of his condition, from the difficulties of mastering or understanding it, or—in many cases—even feeling it.

  5. Clinical applications. This type of relationship is required when the patient is delirious, comatose, immobilized by acute trauma, or anesthetized.

B. GUIDANCE–COOPERATION MODEL. Underlying **most of current medical practice**, this model continues to emphasize the dominant and controlling role of the physician. The prototype is that of the **parent–child (adolescent) relationship**.

  1. Task definition. The physician still defines the illness, treatment, and cure, but the patient is given access to the physician's style and manner of practicing; the patient makes no modifications of his own.

  2. Roles and role images

    a. The physician perceives himself as an exclusively responsible (with respect to the patient), selfless caregiver and lifesaver. Acting parentally (benignly or austerely), he is always in control.

    b. The patient is viewed as suffering and totally helpless. He sees the physician as devoted, heroic, and, at times, omnipotent. **The patient too feels himself to be helpless and places himself in the hands of his physician.**

3. Tacit understandings and behavior codes
   a. The physician has full license to define and decide on evaluation procedures and therapy. The patient's permission, however, must be secured for every procedure.
   b. The patient may not change the physician's view or his treatment; any deviation from this "rule" is labeled by the physician as uncooperative.

4. Gratifications
   a. The physician may satisfy strong needs to nurture, protect, and restore.
   b. The patient satisfies a complementary need to be nurtured and to place his fate in another's hands.

5. Clinical applications. This most commonly used model is employed in situations that are less desperate than those mentioned for the activity–passivity model; for example, it may be employed when the patient has an acute infection or is convalescing from surgery.

C. MUTUAL PARTICIPATION MODEL. This model is based on the belief that equality among human beings is desirable. Its prototype is the relationship between **two adults interacting for professional or business purposes.**

1. Task definition. The physician provides the framework for a precise definition of the illness and its treatment, but the patient's initial and evolving views of his own disorder are constantly integrated with the view of the physician. A "cure" is always mutually defined.

2. Roles and role images
   a. The physician sees himself as an empathic and concerned specialist with particular skills constantly in the process of developing and refining. He sees the patient as a complex person with concerns and a social environment similar, in broad human terms, to his own. The physician learns about the person he is treating.
   b. **The patient** clearly **sees his own condition and** the significance of **his own initiative in coming for and receiving treatment. He perceives the physician as both an expert and one who is humanly concerned.** He feels that these perceptions can be revised by his own experience, and he examines the qualifications, personal limitations, fees, and so forth of the physician.

3. Tacit understandings and behavior codes
   a. The physician has license to lead but not order; he is a resource, a specialist whose competence is actively assessed by the patient.
   b. The patient is to monitor and participate in his own treatment and to learn to resume his status as an expert on his own health.

4. Gratifications. Both physician and patient fulfill personal needs of partnership and discovery. The patient also fulfills needs of active mastery over anxiety and disability.

5. Clinical applications. This model is well suited for the management of chronic diseases such as diabetes or multiple sclerosis, where, over time, the patient may learn as much about the disease as the physician.

D. SOCIAL INTIMACY MODEL. While this model is also based on the desirability of equality among individuals, its prototype is the **relationship between two close friends.**

1. Task definition. There is no sense of purpose in the technical sense; that is, there is no clearcut problem (e.g., pain or disability) requiring a solution. Rather, physician and patient seek to provide security, affection, support, and self-esteem to each other and keep each other from harm.

2. Roles and role images. Physician and patient see each other as affectionate and open and themselves as loving and available. Each expects the other to be accessible and interminably on call.

3. Tacit understandings and behavior codes. Informality, spontaneity, availability, and mutual support are encouraged. Often there is the tendency to deepen the relationship through the mutual sharing of personal information and experience. In contrast to the other models, the relationship is perpetuated as long as possible rather than ended or interrupted when appropriate.

4. Gratifications. A great range of personal needs, including those described for the other models, are satisfied but often to a more comprehensive degree over a longer and uninterrupted period of time.

5. Clinical applications. In view of its contravention of societies' expectations of the physician of functional specificity and affective neutrality (see section III A), **this model clearly reflects stepping over the bounds, and it is not only not functional but in many cases is not ethical.** It represents a developmental dysfunction in the physician and is not applicable to clinical practice.

V. THE CLINICAL INTERVIEW is among the physician's most valuable instruments (see Chapter 13, "Communication and Interviewing"). It is of paramount importance in:

A. Gathering valid and reliable information from the patient and communicating to the patient via **objective and empathic modes** of interaction (see section III D 1)

B. Establishing rapport and developing and maintaining a working or therapeutic alliance

VI. STRESSES ON THE PHYSICIAN–PATIENT RELATIONSHIP

A. "DIFFICULT" PATIENTS. Typically, it is the patient who is identified as difficult when problems arise in the physician–patient relationship [i.e., when the patient does not meet the physician's expectations (see section III C)]. Although individuals of particular personality types (see section II B 4 a) can become, in extreme cases, difficult patients, the following categorization takes into account all personality types.

1. Covertly self-destructive patients
  a. These individuals appear to be covertly suicidal, and they repeatedly defeat the physician's attempts to save their lives.
  b. They engender a sense of futility in the physician, who will sometimes react with overt anger or with covert wishes that the patient would die.
  c. They are exemplified by those with severe emphysema who persist in smoking and by those with liver damage who continue to drink alcohol.

2. Uncooperative patients are often labeled as such by a physician with high priorities of control, omnipotence, and omniscience when they:
  a. Question treatment
  b. Refuse procedures, tests, or treatments
  c. Demand that the hospital make concessions to their needs
  d. Request a second opinion
  e. Do not get well (such failure being viewed by the overly sensitive physician as a "lack of cooperation")

3. Somatizing patients
  a. Somatizing patients have long-standing, recurrent physical complaints in the absence of any significant, underlying physical disease or physiologic abnormalities. Their symptoms stem from psychological problems and are psychologically adaptive efforts to deal with:
    (1) Intrapsychic conflict (e.g., the alleviation of guilt through suffering secondary to chronic pain)
    (2) Problematic interpersonal relationships (e.g., the refusal of sexual relations because of recurrent headache)
    (3) Social or environmental problems (e.g., not returning to an unpleasant job because of continuing symptoms stemming from a work-related injury)
  b. These patients are often perceived by physicians as "not playing by the rules" (by not having a disease that can be diagnosed and treated in accord with "scientific" principles and techniques). This perception may lead to physician frustration, disparagement, annoyance, impatience, or anger to the point that the patient accedes to the physician's (often covert) wish that he seek care elsewhere.
  c. Somatizing patients are generally seeking the relationship with the physician as a key source of the respect, affection, concern, sympathy, and love that they are not getting from parents, spouses, children, or close friends. However, this does not apply either to patients with factitious disorder or to those who malinger (see section VI A 3 d).
  d. These individuals generally fall into one of the following psychiatric diagnostic categories.
    (1) Somatization disorder is characterized by multiple physical complaints involving many organ systems. The disorder extends over many years, and the patient is usually a woman, who is affected prior to the age of 30 years. The disorder occurs in association with obvious, chronic psychological, social, and occupational difficulties.
    (2) Conversion disorder is characterized by the sudden "conversion" and displacement of intense emotions (e.g., anxiety and anger) into a physical symptom. The disorder re-

sults from an acutely distressful perception of an event, and it helps the patient temporarily avoid the conflict situation (e.g., ''hysterical'' blindness or paralysis).

(3) **Psychogenic pain disorder** is essentially a conversion disorder limited to chronic complaints of unrelenting pain.

(4) **Hypochondriasis** is characterized by the overwhelming and fearful **preoccupation** with having a serious disease (rather than symptomatic complaints). Patients with such preoccupations resist the physician's demonstration and repeated assurance that no significant disease is present.

(5) **Atypical somatoform disorder** is diagnosed in a patient who has an unwavering **delusional** belief that he has a serious physiologic or anatomical abnormality that accounts for his disruptive, intense, persistent, single symptom, which is neither obvious to nor diagnosable by anyone else. Typical examples are patients whose delusions are that their feet have a very bad, obvious odor, or their noses are terribly disfiguring, or there are tiny organisms crawling under their skin.

(6) **Factitious disorder** is diagnosed in patients who deliberately pretend to be ill by faking the symptoms and signs of disease; this behavior, which the patient usually continues to deny even after being confronted with the incriminating evidence, results from a serious psychological disturbance.

(7) **Malingering** can be differentiated from factitious disorder only by the fact that the reasons for the deception are readily understandable in view of the details of the patient's circumstances, if and when they become known (e.g., pretending to be sick to avoid standing trial), rather than stemming from a serious underlying psychological disorder. Malingering is not a psychiatric disorder.

4. **Patients with chronic cognitive impairment (chronic organic brain syndromes)**
   a. These individuals have significant **chronic dysfunction of** one or more of their **cognitive abilities** (memory, attention, abstraction, judgment, concentration, calculation, and orientation) as a result of irreversible brain damage from various causes (e.g., Alzheimer's disease, cerebral anoxia, and alcohol abuse).
   b. They often demonstrate ''**sundowning**'': the worsening of confusion and agitation toward evening and at night, apparently resulting from the decrease in sensory input and orienting cues.
   c. They often are perceived as uncooperative and negativistic by physicians who fail to perform a careful mental status examination and therefore do not diagnose milder forms of this syndrome.
   d. Patients may be dehumanized or judged infantile by physicians who, having diagnosed the syndrome, perceive them to be much more helpless, insensitive, uncomprehending, and untreatable than they actually are.

5. **Physicians as patients** introduce even more complexity and stress into the physician–patient relationship as a result of the following issues.
   a. Physician patients often choose a physician with whom they are comfortable or with whom they do not fear a loss of ''equality'' in the relationship, rather than the most competent individual.
   b. The custom of professional courtesy may cause the physician patient to think that he may be exploiting his nonbilling colleague and thus feel reluctant to ask for more time and visits.
   c. The treating physician who is reluctant to treat the colleague as a patient may expect him to write his own history, understand with little or no explanation the reasons for tests and procedures, and manage his own medications.
   d. The treating physician may fear criticism of his knowledge, skills, and judgment by his patient and thus feel anxious and ambivalent about taking care of him.

B. **DIFFICULT CLINICAL ISSUES**

1. **Pain.** The development of rapport and trust between a patient in pain and the physician may be seriously undermined or impeded as a result of the following.
   a. The physician may have exaggerated and unwarranted concerns about turning his patient into a drug addict. The resultant underprescribing (both in dosage and frequency) of narcotic analgesics leads to unnecessary suffering and anxiety in the patient who, while suppressing his resentment, must engage in more pain behavior to get more analgesic medication, which in turn causes more discomfort in the physician.
   b. For the physician who simplistically conceptualizes pain as **either** ''**psychogenic**'' (''imaginary,'' ''functional'') **or physical** (''real,'' ''organic''), the former typically does not merit his full attention.
      (1) The patient suspected of having ''functional'' pain usually perceives the physician's irritation and decreased interest and respect.

      (2) He typically reacts with resentment, anxiety, and withdrawal, especially if he discovers that his physician has acted on the mistaken belief that prescribing a placebo will help define more clearly the nature of the pain.

2. Dying. Helping the dying patient to accommodate psychologically to impending death and avoiding the twin dangers of saccharine reassurance and brutal confrontation are challenges made more difficult for physicians who equate dying with professional failure and a threat to their omnipotence. The relationship of such physicians with their dying patients often deteriorates as a result of the following.

    a. The physician sometimes has a tendency to avoid the patient because he feels that he can no longer do anything for him (and "just" being with the patient does not count).

    b. The physician may be uncomfortable about openly and fully informing the patient of his status, even though the patient may strongly suspect it and often wish to know. This discomfort may be projected onto the patient (e.g., "He will fall apart if I tell him the truth"). Without the physician's initiative in fostering effective and honest communication, there is unlikely to be any meaningful discussion of critical decisions requiring the patient's active participation, such as resuscitation.

3. Informed consent refers to **the patient's right to choose** among several treatment options or diagnostic procedures for his disorder on the basis of a thorough understanding of the potential benefits and risks. (It includes, of course, the right to refuse all treatment.)

    a. For the many physicians who are committed to a paternalistic model of relationship (see section IV B), informed consent is typically perceived as a challenge to their authority and competence. Thus, a patient's request for more detailed explanations about treatments or for second opinions is often experienced by these physicians as a manifestation of distrust, which may elicit from them disappointment, irritation, anger, or explicit threats of transfer to the care of another physician.

    b. It is clear that patients show a wide variation in the extent to which they want to be informed and decide on a therapeutic procedure (the high levels of anxiety and depression demonstrated by some patients actually preclude registration and understanding of the information offered). However, mutual trust and rapport are enhanced when the physician continually invites his patient to participate actively and maturely in decision making, unless there is clear-cut evidence that the patient is too psychologically regressed (e.g., frightened, dependent, or helpless) to do so.

    c. If the physician values knowing the person as highly as he values understanding the disease, he will also come to know about his patient's capacity and wishes with regard to issues of informed consent.

4. Sexuality. Many physicians seem to feel more at ease doing pelvic and rectal examinations (and other discomforting procedures) than asking their patients about sexual functioning. (This may be related to the finding in one study that more than half of the medical students interviewed reported significant anxiety about some aspect of sexuality). The omission of this aspect of history taking and frank discussion often:

    a. Leaves undisclosed data that are important for diagnostic and treatment purposes

    b. Communicates to the patient the physician's discomfort with this subject, thus inhibiting the development of an atmosphere of maximal trust and candor

    c. Generalizes so that the patient may feel inhibited about discussing other personally sensitive topics lest the physician also manifest discomfort about those

C. TRANSFERENCE AND COUNTERTRANSFERENCE

1. Transference refers to an individual's **unconscious** tendency to project onto someone in the present feelings and attitudes originally linked to important people in the patient's early life (e.g., parents and siblings). When intense, it introduces distortions that interfere with the capacity to relate to others. In medical settings, transference may interfere with the development of an effective, working alliance between the physician and patient.

    a. Patients may reactivate an infantile need for a nondemanding, gratifying, omnipotent parent in the relationship with their physicians. When these unrealistic expectations are not met (as inevitably happens), the relationship suffers.

    b. Transference may manifest repressed, negative feelings (typically both negative and positive feelings coexist in transference) through counterproductive action (e.g., noncompliant behavior).

    c. Negative transference reactions (e.g., hostility, suspiciousness, or competitiveness) may elicit from physicians inappropriately angry (rather than curious or understanding) responses. Inappropriately personal or erotic responses may be elicited also to some positive (e.g., seductive or sexual) transference reactions.

2. Countertransference refers to an analogous phenomenon in physicians. The physician's misperceptions of and inappropriate behavior toward patients, which stem from unconsciously determined emotional responses, can undermine the physician–patient relationship as readily as a patient's strong transference reactions.

  a. Examples

    (1) The anxious, perfectionistic physician who practices in constant fear of making a mistake may be unconsciously reliving interactions with very critical, quick-to-punish parents.

    (2) The physician who suspects every patient as potentially litigious may be unconsciously reliving a mistrustful childhood relationship with a sibling or parent.

    (3) The physician who gratifies his patients' every need because he cannot tolerate their disliking him may be unconsciously reliving childhood interactions with an indulgent parent who often and easily flew into frightening rages.

  b. The physician should suspect the presence of countertransference when he:

    (1) Experiences any feeling more intense than normal concern (e.g., anger, guilt, or sexual attraction)

    (2) Feels so drowsy, bored, or preoccupied that it is difficult to pay attention to the patient

    (3) Feels unable to empathize with or understand the patient

    (4) Feels vulnerable to the patient's criticisms and becomes defensive

    (5) Argues with the patient

    (6) Attempts to impress the patient with his knowledge and prowess

    (7) Feels that the patient is not sufficiently appreciative for all that he has done

    (8) Dreads the patient's visits

    (9) Feels unconcerned about the patient

    (10) Departs from his usual routine with similar patients (e.g., sees the patient other than at the usual time or in the usual setting or fails to bill the patient)

STUDY QUESTIONS

Directions: Each question below contains five suggested answers. Choose the **one best** response to each question.

1. The personality style of an individual who expects his physician to inform him about every detail of his tests, diagnosis, and treatment is most likely to be characterized by

(A) impulsiveness
(B) aloofness and seclusiveness
(C) excessive dependency
(D) strong wishes for control and orderliness
(E) chronic suffering and self-sacrifice

2. For physicians who understand their task to be diagnosing and treating significant physical disease, which of the following patients would be perceived as being the most "difficult"?

(A) A somatizing patient
(B) An emphysematous patient who continues to smoke
(C) A patient with senile dementia
(D) A patient who requests a second opinion
(E) Another physician

3. A young physician is seriously considering giving up medicine after one of his patients dies unexpectedly for reasons that remain unclear, even after autopsy. With which professional developmental task is this physician having difficulty?

(A) Balancing nurturant tendencies and executive necessities
(B) Balancing objectivity and empathy
(C) Formation of a professional ego-ideal
(D) Balancing the wish for omnipotence and the toleration of uncertainty
(E) None of the above

physician's inappropriate behaviour towards his patient

4. Clues to the physician that countertransference is present include all of the following EXCEPT

(A) arguing with the patient
(B) feeling empathy and concern for the patient
(C) feeling sexually attracted to the patient
(D) perceiving the patient as being insufficiently appreciative
(E) attempting to impress the patient with knowledge and skill

Directions: Each question below contains four suggested answers of which **one or more** is correct. Choose the answer

    A   if **1, 2, and 3** are correct
    B   if **1 and 3** are correct
    C   if **2 and 4** are correct
    D   if **4** is correct
    E   if **1, 2, 3, and 4** are correct

5. Avoidance is a coping response to illness and can be characterized by

(1) its association with the cognitive response of minimization
(2) "flights into health"
(3) denial as a key psychological defense mechanism
(4) withdrawal from others

6. The sick role concept does not adequately deal with illnesses such as

(1) appendicitis
(2) multiple sclerosis
(3) a skiing-related femoral fracture
(4) a simple cold

7. In a small, private hospital, a nurse who is a patient with puzzling fevers and skin infections has been discovered injecting herself with fecal material. What can be said about this behavior?

(1) When confronted, the patient will readily acknowledge it as playing a role in the production of her illness
(2) After learning of this behavior, her physician is likely to treat her with empathy and emotional support.
(3) It has an easily understood basis
(4) The patient engaged in it for deep-seated psychological reasons

SUMMARY OF DIRECTIONS

A	B	C	D	E
1, 2, 3 only	1, 3 only	2, 4 only	4 only	All are correct

8. Patients requesting a second opinion are more likely to be labeled as "uncooperative" by physicians who

(1) use the guidance–cooperation model
(2) use the activity–passivity model
(3) have a strong need for omnipotence and omniscience
(4) tend to overidentify with their patients

9. Patients who "sundown" can be typified by

(1) wanting to know the details of their illness
(2) becoming more lethargic in the evening
(3) being perceived as "good" patients by nurses and physicians
(4) significant cognitive impairment

Directions: The group of questions below consists of lettered choices followed by several numbered items. For each numbered item select the **one** lettered choice with which it is **most** closely associated. Each lettered choice may be used once, more than once, or not at all.

Questions 10–14

For each description that follows, select the condition that is most likely to be associated with it.

(A) Somatization disorder
(B) Conversion disorder
(C) Hypochondriasis
(D) Factitious disorder
(E) Malingering

10. Preoccupation with having a serious disease despite the physician's repeated assurances to the contrary.

11. Multiple physical complaints involving different organ systems in the absence of significant disease. This condition usually occurs in a woman over the course of many years.

12. A sudden inability to walk in a previously healthy woman who has just discovered her husband's infidelity. She has a normal neurologic examination.

13. The voluntary production of symptoms with conscious intent to deceive stemming from a deep-rooted psychological disturbance.

14. The deliberate and surreptitious raising of blood pressure to avoid induction into the army.

ANSWERS AND EXPLANATIONS

1. The answer is D. [*II B 4 a (2)*] Orderly, controlling individuals generally want very detailed information about all aspects of their illness to help cope with their great fear of losing control and being helpless. They also tend to be thorough, precise, and dispassionate in describing their symptoms.

2. The answer is A. (*VI A*) By definition, somatizing patients do not have a physiologic abnormality underlying their chronic, recurrent complaints. Such patients are typically perceived as being especially "difficult" (i.e., frustrating and infuriating) by those physicians who have come to believe that their efforts, attention, and respect are merited only when significant physical disease is present or is likely to be so. In this narrow biomedical model of practice, the psychosocial aspects of the illness (e.g., the patient's personality) are ignored.

3. The answer is D. (*III D 3*) The physician who excessively strives for and idealizes omniscience and omnipotence and who is intolerant of the significant uncertainty inherent in the practice of medicine is prone to experience a patient's death, especially one that is unexpected and unexplained, as a professional, and perhaps even a personal, failure. Based on such an experience, the vulnerable physician may seriously consider giving up clinical work entirely or may choose a subspecialty limited to the extent that omnipotence and omniscience appear to be achievable.

4. The answer is B. (*VI C 2 b*) Countertransference refers to a physician's misconceptions of and inappropriate behavior toward patients, which stem from unconsciously determined emotional responses. These can undermine the physician–patient relationship as readily as a patient's strong transference reactions. The physician should suspect the presence of countertransference in the following circumstances: when intense feelings (e.g., sexual attraction) are experienced; when feelings of boredom or unconcern are experienced; when feelings of vulnerability result from a patient's criticism; when arguments ensue with the patient; if impressing the patient seems important; or if the time with the patient is dreaded or continually changed. Feelings of empathy and concern are appropriate and desirable emotions in the physician and do not indicate countertransference problems.

5. The answer is A (1, 2, 3). (*II B 4 c*) A habitual way of coping with sickness, avoidance refers to active attempts to escape from its demands and realities. It is typically associated with marked minimization and denial of the illness. Withdrawal from others, however, is not characteristically part of this behavioral pattern; rather, withdrawal often occurs in patients who cope by using capitulation.

6. The answer is C (2, 4). (*II C*) Incurable illnesses, such as multiple sclerosis, require adjustment and adaptation rather than motivation to get well. Minor illnesses, such as a simple cold, typically do not necessitate exemption from usual social-role responsibilities nor contact with a physician. Therefore, the concessions that society makes to the sick individual apply only to those who suffer acute, serious, and largely reversible episodes of illness.

7. The answer is D (4). [*VI A 3 d (5)*] Patients with factitious disorders have deep-seated psychological reasons for their illness-manufacturing behavior, reasons that may come to light only in the very rare cases when they agree to and follow through with psychiatric treatment. After the diagnosis is made, these patients typically continue to deny their involvement in the production of their symptoms and usually evoke much anger and rejecting behavior in their physicians.

8. The answer is A (1, 2, 3). (*IV*) In both the guidance–cooperation and activity–passivity models of the physician–patient relationship, the patient is expected to behave unassertively (like a child) and to accept uncritically the physician's opinions. Physicians committed to these models also tend to have a strong need for omnipotence and omniscience. Thus, they perceive requests for second opinions as a questioning of their medical competence and authority by patients who are obviously being "uncooperative." A physician who overidentifies with his patients, while compromising his objectivity, will empathize with such a request.

9. The answer is D (4). (*VI A 4*) The term "sundowning" refers to the worsening of confusion and agitation in the evening and during the night in patients who have significant cognitive impairment as a result of (usually irreversible) brain damage. These patients are usually unable to understand the details of their illness, and this fact, coupled with their agitation, leads to their typical designation of "difficult" by nurses and physicians.

10–14. The answers are: 10-C, 11-A, 12-B, 13-D, 14-E. (*VI A 3*) Somatizing patients have chronic, recurrent physical complaints without significant underlying physical disease. They fall into several diagnostic categories. The patient who is preoccupied with having a serious disease despite the physician's repeated assurance and documentation that this is not the case is suffering from hypochondriasis.

Somatization disorder, usually starting in a woman before the age of 30 years, is characterized by recurrent physical complaints involving multiple organ systems. Even though no significant underlying disease is present, patients with this disorder often undergo unnecessary surgical procedures and take excessive amounts of analgesic and sedating medications.

The sudden appearance of sensory or motor dysfunction as a response to a stressful event in a patient without underlying physical disease is characteristic of a conversion disorder. The patient's inability to walk probably stems from an underlying conflict about leaving her husband and living independently. The absence of any neurologic abnormalities as the basis for the symptoms is essential for making this diagnosis.

Patients with a factitious disorder deliberately fake the signs and symptoms of disease as a result of serious underlying psychological disturbances. These disturbances rarely come to light because these patients typically refuse psychiatric referral. Rather, they seek other medical settings where they are unknown and may, therefore, engage in this behavior again.

Malingering differs from factitious disorder in that the reason for the deliberate deception is understandable when it becomes known. Effecting abnormalities in order to fail an army induction physical examination is a common example of malingering.

13
Communication and Interviewing

Robert L. Hendren

I. INTRODUCTION

A. COMMUNICATION. Research has shown that the ways in which a physician communicates with a patient significantly affect:

1. The **adequacy** of the clinical interview

2. The **accuracy of detection of a psychological disturbance**

3. The patient's **understanding of and compliance with the physician's advice**

4. The **impact** on the patient of potentially distressing medical and surgical procedures

5. Patient **satisfaction**

B. INTERVIEWING. The **most important skill** of the physician is the ability **to interview patients effectively**. The purposes of the interview are:

1. To **establish interaction** between the physician and the patient

2. To **gather** necessary **data**

3. To **develop the physician–patient relationship**, which is the foundation of any medical practice

II. PRIMARY GOALS OF THE PATIENT INTERVIEW

A. At the **beginning of the interview**, the primary goal is to **establish rapport** with the patient so that a complete history can be obtained. The physician should:

1. Introduce himself and put the patient at ease

2. Show respect for the patient

B. During the interview, the primary goal is to **identify relevant problems** systematically while maintaining an empathic working relationship with the patient. The physician should:

1. Allow the patient to tell his own story while maintaining appropriate control of the interview

2. Use language appropriate to the patient's age and background

3. Use tact in framing questions that relate to sensitive matters

4. Move effectively from one area of questioning to another

5. Use periodic summation

6. Allow the patient to express his feelings

7. Convey understanding and empathy for the patient's feelings

8. Clarify inconsistencies and ambivalences in the patient's statements and responses

9. Obtain adequate and meaningful information

C. At the end of the interview, the primary goal is to close in a way that **leaves the patient feeling satisfied** and sure that he has been understood. The physician should:

1. Inform the patient of what the next steps will be

2. Give the patient an opportunity to ask questions

3. Make a closing statement that will end the interview comfortably

III. CONTENT AND PROCESS OF AN INTERVIEW

A. **CONTENT** refers to the actual **verbal exchange** between the physician and the patient.

B. **PROCESS** refers to what happens during the interview that elucidates the patient's and physician's emotional reactions to questioning and to the subjects being discussed. Process is particularly evidenced by the **sensitivity and sensibility** that evolve, often "beneath the surface" and "between the lines" of the actual verbal exchange.

1. The interviewer should have the following **questions** in mind and should attempt to get **answers** to them through the content, the process, or both of these elements of the interview.
   a. **"Why is the patient here to see me now?"** It is important to understand what specifically motivated the patient to seek help at this time. Perhaps it is a special worry about a serious illness.
   b. **"What are the patient's feelings right now?"** Whereas it is important to know the patient's symptoms in depth so as to make an appropriate diagnosis and to develop a treatment plan, it is also important to be aware of the patient's feelings about the cause of the illness, the prognosis of the illness, and how it will affect his life.
   c. **"What are the patient's reactions to what is happening between us right now?"** These reactions to the evolving physician–patient relationship are often developing at a process level when they are not verbally expressed.

2. **Characteristics of process communication.** Patients who are not intimidated by their illness or by health care providers may offer their feelings freely to the interviewer and speak plainly and openly. However, even when this occurs, unacknowledged feelings may still be present.
   a. A deeply held **fear or apprehension** may be **expressed by momentary anger** at a relatively minor irritation. For example, a patient who expresses anger toward the physician for being late for an appointment actually may be expressing a fear that the physician may not be available when he really needs him.
   b. A patient may **speak about the present by recalling the past**. For instance, a patient who states, "I didn't like my last doctor; he never told me anything about my illness," may be requesting that the current physician share information with him.
   c. Sometimes **important messages hide** behind trivial passing remarks, asides, and casual jokes. The comments that a patient makes before or after the routine history is gathered are often revealing. For example, the patient leaving the office who comments, "Oh, by the way, Doctor, could you speak to my husband? He is very concerned about me," may be suggesting that she needs additional explanation and reassurance about her illness.
   d. **Shifts in conversation away from certain topics** or gradual **shifts toward certain topics** may occur. For example, a middle-aged man with a recent myocardial infarction digresses during the interview to talk about his athletic activities. This likely represents his concern about his ability to be active in the future.
   e. The patient may speak through **body language**. A patient who repeatedly clenches and unclenches his fists while describing his reaction to his illness in a calm, unworried manner may be revealing **underlying concerns** that he is reluctant to express.
   f. If the patient expresses the same concern over and over, the **repetition** should alert the interviewer to the importance of this topic to the patient.
   g. Process communication may be characterized by **repeated requests for information**. For example, a patient who repeatedly asks for information about a recommended surgical procedure may be expressing concerns about doing poorly during the surgery or recovery.
   h. During a patient interview, the **physician may become aware of emotions in himself**, such as boredom, depression, and anger. While these emotions may be due to the physician's own reactions to the patient (see section X B) or to the patient's illness, they are often **reflections of the patient's feelings**.

IV. A.R.T. OF INTERVIEWING.
An effective way to conceptualize the interview that encompasses both the content and the process is to identify three major phases of the interaction—**assessment**, **ranking**, and **transition**.* These three phases are present simultaneously and continuously throughout the interview.

---

*Reiser DE, Schroder AK: A.R.T. of Interviewing. In *Patient Interviewing: The Human Dimension*. Baltimore, Williams and Wilkins, 1980.

A. ASSESSMENT is the phase of the interview during which it is the **most open-ended** and **nondi-rective**. During this period, the patient usually raises concerns, describes symptoms, and offers other information that the physician will investigate further later in the interview.

B. RANKING of the patient's problems begins almost immediately and continues to the end of the interview. Decisions are made regarding **areas to pursue further** based on the urgency of the medical symptoms, the **concerns of the patient**, and the need to establish a working alliance with the patient. Questioning moves from open-ended to direct questions, so that each of the ranked problems can be fully investigated.

C. TRANSITIONS keep the interview flowing smoothly, put the patient at ease, and allow the interview to move from one phase to another with a sense of purpose.

V. GUIDELINES FOR COMMUNICATING AND INTERVIEWING. The most **effective** interview is one that is organized and structured carefully to elicit as much information as possible. The resultant interaction is both verbal and nonverbal (see section III). An interviewer can construct an effective interview by following these guidelines.

A. DEVELOPMENT OF OPEN AND PRODUCTIVE COMMUNICATION with the patient can be aided by specific techniques of asking questions. Interviewing strategies that fit the interviewer's style and with which he is comfortable should be developed.

1. The patient interview is a **professional rather than a personal communication**. It should be approached with a sense of **purpose**, **compassion**, and **curiosity**.

2. The **interview style** should be somewhere between friendly conversation and interrogation. Undirected conversation and rapid, unfeeling questions often interfere with the process of the interview and fail to gain the necessary information; the patient may feel confused and hurried.

B. PERSONALITY CHARACTERISTICS of both interviewer and patient that may facilitate or impede the gathering of information should be identified.

1. The **physician** should examine and attempt to understand his own **thoughts**, **feelings**, and **reactions** that arise during the interview. These reactions should be treated as pertinent and constructive data and should be used to establish communication with the patient.

2. Patient responses and objective **evidence** of the **patient's feelings** should be noted. These include:
   a. Emotional behavior (e.g., laughing, crying)
   b. Motor behavior
   c. Facial expressions and gestures (e.g., smiling, nodding, staring, frowning, sneering)
   d. Speech patterns, including rate, volume, modulation, mumbling
   e. Bodily gestures (e.g., clenching fists, fidgeting, shaking, stiffening)

3. The **patient's emotional response** to illness and some of the psychological and social factors contributing to this response should be explored. This will be facilitated if the physician does a careful patient profile (see section VII H).

VI. TECHNIQUES OF COMMUNICATING

A. FACILITATION is verbal or nonverbal communication that **encourages the patient to elaborate** on something that he has said. The patient's last word may be repeated, a questioning look given, or a question asked; for example, "Can you say more about that?"

B. OPEN-ENDED QUESTIONS are requests stated in general terms for **nonspecific information**; for example, "Tell me more about your pain."

C. DIRECT QUESTIONS are those that ask the patient for **specific information**; for example, "Did you first experience your symptoms after the automobile accident?"

D. SUPPORT comprises both verbal and nonverbal expressions that indicate the physician's **interest** and **concern** and his **willingness to help** the patient. (Support should not be offered before the patient has expressed his feelings.) An example of a supportive statement is, "This procedure will cause you very little pain and will take only a few minutes."

E. EMPATHY is communication that expresses **understanding of** and **sympathy for the patient's**

feelings and his need to express those feelings. (As with support, empathy offered before the patient has told the physician of his feelings is not as effective as it is when offered after.) An example is, "I can see that you are very worried about this procedure."

F. **REFLECTION** is a response from the physician that **repeats**, **mirrors**, or **echoes** a portion of what the patient has just said; for example, "You said your symptoms began after your mother died?"

G. **SILENCE** is a nonverbal communication that may express a range of responses from total disinterest to active concern. Ideally, silence on the part of the physician **leads to very useful information** in that it gives the patient a chance to explore and express deeper, less obvious concerns.

H. **CLARIFICATION** is a response that asks the patient for **further information and explanation**. An example is "Your symptoms occur when you are asleep; how are you aware of this?"

I. **CONFRONTATION** is a technique that brings the patient face-to-face with or calls his attention to some aspect of his behavior, appearance, or manner. These include **inconsistencies and contradictions**. An example of a confrontational statement is, "You plan to continue smoking in spite of the worsening of your emphysema?"

J. **SUMMATION reviews the information** that has been given by the patient; for example, "Let me see if I have this right—your pain began after an accident on the job, becomes worse when you cough or sneeze, and is not relieved by aspirin."

K. **INTERPRETATION** is a **formulation** by the physician of data, events, or thoughts into terms that make the patient aware of their interrelationship. (Interpretations should be used cautiously, especially until the interviewer knows the patient and has established reasonably good rapport.) An example is, "You seem very angry when you speak about your boss at the job where you hurt your back. I wonder if you blame him for what happened?"

VII. COMPONENTS OF THE STANDARD MEDICAL HISTORY

A. **PATIENT IDENTIFICATION** includes the patient's basic identifying information: name, age, sex, race, marital status, and occupation.

B. **RELIABILITY.** Is the patient himself providing the information or is someone else? How reliable is the patient or informant?

C. **CHIEF COMPLAINT.** The patient's major reason for seeking care should be stated as briefly as possible, using the **patient's own words**. (The statement should include the length of time that the problem has existed.)

D. **HISTORY OF PRESENT ILLNESS.** This is the **most important part of the clinical history**.

1. The patient should be permitted to begin his story in his own way, and then the interviewer, striking a balance between specific, nonspecific, and open-ended questions, should **guide** the patient through a **systematic account** of his problems.

2. In chronological order, each major event should be characterized as to date of onset and precipitating factors.

3. All **major symptoms** should be delineated fully in terms of location, quality, severity, duration, persistence or intermittence, aggravating and alleviating factors, and associated symptoms.

4. Symptoms should be **correlated** with each other and with other relevant problems.

E. **PAST MEDICAL HISTORY.** This is a **synopsis** of the **medical events** of the patient's entire life, including childhood illnesses, surgery, medications, drug allergies, substance abuse, psychiatric illness, and all other pertinent information.

F. **FAMILY HISTORY**

1. **This is a summation of** significant **medical information** (e.g., major illnesses, cause of death) for **every first-degree relative** of the patient.

2. This section also includes information on the basic structure of the patient's family (e.g., number of siblings, parents still living).

3. A **diagram** is an effective method for displaying the family history.

G. REVIEW OF SYSTEMS

1. Specific questions should be directed to the patient to assure that a **complete inventory** of his condition has been systematically taken. Symptoms that may have been forgotten or that the patient has regarded as insignificant will thus be elicited.

2. Symptoms pertinent to the history of the present illness are to be recorded in that section of the medical history (see section VII D).

3. All other symptoms are recorded in this section and should be fully detailed as to date of onset, precipitating factors, location, quality, and severity, as those in the history of present illness are detailed.

H. PATIENT PROFILE. This encompasses the **other aspects** of a patient's life, including **major stresses** in his life and the **resources available** to deal with them.

1. Place of birth, level of school completed, occupational history, and marital history

2. Current life status
   a. Home situation
   b. Family constellation
   c. Other significant people in the patient's life
   d. Sexual adjustment
   e. Typical day's activities
   f. Typical day's diet
   g. Social activities
   h. Sense of self-esteem
   i. Competence and mastery of his environment

3. The **meaning of his illness** to him and how it affects his everyday life

4. Past life history
   a. Constellation of historical family
   b. Significant life events
   c. Significant losses and gains

VIII. PSYCHOLOGICAL DEFENSE MECHANISMS emerge when we experience stress. They are **automatic** and **unconscious**, and they affect our perception of internal and external reality as an effort is made to avoid the experience of anxiety or depression. When illness occurs, various defenses arise to help the patient **cope with the threats** posed by the illness. The quality of these reflect the patient's stage of development as well as his character structure and personality style. **Defensive behavior** needs to be recognized by the interviewer, but not all defensive behavior needs to be confronted (unless it interferes with the assessment or with treatment). Instead, the interviewer should try to support the more adaptive defenses. Defenses commonly used by physicians and patients include the following, listed in order from lower levels to higher levels of adaptive functioning (see Chapter 6, section I B 5).

A. DENIAL is an unconscious mechanism that allows the patient to avoid awareness of thoughts, feelings, wishes, needs, or external reality factors that are consciously intolerable. For example, a 50-year-old patient is told that he has advanced lung cancer. Several days later he claims that he has never heard this information.

B. PROJECTION is the unconscious mechanism whereby an unacceptable impulse or idea is attributed to the external world. For example, a patient who is upset and angry about needing to be hospitalized, claims that the nurses are angry at him and are withholding appropriate care.

C. SPLITTING occurs when the patient unconsciously views people or events as being at one extreme or the other. For example, a hospitalized patient views the medical staff as being all "good" or all "bad."

D. ACTING OUT occurs when unconscious emotional conflicts or feelings are expressed in an arena different from the one in which they arose. Generally, acting out is a feeling expressed in actions rather than in words. For example, an adolescent girl who is angry at her family after being grounded, runs away from home without verbally expressing her anger.

E. REGRESSION is a **partial or symbolic return** to more infantile patterns of reacting or thinking. For example, a 4-year-old child resumes wetting the bed at night after a surgical procedure.

F. **COUNTERPHOBIA** is the defensive mechanism of seeking out experiences that are consciously or unconsciously **feared**. For example, a 6-year-old child comes into the physician's office and bravely challenges the physician to give him a shot.

G. **IDENTIFICATION OR IMITATION** occurs when a person unconsciously **patterns** himself after some other person. (Role modeling is similar to identification but is a conscious process.) For example, the son of a man who died of a myocardial infarction 20 years previously begins to experience the same symptoms as his father without the physiologic changes.

H. **REACTION FORMATION** is an unconscious mechanism in which unacceptable feelings, ideas, or impulses are **transformed** into their opposites. For example, a young mother feels resentment toward the demands that caring for her child make on her. However, she repeatedly tells herself and others how wonderful motherhood is. At times she worries unnecessarily that some harm will come to her child.

I. **REPRESSION AND SUPPRESSION** occur when unacceptable thoughts, wishes, or impulses that would produce anxiety are pushed out of awareness. For example, during an interview, a patient, aware of the significance of stomach pains and tarry stools, "forgets" to tell the physician about these symptoms.

J. **DISPLACEMENT** occurs when emotions, ideas, or wishes are transferred from their original source to a more acceptable substitute. For example, a hospitalized patient becomes unreasonably angry with her nurse after her physician informs the patient that she has cancer.

K. **ISOLATION OF AFFECT** is the separation of ideas or events from the feelings associated with them. For example, a patient, in a cool, unemotional manner, describes the circumstances of a serious automobile accident that he experienced, which resulted in multiple injuries.

L. **RATIONALIZATION AND INTELLECTUALIZATION** are defense mechanisms that use reasoning and "rational" explanations, which may or may not be valid, to explain away unconscious conflicts and motivations. For example, a man with coronary artery disease begins to keep careful records of the food that he eats and the amount of exercise that he gets and uses this information to explain the occurrence of anginal symptoms.

M. **SUBLIMATION** is a defense process by which an unacceptable feeling is unconsciously replaced with a course of action that is personally and socially acceptable. For example, a middle-aged man who feels helpless, depressed, and angry about his recently diagnosed coronary artery disease begins an exercise program.

N. **HUMOR** is used defensively to **relieve anxiety** caused by the discrepancies between what one wishes for himself and what actually happens. For example, a stroke patient laughs at his poorly coordinated efforts to walk.

O. **ALTRUISM** is a **seemingly unselfish interest** in the welfare of others. For example, a woman who has had bilateral mastectomies as a result of cancer helps other women soon after their mastectomies, and through this activity she also helps herself to work through her own anxieties and anguish about the illness and the operations.

IX. **EFFECTIVE DEALING WITH DIFFERENT PERSONALITY TYPES** requires recognition of the personality style and the defense mechanisms used by the patient. Eight personality types are described in the chapter on the physician–patient relationship (see Chapter 12, section II B 4 a). The following are suggestions for dealing with each of these types.

A. **DEPENDENT.** The physician caring for dependent, demanding patients should:

1. **Convey an enthusiastic readiness to care** for the patient; failure to do so often aggravates dependent or demanding behavior

2. **Set limits** when necessary, but not as an expression of impatience or anger

3. **Interact in a direct and open manner** to avoid passive-aggressive power struggles

4. **Avoid direct confrontation**; turning the responsibility for the patient's behavior back to him is more effective

B. **CONTROLLING.** The physician caring for orderly, controlling patients should:

1. **Inform** the **patient** methodically and in sufficient detail about his illness and treatment so that he can establish intellectual control over his anxiety

2. **Include the patient** as much as possible in decision-making and in the carrying out of his medical care

3. **Acknowledge and encourage the patient's strengths** to help him feel that he is in greater control

C. **DRAMATIZING.** The physician caring for dramatizing, emotional patients should:

1. Be generous with compliments and not be too reserved, since these individuals have an underlying need for reassurance that they are still attractive and desirable

2. **Discourage** this patient's **readiness for emotional involvement** and proceed calmly and firmly

3. **Offer reassuring explanations** about the illness and medical procedures when anxieties are intense so as to help the patient distinguish reality from alarming fantasies

4. **Allow the patient to discuss his fears freely** so that he can discharge pent-up emotions

D. **SELF-SACRIFICING.** The physician treating long-suffering, self-sacrificing patients should:

1. **Overcome the tendency to avoid these patients**, as this may intensify their behavior

2. Be nonjudgmental, yet **nonreinforcing of the sick role**

3. **Offer support** and guidance **to family members** who must deal with the patient (these relatives can help in the gathering of accurate information)

4. **Establish** gentle, firm **limits** of interaction, as the patient may become excessively reliant on the physician

E. **SUSPICIOUS.** The physician of guarded, suspicious patients should:

1. **Inform these patients** as fully as possible of diagnostic procedures and treatment to lessen suspicion

2. **Adopt a friendly, courteous attitude**, one that precludes getting too closely involved

3. Fully acknowledge the suspicions of querulous patients without reinforcing them

F. **"SUPERIOR."** The physician of **patients who perceive themselves** to be **superior or special** should:

1. Help the patient feel most comfortable by implicitly **acknowledging him as a person of worth**

2. **Strongly affirm his own expertise**, especially when challenged by the patient; the patient needs assurance that he is receiving competent care

G. **RECLUSIVE.** The physician caring for aloof, reclusive patients should:

1. **Respect the patient's need for privacy** and distance but not allow him to withdraw excessively

2. Approach the patient with considerate interest and quiet reassurance, without expecting a reciprocal response

H. **IMPULSIVE.** The physician of impulsive patients should:

1. **Set firm limits** prior to beginning treatment in an attempt to control impulsive behavior

2. **Avoid open confrontations** that are likely to lead to angry words and actions

3. **Hold the patient responsible** for his impulsive actions

X. TRANSFERENCE AND COUNTERTRANSFERENCE (see Chapter 12, section VI C)

A. **TRANSFERENCE** in the patient can introduce distortions in the interviewing process that **can interfere significantly in the physician–patient relationship**. The physician can best deal with this phenomenon by:

1. Not responding in a predictable (e.g., angry, flattered) manner to the patient's provocative (e.g., demanding, seductive) actions

2. Gently confronting distortions or inappropriate behavior

B. COUNTERTRANSFERENCE reactions can result in inappropriate responses to patients.

1. **Awareness** of the inappropriateness or bad timing of the following responses can be helpful in identifying countertransference.

   a. **Evaluative responses** imply what the patient should feel or do and suggest a value judgment of the patient's actions.

   b. **Hostile responses** humiliate the patient and suggest that the patient's feelings or actions are inappropriate.

   c. **Reassuring responses**, if offered before the patient has fully expressed his fears, deny the validity of the patient's feelings.

   d. **Probing responses** create an atmosphere of cross-examination.

   e. **Understanding responses** convey an interest in and an appreciation of the patient's feelings but, if offered too quickly, imply a familiarity that may be unearned, thus creating confusion in the patient's mind.

2. Addressing the problem of countertransference by the physician involves introspection and may involve resolution of the issue outside the physician–patient relationship.

3. If countertransference cannot be resolved, referral of the patient to another physician may be indicated.

BIBLIOGRAPHY

Kahana R, Bibring G: Personality Types in Medical Management. In *Psychiatry and Medical Practice in a General Hospital*. Edited by Zinberg N. New York, International University Press, 1964

Leigh H, Reiser MF: *The Patient: Biological, Psychological, and Social Dimensions of Medical Practice*. New York, Plenum Press, 1980

Reiser DE, Rosen DH: *Medicine as a Human Experience*. Baltimore, University Park Press, 1984

Reiser DE, Schroder AK: *Patient Interviewing: The Human Dimension*. Baltimore, Williams and Wilkins, 1980

STUDY QUESTIONS

Directions: The question below contains five suggested answers. Choose the **one best** response to each question.

1. A 25-year-old male medical student is taking a history from a 56-year-old woman with early Alzheimer's disease. He finds himself feeling depressed and irritated. Thoughts of his own mother who recently died from a degenerative illness keep coming into his mind, making it difficult for him to concentrate on the interview. He is probably experiencing countertransference feelings toward this patient. All of the following statements about this reaction are true EXCEPT

(A) the student should acknowledge that his reactions are natural and allow himself to experience them

(B) the student may need to seek brief psychotherapy to understand and deal with this problem better

(C) the student may need to transfer the patient to another medical student

(D) the student would be most helpful to himself and his patient if he told her she reminded him of his mother

(E) countertransference reactions are not necessarily indicative of serious underlying problems

Directions: Each question below contains four suggested answers of which **one or more** is correct. Choose the answer

A if **1, 2, and 3** are correct
B if **1 and 3** are correct
C if **2 and 4** are correct
D if **4** is correct
E if **1, 2, 3, and 4** are correct

2. A 36-year-old man is admitted to the hospital for evaluation of hematuria. He is guarded and argumentative with the nursing staff, whom he blames for worsening his condition by dislodging his catheter. He appears hypervigilant and often misinterprets responses made to him as rejecting. This patient can be managed in which of the following ways?

(1) Threatening to discharge the patient unless he is willing to cooperate with treatment

(2) Approaching the patient in an outgoing manner, reassuring him with a friendly pat on the shoulder of the respect that you and the rest of the staff have for him

(3) Setting firm limits on the patient's argumentativeness and explaining that he is wrong to assume that the nurses will undermine his treatment

(4) Acknowledging the patient's feelings while offering reassurance that you and the staff will do your best to provide good medical care

3. A 40-year-old accountant is admitted to the hospital for evaluation of stomach pain. He has voluminous notes to read to his physician about his symptoms, asks many questions about his illness, and explains that he makes a real effort to keep himself healthy. He expresses great fear that he has stomach cancer. This controlling, orderly patient can be well managed in which of the following ways?

(1) Informing the patient as thoroughly as possible of what procedures will be followed

(2) Avoiding telling the patient of the possible diagnoses and complications to keep from upsetting him

(3) Acknowledging the strengths of the patient that reduce the risk factors, such as his regular exercise program, good diet, and lack of family history of cancer

(4) Assuring the patient that full control of his evaluation and treatment will be taken by his physician

SUMMARY OF DIRECTIONS

A	B	C	D	E
1, 2, 3 only	1, 3 only	2, 4 only	4 only	All are correct

4. A 23-year-old man is admitted to the hospital after receiving a knife wound to the abdomen in a barroom brawl. He has a history of impulsive behavior and at times is hostile and demanding with the hospital staff. In a moment of anger, he demands to leave the hospital and signs the form for discharge against medical advice. Approaches to this patient include

(1) insisting that the patient stay in the hospital until his emotional lability has decreased

(2) informing the patient of his responsibility for controlling his angry outbursts against the hospital staff

(3) informing the patient clearly of the risks of his leaving the hospital and of the limits on his behavior if he should decide to stay

(4) discharging the patient against medical advice if he continues to be hostile and disruptive

5. The process aspect of a physician–patient interview is characterized by which of the following expressions by the patient?

(1) Speaking about the present by recalling something from the past

(2) Masking important messages in passing remarks and casual jokes

(3) Repeatedly asking for information about a recommended procedure or treatment

(4) Speaking through body language

6. Defense mechanisms are unconscious reactions to stress. True statements concerning defense mechanisms include which of the following?

(1) Defense mechanisms are usually maladaptive and interfere with the patient's ability to get well

(2) Defense mechanisms are unconscious attempts to cope with stress caused by illness

(3) Defensive behavior should be confronted by the physician both to educate the patient and to help him cope with his illness

(4) Defenses such as denial and projection are less adaptive than rationalization and sublimation

Questions 7 and 8

A third-year medical student is assigned to obtain a history and a physical prior to a patient's bilateral mastectomy scheduled for the next day.

7. The student hurries nervously into the room of the 40-year-old woman and quickly begins asking questions and writing on his note pad without looking up. After a few minutes, the patient asks the student to leave the room saying that she is not feeling well. Which of the reasons below would likely account for the early termination of the interview?

(1) The student's discomfort with the thought of the patient's illness and surgery

(2) The failure of the student to introduce himself and explain his purpose for being there

(3) The patient's discomfort with her illness and surgery

(4) The student's overlooking important nonverbal communications from the patient

8. Later, the student attempts to continue the interview with the patient. Which of the following overtures would most likely facilitate the patient's willingness to be interviewed by the student?

(1) Confronting the patient, citing her resistance to the interview as a rejection of the care necessary to help her get well

(2) Offering reassurance that many women adjust very well to mastectomy and that there are support groups available

(3) Offering the interpretation that her resistance to the interview is a reflection of her unwillingness to face the implications of her breast cancer

(4) Apologizing for rushing the interview, then introducing himself to the patient and explaining the reasons for the interview

9. A 64-year-old woman is admitted to the hospital for medical evaluation of her chronic lower back pain. Shortly after her admission, she begins to complain that the staff do not pay enough attention to her and often seem to avoid coming into her room. Her complaining continues for the next several days of her stay, and soon members of the medical staff, who initially responded to her complaints with increased attention, now avoid going into her room unless absolutely necessary. The attending physician could best address this problem in which of the following ways?

(1) Inform the patient of the times of daily physician visits and the times that the nurses will routinely check on her to respond to her reasonable requests

(2) Reprimand the nursing staff for their lack of concern and empathy for the patient

(3) Explain to the nursing staff privately that avoidance of the patient is likely to increase the patient's dependency needs and thus increase her unreasonable demands

(4) Deal with the patient in a very professional even detached manner to let her know that her behavior is disapproved of

Directions: The group of questions below consists of lettered choices followed by several numbered items. For each numbered item select the **one** lettered choice with which it is **most** closely associated. Each lettered choice may be used once, more than once, or not at all.

Questions 10–14

Match each statement or question below with the interviewing technique that it best exemplifies.

(A) Clarification
(B) Open-ended questions
(C) Direct questions
(D) Interpretation
(E) Empathy

10. "Where is your pain located?"

11. "You say your pain occurs only at work? Tell me more about the nature of your work."

12. "The injury must have been very painful."

13. "You seem to be angry about your illness. Perhaps you feel that your mother is responsible for it."

14. "How are you feeling?"

ANSWERS AND EXPLANATIONS

1. The answer is D. (*X B; Chapter 12 VI C*) Countertransference reactions occur when feelings in the physician, stemming from significant past relationships, express themselves in the present relationship with a patient. When intense, they can produce distortions that interfere with the physician's ability to relate to the patient, may require psychotherapy to resolve the basis of the countertransference, and may require transferring the patient to another physician. Telling the patient of his countertransference feelings is inappropriate as it may place the unnecessary burden of the physician's past relationships on the patient. Countertransference reactions are common among individuals who work with patients. They may be indicative of underlying problems if they significantly interfere with the patient's care or cause significant distress in the physician.

2. The answer is D (4). (*IX E*) Guarded, suspicious individuals have difficulty trusting others, and they tend to blame others for their problems. Approaching these patients in an overly friendly manner encourages their mistrust, as does reacting in a punitive manner. The right to their feelings should not be directly challenged, but neither should their feelings be reinforced.

3. The answer is B (1, 3). (*IX B 1–3*) Orderly, controlling individuals experience illness as a threat to their control of their environment. To help the patient regain a sense of control, the physician should inform him methodically and in sufficient detail about his illness and treatment. Pointing out the patient's strengths and involving him in his own care as much as possible will help him feel a greater sense of control and thus lessen his anxiety.

4. The answer is A (1, 2, 3). (*IX H*) Impulsive individuals are often quick to express angry emotions, which can change to more reasonable behavior in a short period of time. These patients should not be excused from taking responsibility for these outbursts; however, open confrontation is likely only to increase their anger and impulsiveness. This patient should be kept in the hospital until his emotions can stabilize, but firm, clear limits on his behavior should be specified. Reacting to the patient in an angry, punitive manner will interfere with the delivery of appropriate medical care.

5. The answer is E (all). (*III B 2 a–h*) The term "process" refers to that aspect of the interview that elucidates the patient's (and the physician's) emotional reactions to the interview and refers to how these emotional reactions can reveal important information. The physician should be alert because messages conveyed by the patient in the process aspect of the interview are often indirect and may be evidenced only by remarks made about the past, body language, casual jokes, repeated requests for information, and by other seemingly unrelated expressions.

6. The answer is C (2, 4). (*VIII A*) Defense mechanisms help the patient cope with the threats posed by illness. While it is important for the physician to recognize a patient's defenses, they usually require confrontation only when they interfere with treatment. Lower-level defenses such as denial and projection are less adaptive than higher-level defenses such as rationalization and sublimation. Higher-level defenses do not usually require interpretation and should be supported by the physician.

7. The answer is E (all). (*II A; V A 2*) The most serious error the student made was not introducing himself to the patient and not explaining the reason for the interview. Other reasons for the termination include his failure to look at the patient, which would have established contact and allowed him to observe her nonverbal responses. It is also likely that the emotional reaction of both the patient and the student to the patient's illness and surgery played a role in the discomfort experienced during the interview.

8. The answer is D (4). (*II A; VI D, E, K*) By far, the best way for the interviewing student to engage the patient positively and to begin the interview again is to apologize for being hurried and abrupt and to show her respect and concern by introducing himself and carefully explaining the reasons for the questioning. Premature and uninformed interpretations of the patient's initial reaction as well as reassurances before she has had an opportunity to express herself are not effective ways to conduct a successful interview.

9. The answer is B (1, 3). (*IX A*) Dependent, demanding patients fear that others will reject them and frequently test the limits of this fear. Treating the patient in a cold, detached way is likely to make her behavior worse, and criticizing the medical staff will likely lead to a further deterioration in their attitude toward her. Setting reasonable limits on her behavior and providing consistent, predictable contacts are likely to be most effective in controlling her demanding behavior and in improving her relationship with the staff.

10–14. The answers are: 10-C, 11-A, 12-E, 13-D, 14-B. (*VI B, C, E, H, K*) There are a number of techniques that can be used to ensure that the communication in a physician–patient interview will be productive. **Direct questions** ask for specific information and usually elicit brief, concise answers, and **open-ended questions** allow the patient to elaborate upon his symptoms and speak generally about his illness. The technique of **clarification** is somewhat directive and should provoke the patient to explain a remark or a conclusion that he has come to. An expression of **empathy** by the physician implies understanding and can be an effective technique; it is best used after the patient has expressed how he feels. The technique of **interpretation** ideally should be used with caution and only when the interviewer and the patient have established a reasonably good relationship. The example of an empathetic comment in this group of questions is an attempt by the physician to help the patient (as well as himself) understand an underlying anger.

14
Ethics, Beliefs, and Values

Richard P. Foa
Seymour Perlin

I. INTRODUCTION. The ethical concerns of medical care have been integral to western medicine from its beginning. It is important for the medical student to recognize that modern medical ethics are built upon a rich tradition of philosophical and religious thought; therefore, this chapter is largely devoted to basic principles of philosophical ethics rather than to current medical ethical debates.

   While medical ethics is not a new field, it is a field that has experienced a dramatic resurgence of interest in the last 20 years. This stems from increasing efficiency in the treatment of disease and prolongation of life. These advances, in turn, stem from enormously accelerated technological progress. This progress has initiated an important intellectual challenge, and we are forced to deal with such critical questions as: What is the real goal of medical care? What are the appropriate limits of medical practice? Are these the same? What are the responsibilities of a physician to the patient and to society? Are they different from what they were in the past?

A. HISTORICAL ORIGINS

1. The oldest medical ethical tradition is **Hindu**, a largely oral tradition dating back as far as the tenth to eighth centuries B.C. Buddhism and other eastern religions also have directives concerning the care of the sick that are important foundational elements of nonwestern medical ethics.

2. **The roots of modern medical ethics are found in Greek philosophy**—both in the Pythagorean–Hippocratic tradition, a tradition commonly considered to have provided the foundational ethical principles of modern western medical practice, and in the ethics of Plato and Aristotle. The historical sources of contemporary traditions, however, are by no means limited to the Greeks. Judeo–Christian ethical thought is extremely important, as are the extensive ethical writings by western secular philosophers of the modern era.

3. Many contemporary medical ethical debates are really continuing discussions of enduring problems that cannot be resolved or ignored. However, specific issues change from year to year, and the ability to deal effectively with them depends on a full understanding of the fundamentals of ethical analysis. Furthermore, while concepts of human biology, health, and disease have changed dramatically over the centuries, basic philosophical and theological concepts of the nature of man have changed relatively little. Consequently, ancient writings about the philosophical character of man provide useful and profound insights.

B. THE SCOPE OF MEDICAL ETHICS

1. Medical ethics extend beyond the physician–patient relationship to include social issues that are multiplying as the cost of care for populations rises inexorably and affects virtually all other aspects of social life. Thus, questions concerning the allocation of limited resources and the balance between medical and other personal and social needs have become medical ethical issues.

2. Ethical questions also pervade the medical–legal tradition.
   a. The legal system is generally considered to be a proper forum for the adjudication of disputes concerning fundamental ethical questions. For example, the courts have made basic decisions on questions of informed consent, refusal of care, termination of care, and abortion.
   b. Ethical questions are fundamentally philosophical rather than legal. Thus, the resolution of an ethical conflict through philosophical argument, when possible, should precede the resolution of any accompanying legal argument. If this is accomplished, the decisions of the courts will more assuredly reflect underlying personal and societal values.

3. Special ethical issues pertain to psychiatry and behavioral medicine, such as:
  a. The determination of mental competence and how to deal with mentally incompetent individuals
  b. The problems of involuntary hospitalization of both mentally and physically ill individuals
  c. The problems of developing and applying technologies that alter how the human mind thinks or how a person behaves
  d. The eternal and universal problems of dealing with dying and death

C. DEFINITIONS

1. A **belief** is a conviction that a particular statement, situation, or causal relationship is true or real. A belief indicates intellectual assent and constitutes a basis of action. It may be based on an examination of evidence or it may be accepted on the basis of faith. It is appropriate to refer to beliefs as religious, philosophical, or scientific in nature.

2. **Values** are beliefs that express the relative importance or worth of particular truths or situations.
  a. Values form a more important basis for determining personal action than the larger category of beliefs, as an expression of our personal selves and as a basis on which individuals judge each other.
  b. Values may also connote worth in a monetary or economic sense, as when costly medical services are referred to as being valuable.

3. **Ethics** are principles of conduct that govern the behavior of individuals or groups and express what is thought to be right or good.
  a. The term ethics derives from the Greek "ethike" or **practical virtue**. For Aristotle, practical virtue, as contrasted to **intellectual virtue**, pertains to the right conduct of human affairs such that man's action will conform to the natural end or goal of human existence— happiness or the good.
  b. Ethics conform to values; different values constitute bases for different ethical principles and may reflect beliefs.

4. **Morals** is a term that is nearly synonymous with ethics. It fundamentally refers to the principles of human conduct whereby right action is distinguished from wrong action according to a set of values. Morals and ethics are terms that often overlap broadly and are used interchangeably, although some distinctions are made between the two in their conventional usage by ethicists. (In this chapter, they are used without any intention of implying an important philosophical distinction.)
  a. Morals is a term more commonly used in a religious context (e.g., Catholic moral theology), whereas the term ethics is used in secular philosophical thinking (e.g., Greek, Kantian, medical, and legal ethics).
  b. "Morals" refers to rules of action that govern behavior more immediately (e.g., it is immoral to cheat and steal), whereas "ethics" refers to broad theoretical principles of right action (e.g., autonomy and beneficence).

II. THE CHARACTER OF MEDICAL ETHICAL CONFLICTS

A. CONFLICTING AND COMPETING VALUES

1. People do not always share the same set of values. For example, a physician and a patient might not agree that the goal of treatment is the elimination of suffering. One might value the prolongation of life above all else and would oppose any treatment that might hasten death, even if greater pain resulted. The other might favor treatments that could directly hasten death and accept death as a desired end to suffering.

2. If values are shared, beliefs about how to achieve ends may be in conflict. For example, a physician and a patient confronting intractable pain may agree that their common goal (or shared value) is the elimination of suffering. One may believe that relief of suffering is best achieved by increasing the quantity of narcotic analgesics. The other may believe that narcotics, by decreasing mental acuity and increasing the possibility of dependency, compounds current and future suffering.

3. Values may be shared in general, but competition among values and disagreement about definition of those values may exist. Members of society may share a number of fundamental values, such as the importance of life and of human freedom.
  a. Greek philosophers and medieval theologians could agree that the proper goal of man is happiness while disagreeing about what constitutes happiness.
  b. Persons may universally value life yet disagree about the nature of a valuable life. Similarly,

persons may simultaneously value life and personal freedom (according to agreed-upon definitions) but still disagree about which is valued more highly.

4. Medical ethical dilemmas may be more often seen arising out of conflicts between two values that are held simultaneously or out of conflicts between the principles and rules that express those values than out of a conflict between fundamentally opposed sets of values.

B. MEANS OF CONFLICT RESOLUTION

1. Often we are unable to resolve medical ethical conflicts. Imperfect institutional mechanisms that have been developed for dealing with such conflicts include, on a large scale, the courts, government policy, and the marketplace, and on a smaller scale, hospital ethics committees. These institutions may be influenced by factors that are outside of the central ethical dilemma.
   a. Political perspectives may influence the delivery of care.
   b. Economic issues may affect selection of appropriate care.

2. Physicians need to recognize ethical problems when they arise, separate them from the economic and social problems that may influence them, and resolve them in terms of the theories, principles, and rules that form the basis of moral reasoning.

III. IMPORTANT MEDICAL ETHICAL TRADITIONS

A. THE HIPPOCRATIC TRADITION

1. **History.** For centuries, the **Hippocratic oath** has been considered the cornerstone of western medical ethics. Despite its central importance, however, much remains unknown about the historical origins of the oath and its purported author, Hippocrates, who lived during the fifth century B.C..
   a. The oath is part of a group of medical writings referred to as the **Hippocratic corpus**, which probably date from the fourth century B.C.. These writings are considered to have heterogeneous origins and may have been used by a small group of physicians functioning within family guilds.
   b. The oath called for more strictly controlled behavior by physicians than was required by Greek law, Platonic or Aristotelian ethics, or common practice.
   c. The principles of the Hippocratic oath became influential with the gradual rise of the tenets of Christianity, with which it is quite compatible.

2. **Basic concepts.** The oath is roughly divisible into two parts.
   a. The first part is a statement of the student's obligations to his teacher and to the transmission of medical knowledge.
   b. The second cites rules to be obeyed in dealing with the sick. The most important of these rules—the **Hippocratic principle**—states: "Whatever houses I may visit, I will come for the benefit of the sick." This defines the main role of the physician.
      (1) The Hippocratic principle may be compared with two other medical ethical principles that are often mistakenly considered to be Hippocratic: "First, do no harm" and "the physician's duty is to prolong life."
         (a) The obligation not to harm, while certainly related to an obligation to benefit, cannot be equated with the primary Hippocratic principle of benefiting the sick. The origin of the idea of a primary obligation not to harm is unknown, but it is of central importance to modern theories of medical ethics that are based on outcomes or consequences.
         (b) The Hippocratic oath does not include any reference to a duty to prolong life. The origin of the principle of the physician's duty to prolong life may actually have been in the writings of Francis Bacon, who perceived three goals for medicine: to cure disease, promote health, and prolong life.
      (2) Restatement of the Hippocratic principle has occurred for centuries. Promulgation has been furthered by the perspective that physicians alone are the legitimate source of the ethical principles that govern practice. Restatements have occurred in the late eighteenth century code of Sir Thomas Perceval, the 1847 code of the American Medical Association, and the 1949 international code of the World Medical Association (which mentions the physician's duty to prolong life).

B. RELIGIOUS TRADITIONS have not viewed the medical profession as having the prerogative to establish its ethical standards. In religious ethical traditions, medical ethics are part of a fabric of ethical principles and rules that govern all aspects of behavior.

1. In **Judaism**, ethics are based on the religious law given to them by God through Moses.
   a. The full expression of the law is the Torah. The other sources of Jewish ethics are the an-

cient rabbinic text, the Talmud, and the ongoing tradition of rabbinical law based on these two texts, which is called rabbinic halakah.

  b. In the medical setting, religious Jews do not turn to the physician for ethical guidance but to the rabbi, who serves as both a legal and ethical arbiter.

   (1) The primary medical ethical principle in Jewish tradition is an uncompromising duty to prolong life, which is based on belief in the infinite value of life itself.

   (2) Secondary principles include the duty to preserve and promote health and the duty to procreate.

   (3) When Jewish principles are intermixed with Hippocratic principles, in which life is not given unlimited value, an uncompromising duty to preserve life may conflict with a primary duty to benefit the patient.

 2. Catholic moral theology, like Judaism, relies on a tradition of canon law as well as the authority of religious experts.

  a. In Catholicism, approaches to ethics based on the concept of natural law are independent of the formal structure of the Church.

  b. As in Judaism, the physician is not privileged to act as moral arbiter. Catholics view man as naturally called to do good and avoid evil in conformance with God's wishes because this is inherent in man's character. Beyond this general principle, there are five specific principles of Catholic moral theology that pertain to medicine:

   (1) An inalienable and inviolable **right to life**

   (2) The principle of **stewardship**, wherein it is recognized that God holds dominion over bodies and that men, in life, are merely stewards of their bodies

   (3) The principle of **totality**, which proclaims that the good of a part must be subordinated to the good of the whole organism

   (4) The principle of respect for the procreative purpose of human sexuality

   (5) The **doctrine of double effect**, which is a mechanism for resolving ethical conflicts that arise when a particular action has two or more effects, including at least one that is good and one that is bad

 3. Protestant ethics may vary from one sect to another.

  a. All Protestants share a rejection of the Catholic concept of natural law and the acceptance of three basic theological beliefs:

   (1) The authority of God's word as expressed in the Bible

   (2) Justification by faith

   (3) The priesthood of all believers

  b. The basic beliefs demonstrate a common preference for a more egalitarian approach to ethical decision-making, one based on a large number of normative rules. Although there may be differences among Protestant thinkers on the exact rules that are to be emphasized (e.g., fairness, keeping promises, steadfast love, and respect for life) and on the weight that rules are to be given as guides to action (guidelines versus governors), a rule-oriented approach is common.

  c. The medical profession is not seen as being privileged to dictate ethical standards, but neither is a physician subordinated to the authority of a religious leader. Rather, all members of the community of believers are on equal footing since they have equal access to the biblical sources of ethical norms.

C. SECULAR TRADITIONS

 1. The western secular liberal tradition that found strong expression in the American and French revolutions arose out of the late seventeenth and early eighteenth century Anglo–European philosophies of John Locke, Jean Jacques Rousseau, and Immanuel Kant. Some of its earlier roots may also be found in the Protestant Reformation and the pressure that movement generated for increasing religious tolerance and the separation of church and state.

  a. The tradition is dominated by notions of individual liberty and equality, or self-determination, and of individual rights that are either established through a social contract or are grounded in natural law.

  b. In the realm of medical ethics, secular liberalism emphasizes certain principles of action, the most important of which are autonomy and justice (see also section VI C 1, 2).

   (1) Autonomy can be viewed as an assertion of the right to be free from any constraints applied by society, the medical profession, or religion. The right to be free from something can be considered a **negative** right. Medical ethical claims that are based on the autonomy of the patient include the right to refuse treatment, the right to privacy, and the important derivative right to provide informed consent, hence permission, for care.

   (2) Justice may be contrasted with autonomy in that it refers to **positive** rights or entitlements; that is, a fair share of the goods and services available to all members of society.

How one determines what is a fair share and how to distribute shares are the questions that lead to multiple conflicting theories of justice. Possibilities include equality of quantity (**egalitarian**), equality of opportunity (**libertarian**), a distribution that yields the greatest net benefit for everyone (**utilitarian**), and others.

2. **The Anglo–American legal tradition** has played an important role in the development of current medical ethical beliefs. The law is a blend of rules and conventions stemming from multiple sources, including the Constitution, statutes, regulations, and legal precedents created by specific court decisions. The power and authority of the courts in resolving disputes has grown enormously because the courts can settle arguments in a way that theoretical ethical debate cannot and because the courts have been increasingly willing to do so.
   a. The courts' influence in the field of medical ethics has grown primarily through court decisions that have established legal precedents and legal arguments pertaining to such issues as sustaining life, terminating treatment, informed consent, mental competence, rights to receive or refuse care, and abortion.
   b. By ruling on medical ethical issues, the courts have expressed society's current belief that issues of medical care are of concern to society as a whole and that medical ethics are no longer a private matter between the physician and the patient.
   c. Law and ethics are not necessarily congruent. What is ethical may not be legal, and what is legal may not be ethical. Furthermore, many aspects of law are unrelated to ethics.

3. **Other traditions.** While the secular liberal and legal traditions perhaps have been most important to the development of contemporary western medical ethics, there are many others. Socialism shares historical origins with the contemporary western democratic tradition. Others, such as the Islamic tradition, have related religious roots. The Hindu, Buddhist, and Confucian traditions are wholly different. As society becomes increasingly pluralistic, these traditions may bear importantly on medical ethical decisions.

IV. GENERAL ETHICAL THEORY

A. **SOURCES OF MORAL AUTHORITY.** Different ethical traditions should be examined to discern their sources of moral authority and how ethical principles and rules are derived from these sources.

1. **God.** In the monotheistic religious traditions of Judaism, Christianity, and Islam, the ultimate source of religious authority is God. The rightness of any action is judged in terms of its conformity with what are believed to be God's wishes or purposes. God communicates these purposes through divine revelation, but the accessibility of revealed truths to all men varies from one religious tradition to the next.
   a. In **Judaism and Islam**, extensive religious–legal traditions **keep ethical discourse firmly within the context of religion**. While God may be the ultimate source of moral authority, ethical conflicts are resolved by the rabbi or imam, who possesses religious–legal knowledge.
   b. The **Catholic tradition of casuistry** provides a quasilegal basis for resolving ethical conflicts through reference to analagous precedents.
   c. **Protestants** believe in more universal, direct access to God's word through the text of the **Bible**.

2. **Natural law**
   a. For the **Greeks**, ethical norms were not supernatural; rather, they adopted **natural law theories**. For example, Aristotle believed that **man has a unique nature and a specific end—happiness**—to which that nature is directed. The desire to fulfill one's end was viewed as natural. Ethical behavior consisted of the development of habits or the perfection of virtues appropriate to the natural character of man.
   b. Natural law is also important in **Catholic** moral theology, particularly that developed by medieval scholastics such as St. Thomas Aquinas. In the Catholic tradition, **man's natural end—happiness**—is not attained simply through the perfection of human intellectual and moral virtues as enumerated by Aristotle. Rather, it comes through the perfection of theological virtues (e.g., faith, hope, and charity), which bring man toward a naturally desired, loving union with God. The absolute source of moral authority is again God, but it is incumbent on man, guided by his intellect and by revealed truth, to obey natural law.

3. **Reason.** During the seventeenth and eighteenth centuries, the period known as the enlightenment, philosophers again turned to man as the sole source of ethical standards, epitomized by the work of **Immanuel Kant**. Kant theorized that ethical standards derived from categorical structures in the mind of man. Reason provided a set of inviolable standards of right and wrong.

4. Social contract theory provides another view of the ultimate source of moral authority. Basic social notions of what is acceptable or unacceptable action derive from an agreement among men when they unite to form social groups for mutual self-protection. The criterion of good in the social contract is what insures the survival of the social order and, thereby, protects its members.

5. Professional assertion as a source of the criterion of right action may be a declaration or oath made by a defined group, such as a profession or guild, as to what standards will govern their behavior as members of the group. Such a declaration may be made without appeal to some other authority. The **Hippocratic tradition** or contemporary statements by the American Medical Association establishing ethical criteria for medical practice are examples of this final approach.

B. THE ENDS OF ETHICAL ACTION. Sources of moral authority are not to be confused with the values expressed in moral actions.

1. In Christian **religious tradition**, God is viewed as the source of authority, but the values that are expressed by the tradition are ends for man, such as closeness to God, holiness, happiness in life, and eternal salvation of the soul. In other religions, they may be the achievement of higher status in the next life following death and reincarnation.

2. In **secular traditions**, whether the source of authority is found in the structure of the human mind, in law, or through other social institutions, the values manifest in a particular tradition may include beauty, truth, peace, pleasure, or some other notion of the good.

3. In **medicine**, values include health, a sense of well-being, alleviation of suffering, cure of disease, and prolongation of life.

C. RELATIVISM views ethical truths as dependent on the individuals, groups, or traditions holding them.

1. Descriptive relativism involves an awareness of the multiplicity of different beliefs about sources, means, and ends and the ability to compare and contrast ethical traditions without choosing among them. This is an important approach to ethics, especially medical ethics, in a pluralistic society. The awareness that a patient may follow a particular tradition will help the physician to tailor care to what the patient feels is in his best interest, rather than imposing upon the patient the physician's own beliefs and values.

2. Normative relativism involves the ability to place oneself within a known tradition while appreciating the validity of other ethical systems for other people. A purely descriptive approach does not help the physician to locate his own ethical values. A physician who is unable to recognize and articulate his own position is unable to provide guidance about what should be done in a situation when that guidance is sought. When a normative approach is taken, one may judge that a particular decision is right in a particular setting on the basis of personally held beliefs.

D. CRITERIA FOR MORAL ACTION GUIDES are needed to distinguish between ethical or moral decisions and those that are scientific or technical. Two contemporary philosophers, **Tom Beauchamp** and **James Childress**, identify three criteria used to evaluate whether the rules and principles chosen to guide actions are moral. Two are formal, referring to the **form** rather than the content of rules or principles. The third is dependent on **content** alone.

1. The first formal criterion states that any moral rules, principles, or judgments must be viewed as "**supreme, final, or overriding.**" In other words, a particular rule or principle must be given greater value than any other rules or principles by its advocate. The pursuit of scientific knowledge or the performance of dance might, by this criterion alone, be given sufficient value to be deemed morally right.

2. Universalizability is the second formal criterion. This means that all situations that are relevantly similar to each other must be governed by the same decisions about how to act. For example, a decision about how to treat one terminally ill patient must be consistently applied to the treatment of all terminally ill patients whose circumstances are relevantly similar in order for the decision to be considered a moral rule.

3. Content is the third criterion. This is particularly relevant to medicine as it requires that the outcome of any moral action benefit others. Actions that benefit only the doer cannot be judged as moral: To the extent that such actions harm others, they are immoral; otherwise, they are **nonmoral**. This criterion would not place within the moral realm many religious activities that involve only the individual in his relation to a deity.

E. VIRTUE-BASED THEORIES VERSUS RULE-GOVERNED THEORIES. Ethical theories and traditions in general may be divided into two major groups according to what is viewed as the central task of ethics.

1. The **development of the character of the individual** involves those traditions or theories that emphasize personal virtues such as temperance, courage, patience, and honesty. In such theories, the central ethical question is "What will I be?" Examples of virtue theories include the classical Greek and medieval Catholic traditions, which are based on a concept of natural law, and the importance of man's learning to conform to his proper nature.

2. The **governance of relationships between people** focuses on relationships that are either utilitarian or deontological.
   a. **Utilitarianism** (or **consequentialism**) originates with the philosophies of David Hume, Jeremy Bentham, and John Stuart Mill.
      (1) Ultimate value is placed on the net benefits generated by a particular action, with the goal being to maximize good. Utilitarians may disagree about what is valued. Some may perceive a plurality of intrinsic goods and will seek to achieve the greatest number, while others may seek a single overarching good such as pleasure or happiness. Regardless of differences in values, utilitarian thinkers agree that moral value is dependent on the utility of actions rather than on some intrinsic quality of the actions themselves.
      (2) An action itself is an instrument or means; thus, it is evaluated not in terms of itself, but in terms of what it accomplishes. The emphasis is on **consequences**.
      (3) There is a division among utilitarians.
         (a) **Act utilitarians** believe that an act is right if no other act available at the same time would result in a better outcome. While certain rules of behavior are developed from past experience, these rules are not to govern activity and may be abandoned at any time if some other action maximizes benefits.
         (b) **Rule utilitarians** accept a set of rules that direct activity more closely. They believe that experience has shown that following rules will result in the greatest good overall, regardless of the exigencies of one particular situation.
   b. **Deontological** (or **nonconsequentialist**) actions are those that are believed to have inherent qualities that make them right or wrong without regard to the outcomes they produce.
      (1) The act of being honest, rather than being inherently neutral, is always ethically correct. A famous example is Immanuel Kant's assertion that it is wrong to lie even if lying results in a manifestly better outcome than telling the truth or remaining silent.
      (2) While utilitarians all justify their judgments on the basis of good outcomes, deontologists differ over what makes a particular action inherently good. Some believe this is a function of human reason, some believe that it is intuition, and others believe that it is a religious tenet.
      (3) Deontologists may be divided into two groups that place different emphasis on the power that particular rules are given in making ethical decisions.
         (a) The **summary rules** position takes rules into account when weighing alternative actions but does not treat them as binding.
         (b) The **rules of practice** position considers rules more seriously binding. This is the more common approach. As in rule utilitarianism, it must rely on some sense of proportionality or ordering of rules in order to resolve dilemmas that arise when two morally binding rules conflict. Approaches to this problem are to balance the rules intuitively or to order them lexically.

V. MEDICAL ETHICS

A. GENERAL CONSIDERATIONS. No physician can escape having to make ethical judgments, especially in the setting of illness. The physician is traditionally placed in the position of "manager" of illness and is relied on for the answers to both technical and ethical questions. Special ethical commitments of physicians to individual patients and to society establish the context in which medical ethical decisions must be made, although they do not indicate which of many possible traditions or theories might be followed.

1. **Public commitments.** The cultural expectation that physicians will provide leadership is reinforced by societal concepts of professionalism and by licensure.
   a. As a professional, the physician is expected to provide rational and dispassionate guidance strictly in the interests of the patient. Physicians are further obligated and society is further reassured by professional oaths, which publicly proclaim a commitment to the well-being of others.

b. By granting a license, society assures itself of the competence of the physician to judge and to act. The license also gives the physician special access to private lives.

2. **Special moral commitments** to patients are contained in the unique character of the physician–patient relationship. A moral obligation may arise out of the fundamental personhood of the patient rather than from the vulnerability of the patient as someone who is sick and in need. The patient who reveals personal secrets to the physician, often including facts not shared within that patient's family, is placing a moral claim on the physician that governs the use of that information. This both compels the physician to respond and limits the range of permissible responses.

3. The physician–patient relationship is often viewed as one governed by an implicit contract or by a stronger, covenantal bond.
   a. Contracts imply only the intellectual assent of both parties, given as long as the arrangement is deemed mutually beneficial; thus, contracts can be made and broken.
   b. Covenants imply a deeper and more permanent relationship, one that cannot be broken at will because it involves the inner identity of both parties. The greater moral commitment implied by a covenant can be seen in its use to describe other profoundly important commitments, such as marital and religious covenants.

4. There has been growing interest in the value of **virtue theory** (see section IV E) in medical ethics, particularly as physicians recognize increasing numbers of situations that they cannot treat. Nonetheless, contemporary medical ethics has been dominated by rule-oriented approaches. This section, therefore, focuses attention on the most important rules—consequentialism and nonconsequentialism—and their implications. While theories based on consequentialist and nonconsequentialist rules rely on different justifications, the rules of action that they emphasize may be the same and the values toward which they work may also be identical.

B. **CONSEQUENTIALIST MEDICAL ETHICS** are utilitarian in nature (see section IV E 2 a) and rely on justification of net benefits and harms.

1. The two consequentialist principles are beneficence and nonmaleficence.
   a. Beneficence involves the obligation to do what is good because it will lead to a good outcome.
   b. Nonmaleficence involves the obligation not to do what is harmful, which corresponds to the previously mentioned dictum, "First, do no harm."

2. Utilitarians may disagree over which of the principles is primary when the two conflict. Many rule utilitarians argue that nonmaleficence is a higher duty than beneficence and that it is always more meritorius to prevent harm than to accomplish good. For example, in considering abortion, the avoidance of harm to the fetus may be preferred to any benefit to the mother that would come with termination of the pregnancy. Alternatively, in a situation in which the mother's health might be threatened by pregnancy, the avoidance of harm to the mother through an abortion would be considered more valuable than the good of carrying the pregnancy to term.

3. Beneficence and nonmaleficence frequently must be balanced, which requires a sense of proportionality (i.e., an appreciation of what actions will bring about the greatest amount of good in relation to harm). Cost–benefit analyses and risk–benefit analyses are examples of utilitarian thinking, each requiring a sense of proportionality as an attempt is made to calculate the ratio of good (benefits) to harm (costs or risks) as they may occur in the projected outcome of a set of actions.

C. **NONCONSEQUENTIALIST MEDICAL ETHICS** are deontological in nature (see section V E 2 b) and rely on justifications involving a set of absolute standards. Important deontological medical ethical principles include autonomy, justice, telling the truth, keeping promises, and avoiding killing. Autonomy, telling the truth, and keeping promises are sometimes combined into a principle of respect for persons.

1. The principle of **autonomy** is of fundamental importance to ethical thinking, stemming from both modern Protestant religious tradition and the secular liberal tradition.
   a. Autonomy is expressed in political and legal philosophies as a right to **self-determination**. The underlying belief is that individuals have sovereign control over decisions that pertain to their bodies and minds; they are free and unconstrained. The only limit to an individual's autonomy or freedom of self-determination within society is the autonomy of another (i.e., infringement on the rights of another individual). In reality, especially in a complex and highly interdependent society, the autonomy of an individual is constantly constrained by the interest of others.

b. In the context of medical care, an individual patient's autonomy must be balanced against the rights and needs of other patients as well as those of health care providers.

   (1) Patients who lack information concerning their illness and care have a diminished capacity to make personal decisions. They have diminished autonomy. This realization is also the basis for ethical arguments for informed consent. Important questions about autonomous action arise when people are fearful, depressed, or mentally incompetent.

   (2) Autonomy is also the principle on which correlative arguments for the right to refuse treatment are based. On the other hand, demands for the right to receive treatment may run up against the autonomous right of a physician to determine what kind of care he will provide and to whom.

   (3) It is important to recognize that something does not become morally right merely because it is done autonomously. Autonomous actions that harm oneself, harm another, or are offensive to another's sensibilities are not to be defended. However, denial of someone else's autonomy must always be considered morally disgraceful.

   (4) The emphasis of autonomy in a medical ethical system asserts that the patient's perception of his best interest is the basis of action. The physician's role becomes **reactive**.

   (5) The opposite of a reactive role is **paternalism**, when the physician acts in the interest of the patient without regard to the patient's differing perception of his needs. When a patient's autonomy is diminished, the temptation to act paternalistically increases.

2. The principle of **justice** determines how the burdens and the benefits of society are distributed among the individuals within the society. The need for justice arises from a relative scarcity of "goods" and a plurality of ideas about what are desired ends, which fosters disagreement about how resources should be distributed. Thus, different theories of justice may argue for distribution on the basis of personal need, merit, effort, or simply through a process of free exchange.

  a. The principle of justice operates at different levels of social interaction and in different relationships.

   (1) **Distributive justice** pertains to the distribution of society's benefits to individuals.

   (2) **Commutative justice** pertains to interpersonal relationships.

   (3) **Compensatory justice** refers to a situation in which someone may claim extra benefits because of prior losses.

   (4) **Retributive justice** pertains to the punishment of those who have violated the law.

  b. Medical ethics must deal with problems of commutative and distributive justice. **Medical malpractice** deals with questions of **compensatory justice**.

  c. Justice may refer to a number of differing theoretical approaches to the problem of sharing resources, none of which is inherently superior to another. Unlike autonomy, justice does not imply a single uniform notion of what an individual should have.

   (1) An idea of what is just may focus on an outcome, which is a utilitarian concept.

   (2) Other ideas of justice may focus on the rules governing distribution, with less emphasis on the final outcome.

   (3) Traditional ideas of justice generally share a concept of a common good to which society is directed. The sense of what each person deserves (i.e., that which is just) conforms with this concept.

  d. The concept of **entitlement**, expressed by **Robert Nozick**, replaces the idea that justice is an expression of what an individual deserves.

   (1) While luck or chance has nothing to do with what an individual may deserve, it has a great deal to do with his entitlements. According to Nozick, entitlement in reality derives from a chance position in **three different lotteries**—a **natural** lottery (e.g., determining physical abilities, gender, intelligence), a **social** lottery (e.g., determining family, wealth, position), and a **cultural** lottery (e.g., determining country, ethnic background). Entitlements are what we may legitimately expect in life stemming from our luck in these lotteries, and justice implies the fulfillment of those expectations. (According to this thinking, Americans may legitimately expect equal treatment under the law and access to high-quality medical care—not out of a sense of common good but because they are American and these things are found here. It is unjust if they do not receive them.)

   (2) Another contemporary theorist, **John Rawls**, thinks that society is or should be governed by an implicit contract by which individuals are committed to rectify the imbalances of those lotteries by deliberately working to benefit those who are least well-off.

   (3) Robert Nozick, however, argues that an obligation to share does not follow as a matter of justice. Individuals are free to take advantage of their advantages, and this is inherently just.

  e. In contemporary medical ethics, the concept of justice has played an important role in arguments for a right to health care and a right to abortion on demand. Such arguments claim a positive right or entitlement for the individual. Issues of justice are also important in determining the allocation of limited health care resources.

3. The remaining principles—**telling the truth, keeping promises**, and **avoiding killing**—are what philosopher **W.D. Ross** calls **prima facie goods** because their moral rightness can be intuitively appreciated at first viewing. This is not to assert that they are absolutely good; instead, they must each be balanced against one another in specific situations. Other ethical principles or duties that are important in medical ethics and that may be placed in the first echelon by some theorists are the duties of **fidelity**, **confidentiality**, and **respect for privacy**, which may be perceived as corollaries of the principles of truth-telling, promise-keeping, and autonomy, respectively. All of these may be grouped under the overarching principle of **respect for persons**.

STUDY QUESTIONS

Directions: Each question below contains five suggested answers. Choose the **one best** response to each question.

Questions 1–3

A 20-year-old man has lost two or three jobs in succession because of his violent temper. He lives with his parents because he has no income and cannot afford to rent his own apartment. He describes himself as enormously frustrated and thinks that several violent outbursts at home have simply stemmed from this frustration. During these outbursts he has broken several of his parents' possessions. He now thinks that his parents conspire with potential employers to keep him from ever working so that they can force him to remain a child. He will not consider hospitalization because he believes that the staff will poison him in such a way that he will never become independent.

1.   The involuntary hospitalization of this patient is justified by the ethical principle of

(A) retributive justice
(B) beneficence
(C) paternalism
(D) autonomy
(E) moral priority

2.   In that any hospitalization of this patient would be clearly involuntary, which ethical principles must be balanced?

(A) Beneficence and paternalism
(B) Patient's autonomy and parent's autonomy
(C) Moral priority and retributive justice
(D) Commutative justice and retributive justice
(E) Beneficence and autonomy

3.   If the patient were to inflict personal injury on his parents or damage their property, questions would arise involving

(A) commutative justice
(B) compensatory justice
(C) retributive justice
(D) distributive justice
(E) none of the above

Questions 4–6

A community recognizes a drug problem among its youth and allocates $100,000 from the city's general funds to establish a treatment program. The money is enough to be useful but is insufficient to deal with the problem comprehensively. One approach is to use all of the money for detoxification and intensive treatment of youthful addicts, a program of little benefit to the larger number of casual and experimental users. The other is to use the money for a combined drug education and surveillance program that will influence drug use among nonusers and casual users but will do little to benefit those already addicted.

4.   This case presents a conflict that can be analyzed in terms of

(A) autonomy versus beneficence
(B) beneficence versus nonmaleficence
(C) consequentialism versus nonconsequentialism
(D) utilitarianism versus deontology
(E) different theories of justice

5.   Devoting money to the detoxification of youthful addicts can best be supported by

(A) the Rawlsian notion of devoting resources to benefit the least well-off
(B) the Nozickian notion of entitlements
(C) a utilitarian calculation of what will yield the greatest net benefit
(D) the Catholic doctrine of double effect
(E) an argument for compensatory justice

6.   Devoting money to a drug education and surveillance program can best be supported by

(A) the classical idea of distributing social goods equally among all citizens
(B) the Nozickian notion of entitlements
(C) the principle of beneficence
(D) the ethical dictum, "First, do no harm"
(E) the principle of respect for persons

7. A severely depressed elderly widow is admitted to the hospital with shortness of breath. Her initial evaluation reveals chronic congestive heart failure and pneumonia. Both are felt to be reversible. The patient refuses treatment, stating that she wants to die. An ethically justifiable response to this circumstance would be to

(A) discharge the patient from the hospital
(B) allow her to remain in the hospital without treatment
(C) provide comfort care, but provide no treatment for the causes of her respiratory insufficiency
(D) treat her reversible medical problems despite her refusal
(E) treat her depression and try to get her to change her mind about other care

Directions: Each question below contains four suggested answers of which **one or more** is correct. Choose the answer

A   if **1, 2, and 3** are correct
B   if **1 and 3** are correct
C   if **2 and 4** are correct
D   if **4** is correct
E   if **1, 2, 3, and 4** are correct

Questions 8 and 9

A 17-year-old college student, away from home for the first time, comes to the emergency room following a seizure. He consents to treatment only after asking that nothing be told to his mother, who lives alone and has been anxious about his being away. He feels that she could not handle the stress of knowing that something had happened to him, and he makes it clear that if she is told, he will terminate further treatment. Computed tomography (CT) reveals the presence of a vascular prominence, suspected to be a large aneurysm. An angiogram is needed, and this requires the mother's consent since the patient is not yet 18.

8. Respecting this patient's wish that his mother not be informed is defensible on the basis of

(1) respect for autonomy
(2) beneficence
(3) keeping promises
(4) justice

9. Informing the patient's mother that he is ill, in violation of his wishes, is defensible because

(1) beneficence is a more important principle than autonomy
(2) the need to respect the mother's autonomy is ethically required
(3) a promise made to a minor is not ethically binding
(4) it is necessary in order to obtain legally valid informed consent for treatment

Questions 10 and 11

A 50-year-old alcoholic comes to the hospital in acute respiratory failure. He has had multiple previous admissions to the hospital's intensive care unit for this problem. Factors contributing to his chronic lung disease include previous tuberculosis, a 60-pack–year history of smoking, and episodes of aspiration pneumonia. When he is not in the hospital, he is noncompliant with medications. Blood gases indicate the need for intubation and mechanical ventilation. A chest x-ray reveals carcinoma of the right upper lobe.

10. Ethical arguments pertinent to a decision of whether to place this patient back in the intensive care unit hinge upon

(1) beneficence
(2) his poor prognosis
(3) justice
(4) nonmaleficence

11. The patient explicitly requests maximal treatment. If he is intubated and ventilated but lapses into a coma, the decision to continue or stop treatment

(1) rests on prognosis
(2) becomes a question of justice and resource allocation (i.e., who else needs the bed in the intensive care unit)
(3) must consider the wishes previously expressed by the patient
(4) can be made without regard to autonomy since the patient is no longer autonomous

12. Under the Hippocratic oath, obligations of the physician include

(1) transmitting medical knowledge
(2) benefiting the sick
(3) maintaining confidentiality
(4) prolonging life

13. The rights of the autonomous person include

(1) the right to refuse treatment
(2) the right to provide informed consent
(3) the right to privacy
(4) the right to a fair share of services

14. Informed consent involves

(1) voluntary action
(2) disclosure of information
(3) competence
(4) comprehension of information

Directions: The group of questions below consists of lettered choices followed by several numbered items. For each numbered item select the **one** lettered choice with which it is **most** closely associated. Each lettered choice may be used once, more than once, or not at all.

Questions 15–18

For each theoretical construct, select the philosopher with whom it is associated.

(A) Kant
(B) Rawls
(C) Bentham
(D) Ross
(E) Nozick

15. The mind determines whether an act is right or wrong

16. Ultimate value is placed on the benefits generated by an action

17. Justice reflects the notion of entitlement

18. "Prima facie goods" are not necessarily "absolutely" good but must be balanced against one another in specific situations

ANSWERS AND EXPLANATIONS

1. The answer is B. *(V C 1)* Obviously, hospitalization of this patient would be involuntary. Arguments for hospitalization would be supported by the principle of beneficence, acting for the good of the patient regardless of whether he can appreciate the intent at the outset. To hospitalize him without his consent would be to act paternalistically toward him. An argument can be raised, however, that involuntary hospitalization violates the patient's autonomy. No matter how strongly one feels that hospitalization would benefit the patient, he continues to have sovereign control over decisions concerning his care.

2. The answer is E. *(II B; VI C 1)* An ethical dilemma can arise from a conflict between two principles (e.g., beneficence and autonomy). It is difficult to balance beneficence, which looks at the good of the end even when the means may be objectionable, and autonomy, which looks at the good of the means even when the outcome may be unsatisfactory.

3. The answer is C. *(V C 2 a, d)* If the patient's behavior threatens the safety and autonomy of his parents in their home or if he were to inflict personal injury or greater property damage, he would be subject to laws restricting such behavior. This would be a matter of legal justice. Notions of justice in ethics are theoretical and primarily relate to questions about the distribution of goods and services. The law and ethics are not to be equated. Sometimes what is legal is unethical; sometimes what is ethical is illegal.

4. The answer is E. *(V C 2)* In this case, the basic question is how a limited amount of social good should be distributed between the two groups in need. Justice is the issue, and how one weighs alternatives depends on the theory of justice to which one subscribes.

5. The answer is A. *(V C 2 d, e)* One of the fundamental principles of Rawls' theory of justice is that resources should be committed to benefit those in greatest need regardless of the cost that such an approach might have for those who are less needy. In this situation, the most acute needs are those of the addicts rather than those of experimenting or casual drug users.

6. The answer is A. *[III C 1 b (2)]* The argument to distribute resources among the numerically largest group who will benefit is egalitarian or democratic, an argument with broad appeal in contemporary western society. In this context, the argument is not far from an entitlement argument, since in a democratic society, all are generally thought to be equally entitled to the benefits of citizenship.

7. The answer is E. *[V C 1 b (1)]* A patient with severe depression has diminished autonomy. Under such circumstances, even though the patient may seem fully rational, it is important to try to remove those factors that limit autonomy in order to gain a true idea of what care to provide.

If the patient in question should worsen and her respiratory insufficiency should become life threatening, strong ethical arguments could be made for providing all necessary care or, alternatively, respecting the patient's wish to die and withdraw care. However, if a patient has an acute life-threatening illness, diminished autonomy, and no prior directives concerning care, the physician must act to preserve life according to the principle of beneficence.

A final decision must take into consideration the factors of prognosis, effectiveness of treatment, discomfort of treatment, and the beliefs and values of the patient when the patient was competent.

8. The answer is B (1, 3). *(V C 1, 3)* Despite the fact that the patient is a minor and therefore is subject to special legal considerations, ethically, as a mentally competent individual, his autonomy must be respected. Keeping a promise is another rule with its own prima facie moral weight. Some ethicists might argue that respect for autonomy is a higher or more powerful moral rule; however, it is difficult to imagine a situation in which respect for autonomy and promise-keeping would conflict with each other.

9. The answer is D (4). *(II C 2; VI C 1, 3)* A purely ethical argument runs into the fact that the parent of a minor legally has the right to determine what is in the best interest of his or her child. Only when the parent makes a decision that is clearly harmful to the child can society, through the courts, remove the child from the legal custody of the parent for purposes of treatment.

10. The answer is E (all). *(V B, C 2 c)* The basic question that is addressed is whether the patient might immediately benefit from treatment. Thus, a decision of whether or not to treat the patient intensively is first a question of beneficence or doing what will directly benefit the patient. This in turn hinges on the medical questions of the patient's prognosis and the nature of the available treatment (i.e., will it cause suffering?). Whether the patient in question or another is placed in the only bed in the intensive care unit is a question of justice.

11. The answer is A (1, 2, 3). *(V C 1)* If a patient who expressed wishes about the nature or limits of care while mentally competent becomes incompetent, the physician remains ethically bound by those previously expressed wishes. However, if treatment at this stage is futile, this fact, the costs of continuing care, and the competing needs of other patients must be taken into consideration in any decision to continue or discontinue treatment.

12. The answer is A (1, 2, 3). *(III A 2)* The Hippocratic oath is a cornerstone of western medical ethics, and it describes obligated behaviors of the physician. These behaviors include obligations to teachers and the obligation to transmit medical knowledge. The oath defines the central role of physicians in terms of benefits to the sick. Nowhere in the Hippocratic oath is there a reference to a duty to prolong life. In addition to reformulations of the oath, there are other traditions (e.g., religious law) that formulate ethical standards for medical practice as well.

13. The answer is A (1, 2, 3). *(V C 1 a–b, 2)* Autonomy is an assertion of the right to be free from constraints. A patient's autonomy involves the independent ability to decide on privacy, to have informed consent, and to refuse treatment. Competence is a presupposition of informed consent. Autonomy and competence, however, do not determine the right to access, which is viewed in terms of theories of justice.

14. The answer is E (all). *(V C 1 b)* Informed consent involves the right of an individual to make a rational choice. However, voluntary action, disclosure of information, competence, and comprehension each may be qualified (e.g., the degree of voluntariness due to internal constraint, an episode of temporary incompetence, lack of full comprehension of medical information, and so forth). The factor of age may also be confounding. Nevertheless, the protection of autonomy requires the examination of each element in the consideration of informed consent.

15–18. The answers are: 15-A, 16-C, 17-E, 18-D. *[IV A 3, E 2 a (1), (2); V C 2 d (2), (3), 3]* Immanuel Kant, one of the philosophers of the period of enlightenment, theorized that human reason provides a set of inviolable standards of right and wrong.

Jeremy Bentham expressed the philosophy of utilitarianism (or consequentialism), which states that an action itself is an instrument or means and is evaluated not in terms of itself but in terms of what it accomplishes.

John Rawls thinks that the principle of justice (how the burdens and benefits of society are distributed within the society) should be an implicit contract by which those who are winners in the social and cultural lotteries rectify the imbalances of these lotteries by working to benefit those who are less well-off. Robert Nozick, however, argues that there is no obligation to share, only that each individual is free to take advantage of all the benefits that are available. He believes that entitlements are what an individual may legitimately expect in life.

W.D. Ross gave the name "prima facie goods" to principles such as telling the truth, keeping promises, and avoiding killing; the moral rightness of these principles is obvious at first viewing.

15
Medical Care

Philip S. Birnbaum
Richard F. Southby
Warren Greenberg

I. ORGANIZATION OF HEALTH CARE DELIVERY IN THE UNITED STATES

A. HISTORY AND STRUCTURE

1. Hospitals

  a. Establishment of public hospitals. In the mid-1770s, cities in colonial America established institutions for feeding, sheltering, and quarantining the mentally and chronically physically ill, the disabled, and those suffering from contagious disease. Medical care was only a peripheral function of most of these institutions, and the quality of life that they provided made them a feared rather than sought-after source of support.

  b. Establishment of voluntary hospitals. At about the same time, usually under the impetus of European-trained physicians, voluntary hospitals were founded in Philadelphia, Boston, and New York. These hospitals were dependent largely on local philanthropy. Because of the quality of care, paying patients also sought treatment in these hospitals and were admitted along with the indigents who had been the sole clients of the publicly operated houses.

  c. Later developments. By the turn of the twentieth century, hospitals of all types numbered about 4000, with a combined capacity of approximately 400,000 beds. Developments in medical science and technology—from infection control and anesthesia to radiology—combined with advances in the training of physicians, nurses, and other health care personnel, completed the transformation of the hospital.

  d. Current status

    (1) There are now almost 7000 hospitals, with a combined capacity of over 1 million beds. All levels of government provide direct care for specific patient groups through the Veterans Administration system as well as through state, county, and municipal hospitals. One-third of all nongovernment hospitals belong to multi-institutional systems (i.e., an organization comprising two or more hospitals with a common ownership, management, or both). The for-profit facilities, which now number about 1000 and which began in the earliest days as private, usually physician-owned institutions, have recently emerged as a major component of the health care system.

    (2) Hospitals have recently added a variety of outpatient and community services to their basic provision of inpatient care. The number of hospitals has begun to decrease for the first time since the depression years of 1929 through 1938. Whether these current events are the start of a long-term trend or are merely a short-term adjustment remains to be seen.

    (3) While the number of acute-care hospitals has remained essentially stable, there has been a significant decrease in the number of hospitals providing long-term care. This development has been partially driven by the eradication of certain chronic diseases, such as tuberculosis, and by the civil rights–inspired de-institutionalization of the mentally ill, which led to the emptying of large numbers of beds in public long-term mental health care facilities.

2. Physicians

  a. Establishment of the profession

    (1) Entrance into the medical profession in colonial America was almost exclusively through apprenticeship.

    (2) Medical education in the colonies was established following the Scottish model of university-based education rather than the English model of hospital-based medical schools. The first medical school in the American colonies was founded in 1756 at the College of Philadelphia, which became the University of Pennsylvania. By 1776, only 5% of medical practitioners held medical degrees.

(3) Until the middle of the nineteenth century, physicians competed for the sale of their services. Licensing of physicians was not required by state or federal government. Entrance to medical school was easy, and many "schools" were for-profit institutions. The annual income of physicians was among the lowest for all professional groups.

b. Foundation of organized medicine. Following the establishment of the American Medical Association (AMA) in 1847, licensure of physicians became mandatory. The Flexner Report in 1910 called for closing the "diploma mill" medical schools and strengthening the curriculum by including medical education in the university setting. Consequently, the number of medical schools was reduced from 162 in 1910 to 69 in 1944, with a corresponding reduction in the number of students. By the mid-1950s, there were approximately 8000 first-year medical students—only 1500 more than in 1910.

c. Recent developments

    (1) By 1950, the expansion of the National Institutes of Health (NIH) extramural research program provided both impetus and support to the development of preclinical medical faculties and facilities.

    (2) The **Health Professions Educational Assistance Act** of 1963 provided substantial federal support for undergraduate medical training. In addition, grants to medical schools provided for the costs of new construction and renovations. First-year enrollments increased from approximately 9000 students in 1965 to more than 18,000 students in 1982. The physician-to-population ratio is expected to increase from 152 physicians per 100,000 population in 1970 to 240 physicians per 100,000 population in the year 2000. Currently, there are approximately 400,000 physicians in the United States.

d. Specialization. As a result of rapid advances in medical knowledge and technology, urban growth, the development of large hospitals, the availability of health insurance, and increased demands for care, the trend toward specialization and subspecialization has accelerated during the past 30 years. Prior to World War II, about 80% of physicians were general practitioners and 20% were specialists. In the years since, these percentages have reversed.

e. Geographic distribution. Despite the recent increase in the number of practicing physicians in the United States, there are still medically underserved areas—the inner cities and rural areas. Efforts to balance the geographic distribution generally have been unsuccessful. Government efforts, especially at the federal level, continue to change this distribution pattern by altering the reimbursement and incentive systems for practitioners.

3. Associated health care personnel

a. During this century, the ratio of physicians to other health care personnel changed dramatically. In 1900, the ratio of physicians to other health care workers was 1 to 1. The present ratio is 1 physician to 20 other health care personnel.

b. Examples of associated health care personnel include registered nurses, physician's assistants, nurse practitioners, nurse midwives, psychiatric social workers, physical therapists, and occupational therapists.

4. Alternate health care delivery systems

a. Health maintenance organizations (HMOs)

    (1) In 1983, more than 12.5 million individuals were enrolled in 280 HMOs in the United States. In 1976, only 6 million individuals were enrolled in 175 HMOs. HMOs have had an uneasy and controversial history of growth since 1929, when physicians Donald Ross and H. Clifford Loos in Los Angeles and Michael Shadid in Elk City, Oklahoma, established the first prepaid health plans in the United States. The early growth was opposed overtly by medical societies and physicians, while physicians reacted to later growth with a combination of indifference, acquiescence, and action to create their own HMOs.

    (2) HMOs represent a major departure from the prevailing fee-for-service mode of physician reimbursement. Payment is based generally on capitation, and under the general HMO concept, individual or family subscribers pay an annual premium to the organization in return for a totally prearranged and agreed-upon package of health care benefits. Such benefits almost invariably include all hospitalization (with limits on mental health services); physician services, both ambulatory and inpatient; preventive medicine services; and, in many cases, dentist, optometrist, podiatrist, and all ancillary services.

    (3) The ability of the HMO to compete with other insurance plans, such as the traditional Blue Cross/Blue Shield indemnity plan, derives from a combination of the comprehensive nature of the coverage offered, the availability of prophylactic services, the use of paraprofessionals such as nurse practitioners and physician assistants, the attempt to control and limit hospitalization, and the use of consulting services and advanced technology.

b. **Independent practice associations (IPAs) and preferred provider organizations (PPOs).** Recently, physicians have grouped into new organizations, such as IPAs and PPOs, under which they contract as a group to provide services to a specific set of patients.

   (1) Frequently, such arrangements include contracts between physicians (including those in subspecialty groups) and particular hospitals for provision of inpatient services. There is a frequent tie between IPAs and PPOs and specific hospitals seeking a defined patient population (e.g., all employees of a given employer).

   (2) The primary concept of IPAs and PPOs is to limit the charges by the group, regardless of the service rendered, and to limit the patient to seeking services only from members of the group.

c. **Ambulatory care** facilities for limited clinical needs have evolved in the recent past. Such freestanding providers attempt to offer services on a more convenient schedule and at a lower price than the hospital-based service that would otherwise (of necessity) be used. These facilities are a relatively new part of the health care delivery system, and their role remains undefined.

5. Public health

a. **Focus.** The field of public health has evolved parallel to the delivery of services to individual patients. Public health practitioners are concerned with the **community**. Their functions include communicable disease control, the determination and administration of food and drug standards, maternal and child health services, environmental sanitation, and health education and promotion.

b. **Organizations**

   (1) Public health services are normally the responsibility of government. Starting as voluntary organizations to meet specific threats to the health of the community, public health organizations evolved by the middle of the nineteenth century into government health departments with full-time officials.

   (2) Responding to the waves of immigration and to the developments in technology, every state had organized some form of health department by 1909. From 1935, the federal role in public health activities increased substantially, in line with significant social, political, and economic changes.

B. FINANCING

1. Private insurance

a. **Blue Cross/Blue Shield** is a nonprofit carrier, insuring approximately 50% of individuals in the private sector. Originally created by hospitals (Blue Cross) and physicians (Blue Shield), the two organizations have been merged in many parts of the United States into Blue Cross/Blue Shield. The market share of Blue Cross/Blue Shield varies from about 20% of the population in California to over 70% in some areas of New York. Blue Cross/Blue Shield also often serves as a fiscal intermediary for the public programs.

b. **Commercial insurers.** There are nearly 1000 for-profit commercial insurers in the United States. Many of these insurers also provide life insurance and pension coverage to their corporate clients. The commercial insurer share of the private sector market is approximately 40%.

2. Public insurance

a. **Medicare** is a federal program that pays for both hospital care (Part A) and medical care [e.g., physician visits] (Part B) for individuals who are eligible for social security (generally those who are 65 years of age or older and disabled individuals under certain conditions).

   (1) Financing is via general tax revenues as part of the overall social security system.

   (2) Physician services are covered by Part B Medicare; however, beneficiaries must pay an annual deductible and 20% of "reasonable charges." (Medicare will pay only a specified amount for a medical service, and this amount is based on customary charges for the type of service given.)

   (3) Provision is also made to cover the cost of treating end-stage renal disease, regardless of the age of the patient.

b. **Medicaid** is a federal- and state-sponsored medical assistance program that pays for hospital, physician, and a variety of other health care services for the indigent, including nursing home care and prescribed drugs. Each state defines the criteria of eligibility as well as the specific services to be covered. The costs of the program are shared by the federal government and the individual states. Neither deductibles nor copayments are required from recipients under this program.

3. Payment methods

a. **Cost considerations.** In recent years, both private and public insurance programs have been much more cost conscious when paying for health care services. The overall level of cost for health care reflects the past policies of society to develop a great capacity both in facilities and personnel for the delivery of health care. Involved are large amounts of fixed costs as well as large numbers of practitioners who generate costs. The recent changes in payment methods, which tend to affect health care utilization rather than capacity, have only an indirect effect on the cost of health care.

b. Payments to physicians

    (1) The most common form of payment is **fee-for-service**: The price set by the physician is paid either by the patient directly or by an insurance carrier on behalf of the patient. The largest payer of physician bills currently is Blue Shield, with Medicare Part B coverage providing for physician services to Medicare beneficiaries.

    (2) Physicians also may be paid on a **capitation basis**, by which a fixed sum per patient per year is assessed, regardless of the volume or intensity of the services actually rendered for the individual patient. This method is seldom utilized by solo practitioners, but it is commonly used in group settings, particularly in HMOs.

    (3) A third method of payment is by **salary**. The physician, as an employee of an organization, is paid a fixed amount for a period of time and renders services to the appropriate population (e.g., military physicians render services to members of the armed services and their dependents for a fixed salary).

c. Payments to hospitals

    (1) Prior to October 1, 1983, hospitals were generally reimbursed on a **cost-incurred basis**, regardless of the extent of the costs. Many Blue Cross plans, commercial insurers, and states in the Medicaid program still reimburse hospitals in this manner. Since October 1, 1983, however, Medicare has reimbursed hospitals on **prospective rather than retrospective costs**.

        (a) The **diagnosis-related group (DRG) system** is a prospective payment system that is used by the federal government (Medicare); at the present time it applies only to hospital services and not to physician services. Under this system, Medicare pays only a set amount for each diagnosis, in conformity with the principal diagnosis that is specified under the DRG system and regardless of the costs actually incurred by the hospital (e.g., if an individual enters the hospital after a heart attack, the hospital will receive only a predetermined reimbursement, despite the length of stay, the number of tests performed, or the severity of the illness). The amount of payment differs according to the wage base that is accorded to the hospital, which is contingent upon the location of the hospital (i.e., if it is in an urban or rural area), the wage level of the area in which the hospital is located, and the number of full-time residents or interns. There is also a special provision for individuals who are so ill that the costs of hospitalization would far exceed any DRG payment.

        (b) The DRG system has reversed the incentives of the hospital that have been reinforced by the retrospective payment system. Under the DRG system, the hospital, which can reduce the number of tests and procedures and the length of stay, can obtain the difference between the Medicare payment and its costs.

    (2) Medicaid and Blue Cross have also recently adopted some innovative reimbursment methods (e.g., in California, Medicaid solicits competitive bids from hospitals to contain costs; in Kansas, Blue Cross has begun to reimburse hospitals using the DRG system).

II. SOCIOLOGY, ECONOMICS, AND POLITICS

A. SOCIOLOGY OF THE MEDICAL PROFESSION

1. Professional status and autonomy

    a. Ascribed status. Society has accorded the medical profession and its individual members what has been termed "ascribed status" upon the completion of specific goals, such as achieving the degree of doctor of medicine, licensure to practice, and board certification.

    b. Autonomy. Society accords to the members of the profession a significant degree of autonomy, perhaps the greatest amount given to any professional in our society. The high status simultaneously gives the physician autonomy in his relationships with patients and with institutional providers such as hospitals and requires that the physician maintain professional behavior and competence.

    c. Collectivity. The medical profession is characterized generally by collegial rather than hierarchical structures.

2. Limitations on professional autonomy

    a. Limitations on the autonomy of the physician have been imposed by society only for the most pressing reasons and where there is an overriding public interest (e.g., reporting a situation that could affect public health and observing drug control laws).

b. Government-directed limitations
   (1) Since 1972, federal and state governments have intruded more often into the practice of medicine and, therefore, have imposed further limits on the autonomy of the physician.
   (2) Governmental limitations may be seen as related to the cost of federal and state programs such as Medicare and Medicaid (see section I B 2). Two associations that monitor physician activities and that may question physician decisions are the Utilization Review organization and the Professional Review organization. The implications of these actions may negatively affect the ascribed status of the profession.
c. Recent developments. HMOs, PPOs, and IPAs (see section I A 4), in which physicians become members of groups with specified protocols of treatment, may negatively affect the status of the physician in that the physician is an agent of the group or the employer rather than being, unilaterally, an agent and an advocate of the patient. Treatment protocols associated with HMOs, PPOs, and IPAs commonly involve criteria relating to such decisions as hospital admission, duration of hospital stay, ordering of consultations, ordering of diagnostic and therapeutic procedures, and specification of particular drugs.

B. SOCIOLOGY OF THE PATIENT

1. The patient in the sick role
   a. Concept. Certain behavior of patients is expected by society in its overall interests. Assuming the sick role is not encouraged; it is expected that the patient will follow the physician's direction for cure and rehabilitation in order to leave the sick (and dependent) role at the earliest possible time.
   b. Changing role. The patient is encouraged increasingly to see himself as a partner, not a dependent, and the physician is expected to enable the patient to participate as actively as possible in decisions about diagnosis and care.

2. The patient as consumer
   a. Choosing among health insurance plans. Increasingly, employees in the private sector have a choice among traditional fee-for-service health insurance plans, HMOs, and PPOs. Because the benefit packages, types of service, and out-of-pocket costs may differ, employees (potential patients) have incentives to become prudent buyers of health insurance for themselves and their families.
   b. Choosing among alternative providers. The growing use of copayments and deductibles by health insurers, whereby the patient may pay a portion or all of the provider's bill, has introduced price sensitivity to physician services by patients, encouraging patients to consider a physician's fees before using his services.
      (1) In response to the choices available to them, patients are requiring information concerning the economic implications of physician decisions. This in turn requires time investment on the part of the physician.
      (2) In general, the patient's freedom of choice tends to remove the physician from the authoritative role characteristic of the ascribed status and also tends to undermine the physician's autonomy.
      (3) Expectations for a successful outcome of patient care have been fostered by the increasing occasions for intervention by health care providers (see section II D). The inability to fulfill these expectations has led to a surge of malpractice claims, with accompanying increases in the costs of insurance. The attention paid to this aspect of the health care milieu has further weakened the public's unquestioning acceptance of physician decision making.

C. SOCIOLOGY OF HEALTH CARE INSTITUTIONS

1. Organizations as open systems. Hospitals and other health care institutions have established sets of goals, encompassing the provision of health care services, teaching health care personnel, and conducting basic and clinical research. In a sociological sense, these institutions are "systems" in that they are goal-oriented and comprise a set of interdependent parts. They are "open" systems in the sense that they must interact with the larger organizational, social, economic, professional, and political environments in which they operate.

2. Institutions as bureaucracies
   a. Definition
      (1) A bureaucracy is a hierarchy of offices that is designed to achieve specified goals in a predictable and efficient manner.
      (2) The term bureaucracy is appropriate in describing most health care institutions because these institutions have established goals and are organized into fairly rigid structures with functions specified by governing bodies.

b. Public and private bureaucracies. The term bureaucracy is equally applicable to both public and private organizations that have hierarchical structures and that operate in supposedly rational, predictable ways. ("Bureaucracy" is often used inappropriately to describe an inefficient civil service organization.)

3. Formal and informal organizations

a. A **formal** organization is the structure as it is described by the official organization chart, which is sometimes referred to as the blueprint of the organization. The formal organization is what the institution is supposed to be, although in reality it may be somewhat different.

b. The **informal** organization refers to the modifications that occur in the formal structure as a result of the personal and social factors that are present in any organization. "Informal" is a way of describing how the institution really functions.

4. The institution as a factor in the socialization process

a. Becoming a patient. An individual entering a hospital or other health care institution is expected to behave in clearly defined ways. Patients are expected to submit to the organizations' requirements, including acceptance of organizational and professional authority, treatment regimes, the institution's timetable, and standards of dress. This process of becoming a patient makes the patient dependent on the organization and its personnel. Attempts to make this socialization process less rigid and more personal reduce the negative impact on patients.

b. The professionalization of providers. Health care institutions create and sustain organizational and social climates that imbue students with appropriate values, attitudes, and behaviors. Senior teachers and staff members serve as role models for students throughout the lengthy period of professional training. This professionalization, which is a form of socialization into certain roles, is achieved through complex formal and informal mechanisms.

5. Physicians and hospitals

a. The physician-hospital relationship. Physicians occupy special positions of influence in health care institutions. This influence is based on the physicians' professional knowledge and authority and the legal system's definition of their exclusive right to practice medicine.

b. Dependency. Hospitals depend on physicians as the source of referrals for treatment and, consequently, revenue for the institution. This dependence exists whether or not the hospital is in any sense the employer of the physician.

c. Distinct responsibilities. Although both the physician and the health care institution administrator are responsible for the patient's welfare, the administrator's responsibility is exercised through the operation and fiscal management of the institution while the physician's responsibility is primarily, if not solely, to the patient.

d. Conflict. One of the consequences of this difference of responsibility is conflict among physicians, other health care professionals, administrators, and members of the governing boards of the institutions. Each group has different demands and expectations, which must be managed constructively for the benefit of patients. Conflicts are inevitable in any organization, but they must be resolved through formal and informal mechanisms in the interests of organizational survival and development and patient care.

D. IMPLICATIONS OF "MEDICALIZATION"

1. Concept. Until recently, the "medicalization" of patient behavior has been predominant (e.g., alcoholism, once defined as a social aberration, is now defined as a disease requiring medical intervention). Medicalization provides justification for the sick role on the part of the patient and provides a basis for the ascribed authority of the physician.

2. Reduction of medicalization. Actions to reduce additional national expenditures for health care may reduce medicalization, thus removing more individuals from the sick role and decreasing areas over which the medical profession has authority.

E. ECONOMIC ASPECTS OF HEALTH CARE

1. Expenditures for health care

a. Trends in health care expenditures. In 1950, health care expenditures in the United States were $12 billion or 5.3% of the gross national product (the total of all goods and services produced in the United States). Expenditures grew to $42 billion or 6.5% of the gross national product in 1965. By 1984, health care expenditures reached $387 billion or 10.6% of the gross national product. Only the expenditures for agriculture and construction exceeded those for health care. Both in absolute terms and relative to the remainder of the economy, growth in health care expenditures has been substantial.

b. Reasons for substantial growth in health care expenditures include the increasing average age of the American population and advances in technology. Most observers, however, suggest that the adoption of Medicare and Medicaid in 1965, which increased the access to health care by the elderly and the indigent, respectively, as well as the widespread increase in private health insurance have been the primary reasons for the increase in costs.

2. Opportunity costs

a. Concept. The concept of "opportunity costs" recognizes that increased expenditures in the health care sector mean that fewer dollars are available for welfare, public housing, defense, and so forth. Even in terms of health care itself, the opportunity cost of additional spending on long-term care might mean reduced spending on acute care; or the opportunity cost of increased spending on preventive care might mean reduced spending on curative care.

b. Impact. Cost containment activities in the private sector might be a result of the opportunity costs of health care expenditures. Firms that have experienced increasing health care costs realize that less money is available for increased salaries or new equipment, which may lead to the institution of cost containment measures. Similarly, state governments that have experienced increasing expenditures for Medicaid have instituted cost containment measures at the urging of education and highway interests, among others.

F. POLITICAL ASPECTS OF HEALTH CARE

1. Care as a "right"

a. Concept. Although a need for health care for the total population was recognized as early as the early 1900s, it was not until the growing civil rights movement of the 1960s and the successful passage into law of the Medicare and Medicaid programs that the concept of health care as a right became accepted in large segments of society and became a political issue. The limits of the right to access and availability as well as the equity and distribution of health care remain to be defined.

b. Rights versus expenditures. The provision of care to growing numbers of individuals and for increasing levels of service have run counter to concern for the increase in the expenditures for health care delivery.

c. Access. Creating access to health care, which was addressed by actions such as the Hill-Burton program (i.e., the Hospital Survey and Construction Act of 1946) to increase the number of hospitals in certain areas (such as rural sections of America) and by the several programs instituted to increase the number of physicians produced by the American medical education system, caused a large increase in capacity and accompanying expenditure levels. Although access to health care was improved for significant numbers of the population, neither the economic nor the geographic access problems were resolved adequately.

2. Limitations to the "right."
Questions of entitlement to health care remain to be resolved, including questions as to the method of rationing, which is implicit in the decision to expand access but to restrict expenditure growth.

a. Attempts that have been made to ease this dilemma include:

(1) Arbitrary limits on benefits, such as 20-day hospitalization limitations under Medicaid

(2) Methods involving the patient in financial sharing, such as copayments and deductibles (under which the patient is responsible for front-end health care costs), with the belief that sharing will tend to reduce the utilization of the capacity

(3) The prospective payment system adopted by the Medicare program in an attempt to decrease the utilization of acute care and high technology services, assuming that decreased utilization will decrease expenditures

b. In effect, fiscal pressures are forcing the political leadership to examine rationing mechanisms ranging from a reduction or control of the capacity to deliver care to clear delineation of eligibility for specific services for specific patient groups.

3. Special-interest groups.
Fiscal pressures run headlong against the special-interest pressures of such groups as the Gray Panthers, representing the elderly, and the various disease-specific groups such as those supporting research and treatment for cancer, arthritis, end-stage renal disease, and so on. The political pressure of minority groups, women's groups, and others merely adds to the difficulty in achieving a rational solution.

BIBLIOGRAPHY

Fox RC: *Essays in Medical Sociology*. New York, John Wiley, 1979

Heydebrand WV: *Hospital Bureaucracy—A Comparative Study of Organizations*. New York, Dunellen, 1973

Raffel MW: *The U.S. Health System: Origins and Functions*. New York, John Wiley, 1984

Roemer MI: *An Introduction to the U.S. Health Care System*. New York, Springer, 1982

Stewart PL, Cantor MG: *Varieties of Work Experience*. Cambridge, Mass., Schenkman, 1974

Stewart PL, Cantor MG: *Varieties of Work*. Beverly Hills, Calif., Sage, 1982

Williams SJ, Torrens PR (eds): *Introduction to Health Services*, 2nd ed. New York, John Wiley, 1984

STUDY QUESTIONS

Directions: Each question below contains five suggested answers. Choose the **one best** response to each question.

1. A health maintenance organization (HMO) is a modality for delivering health care to a specific group of enrolled patients under a premium structure, which most often can be described as

(A) providing for preventive care only
(B) requiring monthly revisions
(C) requiring significant additional payments upon hospitalization
(D) providing full financial coverage for a prescribed comprehensive benefit package
(E) providing for physician services only

2. The most important difference between reimbursement on a diagnosis-related group (DRG) basis and reimbursement on a retrospective cost basis is

(A) differences in wage levels among cities are accounted for in reimbursement under the DRG system
(B) reimbursement under the DRG system is on a prospective, rather than on a cost-incurred, basis
(C) teaching hospitals receive additional reimbursement under the DRG system
(D) physician reimbursement under the DRG system is based on the diagnosis-related grouping of the patient
(E) hospitals can be assured of their annual revenue on a prospective basis

3. The study of conflict in organizations has attracted considerable attention from researchers in recent years. The existence of conflict in health service organizations can be best described as

(A) an indicator of poor management, especially at the senior levels of the organization
(B) a measure of the organization's efficiency
(C) reflecting poor communication throughout the organization
(D) relating to low remuneration and inadequate working conditions for employees
(E) inevitable and constructively manageable to help the organization attain its goals

4. Expenditures for health care in the United States have grown from $12 billion in 1950 to $387 billion in 1984. All of the following factors were significant contributors to the rise EXCEPT

(A) the enactment of the Medicare and Medicaid programs in 1965
(B) the emergence of health maintenance organizations (HMOs) in the early 1970s
(C) the general inflation of the United States economy
(D) the development of technology (including highly effective new antibiotics)
(E) the availability of private health insurance, largely as a benefit of employment

5. The medical profession's status, which has been called an example of "ascribed" status, has been very high in recent years. Many forces are acting to reduce this status. All of the following elements are having a negative effect on the status of the physician EXCEPT

(A) public health reporting requirements, most recently those relating to acquired immune deficiency syndrome (AIDS)
(B) treatment protocols established by provider groups such as health maintenance organizations (HMOs)
(C) actions taken to encourage the patient to take a more direct role in his treatment
(D) the trend to reduce what has been termed the medicalization of patient status
(E) the monitoring of physician decisions by peer review groups such as hospital utilization review committees

6. Between 1950 and 1984, health care expenditures relative to the gross national product have

(A) increased at a slightly greater rate than other goods and services
(B) increased at a slightly lesser rate than other goods and services
(C) increased at approximately the same rate as other goods and services
(D) approximately tripled
(E) approximately doubled

7. The concept of opportunity costs implies that

(A) more money spent on defense might mean fewer dollars to spend on health care
(B) the income earned by physicians will always be greater than the income earned by para-professionals
(C) the availability of insurance increases the propensity to consume more services
(D) insurance firms have incentives to avoid high-risk individuals
(E) health maintenance organizations (HMOs) can have a competitive effect on the fee-for-service sector

8. One of the main purposes of the Hill-Burton program was to

(A) increase the number of physicians
(B) increase the number of hospital beds
(C) provide supplemental insurance for Medicare patients
(D) increase health care coverage for the indigent
(E) provide a system of review of physician hospitalization practices through comparison of individual physician patterns of hospital use with local standards

9. The status of hospitals has been changing in recent years. Although the overall number of hospitals has been decreasing, expansion is occurring in the remaining hospitals in a variety of ways. One area of expansion is

(A) inpatient bed capacity
(B) outpatient capacity
(C) the bed supply in rural areas
(D) the bed supply in urban areas
(E) in areas unrelated to health care

Directions: Each question below contains four suggested answers of which **one or more** is correct. Choose the answer

A if **1, 2, and 3** are correct
B if **1 and 3** are correct
C if **2 and 4** are correct
D if **4** is correct
E if **1, 2, 3, and 4** are correct

10. Diagnosis-related groups (DRGs) measure the relative use of medical resources by patients, who are classified by clinically related disorders and prospective length of hospital stay. True statements concerning the Medicare prospective payment system that is based on DRGs include

(1) the physician in charge of an individual patient comes to prior agreement with the hospital as to the length of stay
(2) under the Medicare program, the hospital is required to ensure that only the resources approved for the DRG will be utilized
(3) a single payment is made to cover all provider (hospital and physician) bills for a patient's stay
(4) in general, the hospital receives a specific payment regardless of the intensity or length of care rendered to the patient

11. Accurate descriptions of socialization include

(1) it is the coverage of all members of society with health insurance benefits to a defined limit
(2) it is the way in which informal organizations develop in institutions
(3) it is the development of community support groups by community health care centers
(4) it is the process by which institutions influence their members to behave in a desirable way within the organization

ANSWERS AND EXPLANATIONS

1. The answer is D. (*I A 4 a*) Health maintenance organizations (HMOs) are designed to provide a comprehensive health care package, which emphasizes preventive care but also includes episodic hospitalization and, under many programs, additional features such as eyeglasses and dental care. Another feature of HMOs is that a single annual premium, which may be paid monthly, is the only payment required of a subscriber and it is set for a period of 1 year.

2. The answer is B. (*I B 3 c*) Medicare's decision not to reimburse on a cost-incurred basis completely changes the incentives of the hospital management. Administrators in hospitals must now be cost conscious or risk incurring deficits in their operations. This cost consciousness will also be reflected in the hospital administrator's relationships with physicians. The fact that differences in wage levels among cities are considered in reimbursement in the diagnosis-related group (DRG) system is of minor importance. Additional reimbursement to teaching hospitals is also a minor point.

3. The answer is E. (*II C 5 d*) Conflicts arise as a result of numerous factors within and outside an organization and are not necessarily associated with poor management. Many factors influence the efficiency of an organization, and firm evidence of a positive relationship between the extent of conflict and organizational efficiency does not exist. Poor communication, low remuneration, and inadequate working conditions may contribute to a conflict situation, but they are not predominant causes.

4. The answer is B. (*II E 1 b*) Health maintenance organizations (HMOs) are generally viewed as mechanisms for controlling or even reducing health care expenditures. However, the Medicare and Medicaid programs, inflation, new technology, and the availability of private health insurance have all been indicted as contributing to the rise in expenditures.

5. The answer is A. (*II A 1, 2*) The public at large has generally accepted public health limitations on the autonomy of the individual physician, and these imposed limitations do not affect the physician's ascribed status. However, health maintenance organizations (HMOs), increased patient participation in treatment, a reduction in medicalization, and the monitoring of peer review groups all tend to diminish the physician's status.

6. The answer is E. (*II E 1 a*) Between 1950 and 1984, health care expenditures as a percentage of the gross national product grew from 5.3% to 10.6%, a doubling of the percentage. This growth, significant as it is in absolute terms, has focused attention of policy makers in both the government and the private sector on health care expenditures largely because of the fact of outstripping the rate of growth of the consumer price index. The implications of such a growth rate, if unchecked, is seen as threatening to both the government's fiscal balance and to private industry's international competitive position.

7. The answer is A. (*II E 2*) The concept of opportunity costs implies that more money spent on defense, welfare, farm aid, education, and so forth means that the money to be spent on health care is less. The relative earnings of physicians and paraprofessionals is irrelevant to the discussion. The hazards inherent in the availability of health insurance (e.g., consumer immunity to the cost of health care services), biased risk selection, and alternative forms of health care delivery are also unrelated to opportunity costs.

8. The answer is B. (*II F 1 c*) The Hill-Burton program was an attempt to increase the number of hospitals and hospital beds. This program (more precisely, the Hospital Survey and Construction Act of 1946) was intended originally to ensure the availability of acute hospital facilities in rural areas. In time, this purpose was sidetracked and hospital construction, expansion, and modernization were supported nationwide by a system of grants and low-interest loans. Hospitals that received support were (and are) obligated to render specific amounts of uncompensated care to patients in designated low-income categories in keeping with a series of complex formulas. At present, it is widely considered that overbedding in many geographic areas has been an unintended result.

9. The answer is B. [*I A 1 d (2)*] Currently, hospitals in both rural and urban areas are attempting to reduce their bed supply and thus close the gap between capacity and the actual number of patients. Although many hospitals are part of multi-institutional systems, there is no evidence of their expansion into areas unrelated to health care as a result of joining such systems.

10. The answer is D (4). [*I B 3 c (a)*] The diagnosis-related group (DRG)–based prospective payment system that is currently used by Medicare covers only hospital services and does not include physician services. A price is paid by Medicare to the hospital, and this price is not affected by any arrangements made by the physician. The DRG system assures the government that, regardless of the resources utilized by the hospital or the length of stay of the patient, the federal payment will not vary from the amount set according to the specific principal diagnosis.

11. The answer is D (4). *(II C 4)* Socialization is the process by which institutions influence their members to behave in a desired way within the organization. For example, when an individual enters the hospital, he is "socialized" into accepting the authority of the institution as well as its treatment regimes, timetable, and standards of dress. Although informal organizations play a part in the socialization of individuals and groups, they are not developed exclusively by the socialization process.

Post-test

QUESTIONS

Directions: Each question below contains five suggested answers. Choose the **one best** response to each question.

1. The right of all citizens (and even temporary residents) of the United States to health care emerged as a political issue during the 1960s and early 1970s. At one time it appeared that a national health insurance law was inevitable and imminent. At present there seems to be little prospect of such a program. A major factor in the failure of the "right" to health care to develop adequate political support was

(A) disagreement within society on a definition of the "right"
(B) inability of the political process to implement a delivery system
(C) realization that there were neither adequate numbers nor geographic distribution of physicians to carry out fulfillment of the "right"
(D) opposition by politically potent groups such as labor organizations and the so-called Gray Panthers
(E) recognition that effecting the "right" to health care would exacerbate the federal financial situation

2. The most essential property of a psychological test for clarifying a psychiatric diagnosis is

(A) standardization
(B) reliability
(C) generalization
(D) validity
(E) specificity

Questions 3–6

A 23-year-old Hispanic woman is evaluated because of symptoms of left lower extremity paresis and paresthesias that have not been explainable organically. She has been in to see her primary care physician almost weekly for the past several months with a variety of complaints, although for the past month she has complained primarily about her left leg. On the consultation request, her physician, Dr. Smith, specifically asks for a determination of whether she has a "hysterical conversion disorder."

During the patient interview it is discovered that the patient and her two young children were abandoned by her husband about 6 months ago. She has since taken a job as a waitress and is working about 35 hours each week. Although she appears fatigued, she retains a spark of liveliness and is quite pleasant to talk to.

3. The biopsychosocial model would suggest that all of the following influences be considered in the evaluation EXCEPT

(A) the Hispanic folk conception of "hot and cold" illnesses
(B) the results of the neurologic examination
(C) the assessment of the patient's personality pattern
(D) the patient's own explanation of her problem
(E) the patient's leisure time activity of doing needlework

4. All of the following questions would direct the inquiry toward exploring her social support system EXCEPT

(A) "You've been through a lot recently, but you seem to be doing quite well, how is that?"
(B) "Who is looking after your children while you work?"
(C) "How well do you think Dr. Smith has been doing in taking care of you?"
(D) "How do you think your life would be different in a year from now if your leg doesn't get better?"
(E) "Do you have a legal case pending against your husband?"

In the interview it is revealed that the patient and her children are sharing an apartment with a man that the patient met 4 months ago. They have decided to marry eventually, but because she has not yet been granted a divorce and in light of their shaky financial situation, they have not set a wedding date.

5. The four of them could be considered a family within

(A) a structural definition of family
(B) a functional definition of family
(C) a definition of nuclear family
(D) a matriarchal family system
(E) none of the above

6. The concept from general systems theory that best describes the patient's symptoms is

(A) a boundary
(B) systemic identity
(C) an environmental perturbation
(D) systemic disintegration
(E) a novel structure

7. Mr. Moses has made frequent suicide attempts via overdoses of the minor tranquilizers that he abuses. None of these attempts have been lethal and have often been angry responses to perceived rejection by others. He also reports wide swings in his feelings, sometimes relative to his indiscriminate sexual relationships with men and women. Which of the following personality disorders best characterizes the patient?

(A) Antisocial
(B) Borderline
(C) Narcissistic
(D) Histrionic
(E) Obsessive-compulsive

8. All of the following statements regarding neurotransmitters are true EXCEPT

(A) Dale's principle (that a given neuron can contain and release only one neurotransmitter and that it can only be excitatory or inhibitory but not both) is no longer considered to be correct
(B) most of the neurotransmitter activity in the brain is probably inhibitory
(C) amphetamines primarily affect dopamine transmission in the brain, with little effect on other neurotransmitters
(D) major catecholaminergic neurotransmitters are derived from tyrosine
(E) neurotransmitters are not considered to be important in the functioning of electrical synapses

9. Which of the following terms best applies to fetal alcohol syndrome?

(A) Sex-linked recessive
(B) Autosomal recessive
(C) Autosomal dominant
(D) Fully penetrant
(E) Congenital

10. A 36-year-old married woman is in the hospital for diagnostic tests. She is overly friendly and at times complains that her physician does not pay enough attention to her. The physician's most effective response is to

(A) withdraw to keep the boundaries of the professional relationship clear
(B) confront her excessive dependency and offer an interpretation of it
(C) allow her to express her fears and provide appropriate reassurance
(D) transfer her to another member of the house staff to avoid excessive involvement
(E) make an effort to spend extra time with her to assure her that she is receiving proper care

11. Exploration is closely associated with what form of learning?

(A) Operant conditioning
(B) Classical conditioning
(C) Autoshaping
(D) Imprinting
(E) Habituation

12. In a patient with primarily a frontal lobe disorder, common findings would include all of the following EXCEPT

(A) normal language and cognitive ability
(B) bizarre delusions and hallucinations
(C) inappropriate social behavior
(D) emotional lability
(E) apathy and indifference

13. Hospitals and other health care institutions are regarded as open systems because

(A) they guarantee access to care for all individuals on the basis of need rather than ability to pay
(B) they provide care on a 24-hour basis
(C) they have clearly defined roles within the health care system
(D) they must interact with the larger organizational, social, economic, professional, and political environments in which they operate
(E) of the relationship of physicians, who are not employees, to the administration of the institution

Questions 14–16

A 45-year-old business executive with advanced cirrhosis of the liver and a history of alcohol abuse claims that he does not have a problem with drinking and can quit anytime he wants to.

14. The primary defense mechanism that he is using is

(A) projection
(B) denial
(C) counterphobic behavior
(D) reaction formation
(E) isolation of affect

15. At other times he says that he drinks only because of the constant nagging of his wife. This defense mechanism is best identified as

(A) rationalization
(B) repression
(C) sublimation
(D) reaction formation
(E) isolation of affect

16. Eventually this patient quits drinking but continues to have the symptoms of advanced cirrhosis of the liver. In spite of the obvious discomfort caused by his illness, he tells everyone how happy he is to have cirrhosis since it has led to the cessation of his drinking. The defense mechanism he is using is best identified as

(A) projection
(B) denial
(C) counterphobic behavior
(D) reaction formation
(E) isolation of affect

17. Psychometric intelligence testing was performed on two people. The first person was evaluated at the age of 4 years and again at 10 years; and the second person was evaluated at the age of 27 years and again at 35 years. Based upon the reliability of the Wechsler scales, which description would best characterize the relationship between the two evaluations for each person?

(A) Stable (person 1); stable (person 2)
(B) Marked change possible (person 1); stable (person 2)
(C) Marked change likely (persons 1 and 2)
(D) Stable (person 1); moderate change (person 2)
(E) Stable (person 1); marked change (person 2)

18. A 70-year-old man who has been treated as an outpatient for 1 week with amitriptyline for a major depression presents to the emergency room complaining of blurred vision, urinary retention, and confusion. What is the most likely cause?

(A) A cerebrovascular accident
(B) Worsening of the depression
(C) An exacerbation of congestive heart failure
(D) A suicide attempt
(E) Anticholinergic side effects of amitriptyline

19. All of the following situations are good examples of operant conditioning EXCEPT

(A) teaching a child to ride a bicycle
(B) maze-learning
(C) bar-pressing in the rat
(D) teaching a frog to eat a worm
(E) teaching a lion to jump through a hoop

20. In the Soviet Union, there have been reports that political dissidents are considered to be exhibiting behavior that is not socially deviant but is symptomatic of mental disease. On this basis, the individual becomes a mental patient rather than a political prisoner. This form of "medicalization" is an extreme, but it is little different in principle from redefining alcoholism as a medical problem. Medicalization, in theory, has which of the following implications for the medical profession?

(A) The profession becomes the arbiter of disputes as to the political appropriateness of alternate treatment choices for specific dysfunctions

(B) The profession is at risk of losing some significant element of the high repute in which it has been held

(C) A greater number of physicians will be needed to cope with the increased number of individuals who would become patients by definition

(D) The status of the profession would be heightened as an increasing number of individuals look to physicians to help ameliorate socially unacceptable behavior

(E) The risk of malpractice claims against physicians would decrease since there would be less expectation of episodic cure as an outcome

21. Hypothalamic releasing factors have been described for many different pituitary and pineal hormones. All of the following hormones have a releasing factor EXCEPT

(A) follicle-stimulating hormone (FSH)

(B) melanocyte-stimulating hormone (MSH)

(C) growth hormone (GH)

(D) adrenocorticotropic hormone (ACTH)

(E) vasopressin (ADH)

22. The physician who becomes tearful when a patient is describing his suffering is having difficulty with which professional developmental task?

(A) Integrating nurturant tendencies and executive necessities

(B) Forming a professional ego-ideal

(C) Balancing objectivity and empathy

(D) Balancing the wish for omnipotence and the toleration of uncertainty

(E) None of the above

23. Constructional ability (i.e., the perception of and copy of designs) is impaired in all of the following disorders EXCEPT

(A) damage to the left parietal lobe

(B) delirium

(C) schizophrenia

(D) early Alzheimer's disease

(E) intoxication

24. An apprehensive patient begins to express concerns to her physician about the pain that may be involved in a bone marrow biopsy he has just recommended for diagnostic evaluation. The physician interrupts and quickly assures her that there will be little pain. He then carefully explains the procedure to her. The patient asks no more questions, but prior to the procedure the physician is surprised to find her tearful and shaky. Based on this information, the most likely reason that his reassurance was not sufficient is

(A) he had not explained the procedure adequately

(B) the patient is unable to tolerate anxiety

(C) the patient is overly demanding

(D) he had not allowed the patient to express her concerns fully about the procedure

(E) he is unconcerned about his patient

25. A pigeon observes a potential sexual partner and begins to approach and show courtship behaviors, but unexpectedly the pigeon is thwarted by the appearance of a much larger and stronger competitor. What type of behavior is most likely to occur under these conditions?

(A) Displacement behavior

(B) Aggressive behavior

(C) Compromise behavior

(D) Suppression behavior

(E) Anxiety

26. A pharmacologic feature that makes triazolam more useful than diazepam as a hypnotic is its

(A) longer absorption time

(B) shorter half-life

(C) metabolism to active compounds

(D) lack of interaction with other sedatives

(E) greater volume of distribution

Questions 27–29

An 85-year-old man with advanced Alzheimer's disease is confined to his bed and chair in a nursing home. Because he is incontinent, he has an indwelling urinary catheter. He has developed a urinary tract infection and has become septic. Long before the onset of his dementia, the patient was known to have said repeatedly, "If I become old and incompetent, I don't want my life unnecessarily prolonged."

27. Which statement concerning the treatment of the infection is true from an ethical viewpoint?

(A) Treatment is ethically unjustified because of the patient's prior directive concerning his care
(B) Treatment is ethically unjustified because it constitutes a waste of valuable resources on someone unable to appreciate the benefits
(C) Treatment is ethically justified because now that the patient is incompetent, prior directives are invalid
(D) Treatment is ethically justified because physicians are obligated to treat all treatable illnesses
(E) Treatment is ethically justified under the guidance–cooperation model of the physician–patient relationship

28. Assuming that this patient is an Orthodox Jew, treatment of the infection is best considered to be

(A) ethically justified because treatment is required according to established Jewish medical ethical principles
(B) ethically unjustified because Judaism forbids unnecessary prolongation of life
(C) ethically justified on the basis of the Hippocratic principle of "First, do no harm"
(D) a decision that is entirely independent of religious beliefs
(E) a decision that can only be made by a rabbi

29. The principle in Jewish medical ethics that would determine the right action in this situation is

(A) the doctrine of double effect
(B) beneficence
(C) the duty to prolong life
(D) the duty to respect patient autonomy
(E) casuistry

30. Increasing stress and anxiety are associated with all of the following conditions EXCEPT

(A) increased blood cholesterol
(B) a reduction of alpha wave abundance on electroencephalogram (EEG)
(C) decreased immune function
(D) increased blood cortisol levels
(E) increased blood flow and temperature in the extremities

31. Which of the following tests is the major projective test of personality assessment?

(A) Rorschach Inkblot Test
(B) Minnesota Multiphasic Personality Inventory (MMPI)
(C) Thematic Apperception Test (TAT)
(D) Sentence Completion Test
(E) Projective drawings

32. In a family with a disease that has an autosomal dominant inheritance pattern, 7 children have been born, 4 of whom have the disease and 3 of whom do not. What is the probability of the next child born having the disease?

(A) 100%
(B) 50%
(C) 25%
(D) Zero
(E) Cannot be determined

33. There appears to be a conflict between two major public policy goals: to provide health care at an acceptable level to all residents of the United States and to contain or even reduce expenditures for health care. These goals may be realized and the conflict reduced by

(A) requiring copayments and deductibles under all forms of insurance for health care
(B) increasing the supply of practitioners and facilities so that the laws of supply and demand will force down prices
(C) acclerating the development of technology so that more rapid and accurate diagnoses may be available
(D) defining an acceptable level of care to be provided and assuring a match between that level and the capacity required to meet the resulting demands
(E) establishing an acceptable level of expenditures and tailoring the capacity of the overall delivery system to that level

Directions: Each question below contains four suggested answers of which **one or more** is correct. Choose the answer

A if **1, 2, and 3** are correct
B if **1 and 3** are correct
C if **2 and 4** are correct
D if **4** is correct
E if **1, 2, 3, and 4** are correct

34. The sensorimotor stage of cognitive development is characterized by

(1) the period from birth to age 5 years
(2) innate reflex patterns initially
(3) the capacity for intuitive thought by the end of the stage
(4) the capacity for object constancy

35. True statements about a psychiatric illness in a family member include which of the following?

(1) A mental illness will attack at least one member in a majority of families
(2) A family support system can protect against depression in the face of adverse life events
(3) The family of a patient can have a significant influence on treatment outcome
(4) The behavior of the family is a major cause of a mental illness in one of its members

36. A 54-year-old night watchman is admitted to the hospital for evaluation of a chronic cough and a lung mass that is suspected to be cancerous. The patient is a loner who has no friends or family. To help this aloof, reclusive individual feel comfortable in the hospital his physician should

(1) allow him to seclude himself in his room with few outside interruptions
(2) not be offended if he does not respond to expressions of interest
(3) try to get him to express his loneliness
(4) make regularly scheduled visits rather than episodically stopping by his room

37. Known associations exist between neuropsychiatric disorders and disturbances in specific neurotransmitter systems, including

(1) Alzheimer's disease and cholinergic dysfunction
(2) depression and noradrenergic dysfunction
(3) schizophrenia and dopaminergic dysfunction
(4) Parkinson's disease and dopaminergic dysfunction

38. The stage of formal operations (adolescence) is characterized by the acquisition of

(1) an understanding of the finiteness of existence and the meaning of death
(2) the capacity for thinking in abstractions and by the use of symbols
(3) the capacity for thinking about the past, present, and future in a continuum
(4) the capacity for reversibility in thought

39. Known causes of major affective illness include

(1) heart disease
(2) corticosteroids
(3) cancer
(4) reserpine

40. "Spectatoring," in which the individual observes himself in the sexual act rather than fully experiencing it, is often associated with which of the following sexual dysfunctions?

(1) Inhibited female orgasm
(2) Inhibited sexual excitement
(3) Ejaculatory inhibition
(4) Premature ejaculation

41. Examples of complementary interpersonal postures include

(1) an enmeshed mother–daughter dyad
(2) a physician insisting on proceeding with a treatment that the patient is expressing reservations about
(3) a physician diligently attending to his moribund patient in the intensive care unit
(4) two medical colleagues arguing a point during rounds

42. Parietal lobe damage or dysfunction may produce which of the following signs?

(1) Inability to copy designs accurately
(2) Poor performance in mental arithmetic
(3) Reading difficulty
(4) Poor score on a continuous performance test (CPT)

43. Occipital lobe lesions are associated with

(1) illusions
(2) unformed visual hallucinations
(3) cortical blindness
(4) formed visual hallucinations

44. Disturbance of short-term memory is found in which of the following disorders?

(1) Korsakoff's psychosis
(2) Depression
(3) Delirium
(4) Organic delusional syndrome

45. Stimulus generalization can be described as

(1) a response learned in one situation that can occur in a different but similar situation
(2) determined by resemblances in size, color, or shape
(3) most commonly established by language
(4) a frequent basis for the development of phobias, especially in young children

Directions: The groups of questions below consist of lettered choices followed by several numbered items. For each numbered item select the **one** lettered choice with which it is **most** closely associated. Each lettered choice may be used once, more than once, or not at all.

Questions 46–49

For each neurochemical mechanism listed below, select the class of drugs with which it is most closely associated.

(A) Tricyclic antidepressants
(B) Benzodiazepines
(C) Monoamine oxidase (MAO) inhibitors
(D) Amphetamines
(E) Butyrophenones

46. Increased presynaptic dopamine release

47. Decreased catecholamine and serotonin metabolism

48. Blockade of postsynaptic dopamine receptors

49. Inhibition of presynaptic norepinephrine and serotonin reuptake

Questions 50–53

For each physician–patient interaction that follows, select the model of the relationship that best describes it.

(A) Activity–passivity
(B) Guidance–cooperation
(C) Mutual participation
(D) Social intimacy
(E) None of the above

50. The physician teaches his eager-to-learn hypertensive patient to take and record his blood pressure and shows him how to practice stress-reduction exercises daily at home

51. The physician responds to his patient's request for the result of his recent blood test by saying, "Don't worry about it; that's my job"

52. The physician treats a comatose patient in the emergency room

53. The physician elicits from his patient dying from acquired immune deficiency syndrome (AIDS) his wishes regarding resuscitation and the use of extraordinary life-sustaining techniques and agrees to respect them

Questions 54–57

Match each attitude toward death listed below to the developmental age with which it is most consistent.

(A) Young child
(B) Latency-aged child
(C) Adolescent
(D) Middle-aged adult
(E) Adult older than age 65 years

D 54. Death as inevitable and personal

B 55. Death as punishment

A 56. Death as abandonment

E 57. Death faced with a sense of integrity

Questions 58–60

Neuroleptic drugs have been shown to block postsynaptic dopamine 2 (D_2) receptors. Match the following effects of neuroleptics with the dopaminergic tract thought to underlie the action.

(A) Tuberoinfundibular tract
(B) Nigrostriatal tract
(C) Both
(D) Neither

A 58. Lactation

B 59. Parkinsonism

D 60. Antipsychotic effects

ANSWERS AND EXPLANATIONS

1. The answer is E. (*Chapter 15 II F 1*) There is no evidence that disagreement over the definition of "right," that the inability of the political process to implement a health care delivery system, that inadequate numbers and geographic distribution of physicians, or that political opposition by special-interest groups have blocked the development of a plan for national health insurance. The federal deficit, the plight of the Medicare trust fund, and a general awareness in Congress that the opportunity costs of providing national health care are too high have led to actions to limit rather than expand the federal responsibility.

2. The answer is D. (*Chapter 8 III D 3*) Establishing validity is the most important aspect of test development. If a test purports to aid in clinical diagnosis, the capacity to substantiate the diagnostic implications of test results must be established in the development of the test. This is done by correlating the results with an outside criterion. This is referred to as the criterion or empirical validity of a test. Tests may be well standardized and reliable, but without demonstrated validity, the results may be meaningless.

3. The answer is E. (*Chapter 11 I C 2*) The biopsychosocial model predicts that to understand illness adequately a wide perspective must be maintained to assess all relevant areas of human experience. The functioning of the nervous system (B), the individual's experience and behavior (C and D), and the relevant community and subculture (A) would all be viewed as potentially significant influences. The patients leisure time activity of doing needlework (E) has no significant relevance.

4. The answer is D. (*Chapter 11 III B*) A social support system refers to the network of people that an individual can call upon during difficult times in an attempt to handle a life crisis. Question (A) and question (B) directly inquire into who is helping the patient. Physicians and lawyers (questions C and E), by the very nature of their jobs, become to a greater or a lesser degree members of their patients' and clients' social support systems. Question (D), although likely to produce interesting information, is more likely to clarify the patient's ability to cope than the nature of her social support system.

5. The answer is B. (*Chapter 11 IV A 1, 2*) There exists a broad array of "family" living situations in contemporary American society. Whether one considers these arrangements to be families or not depends on how one defines a family. Structural definitions typically stress that the members be related legitimately by blood, marriage, or adoption. Functional definitions emphasize the group's commitment to normative family functions, such as mutual need, fulfillment, and nurturance.

6. The answer is E. [*Chapter 11 I B 1 a (1), b, 2, 3, 4; IV F 2*] Unpredictable or novel structures arise in a system attempting to adapt to stress. Clinical symptoms are seen by some family theorists as misguided attempts at adaptation to life circumstances.

7. The answer is B. (*Chapter 9 VIII B 2 b*) Mr. Moses exhibits symptoms that meet the criteria for a diagnosis of borderline personality disorder. Although drug abuse and sexual identity problems can occur in other disorders, as can an oversensitivity to rejection, the cluster of signs and symptoms leads to this particular diagnosis.

8. The answer is C. [*Chapter 1 II C 1 b, 3; III A 1, 3, 5 b (2) (b), B 5 b (1) (c); V A 3 a; VII A 2*] Amphetamines primarily cause the release of both dopamine and norepinephrine. In addition to causing an elevation of mood and heightened sensory experience, amphetamines may cause psychosis and stereotypy. It is probable that dopamine and norepinephrine agonist actions are involved in these effects. Both parts of Dale's principle have been found to be inaccurate in recent years: A number of neurons contain more than one neurotransmitter (often a biogenic amine and a neuropeptide in combination) and may function differently at different synapses. Gamma-aminobutyric acid (GABA) is the most common neurotransmitter in the brain, probably accounting for more than 60% of all neurotransmitters in the brain. Some other transmitters are also mainly inhibitory, such as glycine and dopamine. Tyrosine is the precursor for all catecholaminergic neurotransmitters, including dopamine, norepinephrine, and epinephrine. Finally, electrical synapses are believed to function by the transfer of an electrical charge and not through transfer of chemical neurotransmitters.

9. The answer is E. (*Chapter 4 II B 4; IV C 3*) Although genetic factors are important in the transmission of alcoholism, fetal alcohol syndrome (which is characterized by mental retardation, microcephaly, epicanthal folds, growth retardation, and facial hypoplasia) occurs as the result of moderate to excessive alcohol intake by the mother during gestation. Thus, the condition is congenital but not necessarily genetic.

10. The answer is C. (*Chapter 13 IX C*) Dramatizing, emotional individuals often require reassurance to help them distinguish reality from alarming fantasies. They also need to express their fears to discharge pent-up emotions. However, they are likely to become overly involved emotionally and are best approached in a calm, firm manner. Withdrawing from the patient or transferring her to another staff member is likely to leave her feeling rejected and unattractive, resulting in aggravation of her behavior.

11. The answer is E. (*Chapter 5 III A 2*) Habituation and exploration are closely related. Exploration continues until the animal habituates to the novel stimuli being explored. Excessively novel stimuli are not explored until the animal habituates to these stimuli enough to explore them.

12. The answer is B. [*Chapter 8 II G 1 b (1); Fig. 8-13*] Delusions and hallucinations are rarely found in frontal lobe syndromes. Intellectual functions and language are largely intact, and disinhibition (inappropriate social behavior, emotional lability, or both) is usual. One form of frontal lobe disease (i.e., deep medial lesions) can produce severe degrees of apathy with reduced activity and slowing of all mental processes (abulia).

13. The answer is D. (*Chapter 15 II C 1*) The accepted sociological definition of an open system is interaction on the part of an institution with the larger organizational, social, economic, professional, and political environments in which it operates. Access to care, which is provided on a 24-hour basis, is guaranteed to needy individuals only by some institutions in certain circumstances. The role that a particular institution plays within the health care system does not make that institution an open system, nor does the relationship between physicians and the administration of the institution.

14. The answer is B. (*Chapter 13 VIII A*) Denial, a primitive or infantile defense (i.e., at the lower level of adaptive functioning), has been defined as the disavowing and rejecting of any aspects of internal or external reality that, if acknowledged, would cause anxiety. The patient is denying his obvious drinking problem in spite of the associated physical illness. He is thus avoiding the external reality of the cause of his illness. The other defense mechanisms mentioned may play some part in his coping with his alcoholism, but none are the primary mechanism used by this alcoholic patient.

15. The answer is A. (*Chapter 13 VIII L*) In this instance, the business executive acknowledges his drinking but disavows his own responsibility and justifies his behavior by attributing it to his wife's nagging. The other defense mechanisms, which fall at the middle to the higher levels of adaptive behavior, do not apply in this situation.

16. The answer is D. (*Chapter 13 VIII H*) It is expected that the patient would feel sad, frightened, angry, or guilty about having developed cirrhosis from his excessive alcohol consumption. To avoid these uncomfortable feelings, he is using the mechanism of reaction formation to push them out of awareness and claims to be elated about his illness. If the patient were to describe his self-caused serious illness in unemotional terms and claim he felt no anger, sadness, or unhappiness, he would be using the defense of isolation of affect.

17. The answer is B. [*Chapter 8 III F 1 a (1) (c), (2), (3); Table 8-1*] The Wechsler scales yield reliable test–retest estimates of intelligence; however, intelligence or IQ is not immutable. Level of intellectual functioning may change, particularly during childhood, when important learning and adaptive skills are being mastered. After adolescence, intelligence is relatively stable and would rarely vary more than a few points.

18. The answer is E. (*Chapter 2 III B 1 b, E 1 c; VIII C 1*) Anticholinergic side effects are commonly associated with tricyclic antidepressant therapy. They may include dry mouth, blurred vision, constipation, urinary retention and hesitancy, and (at toxic levels) a delirium. The elderly are especially vulnerable to such side effects, and in treating them the lowest effective dose should be used. In cases in which the patient cannot tolerate the side effects of an antidepressant, electroconvulsive therapy (ECT) should be considered.

19. The answer is D. [*Chapter 5 III B 2 c (2)*] Frogs eat worms without conditioning. When a human observer teaches a frog to eat a worm, the primary adaptation that is taking place is the frog's habituation to the testing situation and reduction of fear responses. Teaching a child to ride a bicycle, maze-learning, bar-pressing, and teaching a lion to jump through a hoop are all examples of operant conditioning, based on the reinforcement of specific behaviors that are not part of the organism's behavioral repertoire prior to conditioning.

20. The answer is D. (*Chapter 15 II D*) The status of the physician has traditionally been high, reflecting, among other factors, society's reliance upon the profession as intervenors on the side of individual patients for their and, therefore, society's welfare. That the risk of malpractice claims would decrease, that more physicians would be needed to serve the increase in patients, and that the profession would be involved politically in determining appropriate treatment choices are all highly unlikely outcomes of medicalization.

21. The answer is E. (*Chapter 1 VII E 1–3, 5, 8*) Releasing factors have been described for each of the pituitary hormones in the question except vasopressin (ADH), which is a hormone of the posterior pituitary gland that can be released by several mechanisms (e.g., osmotic stimulators, hypovolemia) but not by a hypothalamic releasing factor. Luteinizing hormone (LH) and follicle-stimulating hormone (FSH) are released from the anterior pituitary in a process regulated by LH-releasing hormone. The release of melanocyte-stimulating hormone (MSH) is regulated by both MSH-inhibiting factor and MSH-releasing factor. Growth hormone (GH) is secreted and synthesized under the control of GH-releasing factor and GH-release inhibiting factor, which is somatostatin. Adrenocorticotropic hormone (ACTH) is regulated by the hypothalamic corticotropin-releasing factor.

22. The answer is C. (*Chapter 12 III D 1–4*) The physician who weeps when a patient describes pain and anguish is empathizing to an extreme degree. His overidentification with the patient's pain and suffering will interfere significantly with his capacity to be objective and composed in the dynamic process of gathering and assessing all relevant information about his patient and his patient's illness.

23. The answer is C. (*Chapter 8 II F 1, 2*) Damage to the left parietal lobe would impair perceptual analysis of the designs, interfere with pathways to frontal areas, or both. Impaired constructional ability is often an early sign of Alzheimer's disease. In delerium and intoxication, all functions above those associated with the brain stem would be variably affected. Design copying involves many brain stem areas, and inability to perform this task will usually occur early in the course of dementia. Schizophrenic patients do not lose this capacity, although their drawings may have bizarre elements added to the essential design.

24. The answer is D. (*Chapter 13 VI D, E; X B 2 c*) The physician in this example did not allow the patient to express her concerns about the procedure. Thus, his careful explanation of the procedure occurred before her anxiety decreased enough for her to listen fully. Her response is not unusual, and there is no clear indication that she is unable to tolerate anxiety or is overly demanding. It is not clear that the physician is unconcerned about his patient, only that his response failed to recognize the patient's concerns.

25. The answer is A. (*Chapter 5 IV B 3*) Displacement behaviors occur when a strong behavioral tendency is suddenly thwarted, as is described in the question. Displacement is a seemingly irrelevant type of behavior that arises as a substitute. Aggression, for example, is relatively unlikely because the competitor is "much larger and stronger."

26. The answer is B. (*Chapter 2 VI A 2*) All benzodiazepines have hypnotic activity (i.e., the ability to induce drowsiness) when used at sufficiently high doses. Some are superior to others as hypnotic drugs, however, because they are rapidly absorbed, quickly attain peak blood levels, and have a short half-life. This minimizes daytime sedation following a bedtime dose. Diazepam has a long half-life and is also metabolized to active compounds. With daily use it is very likely to have cumulative sedative effects.

27. The answer is A. (*Chapter 14 III B; IV C 1 a, b*) Although it is difficult to declare one course of action ethically right and another ethically wrong without knowledge of the patient's values, a directive by the patient given at a time when he was competent should be given great moral weight. In the absence of a prior directive, the physician must talk to family members or consider the religious practices of the patient. It is wrong for the physician to make such a decision on the basis of his personal values if other information is available.

28. The answer is A. (*Chapter 14 IV A 2, B 1*) There is a strong and well-articulated Jewish ethical principle that places the duty to prolong life above all others. According to Jewish ethics, there is no question concerning the appropriateness of treatment. Note is made, however, of the patient's directive concerning care, which is inconsistent with the religious principle. In this situation, the directive must be weighed against religious principles, and it probably would be given moral priority in a secular health care setting.

29. The answer is C. (*Chapter 14 IV A 2 b, B 1*) The duty to prolong life is of paramount importance in Jewish medical ethics. Treatment efforts must continue until the point that death is irrevocable and imminent. Although the quality of life of this elderly, demented patient is poor, his sepsis is potentially treatable; death will neither necessarily nor immediately follow. Consequently, in Orthodox Judaism, treatment is morally required.

30. The answer is E. (*Chapter 3 VI 2*) Increasing stress and anxiety are associated with decreased blood flow and temperature in the extremities, as well as a reduction of alpha wave abundance on the encephalogram (EEG). Stress is also reportedly associated with decreases in immune function, changes in skin conductance, and increases in blood pressure, muscle tension, and blood levels of cortisol, lactate, catecholamines, and cholesterol.

31. The answer is A. (*Chapter 8 III F 3 b*) The major projective instrument is the Rorschach test. The Thematic Apperception Test (TAT), Sentence Completion Test, and projective drawings are all projective tests, but they are less well studied and yield more limited information. The Minnesota Multiphasic Personality Inventory (MMPI), which is the most frequently used personality test, is an objective instrument, not a projective test.

32. The answer is B. (*Chapter 4 III A*) Every child has a 50% chance of inheriting a condition with an autosomal dominant mode of inheritance. This does not mean that a family with 8 children will necessarily have 4 affected and 4 unaffected members, although this is statistically the most likely possibility. It is also possible that all family members will be affected or all will be unaffected, although these possibilities are unlikely.

33. The answer is D. (*Chapter 15 II F 2*) There would not be a true impact on the overall expenditures for health care even if copayments and deductibles were required under all forms of health care insurance, including Medicaid. Increasing the supply of practitioners and facilities and accelerating the development of technology are cited as causes of the current unacceptably high level of expenditure. The issue of expenditure, but not that of access, is addressed by establishing an acceptable level of expenditures and tailoring the capacity of the overall delivery system to that level. Only by defining an acceptable level of care and guaranteeing that this level and the capacity necessary to meet the resulting demands are matched can an acceptable level of health care be provided to all residents of the United States and the costs of this health care be contained.

34. The answer is C (2, 4). (*Chapter 6 III C 1*) The sensorimotor stage of cognitive development is the first stage, extending from birth to 2 years. It is built initially on the innate reflex patterns of sucking, grasping, eye-following, and crying, and by its end the child is capable of remembering an object even if it is out of direct vision (object constancy). The capacity for intuitive thought does not develop until the next (conceptual) stage of cognitive development.

35. The answer is A (1, 2, 3). (*Chapter 11 I C 2; III B 1, 2; IV D 2 a*) It is estimated that over 50% of families will have to cope with a diagnosable mental illness in one of their members at some time. Families are typically central to any individual's network of social support and can be influential in protecting against depression and other psychological problems, in modulating emotional environment, and in helping a patient comply with medication requirements. Theories stressing the causal role of families in major psychopathology (e.g., the "schizophrenic mother" hypothesis) have received little empirical validation.

36. The answer is C (2, 4). (*Chapter 13 IX G*) The aloof, reclusive individual does not want to be intruded upon. While this wish should be respected, he should not be allowed to withdraw totally. The physician should approach the patient with considerate interest and quiet reassurance but should not expect the patient to reciprocate. Trying to get an emotional reaction from these patients often upsets their deep-seated defensive structure, which may result in a worsening of a relationship with them. Scheduled visits are less disruptive to their solitude than are unscheduled visits.

37. The answer is E (all). (*Chapter 1 III A 5, B 4; IV E 2; VIII A*) A variety of neuropsychiatric disorders are believed to be associated with disturbances in specific neurotransmitter systems, including the following: Cholinergic abnormalities including a reduction in cholinergic neurons are reported in patients with Alzheimer's disease; the catecholamine theory of mood disorders states that reduced activity of the norepinephrine system may contribute to depression; the nigrostriatal tract, which is an important dopaminergic tract, degenerates in Parkinson's disease; and, finally, evidence exists that there is increased dopamine activity in patients with schizophrenia. However, it is not suggested that major psychiatric or neurologic disorders are associated with dysfunction of single neurotransmitter systems. In addition, psychopharmacologic drugs rarely affect a single neurotransmitter system.

38. The answer is A (1, 2, 3). (*Chapter 6 IV C 5*) The stage of formal operations is associated maturationally with adolescence and cognitively with the acquisition and consolidation of truly abstract thought, of thinking entirely by the use of symbols (e.g., mathematics), and of the ability to understand the relationship of the past, present, and future. Acquisition of the capacity for reversibility occurs in the previous stage (concrete operations) of cognitive development.

39. The answer is E (all). [*Chapter 9 IV A 3 b (3) (a), B 3*] Depressive syndromes can be caused by medication and organic or functional disorders. Steroids in high doses can induce mania or depression upon withdrawal. Cancer and heart disease can present as depression, which is secondary to the underlying disease. Reserpine can cause depression, which in some cases is quite severe.

40. The answer is A (1, 2, 3). (*Chapter 10 V B 2, 3*) "Spectatoring" causes distractibility, which interferes with sexual arousal and the maintenance of sexual excitement. This can lead to failure to lubricate or loss of lubrication in women and failure to attain an orgasm in both men and women. Premature ejaculation is usually associated with increased anxiety and sexual tension rather than distractibility.

41. The answer is B (1, 3). (*Chapter 11 II B 1–3, D 1, 2*) Dyadic behavior can be viewed as being composed of a sequence of successive dyadic postures. These postures are defined typically in terms of the focus, interdependence, and affiliation of the behavior observed. Complementary and symmetrical postures are two patterns of recurrent behavioral pairings that have especial clinical import. Complementary postures are those in which the observed behaviors show similar degrees of affiliation and interdependence but differing focus (e.g., a relationship in which one individual is "one down" and the other is "one up"). Symmetrical postures involve pairings of behaviors that evidence similar degrees of affiliation and interdependence as well as similar focus (e.g., a relationship in which both participants regard each other as equals).

42. The answer is A (1, 2, 3). [*Chapter 8 II C 2, 3 c, E 1 a, c (2) (c) (ii), F 1, 2 a, b*] Sustained concentration is believed to be largely a subcortical reticular activating system (RAS) function and is unaffected by parietal cortical damage. Graphomotor, calculating, and reading abilities are heavily dependent upon intact parietal functioning.

43. The answer is E (all). (*Chapter 3 II A 4*) While occipital lobe lesions are most classically associated with unformed visual hallucinations, illusions, and cortical blindness, they have also been associated with formed visual hallucinations.

44. The answer is A (1, 2, 3). (*Chapter 8 II C 2, E 1 b; Figs. 8-2, 8-7, 8-8*) By definition, there is no alteration in consciousness and no loss of concentration or intellectual function in an organic delusional syndrome. Patients with a Korsakoff's psychosis or with delerium always show memory impairment. Many seriously depressed patients also show short-term memory problems; however, this usually does not create a problem in diagnosis because of the prominence of the mood disorder.

45. The answer is E (all). (*Chapter 6 II B 6*) Stimulus generalization is a concept used to explain a universe of both desirable and undesirable behaviors. It is based either on concrete similarities (color, size, and shape), especially in young children (fear of one dog is fear of all dogs), or most commonly on language (e.g., the word "dog" may mean all four-footed animals and later only a certain kind of four-footed animal).

46–49. The answers are: 46-D, 47-C, 48-E, 49-A. (*Chapter 2 II C 1; III C 1; IX E 3*) Amphetamines cause catecholamine release from nerve terminals. This may be related to the ability of the drugs to increase motor activity and to decrease fatigue and appetite. Other effects, especially with toxic doses, include increased blood pressure, cardiac arrhythmias, and (with very high doses) convulsions and coma.

Monoamine oxidase (MAO) inhibitors irreversibly bind to an enzyme involved in amine metabolism, making an increased amount of amine neurotransmitter available at the synapse. These drugs are most often used in the treatment of a major depression that has not responded to tricyclic antidepressant therapy. Tyramine-rich foods must be avoided as they may precipitate a hypertensive crisis in a patient taking an MAO inhibitor.

The antipsychotic agents are thought to act via postsynaptic blockade of central nervous system dopamine receptors. Dopaminergic blockade in the basal ganglia causes the parkinsonian symptoms and other extrapyramidal side effects associated with these drugs. Dopaminergic blockade also stimulates increased prolactin release, which may be associated with galactorrhea. Receptor blockade in the chemoreceptor trigger zone causes an antiemetic effect.

Insofar as depression may be related to inadequate concentrations of amines at the synapse, inhibition of synaptic amine reuptake (resulting in increased synaptic levels of these neurotransmitters) is thought to be a key factor in the effect of tricyclic antidepressants. In spite of this immediate neurochemical effect, however, these drugs do not typically alleviate depression until after 2 to 3 weeks of use. Anticholinergic side effects are often seen with the tricyclic antidepressants, indicating their activity in multiple neurotransmitter systems.

50–53. The answers are: 50-C, 51-B, 52-A, 53-C. (*Chapter 12 IV*) A key aspect of the mutual participation model of the physician–patient relationship is the active role of the patient in carrying out and monitoring his own treatment in conjunction with ongoing discussions with his physician. The hypertensive patient and his physician are clearly using this model in their relationship.

The physician who refuses his patient's reasonable request for detailed information about his illness is emphasizing the dominant, controlling, paternalistic nature of the physician's role. In this model of guidance–cooperation, while the physician has complete freedom to decide on methods of evaluation and therapy, the patient's explicit permission must be obtained for each procedure.

In the activity–passivity model, in which the patient is considered to be essentially inanimate, the patient's permission for evaluation and treatment is not obtainable since he is unaware of his interaction with a physician. A comatose patient being treated by a physician in an emergency clearly exemplifies this model.

For physicians who believe that their main or sole task is to treat and cure disease, whose intense wishes for omniscience and omnipotence make tolerating uncertainty extremely difficult, or whose emotional reactions compromise their ability to empathize, caring for dying patients is particularly stressful. In the mutual participation model of the physician–patient relationship, the physician focuses as much on the personhood of the patient as on his disease processes and continually strives to enhance the patient's understanding and coping skills as well as to comfort him.

54–57. The answers are: 54-D, 55-B, 56-A, 57-E. *(Chapter 7 VI C; VII)* Young children are unable to conceive of death as irreversible. They tend to view death in terms of abandonment and as a temporary state. They seem unable to tolerate the process of mourning. By middle childhood, the finality of death comes to be appreciated. However, the child often feels responsible for the death and considers it as punishment for misbehavior. It is not until sufficient growth has taken place, especially in the realm of psychological independence in adolescene, that mourning can be tolerated or completed.

Young adults and middle-aged adults seem to fear death more keenly than do the elderly. In middle age, death is seen as inevitable and personal, affecting loved ones and oneself; anxiety about death seems to center on separation. Fear of pain and suffering is also involved.

Elderly individuals can face death with equanimity when they are able to review their lives with satisfaction. If choices that are made during life and events that occur during life cannot be integrated with few regrets, the end of life is viewed with despair.

58–60. The answers are: 58-A, 59-B, 60-D. [*Chapter 1 III A 4 a (2), 5 a, b (1); VII D 6 b*] Both lactation, via the tuberoinfundibular tract, and parkinsonism, via the nigrostriatal tract, are associated with the effects of neuroleptic drugs upon postsynaptic dopamine 2 (D_2) receptors. Some of the antipsychotic effects are also thought to be mediated by dopaminergic blockade, but the brain tracts involved are believed to be the mesolimbic and possibly the mesocortical pathways. There is little evidence that the nigrostriatal and tuberoinfundibular tracts are important in the direct antipsychotic effects of neuroleptics. It is, however, useful to add that other neurotransmitter systems are probably involved in the neuroleptic effects.

Index

Alzheimer's disease —
→ cholinergic neurotransmitter
dysfunction

depression — noradrenergic

Schizophrenia →
Parkinson disease ↓ dopaminergic

2 - 8 - 6/2 ①